This Book is Due in
21 Days

OF BRITISH COLUMBIA

WITHDRAWN

the WINERIES

OF BRITISH COLUMBIA

by JOHN SCHREINER

whitecap

Visit our Web site at www.whitecap.ca

Edited by Elaine Jones
Proofread by Lesley Cameron
Cover design and art direction by Roberta Batchelor
Interior design by Margaret Lee / bamboosilk.com
Maps by Jacqui Thomas

Printed and bound in Canada

LIBRARY AND ARCHIVES CANADA CATALOGUING IN PUBLICATION
Schreiner, John, 1936-
    The wineries of British Columbia / John Schreiner. — Rev. and updated ed.
    Includes index.
    ISBN 1-55285-603-8
    1. Wineries—British Columbia—Guidebooks. 2. Wine and wine making—British
    Columbia. I. Title.
        TP559.C3S36 2004   663'.2'009711   C2004-904120-7

We are committed to protecting the environment and to the responsible use of natural resources. We are acting
on this commitment by working with suppliers and printers to phase out our use of paper produced from ancient
forests. This book is printed by Webcom on 100% post-consumer recycled paper, processed chlorine free and
printed with vegetable-based inks. We are working with Markets Initiative (www.oldgrowthfree.com) on this project.

The publisher acknowledges the support of the Canada Council for the Arts and the Cultural Services Branch
of the Government of British Columbia for our publishing program. We acknowledge the financial support of the
Government of Canada through the Book Publishing Industry Development Program for our publishing activities.

Contents

WHY BRITISH COLUMBIA WINES TURNED THE CORNER

JUST WHEN THE BRITISH COLUMBIA WINE INDUSTRY BEGAN ITS remarkable improvement is a matter of opinion. Claude Violet, the founder of Domaine de Chaberton, argues for 1986, the year when Vancouver hosted the world's fair. To satisfy both restaurants at the fair and international tourists, the Liquor Distribution Branch's (LDB) stores listed wines of international quality, exposing domestic wineries to unparalleled competition.

One could set the turning point as early as 1975 when the LDB, for the first time in its 50-year history, began stocking more imported wine than domestic wine. Others set the turning point later. The 1989 free trade agreement with the United States removed overnight much of the sheltered status that domestic wines had enjoyed for two generations. The provincial government and the industry both recognized that world-class wine could never be made with many of the grapes then being grown. After the 1988 vintage, the government paid to have two-thirds of the vineyards ripped out. What remained of the wine industry struggled for the next few years with the fruit from about 566 hectares (1,400 acres) of vines. The vineyards that survived the pullout were planted primarily with the white varieties, such as Riesling and Gewürztraminer, producing successful off-dry white wines. The industry regained some confidence when the so-called farm-gate wineries began opening in 1990. These thrived, along with the handful of estate wineries. That suggested that British Columbians would support their own wine industry if the wines were soundly made.

Conventional wisdom had held that the premium vinifera grapes (with which the imported wines were made) could not grow successfully in British

Columbia. But in 1992, Harry McWatters, the founder of Sumac Ridge Estate Winery, gambled by planting 40 hectares (100 acres) of vinifera grapes on Black Sage Road. It may have been the single largest vinifera planting in Canada at the time. Within a year, however, other growers, most of them new to the industry, were planting adjoining property. For the most part, British Columbia's modern wine industry was born in the 1990s.

Father Charles Pandosy has been called the father of the wine industry because some vines were planted at the Oblate mission he started in 1859 near modern-day Kelowna. That is a purely romantic notion. It is unclear how big his vineyard was or whether it even thrived. The first commercial wine grapes were planted in the Kelowna area in the late 1920s by J.W. Hughes, a well-known horti-culturalist, who sold the fruit to Growers' Wines in Victoria. On the strength of that, Hughes has the better claim as the father of the wine industry. Initially, how-ever, he planted labrusca. Hughes and the growers who took over his vineyards grew grape varieties utterly incapable of producing wines that the rest of the world could take seriously.

Perhaps they did not know any better. The quest for better grape varieties invariably headed in the wrong direction, with winter hardiness being the prime requirement since it was widely believed that the Okanagan is too cold for the great European grape varieties. Thus, the Okanagan ended up being dominated by hardy, but mediocre, grapes not a great deal better for winemaking than those that Hughes planted. The most widely planted white was Okanagan Riesling (now almost eradicated). A variety with labrusca in its history, the hardy and productive vine yielded foxy wines with all the appeal of synthetic wartime chocolate bars.

The quality of the wine did not matter all that much in the 1960s when new wineries opened in the Okanagan for the first time since Calona Vineyards started in 1931. Unsophisticated consumers quaffed alcoholic sweet red wines and berry wines by the gallon. When that was the major market, why would wineries make anything else? The token efforts to make "European wines" had less than credible results. One winery turned a simple table grape, Himrod, into a sweet white wine that it called Canadian Liebfraumilch. When the Germans threatened to sue, the wine was renamed Canadian Rhine Castle.

Eventually, however, British Columbians learned the difference between good wine and poor wine. There were numerous landmark events before the 1986 world's fair. For example, liquor and wine marketing emerged from the long shadow of temperance in 1974 when the government established the Liquor Distribution Branch as a marketing agency separate from the Liquor Control Board. That led to a dramatic expansion in the availability of imported wines. Then, in 1978, the Vancouver Playhouse International Wine Festival began, initially as a showcase for California wine and subsequently for wineries from around the world. The emergence of sophisticated consumers gave domestic wineries no choice but to grow the grapes that gave their international competitors such an advantage.

There is an explanation for the success today of grape varieties that experts formerly said were far too tender for the Okanagan climate. Walter Gehringer, one of the owners of Gehringer Brothers Estate Winery, notes that the winters have become appreciably warmer. The vine-killing frosts — a week of -25°C (-13°F) — that wiped out whole vineyards in the 1960s and the 1970s did not occur in the 1990s. It is certainly premature to say there is a permanent new weather pattern at work, but it is beginning to seem so.

There is a second reason why vinifera varieties, including late ones such as Syrah, Cabernet Sauvignon and even Zinfandel, appear to be thriving in the Okanagan. The vines are being grown quite differently from the hybrids and the older labrusca varieties. The hybrids, typically early-ripening vines, could produce heavy crops and still go into protective dormancy before winter set in. Vinifera trials failed in the 1960s and 1970s because the vines were allowed to grow too many bunches. Grown that way, vinifera vines, typically late ripeners, were still alive with sap that froze when cold weather set in. Once growers stopped over-cropping vinifera, the vines survived the winters — and yielded much better wine.

1990	1995	1998	2001
JOHANNISBERG RIESLING	CHARDONNAY	CABERNET FRANC	MERLOT
VERDELET*	JOH. RIESLING	CHARDONNAY	CHARDONNAY
CHARDONNAY	PINOT BLANC	PINOT BLANC	PINOT NOIR
PINOT BLANC	PINOT NOIR	MERLOT	PINOT GRIS
EHRENFELSER	GEWÜRZTRAMINER	JOH. RIESLING	PINOT BLANC
GEWÜRZTRAMINER	AUXERROIS	PINOT NOIR	CABERNET SAUVIGNON
PINOT NOIR	EHRENFELSER	GEWÜRZTRAMINER	GEWÜRZTRAMINER
VIDAL*	MERLOT	AUXERROIS	CABERNET FRANC
BACCHUS	VIDAL*	PINOT GRIS	JOH. RIESLING
MARÉCHAL FOCH*	CHANCELLOR*	EHRENFELSER	GAMAY
AUXERROIS	BACCHUS	CABERNET SAUVIGNON	SAUVIGNON BLANC
MÜLLER-THURGAU	BACO NOIR*	GAMAY	AUXERROIS
CHASSELAS	VERDELET*	BACCHUS	EHRENFELSER
CHANCELLOR*	MÜLLER-THURGAU	BACO NOIR*	BACCHUS
	PINOT GRIS	CHANCELLOR*	CHANCELLOR*
	MARÉCHAL FOCH*	VIDAL*	SÉMILLON
	SEYVAL BLANC*	VERDELET*	MARÉCHAL FOCH*
	CABERNET FRANC	MARÉCHAL FOCH*	MÜLLER-THURGAU
		MÜLLER-THURGAU	CHENIN BLANC
		CHENIN BLANC	BACO NOIR*
		KERNER	KERNER
		SAUVIGNON BLANC	PINOT MEUNIER
		SÉMILLON	OPTIMA
			VIDAL*
			VERDELET*

* FRENCH HYBRID VARIETIES

Today, about 2,400 hectares (6,000 acres) is under vine, mostly in the Okanagan and mostly with European varieties. Merlot accounts for more than a third of all the red grapes, and Chardonnay, a quarter of the white grapes. The table on the previous page, ranking the major wine grapes in British Columbia by quantity grown, shows the rapid shift in varietals since 1990.

During the last two decades, the number and the nature of wineries have exploded. In 1984, there were just 13 wineries in British Columbia. The 1994 edition of this book profiled 40 wineries or proposed wineries, two of which never developed. This book profiles 126, including fruit wineries, apple wineries and honey wineries. There is a limit to the expansion. Most of the choice land for vineyards has been planted. Even so, there will be more wineries as grape growers push the envelope (as on the Gulf Islands) or as independent growers decide they can make better wine — or more money — from grapes they now sell to wineries.

The important change is not in the winery numbers, however, but in the talent. The majority of the vineyards are managed by professional viticulturists and that has resulted in fundamental improvements in the quality of the grapes. Much of the wine is made by winemakers as well-trained as anywhere in the world, working in well-equipped facilities. British Columbia wines are better now than ever before, but this is just the beginning.

READING THE WINE RATINGS

When I am asked to name my favourite wine, my standard reply is: "The wine in my glass." A real wine lover should not be limited to a handful of wines when there is so much to explore. Of course, some wines please me more than others and these choices are shared with the reader. This is what the ratings mean:

✴ A WINE FOR SPECIAL OCCASIONS.
✴ MEMORABLE WINE TO SHARE WITH GOOD FRIENDS.
✴ WELL MADE.

Some wines are listed but not rated. Don't overlook these wines. They often represent good value even if no stars were entered in my notebook. Perhaps my palate was having a bad day; or perhaps I did not get to taste every wine mentioned in the text. It is important to make up your own mind rather than submit to the tyranny of wine writers.

ADORA ESTATE WINERY

OPENED: 2003

6807 Highway 97, Summerland, BC, V0H 1Z0
Telephone: 250-440-4200
Wine shop: Call for seasonal hours.

RECOMMENDED

* MAXIMUS
* DECORUS
* ELEMENTS MERLOT
* ELEMENTS NO. 8
* DIA

THE FIRST CLUE THAT THINGS ARE DONE DIFFERENTLY AT ADORA comes in the tasting room. A tasting is offered at a modest charge that covers the cost of the elegant wine glass. The view here is that good wine deserves good stemware, not dollar-store wine glasses. "There is nothing worse than a dinky little glass that you can't get your nose into or swirl the wine in," declares Reid Jenkins, one of Adora's three partners. He feels so strongly that Adora wines deserve good stemware that he encourages each visitor to leave with the glass they have paid for.

Adora marches to its own drummer in many ways. Its signature wines, Decorus and Maximus, not only have Latin names but bear vintage dates in Roman numerals. (The back label translates the date.) Every wine is a blend: there are, for example, eight different white grapes in both Decorus and the 2000 vintage of a white called Element No. 8. Even the single variety wines are assembled from grapes purchased from about 15 different vineyards throughout the Okanagan and Similkameen. The grapes are vinified separately and kept in small tanks, sometimes for several years, before blending. While other wineries release wines as early as eight months after harvest, Adora ages its wines anywhere from two to four years before selling them. "In everything we've done, it doesn't matter what the industry thinks the standard is," Jenkins says. "If we don't agree with it, we'll do it another way. We like to buck the trend." Adora, however, is not hiding behind a contrary attitude to camouflage uncertain quality. The wines here are bold and complex.

Jenkins, who was born in New Westminster in 1970, became interested in the Okanagan in the mid-1990s when a Vancouver company he then owned created Web sites for Sumac Ridge and Hawthorne Mountain Vineyards. He developed a friendship with Eric von Krosigk, who was the Hawthorne Mountain winemaker at the time. The Adora project was launched in 1999 by Jenkins and another of his friends, Vancouver car rental magnate Kevin Golka. Together, they enlisted von Krosigk as Adora's winemaking partner.

"When I sat down with Eric and Kevin, my first intentions were to concentrate strictly on sparkling wines in the traditional Champagne method," Jenkins says. By coincidence, he had hit upon von Krosigk's great passion. "Bubbly is really about life," the winemaker enthuses. "It is about subtleties. It's all about elegance and about whispers. You get a kiss of that and a hint of this but you never get overpowered by anything. It's one of those wines that always tastes like more. Try eating just one peanut — or having only one glass of bubble!"

Born in Vernon in 1962, von Krosigk learned winemaking at Geisenheim, Germany's top wine school. While he was in Europe, he also apprenticed with a German producer of sparkling wine. Back in the Okanagan, he was involved in several sparkling wine research projects and became the first winemaker at Summerhill, a winery that specializes in bubble. In his subsequent career as a consultant, he has made sparkling wine for nearly every one of his clients. Adora is no different: the winery has five different sparkling wines, accounting for 20 per cent of its total wine production, which averages about 4,000 cases a year. Jenkins retreated from the original plan of making only bubble after he discovered just how long money would be tied up in aging wine before the business generated a return.

Practical businessmen, Jenkins and Golka plunked the winery on a highly visible site beside Highway 97, near Summerland, just where the highway sweeps around a slow-speed bend. The flat-lying 2.4-hectare (six-acre) vineyard, formerly an orchard, is planted to Chardonnay, Pinot Meunier, Syrah, Merlot and Pinot Noir. The winery itself is a metal-clad building as plain as a mining company's heavy equipment warehouse. Portions of the deceptively large interior have been leased to other wineries for barrel and tank storage. The large tasting room is in the front corner.

"This is a very simple building but it is functional," von Krosigk says. "This is phase one of three phases. The next one is for a proper barrel cellar and Champagne room. And then there will be another building which, long term, will have facilities for a bistro. Our initial focus is putting all our money into production."

He wants to make intense wines, blended to put "the spice points in" and matured slowly. The winery opened in 2003 primarily with white wines — Chardonnay, Pinot Gris, Riesling, Gewürztraminer, Pinot Blanc — and a Merlot from the 2000 and 2001 vintages. "We are not spitting wines out on a 12-month cycle," Jenkins says. White wines are released in their second year; reds in their third or fourth year. "We want the wines to mature and age themselves," von Krosigk explains. "There is quite a difference in the character of a wine if you let time do the work for you, rather than fining it to death so that it is ready six months after harvest."

As a consultant, von Krosigk works for as many as 10 wineries in any given vintage. His mandate at Adora is distinctively different. "There are a lot of styles that I can do here that I can't do elsewhere," he says. The Adora Pinot Blanc, for example, is not the fresh, lemony style demanded by most wineries. "This one is a big, bombastic, really ripe Pinot Blanc with 14 per cent alcohol," he says. "I went for a very different style. It's not what you would say is typical, but I didn't want to be typical. The object here with a lot of wines is to take them where I have always wanted to go, but the normal commercial demands of a given brand make that very difficult."

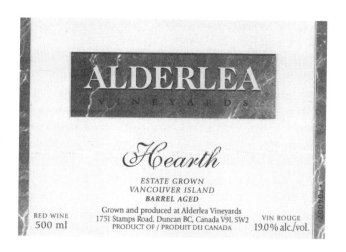

ALDERLEA VINEYARDS

OPENED: 1998

1751 Stamps Road, Duncan, BC, V9L 5W2

Telephone: 250-746-7122

Wine shop: Open 1 pm – 5 pm Thursday through Sunday;
   or by appointment.

RECOMMENDED

* ✳ PINOT NOIR
* ✳ VIOGNIER
* ✳ CLARINET
* ✳ PINOT GRIS
* ✳ HEARTH

AT ALDERLEA VINEYARDS, THE VINES LINE UP LIKE MILITARY CADETS on parade. It is as if they know that Roger Dosman, who runs the winery with Nancy, his wife, flunks the underperformers in his uncompromising pursuit of fine wine. One recent summer, as Dosman marched me through the vineyard, he raged at the irregular growing habits of Agria, and at Dunkelfelder's habit of becoming mildewed. These were among what he calls "the goofy varieties" once tested in his trial block. Those varieties are gone now after a decade of patient trials. More than many growers on Vancouver Island, Dosman has figured out what works best on his site. It shows in the ripeness and intensity of Alderlea's wines.

Dosman is a stickler about a lot of things, including the source of the grapes for his wine. Unlike most island wineries, he will not buy Okanagan grapes. "My commitment is to use only estate-grown fruit," he insists. "That's pretty firm. It costs more to grow it here but that's what I want to do. That's just me. Quite frankly, I think I make some very distinct wines. When you taste our Pinot Noir over the years, you know it's Alderlea Pinot Noir. You just can't mistake an Alderlea Bacchus when you taste the different years. When you buy a wine from a [Vancouver Island] winery that buys grapes from Oliver, well, it tastes like an Oliver wine."

If easier ways of making a living attracted him, Dosman would still be back in Vancouver, running the auto body repair shop he bought from his father in 1976 and operated for a dozen years. "This little winery will never be as lucrative as the body shop," he has remarked. Born in Vancouver in 1948, Dosman has a university degree in urban geography. He never practiced as a town planner, preferring the independence of his own business to being a bureaucrat.

In 1988, he and Nancy decided Vancouver was getting too big and began looking for a vineyard, searching first in the Okanagan and on the Sunshine Coast before buying in 1992 on a quiet dead-end road six kilometres (3.7 miles) northeast of Duncan. (The city's original name was Alderlea.) After cutting down trees, Dosman was able to fashion a sun-bathed south to southwestern slope for the vineyard.

He began planting in 1994. In addition to substantial blocks of Bacchus, Siegerrebe and Auxerrois, Dosman planted about 30 other varieties in a trial plot. Over the subsequent decade, Dosman has adjusted the vineyard continually, phasing out varieties that perform poorly, either in the vineyard or in the market. Siegerrebe, which ripens inconveniently early and is a hard sell, has given way to a bone-dry Gewürztraminer, which sells for considerably more.

The acreage of Bacchus has been reduced to make room for Maréchal Foch, as Alderlea strives to raise its red wine volume to more than half of its production. "I like the Foch," Dosman says. "It's a great wine. This is the grape for Vancouver Island. If you learn how to grow it and how to make wine from it, it will knock your socks off." Shrewdly, Dosman releases the wine, a full-bodied, barrel-aged red, under the name Clarinet. "It was too good to be called just Foch," he explains. Alderlea's signature wines are Clarinet and a full-flavoured, pink-hued Pinot Gris, made in a style that is unmistakably singular.

Continuous vineyard replanting has kept Alderlea's production plateaued at 1,200 cases a year since 1998. The winery should reach about 1,600 cases when Dosman has the vineyard entirely to his liking. He has not yet stopped experimenting. In 2003, for example, he began expanding a modest planting of a promising unnamed new red hybrid vine, a cross of Cabernet Sauvignon and Maréchal Foch developed by Swiss breeder Valentin Blattner.

Alderlea can afford to be small because Dosman makes wines of a quality that fetches premium prices while phasing out the rest. For example, most of Alderlea's lower-priced Auxerrois is being replaced with Gewürztraminer. "It's not that all the wines aren't good," he says. "It's that some are perceived better than others and you get a higher value for them. Sixty per cent of our 2001 crush are wines we sold between $18 and $22. In 2002, it was about 75 per cent."

Such wines as Alderlea's Pinot Noir Reserve are priced right up there with reserve Pinot Noirs from the Okanagan. Dosman goes to exceptional lengths to mature his Pinot Noir, tenting many of the rows each spring to achieve extra ripeness. (Tenting involves covering the vines for a few weeks with plastic, simulating a greenhouse.) "To get a good Pinot Noir, you need a fairly warm year on Vancouver Island," he explains. "Some years it is fine, other years it is just okay. With tenting, you can pretty well guarantee some pretty good fruit, no matter what the season."

Dosman began tenting vines initially to ripen a small block of Merlot. He has used the technique to ripen his modest number of Viognier vines, a variety that needs more heat than is available on Vancouver Island. Alderlea's first Viognier was made in 1998, a hot growing season. It created a buzz among the winery customers; some restaurants offered more than the asking price for larger allotments. That kind of excitement stopped Dosman banishing finicky Viognier from the vineyard, at least as long as the variety is fashionable. "It's a bit of a rage thing," he admits. "When you are a small winery, you have to do something that is a little bit unique and different."

As meticulous a winemaker as he is a grower, Dosman makes fresh, crisp white wines with vibrant fruit and red wines with depth and maturity. And for all the challenge of ripening grapes on Vancouver Island, Dosman even pulls off a good port-style red called Hearth by blending some obscure, early-ripening, "goofy" reds with which he has experimented. Hearth is dark and robust, with cherry and plum flavours. "The wine has certainly been a crowd pleaser," Dosman has found. "We sell almost all by Christmas time." And there is nothing goofy about cash in the till at the year's end.

ARROWLEAF CELLARS

OPENED: 2003

1574 Camp Road, Lake Country, BC, V4V 1K1

Telephone: 250-766-2992

Web site: www.arrowleafcellars.com

Wine shop: Open daily 10.30 am – 5.30 pm from May to November 15.

RECOMMENDED

- ❊ MERLOT
- ❊ GEWÜRZTRAMINER
- ✹ AUXERROIS
- ✹ PINOT GRIS
- ✹ ZWEIGELT
- ✹ RED FEATHER
- BACCHUS

IT IS TOUGH BEING A "BORN FARMER" LIKE JOSEF ZUPPIGER WHEN one lives in Switzerland, where farms are tiny but very expensive. Born in 1950 near Zurich, Zuppiger rented his father's small dairy farm and orchard for 12 years. In 1986, after it was sold, he brought his wife, Margrit, and their five children to Alberta where they owned a farm with about 80 dairy cattle.

It transpired that their children were not born dairy farmers. "I wanted to stay in agriculture," Zuppiger says. "We travelled once to British Columbia, saw the vineyards and liked it." With son Manuel, who was born in 1976, also showing an interest in viticulture, the Zuppigers sold the dairy farm and bought a producing vineyard in 1997. Josef Zuppiger had no experience with grapes but he did not think it would be difficult. "Because I was an orchardist in Switzerland, I had an idea how to do it," he says. "I knew how to prune trees. I also learned it from books and took a course, so I knew how to do it." Almost. That year, there was more rain than usual in the normally dry Okanagan. The inexperienced Zuppiger did not spray as promptly as the weather conditions required and some of the grapes were infected with botrytis of the unwelcome variety. He was more diligent in subsequent vintages. Botrytis did not visit the vineyard again until the 2002 vintage. "We were too busy with the winery and we didn't have time to spray," he admitted later, somewhat embarrassed. Some of the infection, which was not extensive, was prized noble rot. Manuel Zuppiger, the winemaker, took the trouble to hand-select botrytized Pinot Gris berries for a dessert wine. He thought it was the best wine he made that vintage. However, the quantity was small, and it was kept for personal stock.

Initially, Josef Zuppiger had continued selling his grapes to Gray Monk, the patron of the vineyard's first owner. But he realized that he would not prosper and support a family as a grape grower with a vineyard only 6.5 hectares (16 acres) in size. He believes a grower needs a minimum of eight hectares (20 acres) to earn a living from selling grapes. "I would even say a bit more," he says. "But when we have a winery with that acreage, I am sure we can make a living here." Accordingly, Manuel was enrolled in the three-year winemaking program at Wädenswil, Switzerland's leading wine school.

Arrowleaf is located on well-travelled Camp Road. The winery, a simple building designed by the Zuppigers, is perched at the end of a steep driveway. From the veranda of the compact tasting room, there is an attractive view of Okanagan Lake. The vineyard dips sharply southwest, ideal for catching the sunlight that reflects from the lake. A deep gully on the south side of the vineyard, while serving as a local ecological reserve, also assures excellent air drainage. There is little risk that freezing air will pool among the vines. The lean soil, composed of sand, gravel and rocks, ensures that the growth is not too vigorous. As a result, Zuppiger's grapes ripen easily, achieving full varietal flavours.

The original owner had established the vineyard in 1986 with Gewürztraminer, later adding Bacchus, Pinot Gris and Auxerrois. The Zuppigers added Merlot and Zweigelt for their major red wines. To Manuel's disappointment, there was no room in the vineyard for Pinot Noir, a variety he had come to appreciate when he was in school in Switzerland. What little planting room remained was filled with a few vines of Dunkelfelder, an inky German red, useful for blending. There is also some Vidal for icewine or late harvest wine (depending on the winter weather). The Zuppigers intend to buy Pinot Noir grapes from vineyards elsewhere in the Okanagan. As soon as the word got out that they were making wine in 2001, the Zuppigers began hearing from growers eager to sell them fruit. Cautiously, they declined to buy grapes immediately for the same reason that they built a functional winery rather than a fancy one. "We don't want to jump into that right away," Josef said. "We want to see how everything works with the store and how much wine we can sell before we make the next step."

Manuel Zuppiger acquired solid winemaking experience at Wädenswil, where students spend most of the year apprenticing in wineries with periodic breaks to study theory. "It's more practical," his father suggests. "A lot of people go to university and don't find out what hands-on really means." Manuel worked the 2001 vintage in the Barossa Valley with Grant Burge, one of Australia's most awarded winemakers. In British Columbia, he also worked briefly at Tinhorn Creek before beginning to make Arrowleaf's wines in 2001. Burge wanted him back in Australia for the 2002 vintage but, with the new winery under development, he could not spare the time to go.

The wines Arrowleaf released when it opened in the spring of 2003 showed that Manuel had learned his art well. Both the Merlot and the Zweigelt, from estate-grown grapes, are ripe, juicy wines. The Merlot is lightly burnished with oak. "There is a lighter structure to the fruit flavours in the northern Okanagan, so we don't want to drown it with oak," he says. "We basically focus on the fruit and complement it with a bit of oak."

The crisply fruity whites are all aged in stainless steel tanks. (The Zuppigers did not economize when buying tanks because Josef considers the cheaper polyethylene tanks suitable only for water.) The one exception among the winery's whites is a blend of Pinot Gris and Auxerrois. Called Barrique, it is barrel-fermented to produce Arrowleaf's alternative to Chardonnay, which is not grown in the vineyard. Whether that style continues depends largely on the response to it in the tasting room.

"Manuel prefers more dry wines but we kind of persuaded him to make some a little sweeter, maybe, just because the customers may prefer it," the elder Zuppiger chuckles. The Arrowleaf Bacchus is aromatic and off-dry. The Auxerrois, also aromatic, is described as dry but "mellow" because of its fruitiness. However, the winery's debut Gewürztraminer, while also aromatic, is powerful and full-bodied in the style of Alsace.

The winery, with its picnic area, might be at its most attractive in the spring when the surrounding slopes blaze yellow with the so-called Okanagan sunflower. This is the inspiration for the Arrowleaf name. The plant is balsam root, a perennial with bright yellow flowers and large leaves in the shape of arrowheads.

AVERILL CREEK VINEYARDS

OPENING: PROPOSED FOR 2005/2006

6552 North Road, Duncan, BC, V9L 6K9
Telephone: 250-715-7379
Web site: www.averillcreek.ca

ANDY JOHNSTON'S HANDS TELL THE STORY. A COMPACT MAN WITH COILED-spring energy, he extends his vineyard-seasoned palms showing farmer's callusing. They are, he says, no longer the hands of the doctor he was for 32 years before beginning his second career as a Vancouver Island winegrower. "That's why I am Andy, not Dr. Johnston," he says. "I knew a long time ago that I had only so much doctoring in me."

Born in Britain in 1947, he immigrated to Edmonton in 1973, three years after earning his medical degree. A general practitioner, Johnston and a partner ultimately owned a company with 24 walk-in medical clinics in Edmonton and Calgary. "To be a good doctor, you've got to be *100 per cent* a doctor. You have got to be really committed to it. I knew I wasn't going to be, and there was a time coming when it was time for me to stop doing it. I planned an exit strategy, which is Averill Creek winery."

Johnston is a serious wine connoisseur. He has been secretary of the Edmonton chapter of the Opimian Society (a national Canadian wine club); a member of the exclusive Commanderie de Bordeaux tasting group; and a collector of fine wines with a palate for 30-year-old clarets. He was also one of the investors in Villa Delia, Umberto Menghi's cooking school and winery in Tuscany. In 1998, when Johnston disclosed his ambition to make wine, Menghi suggested he start by joining the team for Villa Delia's vintage that fall.

"That was a great experience for me, in a small vineyard," Johnston recalls. The resident winemaker there entrusted many duties to his eager intern. Johnston glows with pride at having managed some critical steps in the production of the 1998 Bambolo, Villa Delia's acclaimed red wine. "That's where I discovered that I can do this," he says.

Johnston levered that vintage into a peripatetic wine course. "I'm a kind of organized person," he suggests. "I didn't like sailing into this without any knowledge, so I spent the next four or five years working in vineyards and wineries around the world." One of the visitors to the Tuscan winery in 1998, noting the doctor's enthusiasm, helped him get a job in the next crush at a winery in Australia. There, Johnston worked with a French winemaker who found him a job the following vintage in a small Bordeaux château. Then, through a Vancouver doctor with shares in a New Zealand winery called Trinity Hill, Johnston arranged to do several vintages in New Zealand. "It's all networking around Villa Delia that got me the jobs I wanted to get," he chuckles. In between southern hemisphere trips lasting a month or more, he helped make wine at Alderlea Vineyards at Duncan.

Johnston considered many options before settling on the Cowichan Valley for his vineyard. He looked at properties in New Zealand. In 1999, he came close to buying a property in Bordeaux with a producing vineyard and a character farm house. Then he looked at Tuscany. "My daughters vetoed that and said I was not allowed to leave Canada," Johnston smiles.

There was another reason for his choice. "One of my hobbies and pleasures in life is sailing. So for me, then, it was Vancouver Island." In the fall of 2000, he armed himself with soil maps of the Cowichan Valley and, with a real estate agent, began scouting properties. At first, he was frustrated: either sites were not suitable or were not large enough. In February 2001, however, his agent came across contiguous treed properties, each about 18 hectares (45 acres), on the south-facing slope of Mount Prevost, north of Duncan. Johnston bought the upper half. (A year later, in an unrelated transaction, a Vancouver doctor named Bertram Perey bought the lower property for his own Mount Prevost Vineyards.)

In 2002, the first six hectares (14.5 acres) of vineyard were planted at Averill Creek (the name comes from a salmon-spawning creek that cuts through the eastern corner of the vineyard). Another seven hectares (18 acres) remains to be planted. Almost a third of the initial planting is Pinot Noir, followed by Pinot Gris, with modest plantings of Gewürztraminer and Merlot.

Johnston leans toward planting more Pinot Noir. He admired the fine wines from this grape that he encountered during another of his winemaking sabbaticals to New Zealand in 2004, when he worked in a Martinborough region winery specializing in Pinot Noir. However, he is also considering planting some Maréchal Foch, having been impressed by the wines that Alderlea's Roger Dosman makes from that French hybrid grape. "I've always been sceptical, I would say downright rude, about Maréchal Foch," Johnston admits. "I never tasted one that I liked at all until I tasted Roger's."

From the start, Johnston decided against planting the bread and butter varieties found in other Cowichan vineyards, such as Ortega and Bacchus. "I think the market really only accepts certain varietals, no matter how good you make your wine," Johnston argues. "I think Roger [Dosman] has a brilliant Bacchus. But no matter what you do with it, you can't sell it for more than $14, $15. So why would I grow Bacchus? If I can't get into the $15 to $25 range, then I shouldn't be in business. It's an expensive place to start a vineyard, the Cowichan Valley. It's an expensive place to make wine, no doubt about it, but I still think it is a very viable proposition."

The natural slope of Mount Prevost dictated the winery design, which Johnston calls "Italian rustic." The building flows down the contour, with the covered crush pad at the top, so that Johnston can avoid pumps and use gravity to move the wines. "The way I've planned it, the Pinot Noir will not be pumped ever, from the time it is crushed to the time it goes in the bottle," Johnston says. The juice flows freely from the crusher into the fermenting tanks, then into the blending tanks and then into the barrels. When the wine needs to be racked, the barrels are moved up the hill and gravity takes over again, all the way through to bottling. All wines benefit from gentle handling but none more so than Pinot Noir.

The winery, to be built in 2005, is designed to process a maximum of 90 tonnes (100 tons) of grapes, producing about 5,000 cases of wine a year. Johnston limits the vine yields severely in order to mature the grapes before the four-month rainy season begins in November. However, those rains fill the vast irrigation reservoir that get the vines through the Cowichan Valley's dry summer.

Johnston may also add a touch of Tuscany by planting a grove of olive trees in a gully not suitable for vines. This is part of Averill Creek's substantial land-scaping, flattering the winery's natural location. The hillside winery commands an extraordinary view south to the distant sparkle of Cowichan Bay. "I can see the planes landing at Sydney," says the sharp-eyed Johnston, referring to Victoria International Airport.

BELLA VISTA VINEYARDS

OPENED: 1994

3111 Agnew Road, Vernon, BC, V1H 1A1
Telephone: 250-558-0770
Toll-free: 1-888-221-0222
Web site: www.bellavistawinery.ca
Wine shop: Open daily in summer noon – 4 pm; or by appointment during winter.

THE TROUT POND IS AMONG THE DIVERSIONS AT VERNON'S BELLA VISTA winery. Armed with a bag of feed purchased for a dollar in the wine shop, visitors can bring the pond's entire population boiling to the surface in minutes. These indulged trout are not for catching but for entertainment and, perhaps like the pond itself, for therapy.

The pond was dug one summer day when Larry Passmore, Bella Vista's owner, needed distraction from deep personal depression. He found that diversion on the seat of his tractor, digging a hole in the hillside below Bella Vista's imposing winery. Eventually, the hole achieved Olympic proportions and he turned it into the trout pond. It is one of very few fish ponds at a British Columbia winery, and certainly the only one built to take the owner's mind away from his troubles. For a few years, life inflicted the trials of Job on Passmore. He has managed to hold onto his dream tenuously. Candidly, he says: "We still have two feet on a banana peel and one in the grave."

He also has a winery in such a splendid location that it has become one of Vernon's favourite locations for weddings and other social functions. Passmore will arrange to have the bridal party brought to the winery by helicopter, a memorable touch which gets around the fact that the driveway is not paved. "I love entertaining," he says. "It gives us the opportunity to make friends. Generally, I would suggest, it is more important to make good friends than it is to make good wine!"

The winery takes its name from the surrounding hillside neighbourhood where most homes enjoy fine views over the valley. Grapes have been growing here at least since 1965. The sun-drenched slope, while in the northern end of the Okanagan, has about 230 frost-free days a year. The grapes often ripen before Oliver-area vineyards. "So many of those vineyards are planted east and west or they are down in frost pockets," Passmore says. He gestures toward his own vineyard. "*These* rows are two degrees off magnetic south. Our average slope here is 12 degrees. It just grows. I wish I owned this whole little bowl."

Passmore, together with 15 minority partners, acquired the 6.5-hectare (16-acre) vineyard in 1991. A small acreage of table grapes was still in production after the previous owner had pulled out most of the hybrid wine grapes in 1988. The fallow acreage was replanted primarily with Maréchal Foch, Gewürztraminer and Auxerrois, with a bit of Chardonnay, Riesling and Pinot Noir. Passmore was launched on the all-consuming dream of running a winery. "This is a business of dreamers," he insists. "What makes it work for everybody is the dream. Very few people who work at Ford work there because they have a dream — unless they are engineers."

Born in Vernon in 1950, he began making his own alcoholic beverages just about the time he was old enough to drink. "I started blowing up beer bottles in 1971," he says, laughing at his amateur mishaps. By the 1980s, he and his wife were running a shop in Vernon that catered to home vintners and brewers, some of whom relied on the amiable Passmore to do the work for them. The customers included the cadre, many of them Vernon professionals, who joined Passmore to develop the city's first winery.

"They were fantastic," Passmore says, speaking in the past tense because he and his partners subsequently became estranged when finances went sideways. "Eight or nine of them were Mensa geniuses and they were wonderful people." In better days, the partners in 1994 erected a grand, colonial-style winery, with 280 square metres (3,000 square feet) on each of three floors. Passmore already had made Bella Vista's first vintage the year before in a small building at the base of the vineyard. "We were doing just fine, down in our service garage," he said at the time. "But we were going to need more space and we thought rather than put the thing together piecemeal, year after year, we'd go out and build a building that would look after our needs in the turn of the century — and grow into it."

Most of the construction was done by Passmore and his partners during a boisterous building bee. "It was a party all summer long," Passmore remembers. "We put this building up by ourselves. We set the windows, we put in the floors, we pounded in the nails, we tied the rebar. We built this thing. We had a campground over there, put in some picnic tables, had a couple of campers. And we always had at least two kegs of Okanagan Springs brew on ice. At the end of the day, what are you going to do? You should have been here, you'd have loved it."

Passmore's party crashed at the end of August that year, when his marriage broke down. The wines of 1994 got made (as they have been in every vintage since) and the winery opened to the public that October. But over the next several years, a period he calls "the dark time," Passmore was consumed with grief and anger, either taking solace in his cellar or taking it out on those around him. "In hindsight, I should have sold it [the winery] immediately and left the country," he says now. "Gone to Provence or Italy and sat down at a bar and stayed there until I was over it. But I didn't want to get away from my dream at all." He managed to alienate partners, friends and even customers. "For a few years, we were a place that nobody wanted to send people to, because of my behaviour."

In time Passmore bounced back. Fundamentally, he is a man of bucolic charm who still sees his winery as a vehicle for delivering good times to everyone in his orbit. An enthusiastic self-taught chef, he still talks about a lively Mother's Day one year when 350 had dinner at the winery. "If I was making money, I'd go and hire a winemaker," he says. "I love entertaining." And the social functions have kept Bella Vista going, along with revenue from the raspberry patch, from the U-pick table grapes and from selling the lambs generated by the flock of sheep that keep the vineyard grass under check. "They've been running sheep in vineyards in Europe for a couple of thousand years," Passmore says. "It's something that works. I use the tractor so much less nowadays than I used to."

When it comes to winemaking, Passmore likes nothing better than blending. "I play with the damn stuff," is how he puts it. "I grab a jug out of this tank and a jug out of that tank and I'll bring it up and I'll start playing with it. And I'm more interested in making a wine that I like than keeping a tank alone and unique."

He has a different take on Pinot Noir than almost anyone else in the business: he likes the grape's versatility in blends with Maréchal Foch. "We make three different wines from the Maréchal Foch–Pinot Noir blend," he says. One is Rocky Mountain Red, a big, black, extractive wine "for serious red wine drinkers." Its companion, lighter and fruity, is called Lady in Red. The third partner in this trilogy is called, simply, Maréchal Foch–Pinot Noir blend, an uncomplicated "drinking" wine. Passmore's approach with whites is similar, although in the past he has produced varietals from both Gewürztraminer and Chardonnay.

One of his favourite wines remains Bella Vista's 1994 Chardonnay, a rich and full-bodied wine. "We made 6,000 bottles and we sold 5,000 bottles at $13.95," he says. (Every wine in the winery usually sells at that one price.) "And it was so good that I put the price up to $20 and stopped letting people taste it. The last 1,000 bottles sold in about six weeks. I couldn't believe it. But we needed the money, so we let it go."

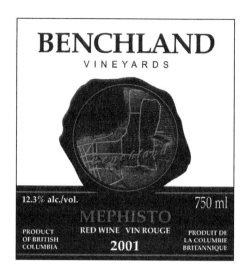

BENCHLAND VINEYARDS

OPENED: 2001

170 Upper Bench Road South, Penticton, BC, V2A 8T1
Telephone: 250-770-1733
Wine shop: Open 11 am – 6 pm Tuesday through Sunday during summer.

RECOMMENDED

* MEPHISTO
ZWEIGELT

KLAUS STADLER IS A STICKLER FOR CLEANLINESS, A LEGACY OF HAVING been a master brewer in Germany. He considers that a winery, like a brewery, is a food-processing facility and must be kept clean.

He could almost do surgery in his winery, which gleams with polished stainless steel tanks and other equipment, most of which, he observes, is the "Mercedes" of its class. Eschewing such cheaper alternatives as plastic tanks, Stadler ferments and stores his wines only in stainless steel tanks, cleaned to the point of sterilization. "If you look at the surface of stainless steel under a microscope, it's smooth, like a paved road," he explains. "And if you look at the surface of plastic under a microscope, it's like mountains. The bacteria are sitting in the valleys. How can you clean it out?"

For the same reason, he has no oak barrels in the winery. "I work with chips because I think it is cleaner to have wine in stainless steel," he says. "If you have a wooden barrel, how do you clean it properly? This way, you have more control over the flavour. I did a lot of research about what is better, barrels or wood chips. I figured out that wood chips, if you buy good quality, are better." So he immerses nylon bags filled with oak chips into those wines where the oak flavour is desired.

The wines are tasted regularly and the chips are removed when enough oak flavour has been transferred.

"It makes sense to me," Stadler says, even if he is in the minority among Okanagan winemakers. He contends that barrels were used to age wine only because winemakers had no other choice. He considers that barrels are dated technology and he is prepared to argue the point. "I say to people, 'What car do you drive? Which model?' They might say 1998. I say, 'Why don't you drive a 1956?' It's the same thing." Clearly, he is a man of strong views — and clean wines.

Born in 1955 in a Bavarian village south of Munich, Stadler became a master brewer. He worked for several mid-sized breweries until 1988, when he opened his own business, combining a brewery, a pub and a distillery. When he became restless for a change of career, he sold the business and came to the Okanagan in 1997. After canvassing potential properties throughout the valley, he purchased an orchard at the eastern edge of Penticton, removed the trees and, beginning in 1998, developed a 3.6-hectare (nine-acre) vineyard.

Stadler originally wanted to develop a distillery after opening the winery. "It is a great area for a distillery," he says of the Okanagan. "We have all the orchards, with apricots, apples, pears, prunes, everything. Somebody has to start. The orchardists are just crying for help to the government. I have the background. I have the experience. I think Okanagan distilled products could be among the best in the whole world." In Germany, he made eight or nine distilled beverages. Before coming to Canada, he had researched the federal government's tax regime for distilleries but not the provincial taxes. "Tax-wise, British Columbia has the highest taxes for alcohol in the whole world," he learned. And the provincial officials were not flexible. "It didn't make sense for me to start this distillery," he says sadly. "But then, you have to play the game. I decided to make high-quality wines. What can you do?"

What he did was plant his vineyard, which slopes gently toward the west and has soil that Stadler compares to a garden. As with the winery, no shortcuts were taken. The vines — Riesling, Pinot Blanc, Chardonnay, Pinot Noir, Cabernet Sauvignon, Merlot, Zweigelt and three rows of Lemberger — all are grafted to rootstock. (Own-rooted vines, he notes, are not even permitted in Germany.) He installed drip irrigation rather than cheaper overhead sprinklers so that water and fertilizers are dispensed with economical precision.

"Drip irrigation costs a little bit more, but in the long run it saves because it reduces the need to spray," Stadler says. "For each spraying, you have to go through with the tractor; you use diesel, you use the tractor, you use chemicals. It all costs money." As well, minimal spraying is an environmental plus. "It is such a nice climate here. It is dry. You don't have to spray a lot," Stadler has learned. "You need the chemicals, without question, but the less chemicals, the better."

Benchland is the first winery in British Columbia, and one of few in Canada, to produce Zweigelt. This red grape, a cross of Lemberger and St. Laurent, was developed in Austria. Because it makes richly fruity and soft wines, it is one of the most widely grown varieties in Austria. Stadler knew the variety from having tasted Austrian reds. However, when he first ordered vines from his supplier, a nursery in Ontario, Zweigelt was not among the varieties being offered.

A few months after he placed his initial order, the nursery told him it could not ship all of the Pinot Noir vines he wanted. The alternatives offered now included Zweigelt. Stadler jumped with excitement but, for several days, he concealed this from the nursery while negotiating a favourable purchase of the vines. He bought 1,600 vines and subsequently doubled the order. "I was so happy to get Zweigelt," he says now.

Benchland's Zweigelt is light to medium in body, with spicy berry tastes. "I make the wine unoaked and the fruity flavour comes out." Mephisto, the winery's premium red, combines Zweigelt, Cabernet Sauvignon and Lemberger in a classic Austrian-style red. "I read about that blend in an Austrian wine magazine," Stadler admits.

The vineyard was planted from 1998 through 2001. In order to make quality wines, he crops the vines carefully, averaging less than half what the vines could yield on his fertile soil. "That's my philosophy of winemaking," Stadler says. "Winemaking starts in the vineyard. If you do not have good quality in the vineyard, you do not get good quality wine."

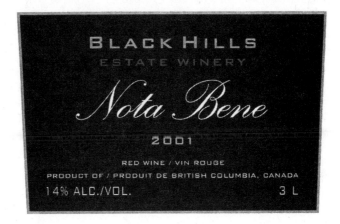

BLACK HILLS ESTATE WINERY

OPENED: 2001

30880 71st Street (Black Sage Road), Oliver, BC, V0H 1T0
Telephone: 250-498-0666
Web site: www.blackhillswinery.com
Wine shop: Open daily 11 am – 5 pm June through September;
   weekends only May and October.

RECOMMENDED

✳ NOTA BENE
✳ SEQUENTIA
✳ ALIBI

VISITING THE WINE SHOP AT BLACK HILLS BRINGS TO MIND THE CHARMING story of an American airline flying into Rome during Vatican II, the Catholic Church's theological conference of the 1960s. For the bishops and cardinals among its passengers, the airline printed menus in Latin. Black Hills, which makes only three wines, has a wine list fit for a cleric. The red wine is called Nota Bene and the white dessert wine is called Sequentia. A dry Sauvignon Blanc-Sémillon wine, made for the first time in 2003, is called Alibi. "The derivation is Latin," Senka Tennant, the winemaker, says.

Fortunately for those who were not altar boys, the winery's Latin is not obscure. *Nota bene,* usually abbreviated now as NB, means "take notice" while *sequentia* is loosely translated as "follow on." True to the name of the wine, Black Hills attracted notice with its debut 1999 Nota Bene. The wine, a Bordeaux blend, earned the winery a cult following.

Why Latin? A couple of the partners in this winery came to appreciate the language in college. Latin was canvassed for the new dry white until the winery owners decided on a name more likely to be familiar to consumers. "The whole process of explaining the meanings became arduous," the winemaker found.

The winery was conceived when four Vancouver business people, in a 1996 mid-life career change for all, left the fast lane in the big city to buy a 14-hectare (34-acre) property on Black Sage Road, south of Oliver. The partners are Peter and Susan McCarrell, and Bob and Senka Tennant. The Tennants were school-teachers for a short time, which helps explain the names of the wines. "I like Latin," says Senka. The winemaker at Black Hills, she consulted during the early vintages with Rusty Figgins, a Washington State specialist in red wine production. "I wish I could have spent a crush with him," she says. "We mostly communicated on the phone. He was a guide." But by the 2002 vintage, which produced the richest Nota Bene so far, Senka Tennant was confidently flying solo.

Wine growing was new to the four partners. Peter McCarrell is a carpenter, Susan is a legal secretary; Bob Tennant, who has a degree in agriculture and plant science, previously was a general contractor and Senka, who has a degree in botany, latterly was a clothing retailer. In the Okanagan, they started from scratch. "Our land had been untouched for 10-plus years after the grape pullout but it was a vineyard," Bob Tennant says. "There were a few broken posts and a lot of weeds and a few hybrid volunteers here and there." They planted three Bordeaux reds, Cabernet Sauvignon, Cabernet Franc and Merlot, and two Bordeaux whites, Sauvignon Blanc and Sémillon. They also planted Pinot Noir and Chardonnay and have chosen to sell those to other wineries.

The property also included a utilitarian Quonset hut, then occupied by an individual who was building cars for demolition derbies. "We weren't thinking of the winery all that much," Tennant says. "Pete and I are from a construction background. We looked at it and we said, this could actually work in this structure. It's about the size we needed. I did some drawings. Our neighbours thought we were crazy. It's turned out to be a very practical space." Not erecting a fancy winery also conserved cash. "We're pretty happy with it as it is," Tennant admits. "We're trying to put our money in our product."

The appearance of the winery has not hurt sales. When Black Hills analyzed its first season, the partners discovered that half of the sales were done in that casual tasting room, from a counter of planks on top of barrels. In its first two vintages, the winery produced about 1,800 cases of Nota Bene and about 150 cases (in half bottles) of Sequentia, the dessert wine. The current intent is to limit Black Hills to a total production of 2,500 cases.

The Bordeaux reds are dedicated to the Nota Bene blend, with the exact proportions depending on vintage conditions. "We're not trying to make our wine identical year to year," Bon Tennant says. "We're not going to adjust things to make it all the same. We expect it to taste different but have a familiarity to it. We want people to look forward to tasting the next vintage and knowing roughly the characteristics to expect — but the season will be a big part of what comes out."

The Sequentia is as different from Nota Bene as Sauternes is from claret. The initial vintages are late harvest expressions of the fine Sauvignon Blanc grown on the property. In 2002 Senka Tennant made a serious study of wine-making with Sauvignon Blanc, including a tour of Sancerre in France. Black Hills's strategy of making just one dry table wine had been undermined by demands from its customers for a white partner to Nota Bene. The outcome was the 2003 Alibi. The crisply fresh blend is 85 per cent Sauvignon Blanc, fermented in stainless steel, and 15 per cent barrel-fermented Sémillon. The 400 cases that the winery released in May, 2004, were sold out a month later, as was the 2002 Nota Bene.

BLASTED CHURCH WINERY

OPENED: 2000

378 Parsons Road, Okanagan Falls, BC, V0H 1R0

Telephone: 250-497-1125

Web site: www.blastedchurch.com

Wine shop: Open daily 10 am – 5 pm in summer and fall; by appointment at other times.

RECOMMENDED

- ❉ GEWÜRZTRAMINER
- ❉ MERLOT – CABERNET SAUVIGNON
- ❉ SYRAH
- ✸ HATFIELD'S FUSE
- ✸ CHARDONNAY MUSQUÉ
- ✸ PINOT GRIS
- ✸ MERLOT
- ✸ CABERNET SAUVIGNON
- EHRENFELSER

NO OKANAGAN WINERY EVER GOT AS MUCH LIFT FROM A LABEL CHANGE as Blasted Church when, under new owners, it relaunched in the summer of 2002 with brilliantly whimsical art on its wine bottles. It was opened two years earlier as Prpich Hills Winery and Vineyard by Dan Prpich, a Croatian-born grape grower. When he retired, he sold the property to Chris and Evelyn Campbell, a Vancouver business couple with experience both in accounting and in hotel management.

Dan Prpich had plunked a winery with a capacity for 10,000 cases a year on the highest point of a 17-hectare (42-acre) property north of Okanagan Falls, but somewhat off the beaten path. Nearby Eastside Road, connecting Okanagan Falls with Penticton, twists picturesquely but narrowly along the east shore of Skaha

Lake, largely for local traffic. Prpich Hills had been operating below the radar screen for two years when the Campbells took over in May of 2002.

To increase visibility, Evelyn Campbell hired Vancouver designer Bernie Hadley-Beauregard to create a lively new wine label. "I told him we had to do something very, very different," she says. "The more outrageous, the better." They canvassed a number of ideas, coming back to Blasted Church because of the solid local story behind it. There is a century-old wooden church in Okanagan Falls that originally was in Fairview, the now-vanished mining community near Oliver. In 1929, when the church was dismantled to move it, the crew solved the problem of loosening the nails from the sturdy timbers with a dynamite explosion inside the building. It worked, at the expense of toppling the steeple. Hadley-Beauregard recounted the story in caricatures on the wine labels (one of which, a popular blend of Chasselas, Optima and Gewürztraminer, is called Hatfield's Fuse).

The Blasted Church label was intended to create a fun-loving image for selling the somewhat average wines that the Campbells acquired with the winery. They planned to come up with an "elegant" name for the new winery. That idea was dropped after Blasted Church struck such a chord with consumers.

The mischievous élan of these labels — "It's just who I am," Evelyn laughs — debunks the image of accountants as humourless number crunchers. Certainly, the Campbells researched the wine business meticulously before getting into it. Chris Campbell, born in 1955 in Vancouver, was an administrator with a major brokerage house. Evelyn, born in Montreal in 1956, was a practicing certified general accountant. They wanted a business that they would run themselves. Once they identified the wine business, with its appealing lifestyle, they spent two and a half years going through the books of wineries that were for sale. "We knew when we put things together that it wasn't going to be a walk in the park," Evelyn says. "The numbers were the reality of it. We did not just want to come to the beautiful vineyard."

Their research had shown that, as novices in growing grapes and making wine, they needed the support of experts. Their first choice as winemaker was Frank Supernak, a graduate microbiologist who had worked in Okanagan wineries since 1984. A founding partner of the Hester Creek winery in 1996, Supernak had spent five arduous years reinvigorating the vineyard there.

Tragically, Supernak died in an accident at another winery on November 10, 2002, a week after the last grapes were picked and processed at Blasted Church. Immediately, teams of winemakers from other Okanagan wineries rallied to help the Campbells deal with tanks of fermenting wines. Chris once made wine at home in Vancouver but admits ruefully that it seldom turned out very well. He needed help. "The support that we got was just phenomenal," Chris remembers. In the eight months it took the Campbells to recruit a new winemaker, Ashley Hooper from Quails' Gate took primary responsibility for finishing 4,000 cases of Blasted Church wines from that excellent 2002 vintage. Blasted Church remembered the Good Samaritan winemakers by putting sketches of them onto the label for the 2002 Pinot Noir.

The search for a winemaker with skills comparable to Supernak's began in December. "For our size, it is a pretty big commitment to have somebody full time but that was our business plan from day one," Chris says. "We were not going the consulting winemaker route." Looking internationally, Blasted Church attracted 75 résumés (including several overpriced California winemakers) before settling on a personable South African, Willem Grobbelaar.

Born in 1976, the lanky Grobbelaar grew up on the 24,000-hectare (59,000-acre) sheep farm that his father operates in Namibia. He went to school in Stellenbosch, the heart of South Africa's wine country. "I guess being among the vines every day — if you look out of the classroom, you see the vines — kind of triggered me," Grobbelaar says. He plunged into his choice with a passion by working two vintages in 1996 — the first at Spier Home Farms in Stellenbosch and the second in the northern hemisphere six months later at Kunde Estate Winery in Sonoma, the first of two winemaker internships he has done in California. "The more experience you have, the better wine you can make," the winemaker observes.

After working two harvests in the same year, Grobbelaar completed a three-year program at Elsenburg Agricultural College, a leading South African viticultural school. "You get a lot of practical experience at Elsenburg," he says. "They have a small cellar. Everything is hands-on. At the end of the year, you should be able to make wine." He was assistant winemaker at Longridge Cellar when he sought the Blasted Church job at the urging of Dr. Hennie van Vuuren, the South African academic at the University of British Columbia's wine research centre.

Regrettably, Grobbelaar was only to make one Okanagan vintage. He was forced to return to South Africa in July, 2004, when the Canadian government refused to extend his work permit. Once again, the Campbells advertised, this time attracting an experienced young Australian, Marcus Ansems, whose papers were in order. Ansems, a graduate of Australia's famed Roseworthy wine school, first came to Canada in 1999 on a three-vintage contract to get the Creekside Estate Winery established in Ontario. He stayed there four vintages, supervising the construction of a winery as well as the planting of several vineyards. He made award-winning wines at both Creekside and its sister winery in Nova Scotia, recruiting a team of skilled winemakers to take over when he returned to Australia. But Ansems had also married a Canadian and that was a factor in his decision to return to Canada. For the Campbells, it was another bittersweet year: bitter because their strenuous effort to retain Grobbelaar failed but sweet because Ansems comes with an impressive track record.

The Campbells have now begun to replace some of their vines with mainstream commercial varieties, including Shiraz and Sauvignon Blanc. In 2004, Blasted Church became one of British Columbia's first wineries to release all wines in bottles sealed with screw caps in order to avoid cork-tainted wines, one of the industry's big headaches. There is another advantage as well. "It eliminates the grief when you can't find a corkscrew," Evelyn Campbell explains.

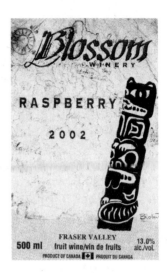

BLOSSOM WINERY

OPENED: 2001

5491 Minoru Boulevard, Richmond, BC, V6X 2B1
Telephone: 604-232-9839
Web site: www.blossomwinery.com
Wine shop: Open daily 11 am – 6 pm.

RECOMMENDED

- ✻ SELECT LATE HARVEST RIESLING
- ✻ RASPBERRY RESERVE
- ✻ RASPBERRY LATE HARVEST
- BLUEBERRY
- DRY BLUEBERRY

THERE IS A BIT OF THE SPIRIT OF JOHN CHANG'S CHINESE GRAND-MOTHER IN EVERY bottle made at Blossom Winery. Chang, who immigrated to Canada in 1999 with Allison Lu, his spouse, grew up on a farm in Taiwan. One room in the family house was set aside for producing fruit wines and other traditional fermented products (pickles, soya sauce) of the Chinese kitchen. The aromas and flavours of the wines his grandmother made are still alive in Chang's memory, powerfully influencing the expressive wines he now makes from the Fraser Valley's raspberries and blueberries.

Over a cup of green tea, Chang explains (through a translator) that one needs to understand Blossom against the culture in which he grew up. Life was very hard in rural China, including Taiwan, and people worked seven days a week from dawn to dusk. Alcoholic beverages served to rejuvenate the weary. "The people believed that drinking alcohol was better for your health," Chang says.

"For instance, if you worked a hard day, and you came home and had some wine, it replenished your body."

While the men worked the land, it was left to women to process the food in the home. That was how women like Soo Gao Chang, his grandmother, became home vintners. They were already fermenting vegetables to preserve them, acquiring a skill easily transferred to fruits and grapes when these were grown on the farm. When Chang came to Canada, he brought along a half-century-old handmade clay jar, about 30 litres (six and a half gallons) in size, in which his grandmother and her peers fermented their wines.

Aside from nourishing the body, the wines were socially important. In a society which then had no disposable income for luxuries, the home-produced wines were used for entertaining and given as gifts. "Because times were tough, you basically took your own wines that you made and shared them with friends," Chang remembers.

His grandmother's technique was that of country winemakers all over the world. The clay jars were filled with alternating layers of fruit (such as plums or whole grapes) and sugar, with sugar being about a quarter of the volume. The jars were then sealed with a cap that let fermentation gases escape but kept the air out, and were left to ferment for seven or eight months before being emptied. The resulting wines might have achieved only five per cent alcohol but they· were sweet, aromatic and richly flavoured. The fruit residue was consumed as well, a candied treat with enough alcohol to flush the faces of grown men and give children an unsteady gait.

Chang's interest in making wines came from watching his grandmother. The taste and aroma of the wines stayed with him as a very pleasant memory. Before coming to Canada, Chang, who was born in 1955, built a business as an electrical equipment dealer in Taiwan. But as a young adult, he had taken up his grandmother's craft of making wines, even to the point of planting a few grapevines. He began to dream of having a winery of his own, not very practical in Taiwan where the single winery was state-owned. But Canada provided him with the opportunity.

In Richmond, Chang and Lu discovered that the local raspberries and blueberries, fruits not well known in Taiwan, were of superior flavour. Chang endeavours to capture the fresh-berry tastes in Blossom's wines, in a setting far more professional than his grandmother's farmhouse. Blossom's strip mall storefront in Richmond, next to a furniture store, has an attractive tasting room for the public. In the back, away from public view, is a processing facility with stainless steel tanks, a far cry from his grandmother's clay jar. Chang did make one batch of apple wine in that jar after coming to Canada but, sadly, the jar developed cracks during a cold winter.

Chang made a number of trial lots of fruit wines in small containers. But before plunging into the business, he retained a veteran winemaker, Ron Taylor, to help Blossom scale up to commercial volumes. Taylor, a microbiologist who had made wine at Andrés for 25 years, had never before made fruit wines. As it turned out, Chang and Taylor learned from each other. Chang acquired the technical skills he needed while Taylor has gone on to a new career as winemaker with two other British Columbia fruit wineries.

The style of Blossom's wines has been informed both by Chang's memories of his grandmother's wines and by his perception of the Asian wine palate. Almost all of the wines, which now include icewines and late harvest wines from Okanagan-grown Riesling grapes, are sweet. Blossom, which makes about 6,500 cases a year, sells as much as three-quarters of its total volume in Asia or to Asian buyers at the winery.

"Sweeter wines sell better in Asia," Chang says. "Chinese people are the only people who are afraid of 'sour' things." The reference is to cuisine with an acidic bite. "The Japanese, the people of Thailand or Malaysia all have sour foods in their diets. Chinese people don't. In China and Taiwan, there is very little sale of dry white wine. For sweet white wine, there is no problem. That's why icewine, whether fake or real, seems to do so well in China and Taiwan."

As Blossom increases its selection of wines, Chang has introduced drier wines from such grapes as Merlot and Pinot Noir and from fruits. In 2002 he made dry blueberry wine, fermented on the skins to achieve the concentration and character of a full-bodied red grape wine. The intent with the drier wines is to increase sales in North American and European markets, where there is a palate for drier wines.

The winery is strategically located in Richmond, near the Vancouver airport, where it is convenient for both exporting and for capturing incoming tours. Blossom has seen as many as 60 buses a month in peak season. However, Chang works equally hard at wine festivals all over British Columbia, overcoming his English deficit with a beaming smile and a generous pour. His ambition one day is to have a winery in the Okanagan. The dream is sufficiently formed that he has a tasting room laid out in his mind.

1999
VINTNER'S RESERVE
Black Muscat
VANCOUVER ISLAND

500 ml · RED WINE / VIN ROUGE · 12.0% alc./vol.

BLUE GROUSE WINERY
DUNCAN, BRITISH COLUMBIA
PRODUCT OF CANADA · PRODUIT DU CANADA

BLUE GROUSE VINEYARDS

OPENED: 1993

4365 Blue Grouse Road, Duncan, BC, V9L 6M3
Telephone: 250-743-3834
Web site: www.bluegrousevineyards.com
Wine shop: Open 11 am – 5 pm Wednesday through Sunday
    (closed Sunday October through March).

RECOMMENDED

* ☀ BLACK MUSCAT
* ☼ PINOT GRIS
* ✷ ORTEGA
* ✷ SIEGERREBE
* GAMAY NOIR
* PINOT NOIR

WHEN HANS KILTZ MOVED BLUE GROUSE'S WINEMAKING FROM THE basement of the family home to a commodious new winery in 2000, he ensured that the new building included a superbly equipped laboratory. "I like laboratories," he says.

That is to be expected. "I had laboratories all my life," he says. Born in Berlin in 1938, Kiltz has four scientific degrees: one in veterinarian medicine, one in tropical veterinarian medicine, one in fish pathology and a doctorate in microbiology. As an employee of the United Nation's Food and Agricultural Organization, he worked both in Asia and Africa, once managing a laboratory with 42 employees. Drawn repeatedly to Africa, where he first began working in 1965, Kiltz returned reluctantly to Germany about two decades later when his two children had reached high school age. That lasted about a year.

"If you are used to life in Africa, you cannot easily get back to a European lifestyle," Kiltz says, explaining how a much-travelled man with his credentials ended up growing grapes on Vancouver Island. "The other problem, of course, is when you are 50, you won't get a job anymore. You are on your own." So in 1988, intending to apply one of his degrees to fish farming, he came to Vancouver Island. As it happened, British Columbia's aquaculture industry went into a slump. However, the farm that Kiltz and his family purchased had been an experimental vineyard that had fallen into neglect when the previous owner got into financial difficulty. Kiltz, who had winemaking relatives in Germany, started making wine for personal consumption. When the rules changed in British Columbia to allow small farm wineries, Kiltz turned his hobby into a business, getting a license late in 1992 and opening the tasting room the following April.

"My scientific degrees helped me to do this," Kiltz says. "It is not much different, winemaking and veterinarian medicine. Both are half science and half art. When you do operations, you have to imagine things because the animal doesn't talk to tell you where the pain is. It's a sort of art, you know."

The vineyard had been planted by John Harper, a viticultural dreamer who died in 2001 after a lifetime of giving sage advice for growing grapes on coastal British Columbia. After operating test vineyards in the Fraser Valley for years, he moved to Vancouver Island. His original Cowichan Valley vineyard became Blue Grouse and his second, near Cobble Hill, became the Glenterra winery.

The 12.5-hectare (31-acre) Blue Grouse property has an excellent southwestern exposure. The vines get adequate sun, ripening without having to be tented. "Why should I tent?" Kiltz asks during a 2003 conversation. "I have been growing grapes here now for 14 years and I have never had a problem ripening them. I refuse to tent. If I cannot grow good grapes without all this extra investment, then I would say I am on the wrong spot here. I think then I should have a greenhouse to grow grapes."

There might have been as many as 100 different varieties growing in Harper's vineyard. Kiltz and his Philippines-born wife, Evangeline, who does much of the vineyard management now, imposed discipline and order on the slope. Gradually, Blue Grouse has selected the varieties — Ortega, Pinot Gris, Siegerrebe and Bacchus — that Kiltz has found to be most successful. The two primary red varieties are Pinot Noir and Gamay.

Kiltz has dabbled a bit himself with trial plots because, with only a third of his property planted, there is room for more vines. "I've got my plate full," he has decided. "There are constantly new varieties coming out. In the past two years, I had other varieties from Germany here. I pulled those out. If I were much younger and had the time to experiment with those, I would certainly try different things. But it's too late for me, you know."

Of course, it is not too late for the next generation. Richard Kiltz, his son, who was born in 1978, has spent four years in Bavaria to train as a winemaker. Sandrina Kiltz, his daughter, has been managing the business and the tasting room since graduating in business administration from the University of Victoria.

A congenial personality, she is more comfortable at public events than her reserved, quietly spoken father. Hans Kiltz can be as laconic as the animals he used to treat as a veterinarian.

He has strong opinions, however, on the controversial question of whether or not Vancouver Island wineries should use only island-grown grapes. He opposes buying Okanagan grapes for winemaking on the island. "It is against our philosophy," he says. "We were one of the first ones trying to establish an identity for Vancouver Island wine." He worries that the character of island wines will be lost among all those wines being made from grapes grown elsewhere.

In the opinion of Giordano Venturi, another Vancouver Island winemaker who shares the same viewpoint, the wines of Blue Grouse are "incredibly well made." Venturi, a consummate artist with bone-dry wines, grumbles a bit that Kiltz is still following the German style of making off-dry wines. But, in fact, Kiltz has moved on. The only wine not fully dry at Blue Grouse is Le Classique, a blend of Ortega and Bacchus that the winery itself calls "a refreshing starter wine or just something to sip before dinner."

The flagship whites at Blue Grouse, now making a total of 3,000 cases a year, are Pinot Gris, always crisp and fresh; intensely fruity Siegerrebe; and Ortega. The latter variety, with an array of flavours running from grapefruit to Muscat, arguably is the signature variety for Vancouver Island.

Blue Grouse also has an exclusive, a wine that Kiltz calls Black Muscat. The variety has been developed from a few vines, perhaps of Hungarian origin, that John Harper left behind. "I gave the grapes to a home winemaker, a friend of mine, and he made a wonderful wine from it," Kiltz recalls. Now, Kiltz produces about 800 litres (175 gallons) annually of an aromatic dry red, aged in American oak barrels. It is exotic, with a powerful aroma, a wine that Kiltz suggests be enjoyed with dishes like foie gras. There never will be much of this wine, and not just because Kiltz is reluctant to offer cuttings to other growers.

"It is not easy," he says. "It wouldn't grow in the Okanagan. Even in our area here, it is very hard to get it through the winter because it freezes back up to one or two buds on each cane. It also doesn't grow like other wine grapes. It is very hard to control it in the vineyard. It is terrible to grow it. Nobody likes to look after it. This is one reason why I have not expanded my plantation."

BLUE HERON FRUIT WINERY

OPENED: 2004

18539 Dewdney Trunk Road, Pitt Meadows, BC, V3Y 2R9
Telephone: 604-465-5563
Web site: www.blueheronwinery.ca
Wine shop: Open daily 10 am – 8 pm (to 9 pm Friday and Saturday).

AT 84, GEORGE FLYNN GAVE NEW MEANING TO THE TERM "ESTATE WINERY."
As he was completing the wine shop at the end of 2003, he explained that "it adds
value to the estate" to establish a winery on the cranberry and blueberry farm he
has owned since 1946. The only fruit winery in the Vancouver area that is north
of the Fraser River, it was inspired by the success of The Fort Wine Company
across the river at Fort Langley.

Born in Moosomin, Saskatchewan, in 1919, Flynn recounts that he made it
to British Columbia "with difficulty" by moving from job to job during the
Depression. When the war began, he enlisted in an army engineering regiment
and was posted to Britain in 1941, where he saw action when the Allies invaded
Europe. "I did swim ashore on D-Day," he says in his laconic style. "More or less
had to. The boat had been blown up." Discharged as a lance sergeant, he
returned to British Columbia.

The eight-hectare (20-acre) property he bought on Dewdney Trunk Road
was then in a largely rural area of the Fraser Valley. Flynn eventually planted
blueberries but earned a living in marine construction, applying the engineering
skills he had acquired in the army. He still reflects on the irony of building docks
and bridges after having once blown them up on another continent. "A lot of loud
noises," he remembers.

After retiring from construction in the mid-1980s, he devoted himself to the
several cranberry bogs that he owned. With cranberry prices strong at the time,

he removed some blueberry bushes to make room for cranberries on his Dewdney Trunk Road farm. In doing so, he was flying against conventional wisdom that said cranberries cannot be grown on ordinary farm soil. Flynn concedes it took a few years to establish his new cranberry bog, but he did succeed.

"Up until the end of the twentieth century, there was nothing but money from cranberries — until everybody in the country started planting them," Flynn says. The collapse in cranberry prices (there has been some modest recovery) was the catalyst behind his decision to research and then build a fruit winery. This was, of course, the same impetus behind the development of The Fort winery, which opened in 2001. Flynn arranged to have Dominic Rivard, The Fort's experienced winemaker, produce the initial wines for Blue Heron Fruit Winery (named for the abundant heron population in the area). "I have never made wine in my life," Flynn says. The products with which the winery opened included wines from blueberries, cranberries, raspberries, peaches and apricots.

To develop the winery, Flynn dipped into the expertise within his family. One son, a union business manager, steered the winery application through the regulators. Another, an engineer, designed the building, a simple and efficient structure with cedar siding and a veranda on the front, not unlike the period architecture around Fort Langley. A daughter, an accountant, helped set up the business systems. George Flynn is satisfied that other members of the large family share a growing interest in the winery.

The production will depend entirely on demand, which may well be brisk. Once a remote rural road, Dewdney Trunk is a thoroughfare bustling with traffic created by urban sprawl on the north side of the Fraser River. Flynn Farms, the parent of Blue Heron, operates a long-established farm market each season for its cranberries and blueberries. "We've sold blueberries here for 35 years," Flynn says, adding proudly: "Anybody can sell a blueberry, but for repeat customers, you must have quality. We have customers that have been coming for years and years."

Now, those customers have an additional reason to return to Flynn Farms.

BLUE MOUNTAIN VINEYARD AND CELLARS

OPENED: 1992

RR1, S3, C4, Okanagan Falls, BC, V0H 1R0

Telephone: 250-497-8244

Web site: www.bluemountainwinery.com

Wine shop: By appointment.

RECOMMENDED

- ❋ PINOT NOIR
- ❋ PINOT GRIS
- ❋ BLUE MOUNTAIN BRUT
- ❋ CHARDONNAY
- ❋ PINOT BLANC
- ❋ GAMAY NOIR

THE FINGERPRINTS OF BURGUNDY ARE ALL OVER BLUE MOUNTAIN, THE Okanagan's most consistent producer of Pinot Noir. Three of the five varieties grown here are Burgundian (and the others are from Alsace, which is next door). Classic Old World winemaking, such as fermenting with wild yeast, is at home here. The vines are farmed according to the quaint principles of biodynamic agriculture followed by some wineries in Burgundy and the Rhone.

The winery is notorious for not receiving visitors unless they have appointments. The reason is that Blue Mountain only makes 9,000 cases a year and there is a waiting list for all of it. Blue Mountain produces only dry table wines and sparkling wines. Before the first commercial vintage in 1991, trial wines were made by Ian Mavety, the windburnt founder of the winery, with his wife, Jane (who polices the winery's waiting list). At the time, most Okanagan wines were either off-dry whites or thin, simple reds. Mavety did not believe he could be competitive making such wines. The wines of Europe were his benchmark.

"Jane and I actually packed our bags and went to Europe," Ian recounts. "We didn't really drink sweet wines, as such. After going to Europe, we realized that we did not have to make sweet wines. We decided that we were no different from others out there not being served by the B.C. wines at that time. That was basically it."

Born in Vancouver in 1948, Ian purchased the Blue Mountain property in 1971, shortly after graduating in agriculture from the University of British Columbia. Then a rundown former orchard, it is now one of the Okanagan's most neatly managed vineyards, and one of the most photogenic. The sandy terrain undulates toward the south, with Vaseux Lake and McIntyre Bluff in the distance. The blue haze that envelops the bluff, as well as the mountains on the eastern side of the valley, inspired the winery's name.

Initially, Ian planted the same hybrid varieties as other Okanagan growers, and the business flourished. Commercially shrewd, he recognized in the 1980s that time was running out for those varieties because British Columbia wine was steadily losing markets to imported wines. He began converting his vineyard to vinifera grapes in the mid-1980s. But he does not denigrate the vanished varieties. Maréchal Foch, he laughs, "financed this property, I can assure you!"

It was a leap of faith to switch from Foch to Pinot Noir. "I planted it because I was told I couldn't grow it," says Ian, whose stubborn independence is legendary. "I'm serious. I was told by a German winemaker that I couldn't grow it. But I knew that I liked the wine and that I couldn't afford it, so it was going to have to be made." There was more to it, of course. When he researched vineyards with comparable grape-growing climates, Burgundy was a good approximate match to the Vaseux Lake bench. It made sense to plant Pinot Noir and its relatives.

"Pinot Gris, Pinot Blanc and Pinot Noir all come from the very same parent," he notes. "Chardonnay comes from a different parent but basically requires the same conditions." The fifth variety in the 25-hectare (62-acre) vineyard is Gamay, which is grown in Burgundy to make Beaujolais. "The reason Gamay is here is that a French nurseryman was here," Ian says, giving another example of how French viticulture has influenced Blue Mountain. "I said, 'Just look around you; with what you see, the soil and everything, what varieties would you plant here?' Without hesitation, he said Gamay."

Blue Mountain's long-time consulting winemaker, Rafael Brisbois, also is French, a native of Alsace trained as a Champagne maker who has worked in California for the past 20 years. A self-taught winemaker, Ian Mavety needed professional advice, particularly from a winemaker conversant with sparkling wines. In the late 1980s, Schramsberg Cellars of California conducted a sparkling wine-making trial in the Okanagan with grapes from several vineyards, including Blue Mountain. After Schramsberg abandoned the project (because the grape supply was inadequate for its proposed volume), Ian added sparkling wine to Blue Mountain's plans. He stumbled across Brisbois in the winter of 1991 while visiting wineries in California's Sonoma Valley. Brisbois was making the sparkling wines for well-regarded Iron Horse Vineyards. Intrigued by the notion of wine in Canada, he agreed to become Blue Mountain's consultant. It was a smart move. Brisbois thought that Blue Mountain's 1990 trial wines were "undrinkable." But the 4,500 litres (1,000 gallons) made for 1991's first commercial vintage were successful; Brisbois said later that the pupil was making better wine than the teacher.

More than a decade later, Brisbois remains involved, as the additional trained palate when Blue Mountain wines are blended. "Ian and Matt Mavety [the founder's son] are almost flying on their own, and they do it well," he says. Matt, who was born in 1975, has an agricultural degree that includes a year of post-graduate level studies in winemaking at Lincoln University in New Zealand.

Matt returned from New Zealand in 1997 to join the winery and the vine-yard. He has influenced the transition at Blue Mountain to biodynamic agricul-ture, an almost mystic type of vineyard management that goes well beyond organic production. Some biodynamic practices are more than a little unusual, involving stag's bladders stuffed with yarrow flowers and manure-filled bovine horns buried over winter. The point of both practices is to produce compost-enriching microbes. Many vineyard and processing activities are done in harmony with lunar cycles. These practices can be found in Burgundy and Rhone vine-yards that both father and son have visited. "It's not just hocus-pocus," Ian snaps. "These things were followed for centuries. Nobody could explain why, but they were proven to work."

Their conviction is that farming with conventional chemical inputs imposes a sterile fertility on the vineyard. At Blue Mountain, natural compost is made with spent grape skins and stems, mixed with manure and straw from a nearby farm. The biodynamic ideal would be to have animals right on the vineyard, adding to the beneficial mix of plant and animal life already there. Beehives have been placed throughout the vineyard and, in recent years, birdhouses have been posi-tioned to attract certain birds. The object is to create an environment in which the vines will flourish, along with all other life, including natural yeasts. The bottom line is to grow wines that express this particular vineyard — very much the Burgundian notion of terroir.

"The best wines," Ian explains, "will be the best expression of your site, resulting from the least amount of intervention. You are trying to peel back all of these other things you are adding that are not organic, that are not pieces of the earth and pieces of the vine. That's how you are going to get to this expression of site. I would hope I would live to see that day when we can line up five, six, seven vintages, and be able to say: *this* is the site."

The test is what is in the glass. Succeeding vintages of Pinot Noir since 1991 have become ever more complex in flavour and structure. "The winemaking prac-tice for the most part is not very different," Ian says. "I think it's the age of the vineyards." The majority of vines are at least 10 years old, a point at which the resulting wines begin showing more depth and character. "You can taste young fruit," Ian says. And it tastes good. He observes that wines from three- and four-year-old vines often win medals at wine shows on the strength of their obvious fruitiness. "But if you examine the wines, they do lack interest in terms of being a complement to a meal," he maintains.

Blue Mountain's white wines have changed. The objective is subtleness rather than power. Others may make plump, ripe wines with 14 per cent alcohol; Blue Mountain farms so that the grapes are ripe and in balance at 12.5 to 13 per cent alcohol. The wines now have almost imperceptible oak, more finesse in structure and crisp, lively fruit. Especially with the Chardonnay, the effort to make it ever more complex begins in the vineyard. "I think Chardonnay is probably our biggest challenge, the most difficult wine that we make," Ian says. "And one that, in this climate, has the most potential, so it's worth the fight. I just love trying to make it — it's such a temperamental bitch."

The Blue Mountain reserve wines are its "stripe label" wines. These are the result not of grapes from preferred sites but from artful blending after the vintage. "You can't walk into your vineyard, isolate a block, treat it a certain way and say, that's going to make my reserve wine," Ian maintains. "That is done in the New World. To me, it's stupid. It does not take into consideration what the climate is going to do that year." Vineyard blocks are picked separately and the wines remain separate until blending decisions are made, typically in December. Occasionally, no reserve wines will emerge from a particular vintage if all the lots are needed to maintain the quality of the regular wines. In 1999, for example, no stripe label Chardonnay was made.

"We are trying to make a more precise wine," Ian Mavety says, explaining the objective of the reserve. "It's not just richer, it's more precise. The acid should be crisper, the flavour should be more defined. Something that, when it is blended, will age gracefully and for a long time." Like fine Burgundies, perhaps.

BONAPARTE BEND WINERY

OPENED: 1999

Highway 97, Cache Creek, BC, V0K 1H0

Telephone: 250-457-6667

E-mail: bbwinery@coppervalley.bc.ca

Wine shop: Open 10 am – 5 pm daily April through September
(closing at 4 pm Sundays and holidays); and open 10 am – 5 pm
Monday through Friday October through March. Call for bistro hours.

THE ONLY WINERY IN BRITISH COLUMBIA'S VAST RANCHING INTERIOR, Bonaparte Bend was conceived on a beach in Hawaii. JoAnn and Gary Armstrong, who never seem to stop working, were passing Christmas vacation time in 1998 walking the beach and mulling ideas for a business at their 65-hectare (160-acre) Cache Creek ranch. For some reason, she remembered a fruit wine that had been brought as a hostess gift to a seasonal party at their home. "I turned to my husband," she recalls, "and said, 'When I get home, I am going to do a business plan on fruit wineries because that is something we might do.' That's what started it."

Born in Idaho, JoAnn grew up on the Gang Ranch, which her father was managing. Located near Clinton, British Columbia, this was once the world's largest ranch (about 400,000 hectares, or 1 million acres) although it has since been broken up among several owners, including a Saudi sheik. Gary Armstrong, born in Montana, is a veterinarian whose clients once included the Gang Ranch, where he met JoAnn. When they married in 1974, he had interests in five veterinarian hospitals in the Interior. He wound up those interests after the couple moved to Cache Creek in 1980. He continues to work as a veterinarian while JoAnn, trained in accounting, looks after the numbers at their various businesses.

Eminently practical, JoAnn Armstrong approaches the Bonaparte Bend venture from a business viewpoint. "Neither one of our families were partakers of the wine industry," she says. It is not that they are teetotallers; the Armstrongs enjoyed wines when they encountered them in social settings. "But it is not something that we purchased or served at home a lot." That has changed little since the winery opened. "We usually have half a glass once or twice a week before dinner," she says. "I guess that's because we are getting up and going back out to work after dinner."

Having decided on that Hawaiian beach that a winery was a good idea, the Armstrongs applied their professional skills. "I did my business plan in February and March, and we started our building May 1, 1999," JoAnn says. The winery is an attractive structure just beside the highway, large enough to house the processing facility, a gift shop and a small restaurant. She could have taken a cheaper shortcut but chose not to.

"I have cattle barns down here," she says of the Bonaparte Bend Ranch, which the Armstrongs purchased in 1993. Overlooking the Bonaparte River, the property is a hobby ranch compared to the vast spread on which she grew up. But the pleasant acreage has been a ranch since 1862. "I could have started the winery in a barn but I didn't think that was the right facility. It was not the image I wanted to portray right off the bat. We decided we were going to do it the right way, right from the start."

They also contacted a consulting winemaker from the Okanagan who, unfortunately for the Armstrongs, bowed out after two long drives to Cache Creek and a few e-mails. "Then I contacted a couple of other winemakers," she says, "but they never did come to meet us or see our facility. It was just obvious that they weren't really interested."

So the Armstrongs did it themselves, with JoAnn poring over winemaking texts and Gary dipping into his veterinarian's invaluable knowledge of chemistry. "We were advised to make smaller batches, test batches," JoAnn says. She does not know whether it was courage or foolhardiness, but they plunged ahead with commercial lots, often as large as 1,400 litres (300 gallons) at a time. "I really wanted to get started," she says. "We had the building. We had the investment. People in the area were asking us what was going on. If we had taken the time to do a bunch of test batches, that would have put us behind another six or seven months. I thought if I was going through the effort, I wanted to be able to have a product for sale. I wanted to get started right away."

In no time, they had a dozen or so different products, including wines from apricots, apples, blueberries, black currants, blackberries, cranberries, raspberries, rhubarb, chokecherries and honey. A blueberry–black currant wine came about when JoAnn blended them to save the cost of separate labels. It has stayed in the line because it succeeded. "It was our original intention to drop some wines, but they all seem to sell equally well," JoAnn says. "All our customers have their own favourites." Some of the fruit is grown on a two-hectare (five-acre) orchard on the ranch and the rest is purchased, although the orchard could be expanded.

Bonaparte Bend sells most of its wines at the wine shop and in the bistro, which is another example of JoAnn's commercial savvy. When she was writing the business plan, she concluded that it would not be economic to staff a tasting room without another activity also generating revenue. The object here is to serve fresh seasonal food in an informal setting. The bistro also lets the winery show off the many applications of its fruit wines. "We put a little bit of the raspberry wine in our raspberry cheesecake sauce," she says. "The rhubarb and the apricot wines — quite often we will put them in our soups."

BURROWING OWL ESTATE WINERY

OPENED: 1998

100 Burrowing Owl Place, Oliver, BC, V0H 1T0
Telephone: 250-498-0620
Toll-free: 1-877-498-0620
Web site: www.burrowingowlwine.ca
Wine shop: Open daily 10 am – 5 pm, May through mid-October; or by appointment.
Restaurant: The Sonora Room. Serves lunch daily, dinner Thursday through Sunday. Closed during winter months.

RECOMMENDED

- ✹ SYRAH
- ✹ CABERNET SAUVIGNON
- ✹ MERITAGE
- ✲ MERLOT
- ✲ CABERNET FRANC
- ✲ CHARDONNAY
- ✲ PINOT GRIS

THE LIGHT WENT ON FOR JIM WYSE IN 1996, AFTER HE HAD OWNED THE Burrowing Owl vineyard for three years. Most of the grapes were being purchased by Calona Vineyards, which, being Okanagan's oldest winery, had plenty of antique processing equipment. But Calona started winning awards with wine from Burrowing Owl fruit. "I knew enough about wineries to know they weren't doing very much," Wyse says. "So I said, we can do much better than this. Why don't we start something that is small and very much hands-on? Let's do what's necessary and see how good we can make this wine."

The Burrowing Owl winery opened for the vintage of 1998 and the wines have been acclaimed and invariably hard to get ever since. Ironically, Calona launched a brand called Sandhill — now emerging as a stand-alone winery — that primarily uses Burrowing Owl Vineyard grapes, and which also has gained acclaim. It is clear that Jim Wyse bought good dirt when he decided to grow grapes, realizing a dream he acquired while wine touring in Europe.

Born in Toronto in 1938, Wyse is a civil engineer with a business administration degree who came to Vancouver in 1968 as a management consultant. He established a real estate development company five years later. In 1991, while working on a project in Vernon, he considered buying the Chateau Ste. Claire at Peachland but prudently walked away from what he characterized as a fixer-upper. (The winery ultimately failed.) Then in 1993 his realtor steered him to Black Sage Road, south of Oliver, where he bought 40 hectares (100 acres). A fifth of the property already grew Pinot Blanc. Wyse thought it was a fine site for premium red grapes. "Our original big leap of faith was to get into the Bordeaux reds," Wyse says. Sixty per cent of the initial plantings were primarily Merlot, Cabernet Sauvignon and Cabernet Franc. Over the next few years, backed by a consortium of investors, Wyse snapped up adjoining properties until Burrowing Owl controlled 116.5 hectares (288 acres). Chardonnay and Pinot Gris were added, and even more reds were planted, including Syrah.

To finance the winery, Wyse struck a joint venture in 1997 with Cascadia Brands Inc., Calona's parent. Cascadia put up the money for the winery in exchange for 50 per cent of the joint venture and the majority of the grapes from the vineyard. The deal was unwound in 2002, with Cascadia keeping two-thirds of the vineyard while Burrowing Owl got the other third and the winery. Cascadia came out of that venture rather well. Its Sandhill wines have won, deservedly so, the positive reputation that had eluded Calona's wines. Some of that, of course, rubbed off from Burrowing Owl's success; Sandhill labels even mimicked the signature owl on the Burrowing Owl labels.

Burrowing Owl has made good wine from the beginning because Wyse, like a good consultant, hired the necessary talent. "We went into this knowing we knew nothing about the business," he says of his family and his investors. "I compared it to real estate development. If you want to 'play' in the real estate game, you go and buy yourself a duplex and run it yourself. But if you want to do it on a businesslike basis, you get a big enough building that you can hire professionals. You buy a 20-storey apartment building with a manager's suite. That's my analogy. We bought a 20-storey apartment building."

To make the wines, Wyse hired a top California winemaker. Bill Dyer, who has a master's degree in enology, had been the winemaker at Sterling Vineyards in the Napa from 1977 until 1996, when he left to consult. "Part of the program for the 'ultra-premium' objective was to have a top-notch world-class winemaker," Wyse says. "We were not going to try to make the wine ourselves. We were going to have a first-class person come in, with great experience and a great reputation as part of this plan." At the same time, Wyse's son, Stephen, equipped himself with technical training to manage the cellar when Dyer is working with other clients or on his own Napa vineyard.

Dyer, whose wife is also a leading California winemaker, said that the offer from Burrowing Owl "tickled his fancy." Surprising his Napa peers with wines made in an emerging region appealed to him. Burrowing Owl's first vintage in 1997 was made under Dyer's eye at the Calona winery because the Black Sage Road facility was only built during the summer of 1998. That gave Dyer a chance to advise on the winery design. Before construction began, he took Wyse and architect Robert Mackenzie to glean ideas from three new Oregon wineries. "It was an education for all of us," Wyse recalls.

Burrowing Owl focuses tightly on the half-dozen varieties that it believes it can do best. Dyer settled on Pinot Gris and Chardonnay as Burrowing Owl's white wines. They are studies in contrast. The Pinot Gris is fermented in stainless steel. "It is intended to be fresh and fruity in style, to reveal what character the grapes have," he says. "I think the variety is a great one for the Okanagan to hang its hat on." Since 1999, Dyer has fermented Chardonnay in barrels, making one of the Okanagan's more opulent examples of this variety.

The début red wines were Merlot and Cabernet Sauvignon. The vineyard's Cabernet Franc was intended for blends until a small single varietal bottling was so well received that it had to be released on its own. However, Dyer began making a Meritage blend in 2000; in that year, only 250 cases were made and it was all sold through the winery restaurant. The response to this superlative wine has been so strong that production is rising to 1,000 cases a year, some of it available for sale to other restaurants and customers. The winery released its first Pinot Noir from the 1999 vintage, having planted that variety because Dyer wanted to make it. Syrah was added in the 2000 vintage and has been a rising star among the varietals. "The general plan is to limit the number of products and to keep our focus," Wyse says. A strategic 2004 purchase of an adjoining producing vineyard has given the winery about 20 per cent more grapes, allowing the winery to reach an ultimate size of 30,000 cases — about three times the original target in 1997.

The reds generally are big, bold and fruity — the style that both Dyer and Wyse gravitate to when enjoying wines. "The Okanagan is infamous for its thin reds," Wyse says. "Well, I wanted to be the opposite of that and Bill also wants to be the opposite of that. Wine writers talk about big extracted wines. I like them, quite frankly. To me, that's the name of the game — to get everything out of those grapes that's in there."

CALLIOPE VINTNERS

ESTABLISHED: 2001

P.O. Box 995, Summerland, BC, V0H 1Z0
Telephone: 250-494-7213
Toll-free: 1-866-366-0100
Web site: www.calliopewines.com

RECOMMENDED

* CABERNET SAUVIGNON
* MERLOT
* MERLOT – CABERNET SAUVIGNON
* SÉMILLON-SAUVIGNON

LIKE THE OKANAGAN HUMMINGBIRD FOR WHICH IT IS NAMED, THIS WINERY changes nests from time to time. The clever strategy of working in someone else's facility permitted Calliope's four partners to make premium wines on a shoestring. "Starting Calliope like this has been good," says Ross Mirko, the quartet's lead winemaker. "Financially, it's been great. We couldn't be in business otherwise."

Calliope (pronounced *ka-LIE-oh-pea*) was conceived by Mirko and his wife, Cherie, also a winemaker, in partnership with Valerie Tait, one of the Okanagan's leading vineyard consultants, and her businessman husband, Garth Purdy. Mirko and Tait use their knowledge of the Okanagan to buy the best grapes they can find. Mirko made Calliope's first vintages, 1999 and 2000, in the Thornhaven winery at Summerland, offering the wines at Thornhaven's shop when Calliope began selling in 2001.

For subsequent vintages, Calliope leased space in the Adora winery at Summerland while moving cellar door sales to the Poplar Grove winery on Naramata Road, operated by Ian and Gitta Sutherland. "They are great friends and they don't use their wine shop all that much," Mirko notes. "All their wine sells out so quickly." However, samples of Poplar Grove's cheeses are available in the wine shop, a bonus for Calliope. "While we were resident in Poplar Grove's wine shop, we were tasting their cheese with our wines," Mirko says. "It was so civilized. Always, people bought cheese or wine, or both. Perhaps just one in 40 walked out with nothing."

By sharing with other wineries, the Calliope partners launched their winery, still one of the Okanagan's smallest, without going into debt. But by 2003, with production approaching 1,000 cases, the partners began debating the future of Calliope. "We need to take the training wheels off and get into business quite seriously," Mirko said. "Right now, it just fills up weekends and evenings." Calliope's wines currently are available only by direct purchase. Calliope moved out of the Poplar Grove Wine Shop after Poplar Grove's own production increased. In addition, Mirko's job as full-time winemaker at Lang Vineyards leaves little free time to staff another tasting room.

The son of an architect, Mirko was born in Vancouver in 1960 and took a degree in psychology before his wine interest was fired by an evening wine appreciation course. In 1988 he joined the quality control laboratory at the Andrés winery in Port Moody, moving two years later to CedarCreek. He took time out to get a postgraduate degree in viticulture at New Zealand's Lincoln University where Cherie Jones, now his wife, was a fellow student. Jones, who was born in New Zealand in 1969, came to Canada in 1995. She made wine at the St. Hubertus winery until 2000 when she began selling winemaking supplies in the Okanagan.

Mirko left CedarCreek in 1997, beginning a hectic career as a consulting winemaker. In the 2001 vintage, he found himself making wine at five different wineries between Kelowna and Osoyoos. "I was in all five places some days," he recalls. "I almost had to give away my poor old Volvo with 370,000 kilometres on it." He shed all but one of his consulting contracts in the 2002 vintage when he took over as the winemaker at Lang Vineyards near Naramata. "I enjoy going to the same place to work every day."

Some of Mirko's partners are equally busy, notably Valerie Tait. Born in 1964, she has an undergraduate degree in biochemistry and a master's in integrated pest management. She started working at the Summerland research station on research contracts while developing her independent consulting business with grape growers in the early 1990s as new vineyards were being planted. "That was my introduction to growers," she says. Calliope was conceived to take advantage of her intimate knowledge of Okanagan vineyards as well as Mirko's winemaking skills.

"We're really still trying to stick to simple winemaking, sourcing the best fruit that we can," Mirko says. In the 1999 vintage Calliope made only two wines: a barrel-fermented Sémillon–Sauvignon Blanc blend and an oak-aged Merlot–Cabernet Sauvignon blend, both with grapes from an Osoyoos vineyard. In order to change the style of its red wines, Calliope began switching growers in 2001 to deal with Chris Scott's Oak Knoll vineyard at Kaleden. The grapes from the latter vineyard, Mirko has found, enable him to produce "fruit forward style" reds with more oak now that Calliope has increased its modest inventory of barrels. The switch in vineyards has cost Calliope its access to Sémillon and Sauvignon Blanc. This white has been replaced with a dry Gewürztraminer, which Calliope began making in 2000.

In 2000, Calliope made an opportunistic purchase of Cabernet Sauvignon from one of the south Okanagan's most seasoned growers, Inkameep Vineyards near Oliver. Mirko received only enough fruit to make 35 cases of wine that, aged 16 months in American oak, developed into what Calliope called a "luscious fruit bomb." The Calliope partners were astonished at how quickly the wine sold, even at a price of $30 a bottle, almost double Calliope's usual prices. "We took a look at that Cabernet and we said, we don't need to get big, we just need to get better," Mirko says. "We're so small. We don't have *any* economies of scale. Our cost per bottle is outrageously high. The only way to make Calliope work is to make wines that fetch higher prices."

CALONA VINEYARDS

OPENED: 1932

1125 Richter Street, Kelowna, BC, V1Y 2K6
Telephone: 250-762-3332
Toll-free: 1-888-246-4472
Web site: www.calonavineyards.ca
Wine shop: Open daily 9 am – 6 pm.

RECOMMENDED

* PINOT GRIS
* PINOT BLANC
* MERLOT
* SYRAH
* GEWÜRZTRAMINER
* SOVEREIGN OPAL
* EHRENFELSER ICEWINE
* PINOT NOIR ICEWINE
* BLUSH
* CABERNET-MERLOT
  SONATA

KELLY MOSS, CALONA'S ASSOCIATE WINEMAKER, WAS A LITTLE INTIMIDATED when she began her first crush at the sprawling Calona winery in the fall of 1999. At the time, the sum total of her winery experience was a university science degree topped up with the winery assistant course at Okanagan University College and six months in the cellar at Quails' Gate. But the shy, young winemaker — Moss was born in Midland, Ontario, in 1973 — was coached through that first vintage not only by senior winemaker Howard Soon but also by Calona's experienced cellar team. The senior member of that team, Emilio Vicaretti, had worked in the cavernous cellar ever since he arrived from Italy four decades earlier.

Moss is only the latest in a long line of individuals associated with Calona to have experienced the winery's deep Italian roots. Many of Calona's loyal customers still think that it is controlled by the Capozzi family, who sold the winery in 1971. Calona is now owned by Cascadia Brands Inc., whose controlling shareholder is Swiss. Snippets of Calona's long and colourful history can be glimpsed from historic photographs and packaging tucked away in the Richter Street tasting room. The tour guides are likely to focus on Calona's current portfolio of well-made, well-priced "Artist Label" table wines. The wines have come a long way from those that generated the lively Calona war stories.

The winery was the idea of Guiseppe Ghezzi, a debonair winemaker who subsequently returned to his native Italy to marry an opera singer. In 1931, Ghezzi organized a syndicate of leading Italians in Kelowna and Vancouver to finance the production of apple wines. (Hardly any grapes were then grown in the Okanagan.) Running out of money, the syndicate turned to Pasquale "Cap" Capozzi, a Kelowna grocer, who tapped the local Italian community for more money. When that ran short, he turned to the wider business community — "all the big fellows," he recalled in an interview years later. The biggest was hardware merchant W.A.C. Bennett, later the premier of British Columbia. Bennett did not drink but he agreed to become president and build a winery that would give apple growers a much needed market. (He sold his shares in 1941 when he went into politics.)

"We make this apple wine for three years," Capozzi remembered later. "And I tell you, [it was] the worst thing in the world when we start. We have to dump the wine ... we can't sell it." By 1935 Calona had switched to grapes, now being grown in the valley, and built its business by, among other things, making altar wine for the Catholic Church in western Canada.

Calona's growth took off in 1961 when Capozzi's three sons — Joe, Tom and Herb — took over the winery. Shrewdly, they went to California and found a winery model in Gallo Brothers. Many of Calona's successful products in the 1960s mimicked Gallo wines (notably alcoholic fruit wines), right down to the bottles. Tom Capozzi even asked Gallo to invest in Calona. When Gallo countered, offering its own shares for 51 per cent, the Capozzis sold their entire business for cash to a Montreal conglomerate in 1971. But together with their colourful father, who died in 1976 (the year after Calona made its 100 millionth bottle of wine), they retained an association with the winery for years.

Calona overhauled its wines dramatically in the 1970s to compete with imported wines. Like most large Canadian wineries at the time, Calona launched a range of more or less dry table wines under labels that sounded imported. Calona labels included Palazzo Reale, San Pietro, Sommet Blanc, Sommet Rouge and Tiffany. Calona's biggest success was Schloss Laderheim, a German-styled white that was launched in 1977 and became Canada's largest-selling brand until it was eclipsed by other wines.

Since then, varietals have supplanted almost all of these so-called pseudo-labels. Among the earliest was the winery's 1978 Maréchal Foch, the first Calona wine to be served at a dinner for the Queen. The hybrid varietals of the 1980s were replaced with vinifera wines in the 1990s, after Okanagan vineyards were replanted with premium grapes. The exception is Sovereign Opal, a white wine made only by Calona. The grape was developed at the Summerland research station by crossing Maréchal Foch and Golden Muscat. It was released to growers in 1976. The only grower to plant a serious quantity was the late August Casorso, whose family belonged to the original Calona syndicate. Since the first vintage in 1987, Calona has found a steady following for the wine, with its distinctive floral aroma and Muscat character.

Calona's current portfolio has been created by Howard Soon. Born in Vancouver in 1952, the son of a Kitsilano grocer, he is a microbiologist who, after five years with a brewery, went to work in Calona's laboratory in 1980 and stayed to become the longest-tenured vintner at any Okanagan winery. Working from a cramped office in a winery so big that he wears a pager, Soon is incredibly busy. He is the winemaker for Sandhill, also owned by Calona's parent. He is the buyer for the bulk wines that Calona imports for its vast array of non-VQA wines, blended by another of Soon's assistants, Rick Weberg. And, along with the associate winemakers, he is responsible for Calona's wines. "During the crush," Kelly Moss says, "Howard is out in the vineyards quite a bit."

In the midst of the 2003 vintage, Moss took leave to have her first child. In a stroke of good fortune, Calona was able to fill her place with Stephanie Leinemann. The Okanagan-born winemaker started her studies at Okanagan University College and then transferred to Brock University in Ontario. Just before joining Calona, she earned a degree in enology and viticulture, graduating with the highest marks in her class.

The intention with Calona's Artist Series wines is to produce quality wines at modest prices. "Artist Series is always good value," Soon maintains. "The price that we sell the Artist Series for is pretty amazing." He recounts the story of the 1999 Artist Series Pinot Gris that sold for $10.95 a bottle. It won a gold medal and was judged best of class at the 2001 Los Angeles County Fair, North America's largest wine competition. Subsequently, the influential wine critics of the *Wall Street Journal*, who had judged at Los Angeles, praised the wine in their column. Among the calls that tied up Calona's switchboard was one from an American offering to dispatch his private jet to pick up two cases.

The wines are called Artist Series because the labels feature original art. This program began in 1991 with the work of Robb Dunfield, a paraplegic who holds the brush in his teeth to paint intricate landscapes. His art appears on both the Sovereign Opal and the Pinot Gris. Since then, numerous other painters have also been engaged, turning the wine bottles into a veritable art show.

Since 1999, Calona has had an entry-level label called Copper Moon for low-priced, uncomplicated wines from British Columbia grapes. "The starter guys are not necessarily looking for varietals," Soon acknowledges. "Our salesmen tell me that some people don't know what a varietal is, and don't really care to find out. They want to taste B.C. VQA wine and be happy. They take it home and drink it on the patio, or wherever, and like it. Not everybody wants the sophisticated wine we are trying to do. We are trying to make some of the best wines in B.C."

CARRIAGE HOUSE WINES

OPENED: 1995

32764 Black Sage Road, Oliver, BC, V0H 1T0
Telephone: 250-498-8818
Web site: www.carriagehousewines.ca
Wine shop: Open daily 10 am – 6 pm March to November 11; or by appointment.

RECOMMENDED

❊ KERNER
✴ KERNER DRY
  EBONAGE BLANC
  MERLOT
  CABERNET SAUVIGNON

WHEN DAVE WAGNER STARTED MAKING BEER AND WINE AS AN AMATEUR in the 1970s, the low-tech nature of the hobby formed his habits for a lifetime. He prefers to avoid complications.

"Technology has changed so much," he acknowledges today. "There are all kinds of new techniques. All those shiny toys are really expensive but would I like to have a whole barn full of them? To be honest, it would take a little bit of the fun out of making wine, to process the hell out of it. You have to leave a little bit up to fate. I think if you do a good job out in the vineyard, half your work in the winery is already done. I still believe that the more you fool with wine, the more you have to correct what you've done. I do things in there," he says, gesturing toward the small winery, "but for the most part, I try to let the wine do its own thing."

Wagner is a low-key grape farmer who manages to hide his passion for wine behind the slow drawl that rumbles from his beard. The passion comes to the surface, however, in his ardour for the Kerner grape. That variety has no greater devotee in the Okanagan. One really needs to visit the tasting room to savour the passion and the wine because Wagner does not appear at many public tastings during the year. "When you are small like this, where I am the winemaker, I can't afford to be running hither and yon, doing all these tastings," he explains. "It takes me away from here too often."

Born in 1952 in New Westminster, Wagner grew up in the south Okanagan, the son of a feedlot operator at Okanagan Falls. He spent a year at university, considering a career as a veterinarian, before dropping out to be a letter carrier and to buy a small farm in the Fraser Valley. The winemaking bug bit him early and hard. Joining an amateur wine club at Abbotsford, he progressed quickly from rhubarb and blackberry wines to grapes, even planting a few vines. The hobby propelled Wagner in 1986 to start a three-year program of science courses at Simon Fraser University with the intent of completing the winemaker program at the University of California in Davis. His timing was unfortunate. There was little prospect of finding employment after two-thirds of the Okanagan's vineyards were pulled out in 1988 and 1989. Instead, Wagner found a job at BC Hydro, reading meters and collecting bills.

But now he was determined to make wine. In 1992, he and his wife, Karen, who is a nurse, purchased a 3.4-hectare (8.4-acre) orchard on Black Sage Road, south of Oliver. "I grew up in the area and I knew what I was looking for," he says. "I knew what I wanted to do, so that's why we bought this site on this side of the valley." He might have preferred a site a little farther south on Black Sage Road, now covered with vineyards, but the available parcels were too large. He wanted to be on the eastern side of the valley where his vines could bask in the heat.

"I think because of the heat we get on this side of the valley, we develop more flavours, better bouquets," Wagner maintains. "One of the main reasons is the afternoon sun, and the fact that, all along this side, the vineyards are pretty much against a rock wall and they get really baked in the afternoon. In July at 8:30 pm, it is still sunny here and 40 degrees." He argues that it is the best place in Canada to grow red grapes.

So it is a paradox that, along with Merlot, Cabernet Sauvignon, Pinot Noir and Syrah, he also grows Chardonnay and Kerner. In 1994, when the Wagners began converting the orchard to grapes, there was much less knowledge about which varieties would grow. There seemed to be some safety in white varieties, especially one like Chardonnay with a consumer franchise. But since then, Wagner has considered replacing his Chardonnay with Syrah. When he planted additional vines in 2003, he stayed with reliable Merlot — and Kerner, his favourite.

"Everybody has a Chardonnay," Wagner recognizes now. "It's not that ours isn't as good as theirs. It's just that Kerner just seems to take away the sales from the Chardonnay. Visitors to the wine shop like the Chardonnay — but then they get into the Kerner, and that's the white wine they'll buy from this winery. If our Kerner is going to be stealing the sales, why bother with the Chardonnay?"

Long before he opened the winery, Wagner already had a passion for Kerner, a German white of which Riesling is a parent. "I'm pretty biased, there's no doubt about it," he says. "When we started with the amateur winemaking club, we made Kerner in 1984 or 1985 and really liked it. It was fun to make the wine. While it was fermenting, it always had such a lovely bouquet, such a nice aroma. It was always fresh and real citrusy. Now when I am fermenting it, I always enjoy the smell. It is either grapefruit or pineapple. It has some nice, complex flavours. It keeps the Riesling edge, too. We have a really good market for the Kerner now. I would really hate to disappoint people and deprive them of their Kerner!"

While Carriage House, now making about 1,200 cases a year, releases its wines as single varietals, Wagner has begun to think about making a big red blend in the future. "I just see people going to blends as the next logical stage of wine drinking." Expect the style to reflect his taste. "I am kind of letting the vineyard set its own style," he says. "But I like dark, heavy wines. I like big, meaty wines."

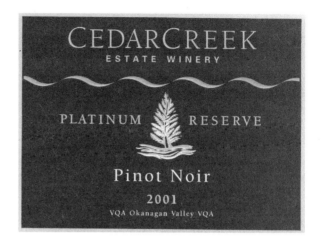

CEDARCREEK ESTATE WINERY

OPENED: 1980

    5445 Lakeshore Road, Kelowna, BC, V1W 4S5

    Telephone: 250-764-8866

    Web site: www.cedarcreek.bc.ca

    Wine shop: Open daily 10 am – 6 pm April through October;
        11 am – 5 pm November through March.

    Restaurant: Vineyard Terrace, open daily 11:30 am – 3:30 pm
        from June 18 to September 12.

RECOMMENDED

- ✹ PINOT NOIR PLATINUM
- ✹ CHARDONNAY PLATINUM
- ✹ MERLOT PLATINUM
- ✹ MERITAGE PLATINUM
- ✸ PINOT NOIR ESTATE
- ✸ CHARDONNAY ESTATE
- ✸ MERLOT
- ✸ PINOT GRIS ESTATE
- ✲ DRY RIESLING CLASSIC
- ✲ EHRENFELSER CLASSIC
- ✲ PINOT BLANC CLASSIC

WITH HIS LACONIC MANNER OF SPEAKING AND HIS HAIR IN A NEAT ponytail, CedarCreek winemaker Tom DiBello comes across as the casual California surfboarder that he was in his adolescence. At high school in Newport Beach, he became so good at predicting the surfing weather that he nearly became a meteorologist. It would have been a serious loss for winemaking. Now DiBello goes back to California to surf the wine competitions with solid results. For example, both of CedarCreek's 2000 Chardonnays won gold medals at the 2002 Los Angeles County Fair, the oldest competition in the United States. They were the only Canadian Chardonnays to win gold in a class usually owned by California. DiBello clearly is an able winemaker. He has also inherited the fruits of a turn-around at the CedarCreek winery and vineyards that enabled the winery to be named Canadian winery of the year after winning 10 medals in the 2002 Canadian Wine Awards.

This apparent "overnight success" was years in the making. Founded in 1980 as Uniacke Estate Winery, the property struggled for six years and then was purchased by businessman Ross Fitzpatrick, now a senator from British Columbia. Bread-and-butter wines at Uniacke included whites made from Okanagan Riesling, an execrable hybrid now eradicated from Okanagan vine-yards. Fitzpatrick got rid of the inventory by peddling it as Rudolph's Riesling just before Christmas one year. Over the next 10 years, CedarCreek's production rose tenfold to about 21,000 cases a year of solid and occasionally notable wine. The winery's 1992 Merlot, for example, so appealed to the judges at the Okanagan Wine Festival that they created a special platinum medal for it, one step above gold. That is why the winery's very best wines today are called Platinum Reserve.

For a long time, CedarCreek was run by remote control because both Ross and his son, Gordon, were running a Vancouver gold mining company. In 1996, after merging the company with another mining firm, Gordon turned his atten-tion to the winery. What little he knew about wine had been learned selling Rudolph's Riesling and backpacking in Europe. Methodical by nature, Gordon spent months analyzing CedarCreek's business. He did not like what he found. The winery relied on sales of its Proprietors' Red and Proprietors' White, inex-pensive everyday wines not profitable enough to sustain the business or inter-esting enough to burnish the reputation. CedarCreek, he concluded, needed to replace the generics with premium wines. To get there, he hired a new winemaker, retained a consultant to overhaul the vineyards and launched a complete recon-struction of the winery.

The winemaker was Kevin Willenborg, a 1985 graduate from the University of California at Davis, who had spent 14 years at the family-owned Louis M. Martini winery in California. Willenborg, in turn, recommended the vineyard consultant, also from California. A significant portion of CedarCreek's original vineyard, which rises uphill behind the winery, was replanted, in part to get the varietal selection right. Pinot Gris, a white that sells strongly, replaced the Pinot Auxerrois, a variety that does not sell well. Parts of the irrigation system were replaced and the soils improved. Meanwhile, CedarCreek's Greata Ranch vine-yard across Okanagan Lake at Peachland was just beginning to produce its first fruit. In addition to having good grapes to work with, Willenborg had the great fortune of arriving for the vintage of 1998. After a long hot season, the Okanagan had produced grapes riper, in some instances, than those of California. Willenborg made big wines. The best were launched as premium-priced Platinum Reserve and Estate Select wines.

When Willenborg returned to California in 2000, he recommended DiBello, a Davis classmate with bagfuls of experience. He started his career in 1983 at Stag's Leap Wine Cellars, one of Napa's best wineries. He did a vintage with Cape Mentelle in western Australia, spent two years selling wine in California and another three years with a small California winery that won awards but went broke. Then DiBello did a vintage in Virginia and four in Arizona before moving to Washington State in 1996 and then to CedarCreek in 2000. "I do everything," DiBello says. "I've been out in vineyards in so many locations and so many climates that I adapt very quickly. I'm not stuck in one mode of thought."

The winery reconstruction was just starting when DiBello arrived and it was urgently needed. Winemaking equipment was old and the cellar was jammed with tanks and barrels. "We used to say that we had to step outside to change our minds," Gordon Fitzpatrick recalls. About $3 million was spent building essentially a new winery, designed for gentle handling of grapes. The tasting room was enlarged and the restaurant terrace added. Here, diners experience CedarCreek wines paired with appropriate food.

The winery was completed just as the 2001 Pinot Noir grapes were delivered. Finicky in the vineyard and in the winery, Pinot Noir takes the measure of any winemaker. "I love Pinot Noir," DiBello says. "It is such a challenging variety. It is such a rewarding one too, the Holy Grail of wines. You just have to do everything right. First of all, you have to be in the right climate and in the right soil for it. The climate for Pinot Noir is a very special thing that doesn't exist in that many places. Everyone likes to make comparisons to Burgundy. I look at it this way: if the Okanagan had been making wine first, all the Burgundians would be trying to imitate what we were doing. We should all be making great Pinot Noir here. It should be our destiny." The Pinot Noirs that DiBello makes possess the classic palate of polished velvet.

A winery with a successful Pinot Noir is likely to get other varieties right as well. CedarCreek makes a range of wines, including Pinot Gris, Riesling, Gewürztraminer and even Ehrenfelser, a white no easier to sell than Auxerrois. "I like making different things," DiBello explains. Powerful Bordeaux reds have begun to appear, including Platinum Reserve quality Merlot, Cabernet Sauvignon and Meritage. In 2001 the winery acquired land north of Osoyoos for what it calls its Desert Ridge Vineyard. This has been planted almost entirely to Bordeaux red varieties, supporting the growing volume of powerhouse reds. Ultimately, CedarCreek intends to establish a satellite winery there, called Desert Ridge.

CHALET ESTATE VINEYARD

ESTABLISHED: 2001

11195 Chalet Road, North Saanich, BC, V8L 5M1

Telephone: 250-656-2552

Web site: www.chaletestatevineyard.ca

Wine shop: Open 11 am – 5 pm Tuesday through Saturday; 1 pm – 4 pm Sunday;
and by appointment at other times.

RECOMMENDED

* ❋ ORTEGA
* ✹ BACCHUS
* ✹ GEWÜRZTRAMINER
* ✹ PINOT BLANC
* ✹ CABERNET MERLOT
* ✹ SAUVIGNON BLANC

IT TOOK RESILIENCE FOR MICHAEL BETTS AND LINDA PLIMLEY TO HANG ON during the roller-coaster ride of their first year and a half as winery owners. The high points included the four medals that Chalet Estate wines won during 2002 in challenging competitions. In the All-Canada Wine Awards, a silver medal was awarded to the winery's 2000 Cabernet-Merlot and a bronze to its 2001 Ortega. The same wine also scored a bronze at the Wine Access Canadian Wine Awards and the 2001 Bacchus won bronze at the Northwest Wine Summit in Oregon. "It put us on the map," Betts says.

The low point was the accidental death (in an Okanagan winery) in November 2002 of Frank Supernak, who had been Chalet Estate's consultant through two vintages. Such a deep bond had been forged between them that, months later, Betts was not prepared to think about recruiting another consultant. Nor was he under pressure to do so. Supernak, a Nanaimo native who had been making wine in the Okanagan since 1987, skilfully mentored many nascent winemakers like Betts, to whom the craft was new.

"He left me in a really good position," Betts says. "He took the trouble to teach me as he went along. As far as the basics are concerned, I've felt very comfortable. He didn't come here like a guru who flitted in and flitted out. He came here, he rolled his sleeves up, and we did everything together. He would go and have me do the tests, or whatever we were working on, and then critique it afterwards. In that way, it was all hands-on learning, right from day one."

Born in Britain in 1940, the lean and wiry Betts was an officer in the Royal Navy's submarines before coming to Victoria in 1967. Much of his civilian life before the winery was tied to the ocean, including living with his family on ocean-going sailboats. "We lived on a boat for almost eight years," he recalls. "But living on a boat in British Columbia weather, especially in winter, loses its glory pretty fast." For several years, he operated a company that built sailing boats. Meanwhile, he learned to fly and started a company that built and sold experimental aircraft to other hobby flyers. He gave up that business in 2000 when the vineyard and winery evolved into an "all-encompassing" pursuit.

Betts and his wife, Linda Plimley — whose family were pioneer automobile dealers in British Columbia — have owned the property that became the vineyard since the mid-1980s. It was a quiet forested spot in the country at the top end of the Saanich Peninsula, across the road from the renowned Deep Cove Chalet restaurant. Betts and Plimley thought of growing walnuts or farming trout before beginning a trial with grape vines in 1998. The idea of commercial vineyards on the Saanich Peninsula had been inspired by two growers on nearby Mount Newton: John Brickett and Peter Longcroft. The latter, who had been a partner in one of Betts's businesses, had just established the Newton Ridge winery (subsequently sold to new owners).

At first, Betts and Plimley, who had planted Ortega, Bacchus and later Pinot Gris in their 1.2-hectare (three-acre) vineyard, thought of selling grapes to home winemakers. "Then I suddenly realized that it would be foolish to spend all this money and hard work just to grow grapes," Betts says. "So the next stage was establishing a winery." Pierre Koffel, the chef who runs Deep Cove Chalet, scoffed at this. However, he bought most of the winery's Ortega after Chalet Estate opened its tasting room in June of 2001. The wine purchases by Koffel, who keeps an 18,000-bottle cellar in the restaurant, gave important support and credibility to the new winery.

Chalet Estate has grown to about 1,750 cases a year, close to the winery's capacity, and almost double the 1,000 cases a year Betts envisaged when he first built the winery. It has expanded twice since, both to accommodate a large barrel cellar and to provide rooms in which the winery can hold functions. "We've discovered unless we can get people to come here, we're not going to be very successful," Betts says. An adept marketer, Plimley has invited Saanich artists to the winery, creating cultural events that reach out to the community. "When we do get people out for the functions we have been holding in the last year, it has been very good for us," Betts has found.

The vineyard is planted to the white varieties that are proving suitable for the Saanich Peninsula. "We could only grow certain varieties here," Betts concluded. "I wanted to gradually get as much product from our own vineyard and other peninsula vineyards as I could, rather than keep buying from the Okanagan. So that restricted me to Ortega, Bacchus, Pinot Gris and possibly Pinot Blanc and Gewürztraminer." The small size of the vineyard prevented Betts from testing either the latter varieties or the red varieties he thinks would work (such as Maréchal Foch). He has been trying to acquire additional acreage.

The red wines in the current Chalet range are made with Okanagan grapes. "I still go up there and collect my own fruit on the day it is picked." He pays the premium necessary to get quality. "We spent $45,000 on grapes in 2002," he says. "But if you don't get good-quality fruit, your wine is just going to be mediocre." He buys varieties that would not mature on the Saanich Peninsula: Cabernet Sauvignon, Merlot, Cabernet Franc and Syrah. "We are dealing pretty well exclusively now with growers on Black Sage Road," Betts says. He also purchases Sauvignon Blanc there, the white he makes in preference to ubiquitous Chardonnay. His Chardonnay experience was discouraging. The Chardonnay grapes he obtained in 2000 were somewhat acidic, presenting winemaking challenges that Betts resolved only with Supernak's help.

"We did two types of Chardonnay at the beginning, oaked and unoaked," he says. "Both were very palatable wines, but then you get a customer who has just had a rich, heavy Chardonnay from California." He decided that if he could not match the mainstream Chardonnay, he would be far better focussing on other varieties.

The winemaking style at Chalet reflects three influences. From Supernak, Betts learned to be conservative in the use of barrels so that the wines never show excessive oak. Guided by his own palate, Betts initially made his white wines completely dry. This accounts for the flinty style of the winery's oaked Sauvignon Blanc — called Fumé Blanc because it is oak-aged — and the rich-textured but dry Ortega.

"We listen to the customers, too," Betts adds. "In the main, people are not very keen on heavily oaked wine anymore. We find too — maybe it's the age of the population around here — but many of our customers like a sweeter wine. So with my Gewürztraminer in 2002, I stopped the fermentation to leave a little bit of residual sugar, so it will appeal to that market."

CHASE & WARREN ESTATE WINES

OPENED: 2003

6253 Drinkwater Road, Port Alberni, BC, V9Y 8H9
Telephone: 250-724-4906
Wine shop: Open daily 11 am – 5 pm in summer; or by appointment.

RECOMMENDED

PINOT NOIR

CHASE & WARREN IS NORTH AMERICA'S MOST WESTERN VINEYARD-based winery. Its vineyard is draped across a rural southwestern slope a mere 10 minutes from downtown Port Alberni. This community in the centre of Vancouver Island is known for its hulking pulp mill. But the region also produces a wide selection of fine seafood, from salmon to shellfish. Vaughan Chase and Ron Crema, the partners behind this winery, see their wines as a complement to the local seafood.

When Chase, who has owned this rural acreage since 1979, set out to grow grapes, one government expert he consulted warned him that the climate might be too challenging. Chase followed his own instincts. He had grown up in the Alberni valley. He knew that the summers are every bit as hot as those of the Cowichan Valley where the majority of Vancouver Island vineyards are. Of course it rains heavily in the Alberni Valley — in the winter. The trick is to get the grapes ripe and picked by October 15 but, with the valley's mild early spring, that can be done successfully. Chase has been doing it now for several years.

Chase left Port Alberni after high school, kicking around in various jobs in Alberta and elsewhere in British Columbia. After marrying, he and his wife, Joanne, lived in Victoria for three years until drawn back to Port Alberni by the affordability of life in this community. "I went to work in the pulp mill for three years," he says. "It drove me crazy so I went back to university and got my teaching degree." Both he and his wife are teachers.

The vineyard was born after Chase planted a few vines of Gewürztraminer about 1991 and made a good wine. Then the slope just below his home was cleared of timber to generate cash for the needs of the Chase family. Chase and Crema, his brother-in-law, had no trouble envisaging a vineyard on that bare slope.

Grape growing is not new in the Alberni Valley, where many home gardeners have arbours, primarily of table grapes. But Chase had to go further afield to research and acquire wine grapes. Conscious that he was pioneering, he tested more than 30 varieties. The vines and the advice came from several sources, including the late John Harper's nursery at Cobble Hill in the Cowichan Valley. "A grand old man," Chase remembers Harper. "If it hadn't been for him, I don't think we'd be where we are."

Developing the vineyard had its challenges, as can be seen from an album of photographs displayed occasionally in the Chase & Warren tasting room. Chase applied 73 tonnes (90 tons) of lime to balance the acidity of what formerly had been the floor of a forest. To take away the winter rains, drainage was put into trenches dug 1.5 metres (five feet) deep. He began planting the vineyard in 1996. All of this work, along with modest winery building, was done on a shoestring, financed by his teacher's salary. Unable to afford bird netting in 2002, Chase lost much of the crop to birds. Anxious to get some revenue before the next vintage was ripe, Chase got the winery open in July 2003. Only about 150 cases of wine were on hand for the opening, but that was enough to get cash into the till and gain local notice.

The two-hectare (five-acre) vineyard's major varieties are Pinot Noir, Gewürztraminer, Chardonnay, Bacchus and Pinot Gris. "What I had in mind here was doing some Champagne," says Chase, a self-taught winemaker. "I wanted to get Pinot Meunier from John Harper, to go with Pinot Noir and the Chardonnay, because that's the traditional Champagne base. John gave me Pinot Blanc instead. I think I only have one Pinot Meunier vine." The sparkling wine project remains to be done, for Chase & Warren opened its doors with a selection of table wines.

Some of the wines employed Okanagan fruit, typically as part of a blend. For example, the winery's Pinot Noir blends fruit from Naramata with grapes grown in the Chase vineyard, where production is still modest. "They say on the island that it is hard to get Pinot Noir with colour," Chase observes. "I haven't had that problem at all."

Because Chase & Warren is a long way from the major wine markets, the wines have been tailored to what Chase perceives are the tastes in his local market. "The original idea was that I would focus on the German varieties, Pinot Gris and Gewürztraminer, because they would suit the seafood that we have in the area," Chase says. When the winery opened, several of the white blends were based on such aromatic Germanic varietals as Siegerrebe, Bacchus and Oraniensteiner.

Obviously, it was a good call, because the wines sold out quickly. "We sold out of Bacchus on the opening weekend," he says. "We didn't have a lot of it, about 10 cases. The same with Müller-Thurgau. The reason we sold out of it was because the wines had oodles of varietal flavour." He attributes that to growing low quantities of grapes on each vine, enabling the vines to deliver vivid cool-climate flavours.

His personal palate is tuned to dry wines but, at this time, that is not where his local market is. "Most people don't like rippingly dry wines," he says. "Having done trials with friends, off-dry styles are probably going to predominate. We have to sell the wine, and to do that, it has to be acceptable. As times goes on, and as I get more experienced, and as people's palates in our area become more educated, perhaps I'll go to more straight-up dry wines."

As the winery opened, Chase already had another 3.2 hectares (eight acres) cleared for additional vineyard — just as soon as cash flow enables him to get at it. He is eager to plant, having found a consuming new passion. "I don't know everything there is to know about winemaking," he says. "I hope I never know everything there is to know."

CHATEAU WOLFF

OPENED: 1998

2534 Maxey Road, Nanaimo, BC, V9S 5V6

Telephone: 250-753-9669

Wine shop: Open all year. Tastings and tours 11 am – 6 pm Saturday and Sunday;
weekdays by appointment.

RECOMMENDED

GRANDE ROUGE

LIKE NEARLY EVERY WINEMAKER WHO WORKS WITH PINOT NOIR, HARRY von Wolff is not satisfied. "I look at my Pinot Noir and I think it lacks that something quintessential that Burgundy has," he confesses. It is a big, fully extracted red wine with a tannin structure designed to give it years to mature. "I know Pinot Noirs can handle 30 years. There is nothing wrong with my Pinot Noir, but if I told you it was a Nebbiolo, you wouldn't question it." Well, you might question it, but that would not take away the Pinot Noir producer's peculiar need to fret and suffer. Pinot Noir is not a destination. It is a work in progress.

Von Wolff, who grew to love Burgundies while at hotel school in Switzerland in the 1960s, made his self-inflicted Pinot Noir challenge more difficult than usual by planting his grapes in 1990 just outside Nanaimo on Vancouver Island. On an island of cool vineyards, his is one of the most northern. It does slope to the southwest, a fine aspect to catch the sun, and it is framed by a heat-reflecting cliff pockmarked with nests of swallows. In recent years, he has taken to draping translucent fabric over the rows each spring, creating a greenhouse effect whose warmth accelerates the vines by at least two extra weeks. The idea is to get the Pinot Noir to the maturity required for his muscular winemaking style before the autumn rain arrives in November. "I'm always looking for a better way," von Wolff says.

He was born in Latvia in 1934, a descendant of a noble family who were extensive landowners before the wars and politics of the twentieth century turned social order on its head in this part of northern Europe. "I am of Baltic German origin," he says. "My family left Silesia in the 1680s. The Protestants in Silesia had to become Catholic. Whoever did not want to become Catholic packed up and left. We went to Russia. The family up to then had been in the wine and vineyard business for 200 years. That is the irony in the thing really, that I would come to the New World and, after a gap of 300 years, start up again."

He came to Canada in 1953 (his father, who had been an officer in the German army, was to remain a prisoner of war in the Soviet Union for two more years), sponsored by an uncle who had a ranch in northeastern British Columbia. Von Wolff worked there for a year to repay his fare, moving on when he concluded he was not going to make it in agriculture without a lot of capital. With that began an 11-year period when, by his count, he had 53 different jobs, from logging to fishing. In one of his longest, he was a steward at one fashionable Vancouver golf club and a bartender at another. When his employer wanted to promote him to catering manager, he decided to get professional training in hotel management. His four years at Luzerne in Switzerland included time for side trips to Burgundy, where the love affair with Pinot Noir began.

After leaving there in 1968, von Wolff spent most of the next decade running hotels in exotic locations from Haiti to the Queen Charlotte Islands and Jasper. He decided to change careers in 1977 because he calculated (correctly) that sharply rising world oil prices were about to throw the hotel industry into recession. "I figured it was time to look for a safe haven," he recalls. "I decided to become a shoemaker." He established himself in Nanaimo. When a partner left to go sailing, von Wolff and Helga, his wife, turned the business into a successful shop selling western gear and accessories. He still wears belts with outsized buckles. For many years, he also wore Stetson hats, until his taste switched to Greek fisherman's caps. Whatever the garb, the big-framed, white-bearded von Wolff manages to carry it all off with flair.

Formerly an amateur winemaker, von Wolff first planted some vines experimentally at his Nanaimo home. Their success sent him and Helga on a prolonged search for vineyard property. They found it in 1987 just beyond Nanaimo city limits. The slope then was entirely forested. He drew on his former skills as a logger to harvest the trees. When the site was ready for vines, he purchased his Pinot Noir and Chardonnay vines from a French nursery. "Fantastic quality," he says.

Currently, there are two hectares (five acres) of vineyard. That was about twice as much as he wanted to plant. He doubled up when it was rumoured that the government planned to impose a two-hectare minimum for the vineyard at a farmgate winery. He developed a plot of land across the road from the winery that has proven less capable of ripening wines than the slope under his cliff. He planted varieties such as Müller-Thurgau, Bacchus, Viognier and Siegerrebe, with varying degrees of success.

The defensive decision to plant a larger vineyard than needed can be understood against the background of his family experience with capricious governments and regulators. Von Wolff's instinct is to stay one step ahead of such trouble. Subsequently, the Vintners Quality Alliance threatened to restrict place names only to VQA producers. It is hardly a surprise that Chateau Wolff, fiercely independent, is non-VQA. Von Wolff quickly registered Nanaimo Vineyards, now a second label at Chateau Wolff. If the VQA ever stops him from putting Vancouver Island on Chateau Wolff's labels, he believes that nothing will stop him from using Nanaimo Vineyards. This is the label under which he releases a popular white called Viva, an unusual blend of Chardonnay and Bacchus.

The black Pinot Noir wines that he says might be taken for Nebbiolo are easily explained. Von Wolff is traditional when it comes to working with this grape. When it is fermenting, he will punch the cap down during the day as often as every two hours. And as patient Helga will report, her husband also rises every three hours at night to continue this practice. The constant immersion of the skins in the fermenting juice draws out the deep colour. It also draws out firm tannins, making the wines very long-lived. In 2003 von Wolff was selling his barrel-aged 1996 Pinot Noir — and the wine still had years of development ahead of it.

Von Wolff is equally pleased with a port-style wine he calls Grand Rouge Liqueur, an artful blend of Dornfelder, Pinot Noir and small amounts of Bacchus, Siegerrebe, Viognier and Müller-Thurgau. Dornfelder is a German red that produces a big, dark wine. Because it matures early and easily in cool sites like Chateau Wolff's Nanaimo vineyard, more of it has been planted there. "I'm really serious about Dornfelder," von Wolff says. "I think it has a good future on the island."

Dornfelder is not the only secret to the Grand Rouge, a wine that has achieved an alcohol of 19 per cent naturally, without being fortified. When asked how that is possible, von Wolff smiles and arches his bushy eyebrows. "It's done with a specific yeast culture," he replies, "which I won't divulge."

CHERRY POINT VINEYARDS

OPENED: 1994

840 Cherry Point Road, RR 3, Cobble Hill, BC, V0R 1L0
Telephone: 250-743-1272
Web site: www.cherrypointvineyards.com
Wine shop: Open daily 10 am – 6 pm. Picnic patio available.

RECOMMENDED

- ☀ COWICHAN BLACKBERRY PORT
- ✹ PINOT GRIS
- ✹ PINOT NOIR RESERVE
- ✹ BLANC DE NOIR
-   AGRIA – PINOT NOIR
-   VALLEY MIST
-   VALLEY SUNSET

THE LINK BETWEEN CHERRY POINT VINEYARDS AND THE COWICHAN INDIAN
Band started when the winery permitted band members to sell wild blackberries
each summer in the winery's parking lot. In 2004, the Quw'utsun' — to use the band's
proper name — acquired the winery and its vineyard from founders Wayne and
Helena Ulrich. The amiable Ulrichs remain under contract as consultants, giving
the entrepreneurial Quw'utsun' time to train their own winery and vineyard staff.

The Quw'utsun', with about 3,700 members living in the Cowichan Valley, is
one of the largest First Nations bands in western Canada. The band owns about
2,400 hectares (6,000 acres), much of it in small parcels throughout the valley, and
a number of businesses, ranging from forestry to tourism. Noting the growth of
the wine industry, the band's Khowutzun Development Corporation in 2001 took
a hard look at planting vineyards. They identified about 120 hectares (300 acres)

suitable for vineyard development. By buying an operating winery that was for sale (the Ulrichs wanted to retire), they secured a business to buy any grapes planted by the band and to provide industry skills. Cherry Point made almost 10,000 cases of wine in 2003, including its remarkably successful Cowichan Blackberry port.

The relationship started with those parking lot blackberry sales. The Himalayan blackberry, which yields lusciously sweet black fruit each summer, grows prolifically throughout the Cowichan Valley. Enterprising berry pickers prepared to wrestle with the nasty thorns on the bushes had little difficulty selling the tasty berries to Cherry Point's customers. At the end of the day, Helena Ulrich often turned unsold berries into pies and jams and Wayne occasionally made a little blackberry wine.

In 2000, a winemaker at Cherry Point made a delicious trial batch of port-style wine. Ulrich decided to gear up. "We just put the word out that we were buying berries and they started to come in," he says. By the end of the 2001 blackberry season, Cherry Point had purchased 2,300 kilograms (5,000 pounds) of berries. By the time the grapes were ready for picking that fall, the port was in tanks. "We started pouring tank sample tastes within two weeks of starting the process," he recalls. "So in the tasting room, we'd have this pitcher off to the side and we would pour samples. We had 300 names on our list to be telephoned when the wine was on the market. I can only remember one person who didn't want his name on the list. There was such universal enthusiasm." After a label had been commissioned from a First Nations artist, the wine was on sale before Christmas. "It is winter cash flow, the first time we've ever had that," Helena observes. "It is a really, really good plan." It was so good, in fact, that in 2002 the winery tripled its blackberry purchase, making about 11,500 half-bottles of Cowichan Blackberry port. In 2003, the winery made 42,000 half-bottles from 19,282 kilograms (42,509 pounds) of berries. Wayne Ulrich stopped purchasing berries when the winery ran out of storage tanks for the wine. "There is no reasonable limit to the amount of blackberries we can get," he says.

The Ulrichs were novices when they planted the vineyard in 1990 on a property that had formerly been a mink farm. Born in 1937, Wayne Ulrich grew up on a family farm at Dundurn, near Saskatoon. After getting an engineering degree, he helped his family run the farm and then became a public servant, first with Alberta's agriculture ministry and then in 1981 with Agriculture Canada in Victoria. It was while reviewing grant applications from wineries in the Okanagan that he and Helena, his Dutch-born wife and owner of a lamp store in Victoria, became attracted to the wine grower's lifestyle.

To begin, they planted about four hectares (10 acres) primarily to Pinot Blanc, Gewürztraminer, Auxerrois, Ortega and Pinot Noir, along with a handful of other varieties. Wayne, who uses a weather forecast as the home page of his computer, recalls each of the Cowichan Valley vintages. In the first year that his vines bore fruit, he had not yet netted them. "That was a wonderful year but the birds ate our crop," he remembers.

The Ulrichs were living on their savings and from the sheep they kept at the time. Anxious to have wine for sale, Cherry Point bought Okanagan grapes and opened its doors in 1994. The winery continued to buy Okanagan fruit for almost a decade while establishing its own vineyard, now increased to about 10 hectares (24 acres). Pinot Gris was included in the new plantings after the winery scored a commercial and critical success with a Pinot Gris from Similkameen Valley grapes.

The blackberry port is not the only example of serendipity at Cherry Point. One of the winery's best-selling white wines is an off-dry blend called Valley Mist. Helena Ulrich has quipped that the wine should be called Valley Mistake. The wine was created after one tank of white wine was topped up by error with a different white wine. Now a blend of Müller-Thurgau, Riesling and Ehrenfelser, Valley Mist has been joined by two partners. One is a Pinot Noir–based red blend called Valley Sunset. The other is a drier blended white called Cuvée de Pinot because it incorporates Pinot Blanc, Pinot Gris and Pinot Auxerrois.

The Ulrichs made a significant contribution to island viticulture in 1992 when they took over grape trials that the provincial government was abandoning. The 32 varieties in the test plot, including table grapes, had been imported from Europe. "The star of the whole works was Agria," Wayne Ulrich says. "We've been excited about it since the first time we picked any fruit." The grape is a vinifera cross created in 1965 by Hungarian plant breeder Dr. József Csizmazia. After Cherry Point bottled the variety the first time, Ulrich sent labels to the breeder so he could see the long-delayed result of his work. Agria is now grown by several wineries, including Larch Hills at Salmon Arm, where an early-ripening red is needed.

The wine has been a style in progress as successive Cherry Point winemakers have determined the best approach to take with these inky red grapes. "Using normal winemaking techniques on Agria, it does come out to be very tannic," Wayne Ulrich notes. "You don't need to depend on long skin maceration to give you the colour in the wine. You've got the colour right off the bat." The wine, in fact, is deep in colour; the texture is fleshy and the flavours are rich. It has become one of Cherry Point's most sought-after wines, with a maximum production of only 200 cases. Most of it is snapped up by members of the winery's Case Club.

Under its new owners, Cherry Point becomes the second Aboriginal winery in North America (the first was Nk'Mip Cellars of Osoyoos). The Cowichan Band has also consulted the world's first Aboriginal winery, New Zealand's Tohu Wines. Opened in 1998, it is owned by a group of Maori development trusts that have been growing grapes for about 25 years. Already a substantial winery, Tohu now produces 25,000 cases a year, with a goal of reaching 120,000 cases by 2007. Tohu should prove an excellent mentor.

COLUMBIA GARDENS VINEYARD AND WINERY

OPENED: 2001

9340 Station Road, Trail, BC, V1R 4W6

Telephone: 250-367-7493

Web site: www.cgwinery.com

Wine shop: Open daily 11 am – 5 pm May through November; weekends to Christmas. Closed during winter.

RECOMMENDED

* ✹ MARÉCHAL FOCH PRIVATE RESERVE
* ✹ PINOT NOIR LATE HARVEST
* ✹ GEWÜRZTRAMINER
* STATION ROAD WHITE
* STATION ROAD RED

AMONG THE INVESTORS WHO PUT CAPITAL INTO CALONA WINES IN THE 1930s were some immigrant Italian smelter workers in Trail, then British Columbia's most prosperous industrial community. Had they known what Tom Bryden knows now, they might have put their money into vineyards in the Columbia River valley south of Trail.

Bryden, together with Lawrence Wallace, his son-in-law, and their families, have pioneered grape growing on a 20-hectare (50-acre) property that has been in the Bryden family since the 1930s. There was, however, a great deal of other agriculture pursued here, including orchards, vegetables, livestock and hay, before 2.4 hectares (six acres) of grapes were planted in the 1990s. Columbia Gardens, which Bryden and Wallace opened in the fall of 2001, is the first winery in the Kootenays.

It will not be the last. A neighbour planted about 1,500 vines in 2002. While he has no winery plans, it shows the interest that Columbia Gardens has generated. "We've had a lot of conversations with other people who are looking at purchasing property out in the Columbia Gardens area," Bryden says. "I think we've broken the ice and proven it can be done." In nearby Creston, for example, the Skimmer-horn Winery is being developed.

The fertile area referred to as Columbia Gardens is on a bench with a good southwestern exposure, overlooking the swift-flowing Columbia. The valley is hot enough for grapes, with mountains on both flanks of the river sheltering the valley from cold winds. Except for one large dairy farm — with a corn field that draws the birds away from Columbia Garden's grapes — the bench now consists largely of hobby farms. For the part-time farmers with jobs in Trail, the city is an easy 15-minute drive on a good highway.

Bryden and Wallace are among those with city jobs that support farming. Bryden, near retirement age, has worked at purchasing and administrative jobs with several of the large employers, including the power company. Wallace, who is in his mid-40s, is a plumbing and heating contractor.

Over the last two decades, Wallace had become an accomplished amateur winemaker. That interest sparked the move to grape growing on Bryden's farm. "Seven or eight years ago, we got tired of the haying end of it," Bryden says. "Lawrence started experimental plots with some grape varieties to see which ones would do well in this climate and geographical region. Then we started phasing in plantings and over the next three or four years, we ended up with a six-acre vineyard. It's kind of grown from a bit of a hobby, to see how the varieties would do, to a commercial operation."

Bryden's philosophical drawl reflects his cautious approach to a radical change of direction for a farm that has been in the family so long. "My grand-parents moved here in the early 1930s." he says. "My grandkids are now living on the same property, the fifth generation to live on this property. It's kind of rare." He and Wallace have taken advice from Okanagan vineyard and winery profes-sionals. They spent time at the Summerland research station while doing their homework and took short industry courses in the Okanagan. "We did a lot of research on weather patterns and temperature patterns over the years," Bryden says. "We compared this to areas like Summerland and Kelowna before we made our leap into bigger plantings."

The reds in the vineyard are Maréchal Foch and Pinot Noir. The white vari-eties are Gewürztraminer, Auxerrois and Chardonnay. As well, there are small plantings of Kerner, Siegerrebe and Schönburger; with their vivid aromas and flavours, the latter two varieties are good as single varietal wines as well as for lifting flavours in blended wines.

The white varieties struggled a little more than the reds before becoming established in the vineyard. The main problem Bryden faced was the soil's fertility. "Probably the biggest thing we had to cope with was vigour," he says. He points to the neatly tended vineyard stretching northward from the tasting room patio. "This used to be a hayfield. We've dealt with the vigour challenge by restricting the water and by not fertilizing. We even went to the extent of planting grass in the rows to take up some of the nutrients." The vines were trellised in a manner designed to limit production. "As the plants are getting older, things seem to be levelling out," Bryden said in 2003. "And we are learning, too."

Columbia Gardens opened in the fall of 2001 with a modest quantity of wines from the 2000 vintage, since Bryden and Wallace wanted to test the local market's response. Sold out by Christmas, they could not reopen the tasting room until the following May when the first of the 1,000 cases of 2001 wine was ready. The current plan is to limit production to about 1,500 cases, a comfortable size for what is intended to be a family operation. "We're taking a cautious approach," Bryden says.

They are also taking a focussed approach, with fewer than a dozen wines, including varietals from Maréchal Foch, Pinot Noir and Gewürztraminer. There are three value-priced blends, of which Garden Gold, a fruity, off-dry blend of Auxerrois and Gewürztraminer, is Columbia Garden's most popular wine. An unoaked Chardonnay was added in the 2002 vintage, along with a dessert wine from Pinot Noir. The intention had been to produce an icewine. The winery missed the brief opportunity during an unexpected freeze in early November. By the time it was cold enough again to freeze grapes for icewine, Wallace and Bryden had taken the less risky course, turning the grapes into a delicious late harvest wine.

The charm of the Columbia Gardens wine shop surprises first-time visitors, who do not expect a tasting room with sophisticated décor this far off the beaten path. The shop is a modern log house, built to an elegant design created by Bryden, Wallace and their families. "We have a couple of ladies involved with this, wives and daughters, that have a knack at decorating," Bryden says. In addition to wines, the shop sells local cheeses, paintings by regional artists and other gifts. Food service with a picnic area is under consideration. "We're not jumping into extra work ahead of time," Bryden adds quickly. "We are trying to do it in a fairly methodical fashion."

The methodical approach included qualifying the wines for the Vintners Quality Alliance seal, something that not all small wineries bother with. The approval of the VQA tasting panel is important to the credibility of this groundbreaking winery. "We're the only one in the Kootenays," Bryden says. "We're new here and we needed some kind of benchmark of quality, just to prove ourselves."

COLUMBIA VALLEY CLASSICS WINERY

OPENED: 1998

1385 Frost Road, Lindell Beach, BC, V2R 4X8

Telephone: 604-858-5233

Web site: www.cvcwines.com

Wine shop: Open daily 10 am – 5 pm June through September; 11 am – 5 pm
    October to December; call ahead January through May.

BEFORE THERE WERE VINEYARDS IN BRITISH COLUMBIA, THE WINERIES of the 1920s turned fruits into wine. Berry wines had a good run before going into decline into the 1960s. The revival of fruit wineries in the modern era, led by Columbia Valley, depended on the stubborn determination of John Stuyt, a Dutch-born horticulturist who once said: "I believe in functioning according to John." The founder of this winery, he ran it for six years until falling victim to ill health in 2003. In that time, seven other fruit wineries were developed in British Columbia, along with two honey wineries and two new apple wineries, travelling a regulatory road blazed by Stuyt.

Columbia Valley's impact on the fruit wine scene has been limited by the winery's perceived isolation. It is based on a 16-hectare (40-acre) farm at the south end of Cultus Lake, in what is called the Columbia Valley. During the summer, the lake is perhaps the most popular resort in the eastern Fraser Valley. But it is very quiet in the off-season.

John Stuyt did not have a winery in mind when he bought the farm in 1989. He just believed that the Columbia Valley is a superior place for growing berries and nuts. Born in Holland in 1930, he came to Canada in 1956, settling on a raspberry and chicken farm near Aldergrove. On a Sunday afternoon drive, he came upon the scenic Columbia Valley and was so impressed with the potential that he bought a farm within five days. He put hazelnut trees on half the property and a host of berries on the rest, including raspberries; blueberries; red, white and black currants; gooseberries and saskatoon berries. The early harvests proved his faith in what he called Bertram Creek Farm. "You should see the quality," he said of his red currants. "It is totally different from Aldergrove. The colour is deep and rich and full."

To add value to the nuts and berries, Bertram Creek Farm began making jams, jellies and other confections. In turn, that gave Stuyt the idea for the winery and the leverage with the regulators to got a license. He did not get much government encouragement, he said, but there was no good reason to put him off since he was already a food processor. In 1997, he hired Dominic Rivard to make the wines.

This clearly was a career turning point for Rivard, who subsequently made wines for The Fort Wine Company, Blue Heron Fruit Winery and Wellbrook Winery as well as several wineries in China. Rivard, born in Quebec in 1971, had started making wine before he was old enough to drink legally. He acquired the necessary skills by taking a British wine course and working in the laboratory of a winemaking supplies company in Vancouver. At Columbia Valley, he also got some help from Todd Moore, a former champion bicycle racer who started making wines at an Alberta fruit winery and has since become a consulting Okanagan winemaker. Columbia Valley provided Rivard with the opportunity to master fruit wines. While some of the early fruit wines were on the dry side, Rivard eventually established a style that he has followed since, balancing the wines with the sweetness necessary to bring out the most intense fruit flavours. Columbia Valley's style remained consistent after Rivard moved on.

Columbia Valley's white currant wine, which happens to be one of the driest, is said to be the world's only white currant wine. The berry itself is rarely planted in North America. Stuyt sourced a white currant variety from Holland, called White Pearl, for his farm. The golden-hued wine is among the most flexible of fruit wines for matching with foods. The winery recommends it with foods ranging from Oriental cuisine to fowl.

Because many of the other fruit wines are finished with a perceptible, but not excessive, sweetness, the food pairing recommendations often include "pour it over ice cream." Raspberry wine, powerfully aromatic and full flavoured, is one of the fruit wines that matches easily with chocolate and chocolate cakes. In 2003, the winery extended its raspberry portfolio by releasing a wine called Velvet Royal, a blend in which red currant adds a vibrant note.

The winery's fruit liqueurs — raspberry, black currant and blueberry — are even richer and sweeter. John Stuyt took particular pride in a hazelnut liqueur that Columbia Valley released in 2002 after a long and difficult period of development. Stuyt saw that product as a legacy that would be around for a good half-century. However, his biggest legacy is the emergence of the fruit wineries in British Columbia. "The fruit wine industry is still getting recognition," he said in a 2002 interview. "But it is here to stay."

CROWSNEST VINEYARDS

OPENED: 1995

Surprise Drive, Cawston, BC, V0X 1C0
Telephone: 250-499-5129
Web site: www.crowsnestvineyards.com
Wine shop: Open daily 10 am – 6.30 pm from April 1 to December 24.
Restaurant: Lunch served on The Cork patio and in German-style lounge.

RECOMMENDED

✵ CHARDONNAY STAHLTANK
✹ OVATION
AUXERROIS
MERLOT
BARCELLO CANYON CUVÉE
BARCELLO CANYON FOCH
SAMTROT

OLAF HEINECKE TRACES HIS INTEREST IN WINE GROWING TO THE HOUSE in Germany's Baden-Wurttemberg wine region where he settled his family after escaping from East Germany in 1982. Like other homes in the subdivision, it had three or four rows of vines attached to it. The grapes went to the local cooperative in return for cash or wine. "That's how it started," he says.

Heinecke, a native of Leipzig, keeps to himself how he managed to leave Communist East Germany. It is obvious that this forceful entrepreneur was a misfit in the Marxist economy. Within a few years of settling in the West, he was a busy property developer. After the Berlin Wall was dismantled in 1989, he even developed a housing tract in the former Eastern zone.

"I sold the company and part of the contract was that I couldn't work in the development business for the next five years," he says. "Then we started travelling." During a vacation to British Columbia, he was surprised to find vineyards. "I never thought there were grapes here, just polar bears and Eskimos." He and Sabine, his wife, moved to the Okanagan in 1995, buying a small Penticton vineyard. That was quickly flipped when he and a friend, a German lawyer, acquired a larger vineyard just above the Nichol Vineyard north of Naramata. They intended to develop a winery there until his partner suggested it would be better to buy an existing winery. In the fall of 1998, they took over Crowsnest Vineyards, then a struggling winery in the Similkameen Valley. Subsequently, when the business partnership dissolved, the Heinecke family took over total ownership of the winery and sold its interest in the Naramata vineyard.

Today, Olaf Heinecke suggests it was a "cuckoo idea" to buy a winery rather than start from scratch on the Naramata Bench. But he has never been one to waste much time on the past. He and his family directed all of their considerable energies to making Crowsnest the star of the Similkameen, raising the annual production from about 500 cases when they bought it to 6,000 or more cases now.

The winery was started by Hugh and Andrea McDonald, who converted a 5.4-hectare (13.5-acre) family orchard to grapes. A graduate food technologist, Andrea was attracted to wine, working first at Okanagan Vineyards and later at what is now Vincor's Jackson-Triggs winery near Oliver until she and Hugh, a trucker, struck out on their own. The winery's name, Crowsnest, was taken from that of British Columbia's southernmost highway. Unfortunately for the McDonalds, not enough wine tourists sought out the few wineries on that part of the Crowsnest Highway.

The Heineckes have been more successful because Olaf mustered his entire family for the business. His son, Sascha, born in 1978, had acquired a diploma in hotel management in Germany; daughter Ann, three years younger than her brother, had taken a winemaking diploma at Weinsberg. Neither had planned to follow their parents to Canada until Olaf let it be known that help was needed in the winery. "Everybody has his own territory now," says Sascha, who became an effective wine marketer.

Winemaking consultant Todd Moore was retained for the 1999 vintage at Crowsnest and stayed on to work with Ann over succeeding vintages. Moore, a former bicycle racer who now juggles winemaking with a career as a fireman, has worked at various British Columbia wineries (in the Okanagan and on Vancouver Island) since 1991. He believes in a minimalist winemaking style, handling wines gently and as little as possible. He chuckles that it was tough to convince the energetic Heinecke family, who like to be hands-on, to practise limited intervention. "These are standard winemaking procedures in the Okanagan," Moore says of the techniques in Crowsnest's cellar. "None of this is revolutionary winemaking."

When the Heinecke family took over, the winery's portfolio was almost entirely white — Auxerrois, Chardonnay, Riesling and Gewürztraminer. That reflected the major varieties in the vineyard, which had not yet been fully planted in 1998. Since then, the modest plantings of Merlot and Pinot Noir have been increased. Some thought was given to adding Syrah but Moore discouraged this trendy variety because it ripens late, making it risky in the Similkameen. While the valley has blistering summer heat, the absence of a lake to temper the climate means there is a greater risk of early autumn frosts than in the Okanagan. Moore thinks it is prudent to stay with earlier-ripening reds such as Merlot. He's had no argument because Crowsnest's Merlots have begun to win medals in competition.

Today, 40 per cent of Crowsnest's production is red wine. In 2002 the winery, hitherto entirely an estate producer, began buying red grapes from an Okanagan Falls vineyard. One variety is a Maréchal Foch from vines planted in 1973, capable of yielding intense, deeply coloured wine with flavours of plum and licorice. This is one of the wines released under the winery's premium Barcello Canyon label. The name comes from the mountain pass connecting Oliver in the Okanagan to Cawston in the Similkameen Valley, passable in summer over a rough dirt road. The other red wine from purchased grapes is made with an obscure German variety called Samtrot, a light, fruity red that is best chilled on a hot summer day. Crowsnest is the Okanagan's only producer of Samtrot.

The most popular wine at Crowsnest is an unoaked Chardonnay that recalls a white Macon in style. To set it apart from a number of other unwooded Chardonnay wines, Crowsnest labels this Chardonnay Stahltank — German for "steel tank." This is one of the Crowsnest wines that has been exported to Germany where, Olaf Heinecke reports, "They were impressed."

D'ANGELO VINEYARDS

OPENING: PROPOSED FOR 2006–07

> 947 Lochore Road, Penticton, BC, V2A 8V1
> Telephone: 250-493-1364
> E-mail: sdangelo@telus.net

WHEN WINDSOR-AREA GRAPE GROWER SAL D'ANGELO WAS NAMED ONTARIO'S Grape King in 1999, it was the first time that the industry's top honour had gone to a vineyardist outside the Niagara region since the award was inaugurated in 1956. It was remarkable that D'Angelo was even growing grapes. Six years earlier, he nearly died during paralysis caused by Guillain-Barré Syndrome. Now, the indomitable D'Angelo, the operator of his own winery and 20-hectare (50-acre) vineyard near Amherstberg in Ontario, is establishing his second winery on the Naramata Bench. "I can be a bit obstinate," he says mildly.

D'Angelo moved to a home on his British Columbia vineyard in 2004 because he feels better in the dry Okanagan climate than in the muggy summer-time heat of southwestern Ontario. But well before his illness, he was attracted to the Okanagan. "I've been going on vacation to Penticton since 1985," he says. It was not until 2002, after extensively exploring the Okanagan's back roads, that he purchased two adjoining orchards and began converting the 11 hectares (27 acres) to grapes. "I should have bought back in 1989," he says wistfully, "when the vineyards were all for sale."

Salvatore D'Angelo, to use his full given name, was born in 1953 in Abruzzi, a wine-growing province on Italy's Adriatic coast. He came to Canada three years later with his parents. "I grew up with the smell of fermenting grapes," he says, recalling his father's rustic wines. "It is part of our culture. I, being the oldest son, had the responsibility every night to go down to the wine cellar and take out a carafe of wine for the evening meal." Eventually, he and his father made wine together, soon arguing about techniques when Sal began applying modern winemaking practices. "It took me a long time to convince him," Sal says. "But the last year we made wine together, he made six barrels of fabulous wine."

With opportunities limited in the Canadian wine industry at the time, Sal became an electrician and then a technical teacher (industrial robotics). In 1983 he planted a small vineyard about 20 minutes outside Windsor, opening his Ontario winery six years later. "I taught school and ran the vineyard and the winery as well for nine years," he says. "I left teaching in 1992. I took a two-year leave of absence and never went back."

He calculates that he was working sixteen-hour days during that period, even finding time to be a martial arts instructor. He thinks that his superb fitness was the critical difference in his recovery from Guillain-Barré Syndrome, an illness that leaves some of its victims in wheelchairs for life. It is a neurological condition that starts with paralysis in the feet and, over a few weeks, ascends toward the chest. Severe cases of paralysis interfere with breathing, sometimes fatally.

"I got stricken in 1993 and I was paralyzed from the neck down for three and a half years," says D'Angelo, who had to be resuscitated once when he stopped breathing. He made what his doctors consider a complete recovery, as the paralysis receded gradually over five years. His illness began a week before the 1993 vintage. D'Angelo stubbornly declined a wheelchair, figuring he would recover faster by forcing himself to walk. When told that he faced four months in hospital, he insisted on leaving four days later to supervise the harvest. "The 1993 Maréchal Foch won three gold medals," he notes.

The extent to which he refused to give in to a potentially lethal ailment is remarkable. On his last day in hospital, a technician spent a morning testing the conductivity of D'Angelo's nervous system. "The technician put me on this cot and we started chatting," D'Angelo recalls. "And after about three and a half hours — it was a four-hour test — he looked at me and said that most people that get on that cot were so depressed they had to be sent to a psychologist. 'And you want to keep selling!' I had snagged his wine order for their annual dinner in Windsor the next month. I got an $1,100 order from him by noon."

His Ontario winery, which makes about 4,000 cases a year, is known for red wines and icewine. He will continue to specialize in reds in the Okanagan. The initial planting in 2003, about 1.8 hectares (4.5 acres) consists primarily of the five Bordeaux varieties, with Merlot being half the planting. More of the same vines will be planted in subsequent years, along with a little Pinot Noir, Shiraz and the Okanagan's largest planting of Tempranillo, a Spanish red that he believes to be winter hardy. He is planting two of his favourite whites, Viognier and Gewürztraminer. "And probably a little bit of Chardonnay," he laughs. "Everybody expects you to have a Chardonnay."

It may have taken D'Angelo a long time to find his Okanagan property but when he did, he found one with unique features. It is a good frost-free site high on a peninsula with the lake on two sides and a dry creek bed on the third. D'Angelo is particularly wary about frost after enduring vine-killing Ontario winters. The contours of the Okanagan property allow D'Angelo to build a gravity-flow winery (where wines are moved gently by gravity, not pumped).

The location, just beyond Munson Mountain, is strategic for wine touring. There are five other wineries within walking distance. Houses on the property have been converted into accommodation for tourists. The Vineyard View Bed and Breakfast, as it is called, opened in 2004, managed by D'Angelo's daughter, Stephanie, who has been studying business. By the time the winery opens, D'Angelo's son, Christopher, will have completed his winemaking studies, having already come first in his viticulture class at Okanagan University College. "I told him you can't come on board without qualifications," D'Angelo says sternly. "If you want to join the family business, you need to be educated."

D'ASOLO VINEYARDS

OPENED: 2003

400 601 West Broadway Avenue, Vancouver, BC, V5Z 4C2
Telephone: 604-871-4329
Web site: www.asolo.ca

RECOMMENDED

PINOT GRIGIO
MERLOT

THIS BEGAN AS ANOTHER OF THE OKANAGAN'S VIRTUAL WINERIES, A PREMIUM label functioning as the storefront for an ambitious real estate project near Oliver called *il villaggio d'Asolo*. Most of the first releases under this label, from the superb vintages of 2001, 2002 and 2003, were made at the nearby Tinhorn Creek winery, with d'Asolo's own polish put on the wines by Daniel Lagnaz, one of the Okanagan's most experienced winemakers.

Behind the project is Vancouver businessman, Bruce Fuller, who has had a fascination with historic villages since his teenage years at Metz, in France, where he explored the gingerbread villages of Alsace. Years later, he was introduced to a community called Asolo, a village not far from Venice. One of Fuller's mementoes is a 1978 photograph that shows him in front of an Asolo wine shop, glass in hand, in the company of half a dozen Italians made cheery by their morning grappa. That is the ambiance that Fuller seeks to re-create. His plans call for developing an Italian-style village near Oliver during the next five years. The proposed site is on Covert Farms, once a large grape producer and still a major producer of vegetables.

The farm, on a plateau near McIntyre Bluff, was developed by the late George Covert, a Californian who bought the property in 1959. As he had done in California, he started by growing onions and tomatoes. In 1962, he began adding grapes. By

1978, the vineyard reached its full extent of 73 hectares (180 acres). The major variety was Maréchal Foch. During the red grape surplus of the 1980s, Mike Covert, George's son, produced grape juice rather than convert to white grapes. That ended after the 1988 vintage, when Covert Farms took advantage of a government incentive to pull out its entire vineyard except for table grapes. Nervous about the winter hardiness of vinifera grapes, Covert planted apples where vines once grew.

Fuller, an ebullient marketer and former vice-president with the Jim Pattison Group, was introduced to Covert Farms in 2003 when he was searching the Okanagan for a development site. The quiet, picturesque farm, about 259 hectares (640 acres) in size, has uncultivated land with potential for residential development. Fuller's concept would weave the housing among terraced vineyards connected by vine-covered pergolas. In other words, a blend of his memories of Europe.

The first step was launching the d'Asolo label and making plans for a storefront winery in Oliver. "If we couldn't move forward with the village," he explains, "we would still have a wine company." The wines, served in top restaurants, are the project's billboard while Fuller works on getting regulatory approvals and financing.

The first release d'Asolo wines, 1,000 cases, were made at Tinhorn Creek and are similar in style to the Tinhorn wines. Perhaps the biggest difference was in the labels. What Tinhorn Creek released as Pinot Gris 2002 appeared as Isabella d'Asolo Pinot Grigio. Tinhorn's Merlot 2001 was relabelled as Franco d'Asolo Merlot 2001. The label names suggest Fuller's romantic nature. Isabella was his mother's name while Franco is an old friend, a Toronto restaurateur who comes from Asolo.

Those two vintages have been followed by 700 cases of 2003 Pinot Grigio and 850 cases of 2002 Merlot. While those wines also were made at Tinhorn, Daniel Lagnaz, who had become the d'Asolo winemaker, finished the wines in d'Asolo's individual style. In the 2004 vintage, d'Asolo expects to have wine made elsewhere because Tinhorn needs its wine for its own sales.

Lagnaz was born in Switzerland in 1954 and trained there. After making wine there, then in Spain and Australia, he came to Mission Hill in 1982. The winery, with a history of receiverships, had been taken over the year before by Anthony von Mandl. Over the next decade, Lagnaz created well-regarded table wines, ciders and eau-de-vie spirits. In 1992, he moved to Mission Hill's Vancouver office as technical director to develop some of the winery's other beverages, including the hot-selling Mike's Hard Lemonade. Lagnaz retired from Mission Hill in 2002 and became d'Asolo Vineyard's vice-president and chief winemaker.

Ultimately, a broader array of wines are to be produced at the d'Asolo winery itself, including a wine in the style of Proseco, a light sparkling wine of Italy. Fuller hopes that some of the wines will be grown on proposed new plantings around the village's Covert Farm site. He is puzzled that vineyards have not been re-established here. "McIntyre Bluff heats up and keeps the property warm," he says. "Our growing periods on the side of the hill will be magnificent." Of course, the vines are essential to his vision of a village whose residents will experience the vintage first-hand each year. "We are building an agricultural village," he says.

DESERT HILLS ESTATE WINERY

OPENED: 2003

30480 71st Street (Black Sage Road), Oliver, BC, V0H 1T0
Telephone: 250-498-1040
Wine shop: Open daily 10 am – 5 pm.

THE GOOD-NATURED TOOR BROTHERS DON'T MIND HAVING A BIT OF fun at a visitor's expense. I began our first meeting by asking who was the elder brother. "Jesse is," Randy said, beginning to chuckle. "I was born about 15 minutes earlier," Jesse chimes in, laughing. "We're twins."

Born in Punjab in 1964, they are the only twins running a winery in British Columbia. Not that it is obvious: they are not identical twins. The winery and vineyard is a family operation that includes their mother, Sukhminder, who patrols the impeccably managed vines with a small tractor. "She pretty well has a name for every plant," Randy suggests. His younger brother, Dave, works off the farm but takes time out to help.

Sponsored by a sister who already lived in Canada, the Toor family immigrated in 1982 after the death of their father, who had been in the farming and trucking businesses. They divided their time between Winnipeg, where a cousin lived, and the Okanagan, where the sister lived. The Toor brothers got their first taste of vineyard life as teenagers, spending several summers working on the former Shannon Pacific vineyard across Black Sage Road from where they now live. Once one of the largest vineyards in the south Okanagan, most of Shannon Pacific's vines were pulled out after the 1988 harvest. The land remained fallow for the next four or five years.

The Toor family moved to their Black Sage Road property in 1988. It was an apple orchard that was struggling because the apples did not grow well on the sandy soil. The Toors tried other tree fruits, but when the vineyard across the road was replanted by new owners, the Toors decided they would switch their nine hectares (23 acres) to grapes if they could find a winery to buy the fruit. At the suggestion of Richard Cleave, a neighbour on Black Sage Road and a veteran vineyard manager, the Toors approached the Domaine de Chaberton winery in Langley.

It was an inspired suggestion. Domaine de Chaberton, which only grew white grapes in its Langley vineyard, was anxious for a source of premium red grapes. The Toor brothers wanted to grow primarily reds. In short order, the winery agreed to help the Toors develop a vineyard in return for a grape supply contract. The apple trees began coming out in 1995 and, within a few years, the entire gentle western slope was covered with vines.

Except for a small plot of Pinot Gris, the vineyard is entirely in reds: Syrah, Merlot, Cabernet Sauvignon, Gamay and a little bit of Malbec. Domaine de Chaberton was able to augment its range of wines substantially, beginning with grapes from the Toor vineyard in 2000. "They grow very good grapes for us, which I was surprised to see, because they had never grown grapes before," said Elias Phiniotis, the winemaker at Domaine de Chaberton. "Whatever they grow, we take."

Once the vineyard was established, the brothers went ahead with their own winery. "It was a little dream, to start a small winery," Randy says. "We love the industry. We love the taste of wine." Desert Ridge was launched with about 1,000 cases of wine, including Chardonnay made with purchased grapes. Phiniotis is Desert Ridge's winemaker. Although the Toors would like to complete their mastery of the grape by learning the art of winemaking, they are in no hurry, intending to keep Desert Ridge's annual production around 1,500 cases for some time.

They have an infectious enthusiasm about British Columbia wines, with considerable pride in what is being made here. On a family vacation in India a few months after opening Desert Ridge, Randy Toor took along some of his wine to show it off and compare it with Indian wines. "Indian wine is not as good as British Columbia wine," he concluded.

DIVINO ESTATE WINERY

OPENED: 1983

1500 Freeman Road, Cobble Hill, BC, V0R 1L0
Telephone: 250-743-2311
Wine shop: Open 1 pm – 5 pm Friday and Saturday.

JOE BUSNARDO, THE VOLATILE OWNER OF THIS WINERY, ONCE SAID IN AN interview that he does not even like making wine. The trouble is, it is hard to know when Joe means one of his extraordinary statements and when he is just being ornery. He is, without question, the most independent-minded individual in British Columbia's wine industry. Sumac Ridge founder Harry McWatters, who can be just as strong-willed, once said of Busnardo: "If you were swimming down the river, you know Joe would be swimming up. And if the river changed directions, so would Joe."

The two men started their wineries around the same time and for a few years were partners in private wine stores in Vancouver and Victoria. Commercially smooth and politically savvy, McWatters mastered the art of getting along with liquor regulators in order to get ahead. Busnardo, on the other hand, got his way (most of the time) by locking horns with regulators. In 1996, he sold his original winery in the Okanagan and moved to a property south of Duncan, on Vancouver Island. "And to fight the system, I brought my license here," Busnardo said. Yet if Joe Busnardo were the kind of man who goes along to get along, he would never have planted premium vinifera grapes in the Okanagan in 1968, against all advice, and would not now be in the midst of grape trials all over again on Vancouver Island.

He was born in 1934 in Treviso, not far from Venice, growing up on a farm where his father grew a variety of produce. Busnardo, who studied at an agricultural college, "never liked any plants but grapes." He immigrated to Canada in

1954 and, a few years later, his father ripped out the vines, planting mulberry bushes to raise silkworms. Meanwhile, Busnardo scraped together the money in 1967 to buy 27.5 hectares (68 acres) of raw land in the Okanagan Valley, south of Oliver. Within a few years, he had as many as 128 different varieties of vines growing here in what was probably the biggest private trial planting of vinifera in the valley. Some of the cuttings came from California and some came from Italy, where a friend had a state-subsidized experimental vineyard. The friend thought Busnardo was mad to try the same thing in Canada without a subsidy.

The nearest winery at the time was Casabello in Penticton. Busnardo sought to sell them his vinifera grapes and was outraged to be offered the same price as the winery was paying for Bath, a mediocre labrusca then growing in the valley. "I said, look, grow your own grapes," he huffed. "I'll keep experimenting on the farm and let the birds eat it." He got a job as a heavy equipment operator, leaving the vineyard to its own devices until 1979. In the previous winter, a severe early freeze devastated vineyards, killing even winter-hardy hybrid varieties. A good quantity of Busnardo's vinifera survived, however, and he took up grape growing again. This time, he would become his own customer by opening one of the early estate wineries.

Self-trained, Busnardo approached winemaking in the tradition of the old country. "I'm making wine the primitive way, the way my father made wine," he has said. "I just throw in the grapes and hope for the best." His brother, Guido, came from Italy a few times to give him a hand. Busnardo did not pay much attention because he considered his brother a connoisseur. Busnardo saw himself as making wine for the people: he even thought of selling 54-litre (11.8-gallon) containers of wine to Italian home winemakers tired of messing around with grapes.

And he made a lot of varieties and blends. "I make 25 wines," he said once. "I have wine for everybody. If a person says he does not like *any* of my wines, he had better stop drinking." His experimentation resulted in some unusual varietals. For example, he planted a big block of Garganega, the Italian white grape found in Soave wine. He grew other Italian whites no one else had, including Malvasia and Trebbiano. Hester Creek, which now owns that vineyard, has had success with Trebbiano. Divino, however, had trouble selling the varietals that, two decades earlier, were unknown among consumers.

Over the years, Busnardo narrowed his vineyard down primarily to a dozen mainstream varieties, including Chardonnay, Pinot Blanc, Cabernet Franc and Merlot. His wine production also ran ahead of the sales and Divino became one of the few wineries able to offer mature wines. At one point in 1993, he had unbottled Chardonnay from every vintage since 1989. He considered distilling some of his wines but changed his mind when he learned the federal government demanded that he deposit a $250,000 bond. "I can't afford you," he told Ottawa. His wines also lost listings in provincial liquor stores. Fortunately for him, he owned or had invested in a number of private wine stores in Vancouver, which kept his business alive.

As challenging as the business was, Busnardo still declined to sell his grapes to other wineries. Harry McWatters, who had been a salesman at Casabello before starting his own winery, once asked Busnardo for five tons of Perle of Csaba to support Sumac Ridge's successful dessert wine from that variety. Busnardo, on the other hand, released a Perle of Csaba only occasionally. He thought about the request for a few days and then said no. He just let the birds eat the succulent fruit.

Busnardo began entertaining offers for his superbly situated Okanagan vineyard in 1995. At the time, he was buying a farm overlooking the busy island highway at Cobble Hill in the Cowichan Valley, heart of Vancouver Island's small wine region. He explained the move to Alan Daniels, a reporter for the *Vancouver Sun*: "I am tired of here. It is too hot. The place is too big. I am getting out."

The new owners of his property relaunched in 1996 as Hester Creek Estate Winery while the Divino winery moved to Cobble Hill, along with 11,000 cases of bottled wine and 53,000 litres (11,660 gallons) of bulk wine. After the transfer of the license was approved, the Liquor Control and Licensing Branch in Victoria said it was suspending the license until the new Cobble Hill vineyard was in production. Fortunately for Busnardo, the Liquor Appeal Board overturned that suspension within six months.

Only Joe Busnardo would consider the move to Cobble Hill as gearing down. With vines brought from his Okanagan vineyard, he has planted almost 12 hectares (30 acres). As always, he has not paid much attention to what varieties are already being grown in the Cowichan Valley, choosing instead to learn for himself what varieties work and what don't. His beloved Garganega is not happy on the island. He has replaced it and some other plantings. "But I am used to that," he shrugs. "In Oliver, some grapes I planted and replanted eight times in 30 years. To come up with a varietal here will take me at least another five years."

Busnardo began making small quantities of wine in 1999 from the Cobble Hill vineyard. In 2001, he released his first two Vancouver Island wines, blends called Bay Rosso and Bay Bianco. "The wine here tastes completely different," he has discovered. "We have to allow that, because in every country and in every area, there is a specific wine. Let's accept it. It is a funny thing, this island. The grape does not have the alcohol or the sugar the Okanagan has. I am used to seeing grapes at 26 Brix in the Okanagan. Here, the same variety will reach 20. So we have a difference of five to six Brix. On the other hand, here we might have a better flavour."

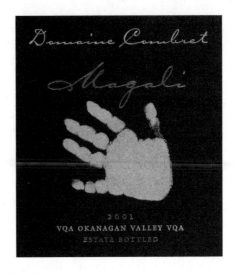

DOMAINE COMBRET ESTATE WINERY

OPENED: 1994

32057 #13 Road, Oliver, BC, V0H 1T0
Telephone: 250-498-6966
Toll-free: 1-866-TERROIR
Web site: www.combretwine.com
Wine shop: By appointment.

RECOMMENDED

* SAINT VINCENT RIESLING
* SAINT VINCENT CABERNET FRANC
* SAINT VINCENT CHARDONNAY
* MAGALI RED
* LINEAGE PINOT NOIR
* LINEAGE GAMAY
  GAMAY ICEWINE

THE ADVERTISING SLOGAN ONCE USED BY A CALIFORNIA WINERY — THAT IT released "no wine before its time" — applies as well at Domaine Combret. It sells 10-year-old Rieslings and six-year-old Chardonnays because Olivier Combret thinks it is "not serious" to sell only young wine. In 2004, the winery released 900 cases of 10-year-old Riesling under its premium Saint Vincent label, a connoisseur's wine that, when it is sold out, will be followed by a similar volume of 1995 Riesling.

"If this wine business in B.C. wants to survive, we have to build inventory," he argues. "We have to be able to offer the consumers old whites and old reds. That's what we do. I'm sure the consumers will appreciate it." It is a position one would expect at a winery with a strong Old World tradition.

The Combret family's wine heritage goes back 10 generations in Provence, to 1638. When they left France in 1992 to start over in New World winemaking, they chose, perhaps surprisingly, the south Okanagan over Chile, Washington State and Australia. After a decade in the Okanagan, Olivier Combret is convinced they chose well. "We have fantastic climatic conditions eight years out of 10 in the Okanagan Valley," he says. "The wineries that are going to make top wines in 10 years out of 10 will be those with the perfect sites. And there are not that many in B.C." Their vineyard, he suggests, is one of those optimal sites.

Their knowledge of the Okanagan started with his father, Robert, who did a master's degree in agriculture in 1958 at the University of British Columbia. He worked in the Okanagan on a thesis about apple storage, not wine, because the wine industry then was primitive. Back in Europe, he often told friends about the amazing "Mediterranean valley" on the other side of Canada. Meanwhile, he continued to run the family's winery, serving as well as president of the Aix-en-Provence appellation. Olivier, who was born in 1971, began working with his father at the age of 12. Olivier was in his final year at the Montpellier wine school in 1991 when the family accepted an attractive unsolicited offer for their winery, Château Petit Sonnailler.

At the time, the British Columbia wine industry was uncertain about its viability under free trade. As a result, the Combrets in 1992 found that virtually everything was for sale. They looked at property on Black Sage Road but decided against it because of the sandy soil. They looked at existing wineries only briefly since Olivier was already designing a "dream winery" on his own. Finally, on a hillside south of Oliver and high above the valley, they purchased 31.5 hectares (78 acres) that included six hectares (15 acres) already producing Chardonnay, Riesling and Cabernet Franc.

While they waited for more vines from Europe, they turned Olivier's design into one of the Okanagan's most efficient wineries. It nestles into the hillside, allowing wines to be made gently by gravity, from crushing the grapes at the winery's upper level to bottling the wine at the bottom level. It has more than enough capacity for the 5,000 cases of wine currently produced at Domaine Combret. But it is just the first stage. Olivier Combret envisages that his dream could be six times as large, including other attractions, when expansion finally concludes.

The vineyard, 80 per cent in red varieties, is about 14 hectares (35 acres), with as much again still available for vines. The varieties added by the Combrets were Gamay, Pinot Noir, Merlot, Cabernet Sauvignon and more Cabernet Franc. Olivier believes that the latter variety has established itself as one of the more consistent reds in the Okanagan, not so vulnerable to winter damage as Merlot.

"Our site cannot be questioned in terms of its capability of producing high-end B.C. whites, reds and rosé, or even dessert wines," Olivier hastens to add. It comes down to terroir, that elusive French concept encompassing all the attributes of a vineyard, from soil to exposure and climate. A profound appreciation of terroir is relatively recent in New World winemaking, where star status usually is accorded the winemaker and his technology. Olivier suggests that the winemaker's contribution to a wine's quality is a mere 10 per cent of the total, while the winery equipment accounts for another 10 per cent. He assigns a further 30 per cent of the quality to the selection of grapes and their management in the vineyard. The remaining 50 per cent comes from the site, or the terroir. For that reason, Domaine Combret's wines are made only with grapes grown on the estate. Year in and year out, the terroir puts its mark on the wines. "Consistency is the key," Olivier says. "That's what gives the reputations to Old World wines."

The winemaker's contribution is likely not as modest as Olivier makes out. Initially, the Combret Chardonnay and Riesling wines won the greatest acclaim. "My first vintage was 1993," Olivier recalls. "My first red wine vintage was 1994. White wine to me was faster to master. Red wines, I had to basically find what kind of process was going to work. It took a while and I made my mistakes. Let's face it, when I came here, I was 21 years old." When he reached the level he was aiming at, in the 1999 vintage, the Cabernet Franc was released the first time under the winery's top label, Saint Vincent.

Saint Vincent was chosen for the winery's premium label because Vincent is the patron saint of vintners. Coincidentally, Olivier Combret was born on the saint's day (January 22), and when his first child was born, the boy was called Vincent. The more popularly priced Combret wines, such as its Chablis-style unoaked Chardonnay, are sold under the Lineage label, inspired by the family's lineage in wine. The lowest-priced wines come out under labels such as Checkmate and Magali. The latter is the name of Olivier's daughter.

All of the wines, even the $20 Saint Vincent Cabernet Franc, are among the Okanagan's more affordable wines. Olivier believes he could easily ask $30 for his meaty, age-worthy Cabernet Franc. "I choose not to," he says. "I choose to make sure that consumers have access to outstanding reds from British Columbia, so we don't go and search for Australian reds, or whatever. If we talk about wanting the consumers to buy B.C., well, we have to give them access, financially speaking, to these wines. If we all aim for $30 or $50 wines, then how do you convince the consumers?"

Behind that attitude is the long-term view of a young winemaker whose family has made wine for almost 400 years. "In the wine industry today, we have to invest a serious amount of money and not expect a return before 30 years, because you are not going to get it," he insists. "You'll find you have to pour all the money you make back into the business. That's the way the wine business works."

DOMAINE DE CHABERTON ESTATE WINERY

OPENED: 1991

1064 216th Street, Langley, BC, V2Z 1R3

Telephone: 604-530-1736

Toll-free: 1-888-332-9463

Web site: www.domainedechaberton.com

Wine shop: Open daily.

Restaurant: Bacchus Bistro is open 11:30 am – 4:30 pm Wednesday through Sunday
and for dinner 5:30 pm – 9:30 pm Friday and Saturday.

RECOMMENDED

* SYRAH
* PINOT GRIS
* ORTEGA BOTRYTIS AFFECTED
* OPTIMA DESSERT
* GEWÜRZTRAMINER
* MERITAGE
* GAMAY NOIR
* MADELEINE SYLVANER
* BACCHUS
* BACCHUS DRY

DOMAINE DE CHABERTON HAD THE MISFORTUNE TO OPEN EXCLUSIVELY
with white wines just as the so-called French Paradox was shaking up the
wine world. The paradox suggested that Europeans nurtured on red wine and
Mediterranean foods had much less heart disease than North Americans. The
resulting stampede for red wines passed by Domaine de Chaberton, whose flagship wine was Bacchus, a white variety. Indeed, all the vines in its 14-hectare
(35-acre) vineyard in the Fraser Valley are white varieties.

Today, however, almost half the wines in Domaine de Chaberton's portfolio are reds, including a bold Syrah, one of the hottest varieties in the new millennium. How Domaine de Chaberton moved from the back of the parade to the front is quite a story.

The owners are both from Europe and are familiar with the Mediterranean diet. Inge Violet is the German-born daughter of an automobile dealer. She met Claude, who was born in Paris in 1935, while he was working at a bank in Munich. Claude Violet's wine heritage is thoroughly Mediterranean. An ancestor, Manaut Violet, established a vineyard in 1644 in Perpignan in the south of France. After generations of grape-growing, another of Claude Violet's ancestors began making a wine-based apéritif called Byrrh in 1866. This was a huge success. By the 1930s, production had reached an incredible 100,000 bottles a day and the expanded Violet cellars included the world's largest wooden vat, with a capacity of one million litres (220,000 gallons), a record that still stands.

After World War II, the Violet family sold its business to a competitor. But Claude Violet, after his brief stint in banking, was back in the wine business by 1968, as a wine merchant in Switzerland selling Spanish wine. A decade later, fed up with Europe's Cold War tensions, Claude and Inge moved to North America to start a winery. Believing Ontario too cold for successful grape growing, they came to British Columbia. Rather than buying land in the Okanagan Valley, they found a farm in the mild Fraser Valley, south of Langley, nearly at the border with the United States. The Violets thought they would be more successful establishing their business close to the big Vancouver market, rather than five hours away in the Okanagan.

That was the decision that set Domaine de Chaberton on its course as a white wine producer. John Harper, the consulting viticulturist who helped the Violets find their farm, then had an experimental vineyard nearby. Based on his experience, he told Claude Violet to plant no red varieties. "So I followed his advice, because he knew the valley very well," Claude says.

The vineyard was planted in 1981 with more than two dozen varieties. The results were assessed four years later to determine the successful varieties, the major ones being Bacchus, Madeleine Angevine, Madeleine Sylvaner, Ortega and Chardonnay. Subsequently, a tongue-twister of a German variety, Reichensteiner, was added. (It is an early-ripening wine grape suitable for the Fraser Valley. Because of its challenging name, the grape is blended, along with the Madeleines, into the winery's generic Chaberton Blanc.)

When the French Paradox turned wine demand upside down, Domaine de Chaberton sought red grapes in the Okanagan. Almost none were available. The red hybrid varieties had been pulled in 1988 and the first planting of red vinifera on Black Sage Road occurred only in 1992. "Here in B.C., red wine grapes were rare," Inge recalls.

The Violets applied for a commercial winery license, in order to import red varieties from the United States. Then in 1997, they found a way to remain an estate winery and make sought-after reds. Randy and Jesse Toor, apple-growing brothers on Black Sage Road, wanted to convert their orchard to a vineyard and approached Domaine de Chaberton for support. An investment by the Violets, along with a contract from Domaine de Chaberton, made the conversion happen. By the 2000 vintage, Domaine de Chaberton was getting Merlot, Cabernet Sauvignon, Gamay Noir and Syrah from one of the Okanagan's prime red grape vineyards. The wines, especially the Syrah, are now winning awards for Domaine de Chaberton.

The Violets give some credit to Elias Phiniotis, their winemaker, for encouraging this deal with the Toors. Widely experienced, Phiniotis was born in Cyprus in 1943 and earned a doctorate in food chemistry from a Hungarian University. He came to Canada in 1976 and, after two years as the technical director of the Wine-Art chain of winemaking shops, settled into a long winemaking career at a succession of Okanagan wineries, including Calona and Quails' Gate. He has made Domaine de Chaberton's wine since the winery opened.

"We think he is a great winemaker," Inge says. "He knows his wine. He has a lot of experience. He is very, very consistent. He has his personal touch, but he adapted very well to the tastes of the public. He is also often in the wine shop, listening to the people. He realizes what people want." The winery sells about 40 per cent of its production, now 35,000 cases a year, directly from its busy wine shop. Everybody in the shop pays close attention to customer feedback.

There has, for example, been a trend toward drier white wines, with the result that Phiniotis is finishing the fruity whites drier than was formerly the case — but not to the point of alienating the original clientele. Thus, the flagship Bacchus is made in two styles, one dry and one with a touch of residual sugar. The trend to unwooded Chardonnay led Domaine de Chaberton to issue one of its own even though, in 1995, the winery gained renown for an exotic Chardonnay aged in acacia barrels. This is a wood that imparts honey and orange blossom aromas, yielding wines that are controversial. Claude Violet loves the Acacia Chardonnay; his wife dislikes it. The winery still makes two barrels of it each year for those who share Claude's passion.

Not wanting to be caught behind the parade again, the winery now secures varieties in the Okanagan that it does not grow in Langley. "All of a sudden, a certain wine becomes really trendy," Inge Violet says. "Like Pinot Gris. It's like a fashion. I never thought, as long as we were in the wine industry, that it can be so trendy in the way of grape varieties. When I was in Germany" — referring to one of her periodic trips back to Europe — "Pinot Grigio from Italy was everywhere."

EAST KELOWNA CIDER COMPANY

OPENED: 2003

2960 McCulloch Road, Kelowna, BC, V1W 4A5
Telephone: 250-860-8118
Wine shop: Call for current hours.

RECOMMENDED

HARD APPLE CIDER

FEW WORK AS HARD AS DAVID AND THERESSA ROSS, THE OWNERS OF this cider company. David, who was born in Kelowna in 1969, is a logger and often away in the bush during the week. That leaves Theressa, with a work ethic developed while growing up on a Sicamous, British Columbia, dairy farm, to look after their two young children and manage the cider company with the occasional help of a relative or two. Between them, the Rosses run their own 3.6-hectare (nine-acre) apple orchard in the rural setting of East Kelowna. "I am out here four days a week, eight hours a day," Theressa says from the rustic tasting room in a corner of the cidery's warehouse. "I would be here seven days a week if I didn't have the orchard to manage too."

Somehow they found time to push through the change in provincial regulations permitting them to make hard cider (as alcoholic cider is called) from dessert apples. When they started working on their plans in 1995, existing rules for apple cider from an orchard-based cidery had been created around Merridale Ciderworks on Vancouver Island. Merridale grows authentic European cider apples; therefore, the regulations specified that land-based cider companies — as opposed to commercially licensed producers — could only use cider apples. Even if David or Theressa liked the bite of English cider, their orchard grows only dessert apples.

Over a period of three or four years, this determined couple pushed and prodded until the government broadened the regulations. "We actually wrote the stipulations to becoming a land-based fruit winery or cidery," Theressa says with quiet pride. "It took a lot of phone calls. The politicians know us all by name. It's the squeaky wheel that gets the grease, right?" The changes were the green light for a subsequent stream of fruit and apple wineries based on their own farms.

The East Kelowna Cider Company sits in the middle of an apple orchard that had been eight hectares (20 acres) in size when acquired in 1942 by David's grandfather, Charles. A photograph of him in the orchard is reproduced on the label of the cider. The orchard was later divided equally between David's father and his uncle, with David and Theressa buying the latter half in 2002.

The sparkling hard cider is David's dream. "Dave loves to create things," Theressa explains. "Ever since he was 12, he has been concocting mixtures of moonshine and that kind of stuff, just for the pure enjoyment of doing it." The motive today involves diversifying the farm. "But even if the fruit price was good, he would probably still be opening a cidery."

Her specialty is the carbonated soft, or non-alcoholic, cider that the farm has produced since 1997, for sale throughout the Okanagan and more recently in Vancouver markets. Theressa has developed four flavours: natural, cinnamon, cherry and peach. Both the soft and the hard ciders are based on the four major apple varieties grown in the orchard: Red Delicious, Golden Delicious, McIntosh and Spartan. "Cider apples are very bitter, or tart," Theressa explains. "When you taste that in the apples, you are going to taste that in the beverage as well. My thing is, if you can eat the apple and it tastes good, why would it not make a good drink? That's just our type of cider."

The blend of apples comprising the hard cider is something that the Rosses keep to themselves. "I don't do any of the blending with the hard cider," Theressa says. "That is my husband's job. I crush it, I ferment it, I do all that, but he does the blending. It is his taste buds that came up with the apples we use here. He has amazing taste buds."

With a modest alcohol content of six per cent, the cider is crisp, fresh and quaffable. "My husband wanted it to be like beer," Theressa says. "He wanted you to be able to sit down and drink a six-pack. I think he achieved that goal without losing the apple flavour. It fits in both worlds. It fits with the beer drinkers and it fits with the wine drinkers."

To husband their modest resources, the Rosses have combined ingenuity and scrounging to create the production facilities. The original equipment to get the juice from the crushed apples consisted of household washing machines. "We have six of them," Theressa says. A petite woman given to easy silvery laughter, she has mastered the art of moving nimbly when apples are being processed. The apples are pulped, a box at a time, in a hand-fed manual crusher. She pours the buckets of pulp into the nylon sacks that are placed inside each machine, where the high speed spinner separates the juice. "You start with number one spinner and by the time you get to number six, number one is done. That is probably about two minutes. Then you take the pulp out and dump it. The spinners are all back to back. I have put plastic eavestroughing behind them and the juice flows down that into a holding tank and then into our big tanks to be settled." With soft cider production rising in 2003, she added a larger juice separator acquired second-hand from a commercial fruit processor. "Our equipment is old-fashioned but it works," she laughs.

She spares herself much of the taxing work of crushing apples for juice by having a commercial processor do the job in the autumn when the apples are picked. Her equipment is pressed into service at other times when more juice is needed. The ability to store apples gives her the flexibility to match cider production against seasonal patterns of demand. Currently, much of the orchard's crop is sold to a large packing house. Premium apples head to fresh markets and the culls are returned for making cider. In time, perhaps, the cidery will need all of the orchard's production.

In time, as well, fruit-flavoured hard ciders might also be developed, although the Rosses are somewhat ambivalent about modifying the pureness of the natural flavours. "That gets away from the craft," Theressa worries. "Do we just add a flavour, like we've done with the soft cider, or do we actually go the extra mile and start crushing different varieties of fruit and blending it with apples? I really don't know what we will do when we get to that point. It depends on how hard we want to work."

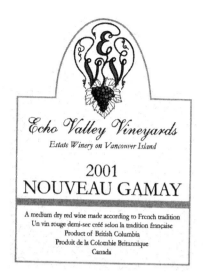

ECHO VALLEY VINEYARDS

OPENED: 2003

4651 Waters Road, Duncan, BC, V9L 3Y2

Telephone: 250-748-1470

Wine shop: Open 1 pm – 5 pm Thursday through Sunday in summer;
    weekend afternoons in spring and fall; by appointment in winter.

RECOMMENDED

CHARDONNAY

PINOT GRIS

GAMAY NOIR

ALBERT AND EDWARD BRENNINK, THE FATHER AND SON OPERATORS OF ECHO Valley, calibrated their former consulting winemaker Eric von Krosigk with samples brought back from a 2002 wine tour in France. The wines included both a red and a white from Beaujolais and a Pinot Gris from Alsace. "Now I know what you are after," Edward Brennink recalls the winemaker commenting after tasting the wines. "Of course, he can't copy them identically," Edward adds quickly. "That was not the intention — but to have something in that direction."

It is hardly surprising that the Brenninks, who opened their winery in the spring of 2003, should have European palates. Both were born in Holland — Albert in 1924 and Edward in 1958 — and lived in Switzerland. "We lived at the Lake of Geneva for 18 years, so we know the wine region there," the elder Brennink says. This is where he formed his appreciation of wine. "Exactly. There is no wine in Holland. It is only imported."

He also developed a taste for Chasselas, Switzerland's major white wine grape and perhaps one day the leading white in the Echo Valley vineyard. Previously, the only source of Chasselas on Vancouver Island was Blue Grouse

Vineyards. When Blue Grouse pulled out its 20-year-old Chasselas vines in 2002, the Brenninks transplanted a number around the border of Echo Valley's test vineyard. "We have two rows of Chasselas because we are going to plant it," Albert says. "I decided that before I started. That's the famous white wine in Switzerland and I'm just fond of it."

Albert Brennink practised as an architect in Europe until retiring to bring his family to Canada in 1979. He specialized in reconstructing churches and schools, repairing the extensive wartime damage those buildings had suffered in Holland and Germany. He kept his office in Holland, commuting regularly to Switzerland where the family had established a home for health reasons. (Mrs. Brennink had a chronic bronchial condition that resolved itself in the crisp mountain air of Switzerland.) When immigrating to North America, the family purchased a farm on Vancouver Island, attracted by the mild climate.

The 65-hectare (160-acre) farm is close enough to Duncan that the journey was once a brisk 15-minute gallop for a former owner, an avid horseman. This was an early island homestead. The original cook shack, held together with forged nails, still survives. Located at the very end of Waters Road, the farm seems remote because it nestles in its own valley below the Koksilah Ridge, surrounded by forest. "This was the only farm for sale at the time," Edward says. "My parents fell in love with it — the beauty of it, the remoteness, the peace and quiet." An enthusiastic and energetic horticulturalist, the elder Brennink has created an extensive, soul-soothing heather garden near his house.

Albert Brennink spent two decades pursuing other agricultural avenues before settling on grapes. For a time, his sheep produced wool for the island's coveted Cowichan sweaters. When cheaper New Zealand wool took that business away, he raised hardy Highland cattle, successfully exporting breeding stock to Europe until beef markets there were devastated by mad cow disease. He still keeps a small herd, more for what they add to the pastoral landscape than to the family's income. In 1999, the Brenninks began clearing 10 hectares (25 acres) of second-growth forest to prepare for a vineyard, inspired by the success of grapes at nearby Vigneti Zanatta.

Edward Brennink, lean and almost as tall as his towering father, has followed an eclectic career path in Canada. After studying hotel management for a year, he worked at hotels in the British Columbia Interior and in the resorts of Banff and Jasper. But with a taste for farming, he and his wife operated a successful Keremeos orchard and fruit stand for several years. After selling that, the versatile young Brennink became a driving instructor in North Vancouver.

"Then in 1996 my father said, 'Won't you come back here?'" Edward says. "He described all his plans. We said okay, let's do that." The plans, of course, were for the vineyard and the winery.

The Brenninks moved cautiously, getting advice on suitable grape varieties first from other Cowichan Valley wineries and then retaining consultant Eric von Krosigk in 2001. At his suggestion, a test vineyard was started on the slope immediately below Albert Brennink's comfortable home. There is an architect's touch even in the vineyard: the 20 rows of vines are in a fan shape, narrow at the top, wide at the bottom, so there is a view down every row from the top. Twenty varieties — 10 red, 10 white — grow here, including long shots such as Cabernet Sauvignon and Syrah, as well as Ortega and Siegerrebe, proven ripeners on Vancouver Island. "You know what my idea is about these 20 rows with 20 plants in each row?" Albert Brennink chuckles. "If we make a blend of them all together, we'll have a nice rosé."

The vineyard itself is being planted over four or five years, beginning in 2003, with white varieties on the flat valley bottom and reds on the warm south-facing slope. The soil, the toe of a glacial moraine, is lean and rocky, with little topsoil. It is suitable for grapevines but, Edward suggests, not much else. "The only other thing we could do here is grow broom grass or Christmas trees." The summers are so dry and the soil drains so quickly that two wells and a creek are harnessed for irrigation.

The vines planted initially mirror the 1,700 cases of wine that von Krosigk made for Echo Valley in 2001 in the Okanagan from purchased grapes. There was Kerner, which the elder Brennink describes as "one of our favourites." The other début whites were an apple-fresh Pinot Gris and a minimally oaked Chardonnay. The winery also opened with two red wines made from Gamay Noir grapes — a fresh, early-bottled version called Nouveau Gamay and a moderately barrel-aged Gamay Noir. The Brenninks prefer a light touch with oak, where it is appropriate. "That is what we found out when we were in Beaujolais, that they do not use new barrels," Edward says. "Eventually, you have to replace your barrels when they get too old but you would only put your wine in them for a very short period of time. A month at the most, so it wouldn't take up too much of that tannic harshness."

Echo Valley skipped the 2002 vintage out of fiscal prudence but had wine made in 2003. "The first thing we have to do is sell what we have here, or at least a good portion of it," Edward says. "We would certainly like to stick with the current line-up of wines. The one we would like to add would be Chasselas if we can get a supply of grapes. In the reds, we might add Pinot Noir."

ELEPHANT ISLAND ORCHARD WINES

OPENED: 2001

2730 Aikens Loop, Naramata, BC, V0H 1N0

Telephone: 250-496-5522

Web site: www.elephantislandwine.com

Wine shop: Open daily 10:30 am – 5.30 pm from May 1 to October 15.

Patio picnic area.

RECOMMENDED

* ✳ FUJI ICE
* ✳ STELLAPORT
* ✳ CASSIS
* ✳ CRAB APPLE
* ✳ APRICOT DESSERT
* ✳ PEAR
* ✳ CHERRY
* ✳ BLACK CURRANT
* APPLE

EVEN AMONG THE HIGHLY INDIVIDUAL WINERIES OF THE NARAMATA bench, this winery takes visitors by surprise. Here, the wines are made exclusively with fruit other than grapes. But what remarkable wines they are! They are aromatic and fresh expressions of underlying fruit, which includes apples, cherries, apricots, pears and black currants. The wines are almost always dry and food-friendly.

"A lot of people have a misconception that you cannot produce good dry fruit wines," says Del Halliday who, with his spouse, Miranda, opened the wine shop for public sales in 2001. "And a lot of people when they come into the shop expect all the wines to be sweet. In fact, some of our dry wines have been our most popular. People who enjoy dry grape wines are easily won over to our dry wines once they have a chance to try them."

Both the wines and the winery's unusual name express the dreams of Miranda Halliday's grandparents, Catharine and Paul Wisnicki. The property on which the wine shop and orchard are located was purchased as an investment three decades ago by Catharine Wisnicki, now a retired architect. Her husband scoffed that it was a white elephant and said the house she designed for it was fashioned just for the eye. *Elephant eye-land* was born, to become Elephant Island.

Prior to his death in 1992, Paul Wisnicki, a home fruit winemaker, had begun a business plan for a cottage distillery in the Okanagan. Completing the plan led the Hallidays to conclude that a distillery would not be viable — but that a fruit winery might be. They registered Elephant Island in 1999 and set out to prepare themselves for a business in which neither had any background. They acquired cellar experience working at the nearby Red Rooster winery while Del Halliday took winemaking courses at Okanagan University College from Christine Leroux, a Bordeaux-trained winemaker who subsequently agreed to make the Elephant Island wines.

Miranda Halliday, born in Powell River in 1973, is a geologist. Del, born in Victoria in 1972, went to Loyola College in Maryland on a lacrosse scholarship. He earned a marketing degree and a spot on a professional American lacrosse team. While lacrosse salaries are among the most modest in professional sport, Del describes his athletic sideline as a "good part-time job" during the winter months when there is limited activity at the winery.

Their first task was refining grandfather Paul's winemaking recipes. "He did it for several years in a real sort of home winemaking style," says Del, who began trials with a number of fruits before hiring Leroux as the winemaker. An Ontarian who grew up in Quebec, she studied enology at the University of Bordeaux and worked subsequently in Bordeaux, Australia, California and at Inniskillin Okanagan for two years. Since 1998, she has been one of the Okanagan's busiest consulting winemakers. "She's introduced quality winemaking practices," Del Halliday says. "What we're doing now compared to what we were doing in our research and development is completely different." Miranda Halliday says that Leroux "is by far the best investment we've ever made. She gives credibility to our product."

Del's research, however, had narrowed down the winemaking choices. First, he had to ascertain the best varieties. "For instance, for our apple wine, I tested over 30 varieties of apple and made wine and blends until we settled on our apple blend, with three varieties," he says. This wine is based on Granny Smith and Golden Delicious apples and an unidentified crabapple, all of which combine in a light, crisp wine that, Halliday has found, goes well with shellfish.

The other fruits assessed at Elephant Island were pears, cherries, black currants, crabapples and apricots. Encouraged by their initial success, the Hallidays subsequently added wines made from raspberries, blackberries and quince. A century ago, there were quince orchards in the Okanagan Valley until the bulbous, pear-shaped fruit was replaced by more popular tree fruits. Del Halliday's test lots of quince wine in 2002 were made with fruit scrounged from old trees now growing wild. The wine, a dry, aromatic white, was so successful that Elephant Island has planted just over half a hectare (1.5 acres) of quince trees.

The Hallidays have worked out food matches with their wines. Del recommends the dry wine made from the Stella cherry with "heavier meats and cheeses. Game meat. We eat a lot of venison and the cherry wine is the natural pairing." Because the wine is fermented on the pits, it has a flavour suggesting an oak-aged wine. He recommends lamb with the black currant wine, a rich, tablecloth-staining red with dense, spicy flavours. Miranda Halliday is working on a cookbook with recipes tested to pair with the wines.

"We tried several varieties of apricot before we settled on the Goldrich," Del Halliday says. The variety, which matures to a high sugar content, has become obscure because its acidic skin makes it unappealing on the fresh market. However, that combination of sugar and acid is ideal for making a lively dessert wine. It has become one of the top-selling wines at Elephant Island. While sweet wines are in the minority in the tasting room, they are made with a creativity that sets them apart. The winery has made an icewine-style apple wine, using Fuji apples that were picked when frozen. Halliday believes Fuji is best able to hang well beyond the usual harvest without significant oxidation. The winery's 2002 Fuji Ice was made from apples picked on March 1, 2003, the same date when it was cold enough for other producers to pick grapes for icewine.

The winery's wood-aged Stella cherry port and its Cassis (made from black currants) employ classic port wine techniques, where fermentation is arrested by adding grain spirit. Importantly, no water is added to the fruit juices at fermentation, with the exception of black currant (whose citric acidity can only be defanged with water). "I know that it's a pretty common practice with fruit wine production to use water," Halliday says. "What better way to dilute flavours and dilute wine? We're doing everything we can to use the pure fruit and that's it."

Elephant Island "legitimizes" its products — as Miranda puts it — by following the same authentic standards that govern grape wines, including icewine rules. "Certainly, our goal has always been to put ourselves in the same category as the high-quality grape wines," she says. "The methods that VQA prescribes are intended for the production of a quality product. So it only follows that we would look to those kind of parameters to make wine from a different fruit."

FAIRVIEW CELLARS ESTATE WINERY

OPENED: 2000

13147 334th Avenue (Old Golf Course Road), Oliver, BC, V0H 1T0
Telephone: 250-498-2211
E-mail: beggert@img.net
Wine shop: Open 1 pm – 6 pm Monday through Saturday.

RECOMMENDED

* MERITAGE
* MERLOT-CABERNET
* CABERNET-MERLOT

BILL EGGERT IS USED TO CUSTOMERS SUMMONING HIM BY TAPPING THE car horn a few times in his driveway. The tasting room is not always manned at this busy, one-man winery. During the long Okanagan summer, the place to look for Eggert, the owner, is in the well-tended 2.4-hectare (six-acre) vineyard. When he began planting this vineyard in 1993, he only intended to be a grape grower. Later, he figured that he could make a better living selling wine than he could selling grapes. Fairview quickly became known for its big, sturdy reds. "I do not consider myself a professional winemaker," he says. "It's all done in the vineyard."

He is a far better winemaker than he lets on, although he gives credit to his winemaking mentors in the Okanagan, Tinhorn Creek's Sandra Oldfield and Inniskillin Okanagan's Sandor Mayer. Fairview's wines are invariably sound. He did have a scare a few years ago when an outside laboratory that was analyzing his wines told him one tank had excessive volatile acidity (a precursor to vinegar). Shaken, Eggert sought a second opinion from a different laboratory. He was vastly relieved to find the first laboratory was wrong and that he would not have to dump a tank of wine after all. Since Fairview's full production, achieved in 2003, is 1,500 cases of wine a year, he could hardly afford to dump any.

Eggert makes only reds because that is what he likes and that is what grows best in his vineyard. "I have some of the best land for supporting reds and I honestly didn't want to waste any of my land on whites," he says. "It boils down to the site. We're in the hottest area in Canada where they grow grapes. When you compare the heat units to Bordeaux, we're 50 to 100 more heat units higher." His vineyard is planted almost exclusively with Bordeaux varieties and his most popular blend, called Cabernet Merlot, mirrors what is in the vineyard: 50 per cent Cabernet Sauvignon, 30 per cent Merlot and 20 per cent Cabernet Franc. He got rid of Gamay, a planting error, because the wine was wimpy, definitely not the Fairview style.

The wines, bold and honest, seem to express Eggert's gregarious personality. A big man with unruly black hair, Eggert was born in Ottawa in 1957 and raised in northern Ontario, where his father was a mining engineer. An uncle had a vineyard near Beamsville, south of Hamilton. A few summers there fired Eggert's love of grapes as well as his taste for the wine that was always on his uncle's table. (Eggert came from an open-minded family: his father told him that if he was allowed to taste Communion wine in church, he could also have it at home.) Eggert got an agriculture degree at Guelph and worked in the vineyard until he failed to convince his uncle to replace the hybrids with vinifera grapes. He moved out to the Okanagan in 1983.

He spent a year at Covert Farms, a large commercial operation at Oliver that once had 73 hectares (180 acres) of grapes. He went back to Ontario in 1984, spending a year and a half with a winery before returning to the Okanagan. He worked in vineyards when he could and at construction jobs when he could not, until purchasing his own property.

The Fairview vineyard occupies a wedge of plateau overlooking the first tee at the Fairview Golf Club. The site, which marks the northern start of what Okanagan winemakers call the Golden Mile, was well chosen. "We have a good quantity of gravel in the soil for drainage," Eggert has found. "We have the sand but we also have a good percentage of clay for retaining nutrients. And we have silt also." He maintains that wines made on the Golden Mile often are more complex than those grown on the sandy eastern side of the valley. "It's not just the soils. It is the morning sun. We get that sun exposure early in the morning on the grapes and there is more time for the vine to develop flavours."

Fairview opened in the spring of 2000. The public face is a small, rustic tasting room and a weather-beaten picnic bench under the trees in front of the winery. But the cellar is equipped with stainless steel tanks — Eggert refuses to use plastic tanks — and the best barrels he can afford. "I was quite reasonable in my expectations, in terms of sales," he says. "I did not come at it with full production and spend a whole bunch of money on winery equipment. I did it the other way. Started out small with 300 cases." He doubled that in his second vintage and kept increasing production as he developed a following. "I didn't rely on a huge marketing campaign. I think my price is probably 30 to 40 per cent lower than people who do a huge marketing campaign. But I'm building up a good solid core of customers now that appreciate it."

Eggert's longer-term plans include a larger tasting room, a conference centre at the winery, new processing equipment and more expensive barrels — but all within his budget. "I'd rather be small with no debt, than big with debt," he says. "Some people have to have that complete set-up from the beginning. I've never got a phone call from my bank, *never.* I phone them but they never phone me. That's the way I want to keep it."

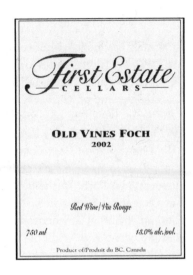

FIRST ESTATE CELLARS

OPENED: 1979

5031 Cousins Road, Peachland, BC, V0H 1X2

THIS IS A WINERY WITH THE LIVES OF A CAT. THE ORIGINAL ESTATE WINERY in the Okanagan, it has opened, closed and reopened under a succession of owners and a variety of names. Frank Silvestri, the most recent owner setting out to revive the winery, is a Calgary trucking company owner with roots in Italy.

The winery was launched in 1979 as Chateau Jonn de Trepanier by a colourful character named Marion Jonn. Born in Bulgaria, he claimed a family tree going back to Roman legionnaires. In 1972, he bought 14 hectares (35 acres) on the side of the mountain above Peachland and planted grapes. At first, he sold grapes primarily to home winemakers, for he was a keen amateur winemaker himself. However, it was not long before he was scaling up production for a winery. A risk-taker, he took most of his 1977 vintage over to what is now the Mission Hill winery, producing about 55,000 litres (12,000 gallons) of wines from Okanagan Riesling, Rougeon and Maréchal Foch. When British Columbia's estate winery regulations were announced in April, 1978, he built his own winery and, the next summer, became the first of the vineyard-based wineries to open, with an adequate wine inventory.

The winery was open only a few months when, just prior to the 1979 vintage, Jonn sold it to Bob Claremont, who used to be the winemaker at Calona Wines. Although it was suggested that Jonn was frightened off by the business risk he had taken on, he was, in fact, going through a divorce and had to sell in order to divide the assets.

Claremont had been a pivotal figure at Calona. A graduate in microbiology from the University of Guelph, he started making wine at the Jordan winery near

St. Catherines and then moved on to the large St. Julian winery in Michigan in 1967. When Calona Wines was taken over by Standard Brands of Montreal in 1971, the new owners hired Claremont to overhaul Calona's rustic wine portfolio. Claremont came up with several wines modelled after European wines. Schloss Laderheim, which he patterned after popular German whites, was launched in 1977 and for a few years was the largest-selling table wine in Canada.

Chateau Jonn de Trepanier was renamed Claremont Estate Winery and changes were made in the vineyard to reduce the acreage of red varieties, notably Rougeon and Foch. At the time, there was a significant surplus of red wines in the Okanagan. Fortunately, Jonn's block of whites, in addition to Okanagan Riesling, included Gewürztraminer and Muscat. Claremont added Johannisberg Riesling, along with small plantings of other premium vinifera grapes, including the Okanagan's first Sauvignon Blanc. Unfortunately, the vineyard lies at a high elevation and in a draw with breezy air drainage down from Trepanier Creek. The tender Sauvignon Blanc did not succeed.

Claremont had other problems as well. He had not been well enough financed when he bought the winery and, in 1986, it went into receivership. Claremont returned to Ontario, picking up his winemaking career there until 1994, when a heart attack claimed his life at 51.

The winery resurfaced as Chateau Ste. Claire, named after an order of nuns by Goldie Smitlener, the new owner. A native of Croatia, she purchased the winery in order to move her young family away from the Vancouver area where she had run a restaurant. She was an unusual winery owner in that she did not drink; wine just did not agree with her. But she certainly was familiar with the culture, having grown up among vineyards near Zagreb. "The lifestyle, it never gets out of your blood." Shrewd in business, she did well in flipping vineyard property in the south Okanagan in the early 1990s.

However, the winery itself drifted indecisively for a few years, to the point where even the vineyard was so neglected that the next owner of the winery, in 1998, said three to five years would be required for it to recover. Gary Strachan and partner Nancy Johnson took over, renaming the property First Estate Cellars because it had been the Okanagan's original estate winery. Strachan, a native of Toronto, has been a research scientist for many years at the Summerland Research Station. A specialist in yeast genetics, he made many experimental wines at the station in the 1980s in trials to assess grape varieties.

Because of the state of the vineyard, First Estate was relaunched initially with 1996 vintage wines purchased from other wineries, including a Maréchal Foch, a Gewürztraminer and an Auxerrois. Strachan intended to plant mainly Pinot Noir and Chardonnay, while converting a block of Okanagan Riesling — one of the Okanagan's last plots of this mediocre wine grape — to Johannisberg Riesling. Unfortunately, the winery ran short of money, went into receivership and reverted to Goldie Smitlener in 2000.

The Silvestri family bought the property a year later and have been busy ever since at rejuvenating the 7-hectare (17-acre) vineyard (now growing Foch,

Gamay, Pinot Noir, Pinot Gris and Gewürztraminer). While 9,000 vines were replaced, the mature Foch survived neglect in the vineyard, enabling the winery to début with an oak-aged Old Vines Foch. Alferino Silvestri, who looks after the vineyard, brought his family to Canada in 1952 from Bologna. One of his Canadian careers involved training race horses. His son, Frank, was to name his trucking company Remwan after one of those horses.

Frank Silvestri, who was born in Bologna in 1948, had harboured the ambition to own a winery for some time. In fact, he had come close to buying it a decade earlier but could not come to terms with the hard-bargaining Goldie Smitlener. Now, he is taking charge of making wines in a traditional no-preservatives style that he was born into. "Back in Italy, everybody makes wine," he says. He expected to have the wine shop reopened during summer or early fall of 2004.

FOCUS OKANAGAN VALLEY

OPENED: 2003

1670 Dehart Road, Kelowna, BC, V1W 4N6
Telephone: 250-764-0078
Wine shop: Open noon – 5 pm Tuesday through Saturday and long-weekend Sundays.

RECOMMENDED

✹ FOCUS RIESLING

AT LAST, HERE IS A WINERY FOUNDED ON THE KISS PRINCIPLE: KEEP IT simple, stupid! Roger Wong makes wine exclusively from the Riesling grape.

This might seem a risky concept. While Riesling undeniably is a great variety, it was eclipsed by Chardonnay during the last quarter of the twentieth century. But recently, it has become fashionable among consumers to affect boredom with Chardonnay. The long-heralded Riesling Renaissance is actually beginning. Wong appears to have caught a wave.

"I feel that Riesling is the best grape for this region," Wong says. And that is the idea of Focus. It is Wong's dream one day to launch Focus in other wine regions, always dedicated to what he would consider the greatest grape of that region. "If you look at the Old World, you don't go to Burgundy looking for a nice Gewürztraminer," he says. "But all the New World areas profess they can do everything. One winery can do it all." He does not agree with that. "One particular grape is going to do better for a winery, or a site, or a region. You might as well stick with that and become an expert at it."

Born in 1965 in Vancouver, Wong spent 10 years running computer networks for a federal government department after getting a geography degree from the University of British Columbia. But his passion was wine. He began making wine as an amateur before he had reached the legal age for drinking it. By 1995, tired of being a civil servant, he quit and went to the Okanagan. That fall, he talked Sandra Oldfield at Tinhorn Creek into letting him help with the crush. "I just showed up," he remembers. "I met Sandy and we walked through the empty shell of a winery. We agreed that I would just live with them in their basement, and I would help through crush."

In the spring of 1996, when Tinhorn Creek planted its vineyard on Black Sage Road, Wong joined the crew digging irrigation ditches. He admits that the hard labour was tempting him to rethink his career switch until he was promoted to cellar work in the winery. Oldfield, who has mentored other rising young winemakers in the Okanagan, encouraged Wong to learn winemaking. He was sent for short courses to the University of California at Davis, Oldfield's alumnus. He enrolled in Davis correspondence courses in viticulture, supplementing that by working with Hans Fischer, then Tinhorn Creek's veteran vineyard manager.

Tinhorn Creek also arranged for Wong to qualify as a member of the tasting panel for the Vintners Quality Alliance (VQA). "That was a really good education," Wong says. Here, he learned the discipline to distinguish quality wine and became thoroughly familiar with Okanagan wine styles.

In 1998, Wong became the winemaker at Pinot Reach, the small winery that Susan Dulik had opened the year before in an East Kelowna vineyard owned by her family for two generations. Wong now turned for mentoring to Susan's father, Den, a respected grape grower. "His 50 years of experience," Wong says, "is something you can't learn in the classroom." Because the winery was small, Wong was able to spend much time in the vineyard. "The wines are made out there," he says. "If perfect grapes arrive, winemaking is just an accessory. You can control so much by being in the vineyard. A winemaker needs to have dirty shoes."

The Riesling in that vineyard had been planted in the 1970s. Recognizing the quality delivered by mature vines, Wong made what came to be known as Old Vines Riesling. Wong is somewhat self-conscious that most of his training has been hands-on rather than academic. But he knew he had arrived as a winemaker when Pinot Reach's 2000 Old Vines Riesling scored gold at the Riesling du Monde competition. The wine scored an even bigger triumph by meriting a mention for Pinot Reach — one of only two British Columbia wineries to get mentioned — in a new edition of Hugh Johnson's *World Atlas of Wine*.

The Focus Riesling, launched with the 2002 vintage, was produced at Pinot Reach and marketed initially under the Pinot Reach license. He made only 3,200 bottles of a dry, full-flavoured table wine that won a silver medal at the Okanagan Wine Festival that fall. The 2003 Focus vintage was nearly derailed by the forest fire that raged through nearby Okanagan Mountain Provincial Park that summer. The smoke hung thickly over the Pinot Reach vineyard for weeks, so impregnating the grapes with the taste of smoke that none could be used for wine. Wong was able to buy grapes from two good Riesling vineyards at Naramata and Okanagan Falls. He had a similar volume of the dry Focus Riesling, along with about 600 bottles of sparkling Riesling and about 2,400 half-bottles of late-harvest wine. "The idea with Focus is only Riesling, ever." The Dulik family sold both Pinot Reach and the vineyard in 2004. The new owners retained Wong as the winemaker, likely providing him access again to grapes from those old Riesling vines.

Focus also stands apart with its packaging. Like Venturi-Schulze on Vancouver Island, Wong put his wine in heavy Champagne bottles closed with a crown cap, not a cork. When Venturi-Schulze did it in the 1990s, the winery was forced to quit VQA because VQA allowed only cork closures. That restriction was removed in 2003 and Focus became the first wine without a cork to pass through the VQA panel.

Both wineries use caps to avoid releasing so-called "corked" wines. It is a term referring to the musty, root-cellar taint that occasional bad corks impart to otherwise sound wines. "I have been having problems with corks for many years," says Wong, echoing an industry-wide complaint. "I am quite anti-cork, personally."

THE FORT WINE COMPANY

OPENED: 2001

26151 84th Avenue, Fort Langley, BC, V1M 3M6
Telephone: 604-857-1101
Web site: www.thefortwineco.com
Wine shop: Open daily 10 am – 6 pm.

RECOMMENDED

✳ RASPBERRY PORTAGE LIQUEUR
✳ WILD WEST BLACKBERRY PORT
✸ CRANBERRY
✸ RASPBERRY
✸ BLUEBERRY

IN 1999, THE YEAR AFTER WADE BAUCK INVESTED IN A SEVEN-HECTARE (17-acre) cranberry farm just east of Fort Langley, the price of cranberries dropped about 400 per cent. Rather than wait out the market oversupply of berries, Bauck found a partner to create The Fort Wine Company and turn the cheap berries into profitable fruit wines. Within two years of opening, The Fort was British Columbia's largest fruit winery, making about 13,000 cases annually. To support further expansion, Bauck, a veteran towboat captain, replaced his original partner in 2003 with a pulp and paper executive named David Gandossi. The pair are among the most aggressive owners in the burgeoning fruit wine sector in British Columbia.

"The goal here is to be large," says Dominic Rivard, the initial winemaker at The Fort. "We don't have the mentality of a mom and pop operation. We are thinking as a business. Our goal is to sell wine all over the world, if possible." At least half a dozen fruit wineries have been started since The Fort opened.

Rather than viewing these as competitors, Rivard welcomes their help in validating fruit wines with consumers. "We all want to see these fruit wines become mainstream products."

Born in Quebec in 1971, Rivard began making wines at home while still a teenager. By the time he was 19, he was a sommelier in Ottawa. After coming to British Columbia in 1994, he worked in the laboratory of a winemaking supplies company, took the diploma course of the London-based Wine and Spirit Education Trust, and enrolled in science courses at the British Columbia Institute of Technology. By 1996, he was involved in establishing a joint-venture winery in China and in 2004, now with four winery clients in China, Rivard turned over The Fort's winemaking to his protégé, Derrick Power. Born in Hamilton in 1970 and trained as a carpenter, Power was in the crew that built the winery. Becoming fascinated with wine, he moved into the cellar with Rivard to discover "the best job I have ever had in my life."

British Columbia's first modern-era fruit winery, the Columbia Valley Winery, opened in 1997 on a farm at the south end of Cultus Lake, with Rivard as the winemaker. Three years later, he moved to the bigger opportunity offered at The Fort. Unlike the Cultus Lake winery, which is in a somewhat remote location, The Fort is just down the road from one of the Fraser Valley's busiest tourist attractions, the restored Hudson's Bay trading post at Fort Langley. In appearance, the winery echoes the fort, and has a tasting room with, as winery literature puts it, "the ambiance of an 1800s saloon."

Rivard has packed a lot of experience into his short winemaking career. A winemaker in a grape winery only does one vintage a year (unless he travels to the southern hemisphere). The winemaker in a fruit winery ferments new batches year-round. Unlike grapes, fruits generally are frozen and thawed as required. This is done not just for convenience: it promotes a more efficient release of juice, colour and flavour from virtually all fruits and berries. By the time Rivard joined The Fort, he had fermented dozens of lots of wine, learning along the way. "Over the years, I have been trying to improve myself," he says. "I learned new tricks and I learned from mistakes."

A case in point is The Fort's flagship cranberry wine (about one-third of its sales) which is richer in both hue and flavour and tastes less tart now than initial vintages. "Cranberry wine is actually a very difficult wine to make," Rivard has found. The ascorbic acid in the berries inhibits fermenting the wine to dryness. The conventional way of moderating the acid is diluting the juice. "I used to dilute it quite a bit with apple juice but now I don't have to," the winemaker says. "I found a way around that. It is something I don't want to tell to too many people." The result of the technique he keeps to himself is an intense wine with purity of fruit.

Cranberry is one of more than a dozen wines made here, including wines from blueberries, blackberries, raspberries, peaches, apricots and apples. The apple wines feature an iced apple dessert wine. Rivard has also been developing apple wines infused with various spices and experimented with kiwi fruit wine.

Rivard's style is his own. "In recent history, I was one of the first to make fruit wines in British Columbia," he notes. "I have never copied anybody else. I try to make full-flavoured wines. That's why most of my wines are not bone-dry. I want a fruit wine to be as fruity and full-flavoured as possible." However, The Fort's range includes a growing number of relatively dry wines aiming for a role as dinner wines, not just as social wines.

The Fort will always offer sweet wines because Rivard has a fondness for making what he calls liqueur or fortified fruit wines with 16 to 18 per cent alcohol. It is a style adopted by a number of wineries because the fortified wines are much richer in flavour. The wines in this range from The Fort include blueberry, raspberry, cranberry, and one of Rivard's favourites, a barrel-aged blackberry product called Wild West Blackberry port. It is made with cultivated berries but Rivard is experimenting with wild berries and is looking for a reliable supply of the fruit. It is, in his view, one of the few fruits, if not the only one, that is enhanced by oak aging. "Blackberry wine is good with game," Rivard says. "The port can be paired with cheesecake or chocolate or strong cheeses, like a very old Cheddar."

While The Fort will remain primarily a fruit winery, a .8-hectare (two-acre) vineyard, largely devoted to table grapes, is being planned near the winery. The vineyard is essentially decorative because the low-lying plot not far from the Fraser River is ill-suited for wine grapes. The vineyard will entitle The Fort to purchase wine grapes from the Okanagan. Rivard recommended barrel-aged Chardonnay, Merlot and Cabernet to the wine shop selection, "just to have a bit of dry grape wine for the people who demand it."

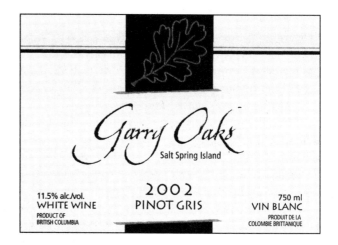

GARRY OAKS VINEYARD

OPENED: 2003

1880 Fulford-Ganges Road, Salt Spring Island, BC, V8K 2A5
Telephone: 250-653-4687
Web site: www.saltspringwine.com
Wine shop: Open noon – 5 pm Friday through Sunday; or by appointment.

RECOMMENDED

✹ PINOT GRIS
✵ LABYRINTH
✵ PINOT NOIR ESTATE – LIMITED EDITION
✴ PINOT NOIR
✴ FETISH
✴ BLANC DE NOIR
　 GEWÜRZTRAMINER

FARMING GRAPES ON SALT SPRING ISLAND IS A RETURN TO THEIR ROOTS for Elaine Kozak and Marcel Mercier, the brainy professional couple that began selling their wine here in 2003. In his youth in Edmonton, Mercier achieved local fame for growing giant pumpkins. At university, where he did postgraduate work in science, an aptitude test suggested he really should become a farmer. Kozak, a granddaughter of homesteaders from Ukraine, grew up on an Alberta farm. Her parents were proud when their daughter became a professional economist. When she and Mercier, in a dramatic career switch, bought a derelict orchard site on Salt Spring in 1999, her mother despaired: "What am I going to tell my friends?"

Mercier and Kozak make wine that should be an answer for anyone's friends. They are conscious that their vineyard is on an island with no track record for wine-growing. "Everything we do is geared to producing wine that can stand on its own as a very fine product," Kozak promises. "This is a new area that has yet to establish itself as a place that can grow good wine. We are very concerned that other people on the Gulf Islands also produce good wine and make a good start. If they don't, there will be a sense that this is too marginal an area. We don't think it is."

Mercier's professional expertise is land and environmental management. "I've led a lot of projects on these systems throughout Canada and throughout the world," he recounts. "I worked throughout Asia, Africa, Latin America, Central America and Europe." He was a founding vice-president of the Asia Pacific Foundation in Vancouver in 1985 and then returned to his career as an industry consultant.

Eventually, the demands of travel got to him. "You'd go into a hotel in Kuala Lumpur and all of a sudden you couldn't breathe," he remembers. "I have a bit of asthma. I realized it was time for a decision here." Kozak, successful as an executive in the public sector, also was ready for something different. In 1999, they decided to become wine growers. Having formerly owned land on Pender Island, they chose to remain on the west coast, but on the largest of the Gulf Islands. "A lot of interesting people from very different backgrounds have moved to this island," Mercier observes. "You do have a fairly vocal group. A lot of the people here are really skilled. When an issue comes up, things get done." Mercier and Kozak fit the Salt Spring character well.

"What made us do this?" Mercier says. "There are three things. We wanted to be in a healthy environment. We wanted to have a very strong intellectual challenge. And we wanted a very strong business challenge. We always had intellectual and business challenges in our careers but we didn't have a lot of opportunity for working outside. This brings it all together."

Their property, called Garry Oaks after the trees that have been preserved on the south-facing hillside, once was part of a 32.3-hectare (80-acre) orchard. Mercier and Kozak have retained a few of the heritage fruit trees. At the time they bought the land, it had been zoned for gravel. They speculate that their vineyard sits on about $1 million worth of gravel. They are quick to add that running a gravel pit is not an option should the winery not give them a living. "We'd be tarred and feathered," Kozak laughs.

Despite its size, Salt Spring Island has limited sites suitable for grapes. The northern half of the island, besides being short of water, is cooler than the southern half where Garry Oaks and two neighbouring vineyards are. Since 2000, when they began planting, Mercier and Kozak have developed three hectares (seven acres) with the varieties they believe will ripen early enough to succeed: Pinot Gris, Pinot Noir, Gewürztraminer, Léon Millot and Zweigelt. As well, there are a small number of vines of Gara Noir, an experimental cool climate red developed in Switzerland. With a little more room in the vineyard, consideration is being given to planting Schönburger, an aromatic German white grape.

"We are not trying to force varieties by going to extraordinary measures," Kozak says. Mercier did make one move to better the odds of ripening the grapes:

nearly all the vines are grafted onto a rootstock specially chosen for accelerating the vines while controlling the vigour. There is evidence it is working. The young Pinot Gris vines produced their first small crop in 2001, before nets had been deployed. Birds swooped onto the vineyard in mid-October, forcing Mercier to pick two weeks earlier than planned. "It turned out wonderful," he says of the trial lot of wine. The grapes were sufficiently ripe and the wine was nicely balanced.

Kozak and Mercier have changed careers methodically. "Once we got on this track, I figured out what I needed to know," Kozak says. "We'd always drunk a lot of wine and toured wineries but I knew I had to be able to talk to people who were knowledgeable about wine; and I knew I needed to understand the product and how to assess its quality." After their 1999 decision to plant vines, Kozak earned a higher certificate from Britain's Wine and Spirit Education Trust — the first step, if that were her objective, to becoming a Master of Wine. She also earned a diploma in enology from the University of Guelph, equipping her technically to make wines with Ross Mirko, the consultant to Garry Oaks. At the very least, she and Mercier, an amateur winemaker, can debate questions of style with Mirko. "Our reference points are more Europe than the New World," Kozak says — but then quickly makes an exception for New Zealand, which makes classic cool climate wines, and is where Mirko trained.

"We will, as many start-up wineries do, be buying fruit to supplement our own for the first few years," Kozak says. "The economic reality is that we couldn't wait for seven years" for the Garry Oaks vineyard to be fully productive. By that time, they hope that the winery will have become well established among Salt Spring's many attractions.

GEHRINGER BROTHERS ESTATE WINERY

OPENED: 1986

Number 8 Road at Highway 97, Oliver, BC, V0H 1T0

Telephone: 250-498-3537

Toll-free: 1-800-784-6304

Wine shop: Open daily 10 am – 5 pm June through mid-October; 10 am – 5 pm
   Monday through Friday the rest of the year; open during the May long weekend.

RECOMMENDED

- ✱ OPTIMUM PINOT GRIS
- ✱ RIESLING DRY
- ✱ RIESLING PRIVATE RESERVE
- ✱ PINOT GRIS PRIVATE RESERVE
- ✱ RIESLING
- ✳ AUXERROIS
- ✳ EHRENFELSER
- ✳ DRY ROCK SAUVIGNON BLANC
- ✳ PINOT NOIR PRIVATE RESERVE
- ✳ SCHÖNBURGER-GEWÜRZTRAMINER

WALTER AND GORDON GEHRINGER BELIEVE THAT THE WINTERS ARE
gradually becoming warmer in the Okanagan Valley. It is a conviction arising
from their quarter-century experience in growing grapes there. In the early
1980s, they routinely covered young vines with sawdust as protection against the
winter cold — and even that was not enough to protect their first planting of
Pinot Gris. "Nobody has to bury a vineyard in its first year anymore," Walter says
now. "The winters are warmer." While they started only with hardy German
grape varieties, the brothers now grow Bordeaux and Burgundy grapes as well.

As a result, their tasting room offers something for every taste, with the exception of sparkling wine.

When the winery first opened, the brothers followed an unabashedly German winemaking style, complete with baroquely scripted labels. This reflected the family's roots as well as the grapes they planted. Their father, Helmut, came to the Okanagan from Germany in 1952, becoming a car dealer. His brother, Karl, soon followed him and ran the resort at Cathedral Lakes. The senior Gehringers provided critical support when Walter and Gordon were becoming winemakers.

Walter Gehringer, who was born in Oliver in 1955, went to Germany in 1973 where he apprenticed with the renowned Guntrum winery. He enrolled at Geisenheim, Germany's leading wine university, and in 1978 became its first Canadian graduate. Gordon, who is four years younger, followed Walter to Germany, enrolling at the wine school at Weinsberg. The latter is a strongly practical school while Geisenheim is more research-directed. "Looking at things from two different angles might help us," Walter had suggested to his brother. "If you take the same educational path, all you are going to do is agree with me."

Back in Canada, Helmut and Karl undertook a seven-year study of the climate in the south Okanagan before purchasing the south half of what is now the 26-hectare (65-acre) Gehringer property in 1981. The north half, now called Dry Rock Vineyard, was acquired in 1995. The property is on a plateau on the west side of the Okanagan Valley. Hybrid grapes were already growing there. With one exception, these were replaced with premium German whites. The exception was Verdelet, a low-risk bread-and-butter variety with which Walter Gehringer had developed a sure winemaking touch. But it, too, was pulled out as soon as the winery succeeded with its Riesling, Auxerrois, Ehrenfelser — and Schönburger, a sentimental favourite with Walter.

Schönburger produces a spicy white wine not unlike Gewürztraminer. The grape was bred in Geisenheim under the direction of Dr. Helmut Becker, a teacher much admired by Walter Gehringer. It was one of the varieties that Dr. Becker recommended when he was consulting in the Okanagan in the late 1970s. Gehringer Brothers is one of a handful of wineries that grow the grape, making only a few hundred cases a year. Most wineries finish it in the delicate off-dry "German" style. When Gehringer Brothers opened in 1986, most of its wines were in this style. The brothers knew their market: the tasting room was usually sold out by Christmas.

As tastes changed in the 1990s, the winery responded with drier versions of its whites. However, the big change occurred after the brothers bought the adjoining northern half of their plateau. They called it Dry Rock for the obvious reason: this vineyard, like the rest of the plateau, is dry and strewn with rocks. Because they perceived that the climate had warmed, they planted entirely different grape varieties on the north side, including Chardonnay, which they had spurned initially because it is not a German wine grape. That variety, along with Sauvignon Blanc, Merlot, Cabernet Franc and Cabernet Sauvignon — all mainstays of French winemaking — went into Dry Rock. It was "a definite change in direction from where we initially were, allowing us to round out our winemaking style, rather than just making Germanic whites," Walter says. "We've evolved to make wines for certain wine styles, so that I can pretty well boast a wine for anybody's palate. From a fairly narrow portfolio, we have gone to a wider range."

That includes icewine, first made by the winery in 1991. That fall, a sharp freeze snapped across the Okanagan on November 1, six weeks to two months earlier than the typical icewine freeze. The Gehringers quickly picked the Riesling grapes still remaining on the vines. When the cold weather persisted, they bought some frozen Ehrenfelser the next day; and finally, on the third consecutive frigid day, they pressed some Chancellor for a red icewine. Since then, Gehringer has become a leading icewine producer, in part because the brothers are always prepared for the unexpected. In the vintage of 2002, the unexpected happened again when the temperature plunged at the end of October. This time, it only stayed cold enough for two hours early on the morning of October 31. Because their pickers were standing by, the Gehringers harvested part of their grapes on what was the earliest icewine picking date in the Okanagan's history. No other Okanagan winery picked for icewine that morning.

The Gehringer wines show impeccably clean and fresh fruit. That applies equally to the whites and to the reds because, for many years, the brothers disdained using oak. They have revised their approach as they have begun making more red varietals, notably Pinot Noir and a Cabernet–Merlot blend. But even having made this change, the brothers still aim for an unpretentious style. "I'm not looking for that real heavy red," Walter says. "I'm looking for that pleasant, nice glass of red — something you can drink sooner."

While he believes the winery can grow those varieties in Dry Rock successfully because of climate warming, Walter remains nervous about how permanent the change is. "We're far out on thin ice," he worries. "If you take the average winter temperatures from way back when, then easily half the acreage would be toast, or heavily damaged."

GERSIGHEL WINEBERG

OPENED: 1995

Highway 97, between Road 20 and Road 21, Oliver, BC, V0H 1T0
Telephone: 250-495-3319
Wine shop: Open daily 9 am – 9 pm.

RECOMMENDED

VIN DE CURÉ

THE HAND-DRAWN SIGN IS THE FIRST THING THAT CATCHES THE EYE from the highway midway between Oliver and Osoyoos. In untidy scrawl, it proclaims "The Wonderful Wines of British Columbia." Because the sign is on the Gersighel vineyard, winery owner Dirk De Gussem gets away with a small, but effective, billboard that certainly would not conform to the Ministry of Transportation's rules if erected on public land. Of course, De Gussem, who has been known to preside shirtless in the tasting room on blistering Okanagan days, has never had much time for bureaucracy. He once gave up on trying to develop a vineyard in South Africa because the rules constraining the wine industry there were, in his view, "Communist."

Born in 1946 near Flanders Fields in Belgium, he grew up on a potato farm. He was introduced to vineyards in 1966 when he went to Pomerol in France to pick grapes. After that, the family farm no longer satisfied him. He left it in 1970 and spent much of that decade following a vineyard dream. Three years were spent at Limoux in southwestern France and one year was spent in Spain. "I went all over Europe to find a place to grow grapes and make my own wine," he remembers. "But over there, it is too expensive, or it is too dangerous. We went to Yugoslavia, Hungary, Romania — what the heck!" He only needed six months in South Africa in 1981 to dismiss that country. Ultimately, he decided Canada offered the freedom he was looking for.

He is somewhat mysterious about the circumstances that brought him and his family to the Okanagan in 1986. He provided a clue in a note on the back cover of a privately published romance that he co-authored four years ago: "Flemish-born Dirk De Gussem … took flight to the Canadian West, freed from a family feud and hereby from being put behind bars in Belgium." Perhaps the drama might be disclosed over a bottle or two of wine.

De Gussem bought a 2.8-hectare (seven-acre) property on the west side of the highway, then an orchard with some grape vines. Wedged on a narrow bench sloping up from the road toward a steep mountainside, it is the last bit of vineyard that can be included in the so-called Golden Mile, that swath of vineyards extending south from Oliver on the west side of the Okanagan Valley. Of course, De Gussem prefers to describe this as the "Miracle Mile."

In 1989, just as two-thirds of the Okanagan's vineyards were being pulled out, De Gussem swam upstream, replacing his fruit trees with vines. He planted premium varieties, including Pinot Noir, Chardonnay, Gewürztraminer, Pinot Blanc and Riesling. He either planted or retained some interesting Muscat family grapes, including Perle of Csaba and Tokay. A few years ago, some vines were grafted over to Viognier.

Some of the vine choices were determined by De Gussem's interpretation of his site, where the towering mountain shields the vines from the hot late afternoon sun more than in any other Golden Mile vineyard. "This is Burgundy country here," he maintains. "I lived in France for three years. I knew the Burgundy country." That was why he planted primarily what he considered Burgundy varieties.

He makes a distinction between his side of the valley and the Black Sage Road side across the valley, where the soil is sandy and the temperature is hotter. "When it is too hot, you have problems with Pinot Noir," he suggests. But Pinot Noir has hardly been a picnic in his vineyard either. In 1994, the first year he expected to get a significant crop from his vines, the birds beat him to the harvest. De Gussem got protective nets the next year. "Pinot Noir is a difficult grape to grow," he discovered. "You have to net them; and you have to pick them twice." Then, tossing off a typically obscure aphorism, he adds: "You have to look after them like a chicken on a bed."

De Gussem's flair for writing — he has written poetry in both Flemish and English and would prefer to write poetry if he did not have to work — is expressed in the name of the winery. Gersighel is assembled from the first three letters of the given names of each of his children: Gerd, Sigrid and Helgi. The two sons, Gerd and Helgi, share winemaking duties, while their father looks after viticulture.

Gerd De Gussem describes his winemaking style as French and straightforward. There is no oak in the winery. "I am not a fan of oak," he says. "Clean, crisp and simple" is how he prefers the wines. Most of the white wines are finished dry except when very warm vintages permit the winery to produce late harvest versions of its Riesling.

Gersighel is one of the few Canadian wineries to use the old European method of making dessert wine by air-drying grapes to concentrate the sugars prior to fermentation. The wine is called Vin de Curé and it is made with Pinot Blanc, the white variety making up a third of the vineyard. The first was made in 1996. "We don't make it every year," Gerd says. A new vintage is made when passing wine tourists, drawn to the unadorned tasting room by the bucolic sign, have tasted and purchased most of the previous vintage.

In 2001, another sign went up on the Gersighel property, this time proclaiming that the entire winery is for sale. No one would be surprised if the dashing but mysterious Dirk De Gussem took his leave as he is pictured on the back of his romantic book — boldly astride a horse.

GLENTERRA VINEYARDS

OPENED: 2000

3897 Cobble Hill Road, Cobble Hill, BC, V0R 1L0

Telephone: 250-743-2330

E-mail: glenterravineyards@shaw.ca

Wine shop: Open daily 11 am – 6 pm March through October;
winter hours 12 pm – 5 pm "or by chance."

RECOMMENDED

✻ MERITAGE

✸ MERLOT

✸ CHARDONNAY

VIVACE

WHEN JOHN KELLY BECAME INTERESTED IN WINE IN THE 1970s, HE DRANK mostly low-priced Spanish reds because they were good value for the money. His wine horizon expanded considerably in the vineyards of Bordeaux during a 1988 European backpacking trip. "I was still buying inexpensive wines, of course, because I was on a budget," he recalls. "When I got back, I started paying more for wines to educate my palate. It was an expensive education. You've got to drink the good stuff to know what it's supposed to taste like." That preparation served him well. He and partner Ruth Luxton opened this tiny Vancouver Island winery with award-winning wines.

Born in 1955 in Glasgow, Kelly has lived in Canada since 1969, so long that he has lost most of the Scots inflection in his soft, lilting speech. He honours his heritage in the winery name. *Glen* is what Scots call a valley while *terra* acknowledges that his mother's homeland is the Mediterranean island of Malta. Kelly nurtured his growing interest in wine while running a successful, if mundane,

Vancouver business that made traffic signs. "Around 1995, I was fed up with what I was doing and I thought it was time to make a change," he remembers.

Luxton has come to wine through the food industry. "I'm a chef and I have a full-time job here on the island," she says. When they lived in Vancouver, she worked with several catering companies before starting her own. On Vancouver Island, she runs the kitchen at a country club during the summer and does much of the vineyard pruning in the winter. Winemaking is Kelly's passion.

Kelly's experience in Bordeaux provided lasting benchmarks. "One of my favourites of all time is Pichon-Lalande," he says, referring to a distinguished château in Pauillac. "The blend always seems right to me." However, California — and especially the Chardonnays there — influenced his tastes even more. Prior to moving to Vancouver Island in 1998, he and Luxton toured California wineries almost every year. Eventually, he inquired about taking winemaking courses at the University of California at Davis. Deterred by the cost there, he enrolled in the two-year program at Okanagan University College in Penticton, where he could study during the week and run his Vancouver business on weekends.

When Kelly and Luxton looked for vineyard property, they chose Vancouver Island over the Okanagan because they prefer living on the west coast. The Cowichan Valley, they concluded, was the only region outside the Okanagan with enough wineries to attract wine tourists. "We had to be where there are other wineries, so we could at least have half a chance of succeeding," Kelly says.

Their conveniently located seven-hectare (17-acre) property backs onto the Island Highway, with an entrance through the vines from Cobble Hill Road. It was called Ayl Moselle by the previous owner, John Harper, one of the island's pioneer grape growers. In the 10 years prior to selling in 1998, Harper conducted extensive grape-growing trials here. Harper, who died in 2001, worked the vineyard until he was 84 and in declining health. His workshed, about the size of a two-car garage, was turned into a compact winery by Kelly and Luxton. While the tasting room gets tight when half a dozen people arrive together, it does offer a close-up look at the winery's French and American oak barrels. "We do it all here," Luxton says, gesturing toward barrels an arm's length away.

At first, Kelly intended to pull out the Harper vines — there are about 40 varieties in a .4-hectare (one-acre) block. He soon realized it would be folly to get rid of mature vines before planting his own vineyard. Creatively, he makes two artful blends from the fruit. Vivace, a fruity white in the style of a Muscat wine, includes at least 10 white grape varieties. Brio, described as a hearty red blend, includes Dornfelder, Zweigelt, Agria, Lemberger, Dunkelfelder and Haroldrebe.

From 1999 to 2003, Kelly planted about two hectares (4.5 acres), with room to double the vineyard as the business grows. The varieties are Pinot Gris, Pinot Blanc, Pinot Noir, Gewürztraminer and Merlot. Husbanding his resources, Kelly began netting the vines against birds only when the vines were in their fourth year. However, he saved enough grapes from the "relentless" birds to make limited quantities of estate-grown varietals. His first Vancouver Island wine, a

2000 Pinot Noir, won a silver medal at the Northwest Wine Summit. "Against all those Oregon wines," Kelly says with quiet pride.

Like several other island wineries, Glenterra launched itself primarily with wines made from grapes purchased in the Okanagan. Kelly could not afford to wait until his own vineyard was producing. Glenterra endured some criticism for this from several Cowichan wineries that are exclusively estate producers. Kelly shrugged it off as "petty political crap" as he sought out the grapes needed to make good wine. His first Meritage, a blend of Bordeaux red grapes from the 1999 vintage, earned Glenterra a silver medal at a subsequent All-Canada Wine Competition. "I am into Bordeaux," he says over his 2001 Meritage. "I will probably always do one, occasionally."

He has also made barrel-fermented Chardonnay wines from Okanagan grapes, big and ripe in the California style. While there is a little bit of Chardonnay in the Harper test vineyard, the varietal that might take greater prominence in Glenterra's range is Pinot Blanc, a grape that Kelly finds as versatile as Chardonnay.

"We've pretty well got it figured out, as far as the varieties we want to work with," he says with cool confidence. "We'll probably put in a little more Gewürztraminer, a little more Pinot Blanc, a little more Pinot Noir. I don't know if I am going to put in more Pinot Gris because everyone has it."

2001
Pinot Noir
BRITISH COLUMBIA
~
Limited Vintage

RED WINE   VIN ROUGE
750 ML 12.5% ALC./VOL.

GLENUGIE WINERY

OPENED: 2002

3033 232nd Street, Langley, BC, V27 3A8
Telephone: 604-539-9463
Toll-free: 1-866-233-9463
Web site: www.glenugiewinery.com
Wine shop: Open 10 am – 6 pm Monday through Saturday; 11 am – 5 pm Sunday.

RECOMMENDED

✴ PINOT NOIR
✴ GAMAY
✴ CHARDONNAY
  PINOT BLANC

WHEN IT COMES TO HIS DRINKS, GARY TAYLER'S TASTES RUN TO SINGLE
malt scotch and Pinot Noir. The former may be genetic, since his roots go back to
the Campbells of Scotland. The preference for Pinot Noir was reinforced during
two stints as a grape grower — first in the Okanagan and latterly in the Fraser
Valley where he and his family opened the Glenugie winery in 2002.

The Scots heritage is stamped all over this winery, starting with the name,
pronounced *Glen-EWE-gie*. The grandparents of Gary's wife, Christina, who was
born in Scotland, had a farm called Glenugie in the Ugie River valley, north of
Aberdeen. "So we took the name over from Scotland for the farm here," Gary
says, referring to his property near Langley. "We initially became Glenugie
Vineyard. When we did the winery, it was Glenugie Winery." The heritage is
further honoured by the winery's labels, richly adorned with the Campbell of
Argyll tartan. The winery's spacious tasting room displays the crests of four clans
to which the family belongs.

While he has Scots blood, Gary Tayler was born in Edmonton in 1939 and was raised in the Okanagan and in Vancouver. In 1976 he returned to the Okanagan, establishing his first vineyard south of Penticton on the east side of Skaha Lake. Penticton-based Casabello winery (which no longer exists) agreed to buy his grapes. On the advice of Tom Hoenisch, Casabello's winemaker at the time, Tayler planted mostly Johannisberg Riesling. To make wine for his own consumption, Tayler also planted a small block of Pinot Noir, his red wine of choice.

He grew grapes until 1988 when grape prices collapsed (he was getting about $300 a ton for Riesling). When growers were offered government cash to stop growing, Tayler simply assigned his payment to the finance company holding his mortgage. He moved to the Fraser Valley and resumed a construction career, with considerably more success. "I built apartments and townhouses and commercial strip malls," he says. When he retired from construction, he decided to plant a few vines on his Langley farm in 1997.

"It started with the idea of a few Pinot Noir, to make my own red wine again," he says. "But the 125 grape vines suddenly exploded to 8,700 plants." He figured he would sell his surplus grapes from the two-hectare (five-acre) vineyard to other wineries. However, the other Fraser Valley wineries had all the Pinot Noir they needed and it was impractical to ship the fruit to the Okanagan.

"So I polled the family," he recalls. The decision was to start their own winery, with appropriate roles parcelled out among the family. Michele Tayler, the oldest daughter, with a degree in agriculture from the University of British Columbia, took on managing the vineyard with her father. The younger daughter, Lara Galloway, with a university marketing degree, agreed to become the winery's head of marketing. As a builder, Gary Tayler managed the construction of the winery, set prominently at the edge of busy 232nd Street. He counts on that visibility to draw consumers into the tasting room for direct sales of the Glenugie wines and to enjoy the adjacent picnic facilities.

The solidly built winery is what one would expect from a veteran builder. "You can't start off in a garage anymore," he says. Glenugie is constructed with the ultimate capacity to make 10,000 cases of wine. There is something of the look of a brick-clad Highland fortress to the building, perhaps because all the windows are narrow slits not much wider than a hand. It is a security feature, Tayler explains. A thief trying to break in would find it impossible to get even his head through any window.

Even though Tayler has considerable experience as a home vintner, he retained the consulting services of Elias Phiniotis. Born in Cyprus in 1943, Phiniotis is one of only two Okanagan winemakers with a doctorate (the other is Summerhill's Alan Marks). Phiniotis has worked with numerous British Columbia wineries since 1978 and for many years has been the consulting winemaker at Domaine de Chaberton, the first winery in the Langley area. Tayler credits the founders of Domaine de Chaberton, Claude and Inge Violet, for being helpful in a number of ways in getting Glenugie launched, in addition to sharing a winemaker.

Glenugie opened in 2002 with four wines made from two varietals, using both grapes from its own organic vineyard and from the Okanagan. Subsequently, Glenugie's range was increased to include Pinot Blanc and Gamay. The debut wines include two Chardonnays, one unoaked and one lightly oaked, both from Okanagan fruit. There were also two Pinot Noirs. A full-bodied version was made in 2001 from grapes grown in a vineyard near Osoyoos. Tayler liked the wine so much that, initially, he kept the grower's name a close secret.

The other Pinot Noir comes from the vineyard just beyond the winery, a flat lying plot of fertile clay under a massive hydroelectric line. Tayler wonders whether the high tension wires actually accelerate growth in the vineyard, although the vigour might have other causes as well. "Being organic, I put down chicken manure and the vines seem to love that," he says.

The vineyard produces fruit with a distinctive, bright, berry flavour, making a wine that is lighter than the Okanagan Pinot Noir but still shows the texture and character that make Pinot Noir so beguiling. Tayler recognizes that the Fraser Valley, with less sunshine than the Okanagan, is a more challenging place in which to grow red varieties like Pinot Noir. Thus, like many growers on Vancouver Island, he has begun tenting the wines in spring, aiming to accelerate them and to achieve slightly more sugar at harvest.

It is Tayler's plan that he and his wife will remain involved with Glenugie for five years before withdrawing in favour of the rest of the family. An unfortunate bottling line accident that injured one of the staff left Gary Tayler down on the wine business for some months, seriously considering selling the property. But his natural optimism reasserted itself after several Glenugie wines, including a Pinot Noir, won gold medals in competition. Then visits to the tasting room picked up. The average Sunday afternoon, Tayler discovered, could be counted on to generate more revenue than he once got from an acre of grapes.

GODFREY-BROWNELL VINEYARDS

OPENED: 2000

> 4911 Marshall Road, Duncan, BC, V9L 6T3
> Telephone: 250-748-4889
> Web site: www.gbvineyards.com
> Wine shop: Open daily 10 am – 5 pm.

RECOMMENDED

- ✹ FRANCESCA PINOT GRIGIO
- ✹ MERLOT
- CHARDONNAY
- BLACKBERRY CHAMPAGNE

AN AMAZING COINCIDENCE EXPLAINS THE DOUBLE BILL IN THIS WINERY'S name. In 1998, when David Godfrey bought this property near Duncan for his vineyard, he was surprised by what a title search revealed. The property had been settled in 1886 by a homesteader called Amos Aaron Brownell. "He was my grandmother's second cousin," Godfrey says. "So we felt we had to put the Brownell in the winery name." To the best of his knowledge, none of his Brownell relatives remain on Vancouver Island, although many live in eastern Canada, beyond the reach of the winery's products. "My mother had 254 first cousins," he says.

By establishing a vineyard, Godfrey is resuming a long farming tradition in his family. His grandparents homesteaded in Saskatchewan. During the Depression, the Godfreys lost the farm. The grandparents moved to the Saanich Peninsula on Vancouver Island, and the rest of the family headed east. David Godfrey was born in Winnipeg but grew up near Toronto, becoming a university English professor. "The family myth was to get the farm back so I actually went out to Saskatchewan and tried to buy it back," he recalls. "But that was when regulations said you had to be a Saskatchewan resident to buy a farm." So he bought a small farm north of Toronto.

In 1976, Godfrey came west again. He taught at the University of Victoria and became a technology writer. He co-authored a book in 1979 called *Gutenberg Two* that, among other topics, listed every store in Canada selling computers (he recalls the first list was a mere two pages long). The book went through at least four editions before he got bored with revising it. By then, Godfrey had started a company providing Internet service in Victoria.

In the early 1990s, the Godfreys decided to buy a farm again and plant a few grape vines. Godfrey had become a keen home winemaker while doing graduate studies in the United States. He thought it was time to have his own supply of grapes and eventually make wine commercially. "We were going to start small," he says. "We were going to sell our house and buy a house with five acres." Winemaker Eric von Krosigk, whom they enlisted as a consultant, argued that they would need four times as much vineyard if the operation was to be economic.

The Godfreys scoured Vancouver Island and Salt Spring Island for a vineyard site for five years until they found the old Brownell homestead. The first five hectares (12 acres) were planted in 1999; subsequent development will take the vineyard to nearly eight hectares (20 acres).

"The first year, that was the big debate," Godfrey remembers. He would have preferred varieties aimed at yielding what he calls a "big" red but prudently planted mostly the vines that were already doing well elsewhere in the Cowichan Valley, notably at nearby Vigneti Zanatta. "We really benefited from everyone else having experimented for almost 10 years. So we planted an acre of Bacchus and an acre of Maréchal Foch. Those are our insurance crops. And we planted three acres each of Pinot Gris and Pinot Noir and two acres each of Chardonnay and Gamay Noir. Except for the Chardonnay, somebody was already growing them and doing quite well." In subsequent plantings, Godfrey added Agria, Lemberger, Dunkelfelder and even a little bit of late-maturing Cabernet Sauvignon, a sentimental favourite of his.

Godfrey also tapped a good Vancouver Island source of blackberries in 2002, producing 1,900 litres (418 gallons) of wine. Some has been sold on its own and some has been turned into a light, refreshing sparkling wine.

Godfrey-Brownell opened with wines made from Okanagan grapes. That had not been Godfrey's initial intent. "That was part of my education," Godfrey says. "Eric took me around dozens of vineyards in the Okanagan to look at what to do and what not to do. Two things happened. One, we bought some Merlot in 2000. Basically, I was buying varieties that I had planted so I would be able to have some continuity. But we came across this Merlot and it was just wonderful; so I think I may very well always buy Merlot, and maybe Syrah, from the Okanagan. And then we also came across a couple of really good smaller vineyards with interesting varieties that they are having trouble selling. So there are a couple of vineyards that we will establish a long-term relationship with."

The object is to grow the winery until the annual production reaches about 5,000 cases. "That is a nice, manageable operation," he believes. "You can do the promotion, you can have the quality, you can have the staff, you can have the equipment. But you don't have so much wine that you have to worry about how to crack the New York market."

Something of a showman, Godfrey is trying to turn the winery into a destination for tourists. He intends to establish a farm store, selling herbs and other produce, possibly even olives when he gets around to planting an olive grove. "We try to give everybody that wants it the winemaker's tour," he says. "Take them in and let them taste what's in the barrel, not just what's in the bottle. It's fascinating because you are running 6,000 to 7,000 people a year through your winery, tasting wine at different stages. That's the best kind of market research you can possibly do."

GOLDEN MILE CELLARS

OPENED: 1998

13140 316A Avenue, Road 13, Oliver, BC, V0H 1T0
Telephone: 250-498-8330
Web site: www.goldenmilecellars.com
Wine shop: Open daily 10 am – 6 pm from May 1 to October 3;
    by appointment in winter.

RECOMMENDED

✳ MERLOT
   CHARDONNAY-SÉMILLON

SINGULAR IN DESIGN TO THE POINT OF BEING ECCENTRIC, GOLDEN MILE
Cellars looks like a small castle in Bavaria. Set well back against the side of a
mountain, the winery is not readily visible from the Highway 97 wine route.
Golden Mile kept such a low profile during its first five years that some in the
south Okanagan were unaware of it until they were invited to an open house in
December, 2003, by the new owners, Pam and Mick Luckhurst. Entrepreneurs
with no wine background but a rapidly developing passion, they intend to make
the splash that one would expect from lords of a castle.

Sitting in one of the castle's authentically draughty rooms, Mick Luckhurst
marvels at the incongruity of his career. He was born in 1950 in Port Alberni, a
fishing and forestry city on Vancouver Island. "That's a long road to come, from
Port Alberni to a winery," he suggests. Armed with a marketing diploma from
the British Columbia Institute of Technology, he has been a lumber broker, a real
estate developer and the operator of a building supply business in Nanaimo. Pam,
born in Manchester in 1954, was a Pacific Western Airlines flight attendant when
she met Mick. Now the partner in his business ventures and mother of their two

children, she does the books and, at the winery, looks after marketing and the tasting room.

They bought a winery after being swept off their feet by the industry. Having endured three cold winters in Edmonton, where they were building houses, they moved to a home on Osoyoos Lake in the spring of 2003. This was the second time Mick Luckhurst had fled the weather; previously, he and Pam moved from Vancouver Island to Edmonton to escape the rain. A gregarious couple, they entertained friends throughout the summer at the Osoyoos lakefront, often taking them wine touring, something the Luckhursts had never done before.

By summer's end, Mick found he had been, as he puts it, "sucked into the vortex of the romance of it all." He had intended to continue as a property developer but his heart was no longer in it. "There is no passion to that business, building a house," he says. "It is just a grunt and we were looking for a little more than that." A summer of visiting wineries convinced them that the wine business is dynamic and growing, to say nothing of the attraction of the scenic qualities. "The vineyards are like waterfront," Mick says. "They are serene. They are just art for the eye. But if this was potato farming, even if those potato fields were serene, I wouldn't do it, because there is no romance in it. This just looked like it was interesting as all get out."

It was a whirlwind romance. By September, the Luckhursts had decided to become wine growers. A quick canvass of properties led to Golden Mile and a handshake purchase agreement in October with Peter and Helga Serwo, builders of the castle. The Luckhursts took over in November and soon were announcing themselves to their neighbours. Impressed, Helga Serwo called them "young people with new ideas."

Like Mick Luckhurst, Yugoslavian-born Peter Serwo once was a builder, first in Germany and then in the Okanagan after he and his wife immigrated in 1966. After living on a hobby farm at Kaleden, the Serwos moved to a larger farm south of Oliver in 1970, growing peaches but switching to grapes in 1980. He was one of the earliest growers to plant premium vinifera grapes. The Serwos were approaching their 70s when he designed and built the castle to serve as a winery. A daughter went to Germany to study winemaking but when she decided to stay there, they sold Golden Mile.

Under the Serwo ownership, Golden Mile was selling most of its grapes, only making between 1,000 and 1,500 cases of modestly priced wine annually. Mick Luckhurst certainly is more ambitious. He purchased an adjoining vineyard so that the property has about 8.5 hectares (21 acres) of vines and he plans to acquire another two hectares (five acres) of raw land nearby. Ultimately, the vineyard will support about 6,000 cases of estate-grown wine.

Luckhurst moved fast but he had done his homework. "I knew that, with this location, it was an exceptionally good vineyard," he says. Most importantly, the vines are the right age to produce superb wines. Luckhurst used that leverage to lure winemaker Lawrence Herder away from a well-paying senior post in the Jackson-Triggs cellars. The commitment from the owners is that Golden Mile will allow him to make eye-popping premium wines. It will take a while to get there. Because no wine was made there at all in 2003, about 20,000 litres (4,400 gallons) were purchased from other Okanagan wineries and finished at Golden Mile, enough to sustain the tasting room until Herder's first wines are released in 2005.

"I came here largely because I think I can make super premium wines at this location," Herder says. He knew the vineyard already because Jackson-Triggs had been the major buyer of the grapes. The vineyard has Chardonnay and Chenin Blanc vines that range in age from 18 to 25 years, Riesling that is about 12 years old and Merlot that is five to seven years old. There are also Pinot Noir, Syrah, Viognier and a small assortment of other varietals. "Superb blending materials," Herder beams.

Born in 1967 in San Diego, Herder is a graduate of Fresno State University. For several years, he operated his own vineyard and winery at Paso Robles in California. He sold it to manage a printing company that his wife's family had in Burnaby. For him, it was a business that, like Luckhurst's house building, held no passion. In 2002 Herder started developing a vineyard near Cawston in the Similkameen Valley, for his own small winery there.

He did two vintages at the giant Jackson-Triggs winery north of Oliver, enjoying everything about the work but the scale. He is a hands-on winemaker who prefers to work in small batches and craft powerful wines. "I believe my potential for creating better wines is here," he says of Golden Mile. "My wines are not going to be wines that are ready in 10 months. I build wines more for the two- to five-year range. We'll be doing barrel aging for 12 to 18 months, including Chardonnays, and releasing wine when it is ready to release, and not just because it is time to sell more wine."

GRANITE CREEK ESTATE WINERY

PROPOSED OPENING: 2004

2302 Skimikin Road, Tappan, BC V0E 2X0
Telephone: 250-835-0049
Web site: www.granitecreek.ca

NO ONE WAS HAPPIER THAN RECLINE RIDGE WINERY OWNER MICHAEL SMITH when the Kennedy family planted vines in 2003 a short walk down Skimikin Road from his winery. As the lone winery here since 1999, Recline Ridge has struggled at times to get tourists off the TransCanada Highway for a wine tour. Two wineries almost side by side are a stronger attraction. They are also stimulating others. Several vineyards around Shuswap Lake, planted recently to sell to the established wineries, are expected to become wineries themselves before the end of the decade.

Granite Creek is a partnership of two of the three generations of the Kennedy family that have farmed in the Tappan Valley since 1959, when Robert Pemberton Kennedy moved there from the Fraser Valley. Gary Kennedy, Robert's son, was completing a doctorate in agricultural engineering at the University of British Columbia when a family crisis required him to come back to the farm. Doug Kennedy, Gary's son, was born in Vancouver in 1972 while his father was at university.

The vineyard and the winery are being promoted by Doug and his Polish-born wife, Mayka. Trained in computer science, Doug started his business career in northern British Columbia with Schlumberger Ltd., an international oilfield service company operating in 100 countries. Doug soon found himself promoted to management and working in central Africa. The Granite Creek winery has been developed as a way for him to return to the Kennedy farming roots in the Tappan Valley.

"My wife and I have been home winemakers for years," Doug says. He and Mayka, also a Schlumberger employee, have travelled Europe's wine regions extensively. They began planning a winery about the time that Recline Ridge became the second winery to open near Salmon Arm. The first winery in the area was Larch Hills, which opened in 1997. "With everybody being so positive about what can be done here, it is something we got behind," Doug Kennedy says.

In 2003, the Kennedy family planted four hectares (10 acres) of vineyard. There is considerable potential for more vines as the winery grows. Doug believes that the expansive Kennedy farm, once a dairy and livestock operation, has ten times as much land available that is suitable for vines. Doug believes that the farm has the appropriate climate. "We tend to be slightly warmer than a lot of Kelowna during the year," Doug says, "and cool enough in the evenings that we get good flavours in the grapes in the fall."

The vineyard is planted primarily with Gewürztraminer, Maréchal Foch, Kerner and small test plots of Pinot Noir and about ten other varieties. As a professional agrologist, Gary Kennedy is proceeding cautiously to determine the vines best suited to the site. Doug hopes that Pinot Noir in particular will be one of the successes of this test. "If it works out, it could create quite a unique wine in our area," he says. The comment reflects the characteristic winemaker's infatuation with Pinot Noir, a notoriously challenging variety that makes great wine in the right growing conditions.

Granite Creek's initial wines, with Summerland consultant Gary Strachan advising the Kennedy family on winemaking, are from grapes purchased in the Okanagan in the 2003 vintage, including old vines Ehrenfelser from the Inkameep Vineyard. The winery is releasing both a table wine and a late harvest version of this fruity German white. Once widely grown in the Okanagan, Ehrenfelser is made now by only a few wineries. "It appeals to a unique niche of people," Doug says. "It is something that we really liked and we wanted to get behind it."

Granite Creek's other wines include Chardonnay, Pinot Gris, Maréchal Foch and Merlot, including a port-style wine made from Merlot. Since some of these varieties are not suited to Salmon Arm vineyards, Granite Creek is likely to continue its relationship with Okanagan growers. Doug Kennedy's objective is to grow Granite Creek's production from an initial 2,000 cases a year to about 5,000 cases and eventually to build a gravity-flow winery.

"We are not going to waste time doing volume here," he says "The only thing we are going for is quality. We want to get a name for the best thing we can produce."

GRAY MONK ESTATE WINERY

OPENED: 1982

1055 Camp Road, Okanagan Centre, BC, V4V 2H4

Telephone: 250-766-3168

Toll-free: 1-800-663-4205

Web site: www.graymonk.com

Wine shop: Open daily 9 am – 9 pm July and August; 10 am – 5 pm in spring and fall;
11 am – 5 pm in winter except for Sunday closings January through March.

Restaurant: Grapevine Patio Grill open 11:30 am – 5 pm April through October.

RECOMMENDED

* ❋ ODYSSEY MERLOT
* ❋ ODYSSEY PINOT GRIS
* ❋ ODYSSEY PINOT AUXERROIS
* ❋ PINOT AUXERROIS
* ❋ GEWÜRZTRAMINER ALSACE CLONE
* ❋ PINOT GRIS
* ❋ SIEGERREBE
* ❋ ROTBERGER
* ❋ CHARDONNAY UNWOODED
* ❋ EHRENFELSER ICEWINE

ONE OF THE NOTABLE THINGS ABOUT GRAY MONK IS THE GOOD-HUMOURED joking that goes on in the tasting room when founders George and Trudy Heiss are there. Everyone gets a warm reception. George recounts a morning when three decidedly unkempt men — an older man accompanied by two strapping youths — marched into the Gray Monk tasting room, the image of classic free-loaders. While the youths looked bored, the older man methodically tasted Gray Monk's extensive selection and then named the five varietals he wanted. When

Heiss began packing up five bottles, the man said he wanted a *case of each wine*. It turned out that the three were unshaven and dishevelled because they were returning from a few days in the bush. They had stopped at Gray Monk to replenish the older man's wine cellar. The youths were there to carry the wine up the steep stairs to Gray Monk's parking lot. "You can never judge," Heiss says.

Dealing with people was something George and Trudy Heiss learned in their previous career as hairdressers in Edmonton, where they met. "Having been in the service industry all along, it is easy for us to be very service-oriented," George says. "I have worked all my life with people, and very closely with people, because hairdressing is one on one, and maybe" — with mischief in his voice — "with the more difficult set of the human race, the females!"

Born in Vienna in 1939, George grew up with parents who were world champion hairdressers. George's career choice was made for him when his father announced it was time for him to learn the trade. He became very good at it. In Edmonton, where he and German-born Trudy had separate businesses, George dealt with as many as 35 customers in a day and was booked months in advance. The trade continued to be useful when he and Trudy moved to the Okanagan in 1972 to become farmers. Until they could earn a living from wine, they continued styling hair, doing their farm work during evenings and weekends. "There were many days when I was still on the tractor at night with the lights on," George recalls.

They had been preceded to the Okanagan in 1968 by Trudy's parents, Hugo and Anna Peter, who had a small vineyard overlooking Okanagan Lake near Winfield. When Hugo alerted them three years later that a nearby orchard was on the market, they decided to switch from hairdressing to grape growing. "My parents thought we were crazy," George recalls. It was a reasonable conclusion, since he knew nothing about vineyards. "I knew how to get the content in a bottle out of the bottle and into myself," he laughs. "We were so bloody ignorant. We had not even figured out at that time the positive influence of the lake on our vineyard. That was way beyond us. One thing we did figure out right off the bat: if cherries, apricots and peaches survived here, grapes would definitely survive."

They plunged ahead, learning to do everything, including burying about 6.4 kilometres (four miles) of irrigation pipe. "That's when we coined the phrase that we don't mind learning from the ground up but why does it always have to be from 16 inches under the ground?" he says. The winery that agreed to buy his grapes told him to plant French hybrids, including Maréchal Foch and Seibel 1000. Both were ripped out when he saw how unsatisfactory the wines were. "I don't think they were imported from France," George fumes. "I think they were deported from France."

In 1975, his father-in-law had the Alsace research station at Colmar ship George the premium varieties that have become Gray Monk's foundation: Pinot Auxerrois, Gewürztraminer, Kerner and Pinot Gris. The latter is known in Austria by a name that translates as Gray Monk; hence the winery name. The 1976 and 1977 blocks of those vines, now fully mature, yield such rich, intensely flavoured grapes that the fruit has been used since 2000 for Gray Monk's Odyssey, or reserve, label.

Confirmation that George Heiss was on the right track came in 1977 from the renowned Dr. Helmut Becker, then head of grape breeding at Germany's Geisenheim Institute. During a brief tour of the valley, Becker offered George 34 different varieties from Geisenheim. Heiss passed this opportunity to all the Okanagan growers. The subsequent Becker Project (involving two test vineyards) identified varieties suitable to the Okanagan. Hugo Peter was the project's field man.

Having decided to open a winery, the family sent George Jr., who was born in 1962, to Germany in 1980, where he studied at Weinsberg and apprenticed with the historic Guntrum winery. "People asked us why we would send George to Europe, not to California," his father says. "When you look on the map, Europe's problems are similar to ours but California's problems are totally different." Until George Jr. returned in 1984, Gray Monk early vintages were made by Lynn Bremmer, then the winemaker at the new Brights winery near Oliver. Today, the vineyard she and husband, John, cultivate south of Oliver grows the premium grapes for Gray Monk's Odyssey Merlot. The Heiss family itself has 18 hectares (45 acres) of north Okanagan vineyards. George Jr. has taken over the Hugo Peter vineyard, while his brother Stephen, born in 1967 and now handling Gray Monk's marketing, planted a vineyard nearby.

The winery opened in 1982, offering Germanic-style wines with lively fruit flavours supported by a touch of sweetness. Gray Monk dominated Okanagan wine competitions for years until other capable wineries emerged (it still does very well). The style of Gray Monk wines has evolved with the changing palate of its customers. The Odyssey wines, for example, are drier and a step ahead in complexity. The red wine program expanded after Christine Leroux, a French-trained consultant to several Okanagan wineries, was hired in 1999 to help George Jr. cope with a total production that has now risen to about 60,000 cases a year. Leroux convinced Gray Monk, once resistant to barrels, to start aging its red wines in oak.

George Jr. has always done his magic with stainless steel. Invariably, the wines are clean, fresh and wonderfully aromatic. The range of varietals is large and each wine has a following. For example, Trudy Heiss's personal favourite is Siegerrebe, an off-dry white with aromas of rose petals and spice and flavours of tangerine and pink grapefruit. There are loyal fans for Rotberger, a fruity rosé made exclusively at Gray Monk, which is believed to be the only winery in North America growing this obscure German variety. About 1,200 cases are made each year.

The winery's greatest commercial success, Latitude 50, is a white blend — mostly Bacchus and Riesling — launched in 1991 and now more than a third of the winery's production. This wine, along with more recent red and rosé companions, is popularly priced. "I would like everybody to be able to afford our wines," George says. "That's why we started the Latitude 50 series. I want to be able to give the consumer a wine that's affordable."

There is not much that George Heiss Sr. would do differently if he were starting out again. "I might lay out the winery a little differently than we did to start with," he says, after a moment of reflection. In 1980, an architect friend helped the Heisses sketch out a building that would sit, slightly banana-shaped, midway down the slope of the vineyard. One of the most attractively sited Okanagan wineries, it has been expanded several times, always true to the original shape. "The shape we built it made it quite a bit more expensive to operate," Heiss discovered. "The square box is more efficient. But the square box offends my artistic side."

Pinot Noir
VQA OKANAGAN VALLEY VQA
2001

GREATA RANCH VINEYARDS

OPENED: 2003

697 Highway 97, Summerland, BC, V0H 1Z0

Telephone: 250-767-2605

Web: www.cedarcreek.bc.ca/greataranch.htm

Wine shop: Open daily 10 am – 6 pm May through October; 11 am – 4 pm November, December, March, April; closed January and February.

Restaurant: Veranda picnic facilities with delicatessen service.

RECOMMENDED
_____

✹ SELECT PINOT BLANC

✺ SELECT CHARDONNAY

✷ SELECT PINOT NOIR

✷ GEWÜRZTRAMINER

✷ EHRENFELSER

IT WAS NOT TOO LONG AFTER THE GREATA RANCH VINEYARD WAS PLANTED in 1994 that motorists passing on Highway 97 began stopping at vineyard manager Merle Lawrence's home, assuming it to be a wine shop. In 2003, Cedar-Creek Estate Winery, owners of the vineyard, responded to an obvious demand by opening a farm winery, building a tasting room resembling a rambling farmhouse with a shaded veranda. The design, complete with the eye-catching red roof, echoes the heritage appearance of the nearby bunkhouse and the manager's home. The heritage is real. In another era, Greata Ranch was one of the valley's leading orchards.

The property takes its name from George H. Greata, a British immigrant who came to the Okanagan in 1895. The ranch occupies a bench on the west side of Okanagan Lake, eight kilometres (about six miles) south of the current village of Peachland. In Greata's day, it was an arid tangle of trees and sage until he built a wooden pipeline for irrigation water from Deep Creek, just south of Peachland. In 1901, he planted 20 hectares (50 acres) of apples.

Greata (pronounced *Gretta*) sold the ranch in 1910 to a British investment syndicate. John T. Long, a British immigrant already working at a Kelowna orchard, was named the manager. Thirteen years later, Long and his family bought the property and built the business to national prominence. After a large 46.6- kilometre (29-mile) irrigation line was built to Brenda Lake, Long expanded the orchard until, in 1945, the ranch boasted 55 hectares (135 acres) of fruit trees. The ranch was producing more than 454 tonnes (500 tons) of fruit a year for its own refrigerated packing house. Greata Ranch had its own dock where railway cars loaded with fruit were transferred to barges and shipped to the nearest railhead.

The Long family (descendants still live in the Okanagan) sold the ranch in 1965. Unfortunately for the new owner, a very hard winter that year devastated the fruit trees. The orchard now slipped into a long period of neglect. Squatters built shacks along the lakefront. A condominium project begun in the early 1980s failed. People began dumping appliances and old vehicles on the land. By the time Greata Ranch was purchased in 1994 by Senator Ross Fitzpatrick, the owner of CedarCreek, it had become derelict.

Fitzpatrick was looking for an additional vineyard for CedarCreek. Other wineries had not taken much notice of the property. Sloping toward the east and with the high hills on the west that cut off the evening sun, the property looked like a challenging place for growing grapes. Fitzpatrick, however, had insights that suggested otherwise. His father, Bud, once managed a packing house in Oliver and sometimes took his son along on trips to buy fruit. "This was a big beautiful peach orchard," the senator remembers. That was the clue that grapes could grow here. "I really relied upon my recollection of coming up to the orchard with my Dad, and of the great peaches that were produced. This was too far north to grow really good peaches but they did it successfully at Greata, so I took a chance."

It seems that Greata Ranch benefits from a local microclimate. The valley narrows dramatically here as the lake executes a dog leg toward the north. The granite cliffs on the east side radiate the heat of the day back across the water onto the vines in the evening. The funnel effect of the narrow valley creates beneficial morning and evening breezes that ward off frost. "You get really good air circulation," Fitzpatrick says. "We never have any hint of frost. Our leaves will be the last to turn." Thus, the vineyard, despite its exposure, grows quality grapes as it once produced quality peaches.

The entire property now is 44 hectares (108 acres) but only 16 hectares (40 acres) have been planted to grapes. On some of the remaining land, Fitzpatrick intends eventually to develop a carefully planned residential community, something that he has termed a "Tuscan" village. This would take advantage of the quite remarkable views over the lake and of the beachfront, from which most traces of shacks and packing house wharves have been removed.

The varieties chosen were those central to the wines at CedarCreek: Pinot Blanc, Pinot Noir, Chardonnay, Gewürztraminer and Merlot. The first significant harvest was taken off in 1998. The fruit was of such quality that CedarCreek was able to launch its Platinum series, as it calls its reserve wines. The first wine released with a Greata Ranch label was the 2000 Estate Select Pinot Blanc. In the spring of 2002, this wine won gold medals both at the Okanagan Spring Wine Festival and at the Los Angeles County Wine Fair. The Los Angeles judges also named the wine as the best in the Pinot Blanc class.

Capable of producing about 91 tonnes (100 tons) of grapes at full maturity, the Greata Ranch vineyard now supplies two wineries. Soon after opening its wine shop in the spring of 2003, Greata Ranch was offering a dozen wines, including an Ehrenfelser from purchased grapes. The wines are differentiated from those at CedarCreek by their modestly lower prices. Ultimately, what should set Greata Ranch apart are the fresh, vivid flavours of which the Greata Ranch fruit is capable.

HAINLE VINEYARDS

OPENED: 1988

5355 Trepanier Bench Road, Peachland, BC, V0H 1X2
Telephone: 250-767-2525
Toll-free: 1-800-767-3109
Web site: www.hainle.com
Wine shop: Open daily 10 am – 7 pm.

RECOMMENDED

- ✹ ICEWINE 1983 AND 1984
- ✺ ZWEIGELT "Z"
- ✺ DEEP CREEK RIESLING
- ✺ DEEP CREEK 23
- ✹ DEEP CREEK PINOT GRIS
- ✹ DEEP CREEK PINOT BLANC
- ✹ DOLCE AMORE
- DEEP CREEK CHARDONNAY
- DEEP CREEK PINOT MEUNIER

AT $200 FOR A 200-MILLILITRE (SEVEN-OUNCE) BOTTLE, THE HAINLE 1983 Okanagan Riesling Icewine almost certainly was the most expensive wine in any Canadian winery when it was released 19 years after it was made. The price was audacious because the wine, of which only 1,000 bottles were made, was rich in history as well as flavour. That history is one reason why Walter Huber did not change the winery's name when he purchased the winery from the Hainle family early in 2002.

Walter Hainle (the name rhymes with finely) is credited with making the first Canadian icewine. The tradition of making dessert wines from frozen grapes originated in Germany in the eighteenth century. A German textile salesman who

had brought his family to Canada in 1970, Hainle dabbled in home winemaking. In the fall of 1973, an unexpected frost caught the Okanagan vineyard from which Hainle was buying grapes. Remembering the German tradition, Hainle made between 30 and 40 litres (6.6 to 8.8 gallons) of icewine for personal consumption. Within a few years, he began planting a vineyard near Peachland. Tilman, his son, returned to Germany to learn winemaking. Walter and Tilman also kept on making icewine. When the family opened their winery in 1988, they offered icewines starting with the 1978 vintage.

Occasionally, Tilman moves a batch of icewine that he is not pleased with to the back of the cellar, hoping that time will bring it around. That happened with 200 litres (44 gallons) of 1983 icewine and about 100 litres (22 gallons) of 1984 icewine. When the winery changed hands early in 2002, a cellar inventory uncovered these two icewines. Both had transformed over two decades into wines of great character. The bouquet of the 1983 (the last year before Hainle switched from Okanagan Riesling to Johannisberg Riesling for icewine) reminded Tilman of the rich butter and caramel aromas of a pastry shop. The winery quickly bottled these neglected treasures. The aggressive prices (the 1984 is $195) are justified by the rarity of the wine and the history. "Hainle Vineyards has a great history behind it," says Shelley Huber, the marketing director. "That kind of leads the conversation."

The Huber family also has a rich history, with an ancient family crest to prove it. The son of a successful car dealer, Walter Huber was born in Munich in 1959. He was a management trainee with Mercedes-Benz when his family invested in a fishing lodge near Dryden, Ontario, and sent him to run it in 1980. "It was quite challenging, that first year," he recalls. "I had yes and no, and that was about as much English as I knew." Quickly fluent, the personable Huber developed the lodge into one of Canada's best.

In 1991, the Huber family bought orchard property on the mountainside just above Peachland, initially as a residential property. A shepherd, whose flock was retained to keep the grass down, talked Walter into a trial vineyard plot with 600 vines. Apparently, that stirred the memory about his family's previous foray into growing grapes. In 1167, he says, an ancestor who had served a minor king bravely, was awarded farmland in what is now Austria's Burgenland, where he planted grapes. Subsequent generations of Hubers grew hops for beer in Bavaria. Now, the success of his 600 vines spurred Walter into the wine business. He began planning a winery near Peachland and was prepared to become a professional winemaker by the time it opened in 2006.

"Accidents happen all the time," Walter marvels, telling the story over lunch in the winery's cozy Amphora Bistro. In December, 2001, he was working with a crew, terracing the Peachland property ("the vineyard looks like in Europe," he notes) when a curious neighbour asked what was happening. When Walter explained, the neighbour informed him that the nearby Hainle winery was for sale. "I came over and talked to Tilman and his sister. We started negotiating and we ended up with the winery."

The opportunity came along sooner than he expected, for he wanted to sell the fishing lodge first and learn winemaking. Tilman Hainle agreed to remain as the winemaker, allowing Walter to apply his aggressive management to the rest of the business. Under Hainle ownership, the winery had never made more than 5,000 cases a year. Walter Huber is expanding that to between 12,000 and 15,000 cases, at which point this compact winery, with its cellars tight against the mountainside, will be at capacity.

Walter Huber is a decisive man by nature. Not long after taking over the winery, the strawberry blonde marketing director of a Kelowna radio station arrived to sell him some advertising. A whirlwind courtship ensued. Within five months, Shelley and Walter Huber were married and she had become the winery's marketing director (since Walter still has the fishing lodge to run). Shelley, a Revelstoke native who was a figure-skating coach in her teens, has tackled Hainle's marketing with imagination. She resolved the challenge of selling the winery's tongue-twisting Zweigelt, a full-flavoured red wine, by re-labelling it as "Z."

While the winery has new owners, the character appreciated by Hainle fans has remained. Tilman Hainle's initial style was to make wines, most produced organically, that were quite dry, often structured to age a few years before showing all their complexities. His style is not fixed in amber, however. Under Huber ownership, many wines have been released while still young and fruity, notably under the new Deep Creek Wine Estate label. In the winter of 2004, Tilman worked the vintage at the Mountadam winery in Australia, a producer known for its Chardonnay and Shiraz wines.

Above all, the Hainle wines are crafted to go with food. The Amphora Bistro, the winery's 90-seat restaurant and patio, was opened in 1995 (only one other British Columbia winery then had a restaurant) to show off the Hainle wines with meals. (It had to be closed in the summer of 2004 to enlarge the wine shop.) Tilman Hainle is as intensely interested in food as he is in wines. "I work with the kitchen to augment the offerings," he says, referring to the vegetables and herbs grown in his own garden. In the spring, he scours the north Okanagan for wild asparagus. And he is fired up about baking bread. He got what he calls the "bread bug" in 2003 after being served exceptional sourdough bread at an Oregon resort. He talked the resort's bakery into giving him its sourdough culture. "I smuggled it back across the border and that's what got me going," he confesses. "I've been teaching myself to make sourdough bread."

HARMONY-ONE VINEYARDS

OPENING: PROPOSED FOR 2006

1143 Highway 3, Cawston, BC, V0X 1C0

Telephone: 250-499-2144

REASONABLY NEW TO GRAPE-GROWING, GEORGE HANSON WAS LOOKING for a bit of reassurance in the fall of 2003 when some of his Merlot grapes were slipped into a grape tasting being done by the staff at the Jackson-Triggs winery. He was ecstatic that his Merlot topped the tasting. "They thought they were from Black Sage Road," he chuckles.

It is one of Hanson's ambitions to elevate the Similkameen Valley's reputation for grapes to the same level as that of Black Sage Road, both with his grapes and with the wines he plans to release. Moving cautiously, Hanson in 2003 engaged winemaker Lawrence Herder, a neighbour, to make the first 150 cases of what is planned to become a red Meritage. Hanson intends to double that production in 2004. The plans beyond that remain tentative, but with an ultimate target of producing about 4,500 cases a year. He wants to open the tasting room in 2006 with wines that attract attention. "That's the way to build a reputation," he says. "Start out well."

Born in Alberta in 1957, Hanson spent 25 years in the Yukon, becoming a manager in the territory's telephone system. "I got an early golden handshake from the telephone company and decided to pursue my dream," he recounts. His interest in wine, he says, began when a brother married into an Italian family that included a father who was a good winemaker. Hanson learned how to make wine (although he plans to employ a professionally trained winemaker). He also began travelling to wine regions to further his passion. "I thought it would be a nice thing to do when I retired at 55," he says. "It promises a good lifestyle."

The unexpectedly early severance from the telephone company, more than

a decade before he intended to retire, enabled him to look for vineyard property. After several unsuccessful bids on property near Oliver, he chanced on his Similkameen property, then a hay meadow, on the very day in 1999 when the owner put up the for sale sign. Hanson bought it immediately — and just ahead of two wineries that were also interested. It is well located beside the highway, on a westward-sloping plateau with panoramic views of the mountains across the valley. A natural gully on the property is ideal for an underground cellar and a gravity-flow winery. "The site is phenomenal," he believes.

Hanson pegged the torrid Similkameen as red wine country from first-hand experience with the heat. He recalls one recent summer when, for 43 consecutive days, the noon temperature was above 40°C (104°F). It makes it easy to stress the vines by so-called deficit irrigation. By applying minimal irrigation water, Hanson produces grapes with small but intensely flavoured berries, as the taste test at Jackson-Triggs showed.

Starting in 2000, he has planted six hectares (15 acres) of vines — Merlot, Cabernet Franc, Cabernet Sauvignon and a little Shiraz. His only white variety, about .8 hectares (two acres), is Chardonnay. He figures there will always be a demand for this white among consumers in his tasting room.

Perhaps it developed during those long Yukon winters, but Hanson has a streak of poetry in his nature, as reflected in the name chosen for both the vineyard and the winery. After thinking about names for a long time, it occurred to him that his role is much like that of an orchestra conductor — creating harmony.

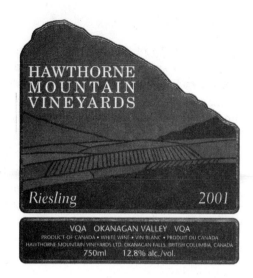

HAWTHORNE MOUNTAIN VINEYARDS

OPENED: 1986

Green Lake Road, Okanagan Falls, BC, V0H 1R0
Telephone: 250-497-8267
Web site: www.hmvineyard.com
Wine shop: Open daily 9 am – 5 pm.

RECOMMENDED

- ✳ SEE YA LATER RANCH WINES
  (INCLUDING BRUT, CHARDONNAY, PINOT GRIS, EHRENFELSER ICEWINE)
- ✳ HMV PINOT GRIS
- ✳ HMV RIESLING
- ✳ HMV GEWÜRZTRAMINER

WHEN HAWTHORNE MOUNTAIN VINEYARDS LAUNCHED ITS FIRST TRUE RESERVE-quality wines from the 2000 vintage, the bottles were mundanely identified as "Gold Label." The See Ya Later Ranch labels that replaced Gold Label two years later have the irreverent pizzazz that the property's eccentric past deserves. The label shows a flying dog with the wings and halo of an angel. This is the only winery in British Columbia with a pet cemetery beside the century-old heritage tasting room.

Now owned by Vincor International Inc., Canada's largest wine group, Hawthorne Mountain was opened in 1986 as LeComte Estate Winery by Albert LeComte, a former sign company owner who had become a wheeler-dealer in Okanagan real estate. As colourful as he was, he paled compared with an earlier owner of the property, the dog-loving Major Hugh Fraser.

Fraser, who was born in Montreal in 1885, was an officer with the Canadian troops in World War I, two years of which he spent as a prisoner of war. After demobilization in 1919, he bought the farm that had been homesteaded in 1902 by two brothers called Hawthorne on a mountainside overlooking Okanagan Falls. When the major brought his English bride to what was then a very remote farm, it was not long before she departed, having left — so the story goes — a breezy note reading "Gone back to London, see ya later."

The major was not alone, however. His companions included a pair of collies, Jimmy My Pal and Rex, the first of a dozen dogs that later were buried on the farm. Their headstones were lined up beside the barn that Albert LeComte later converted into a rustic winery. During a recent winery expansion, the headstones were moved under a tree in front of the tasting room. Major Fraser planted the first vines on the property in 1961, shortly before retiring and moving into Penticton. He continued his affection for animals there. A local writer who profiled him for the Okanagan Historical Society in 1970, the year of Fraser's death, noted that the major still had two collies and a 19-year-old parrot. (The See Ya Later label takes some liberties: the dog looks more like a terrier than a collie.)

The varieties in the original vineyard clearly included some obscure labrusca vines of dubious wine-making quality. When LeComte bought the farm with its 8.5-hectare (21-acre) vineyard, the varieties included Okanagan Riesling, Chelois, De Chaunac and a substantial block of Buffalo, a labrusca. The latter was pulled out in 1984 when no winery would buy the fruit. When he started upgrading the vineyard, LeComte had the good fortune to plant Gewürztraminer. Even though LeComte's winemaking could be inconsistent, his Gewürztraminers won awards. It seems that Hawthorne Mountain, the highest-elevation vineyard in the Okanagan, produces superb Gewürztraminer, now the major variety in the vastly enlarged 69-hectare (170-acre) vineyard. Most of the fruit is sold to a sister winery, Sumac Ridge, for its best-selling Private Reserve Gewürztraminer.

LeComte always had too many irons in the fire, including Mexican real estate, to tie himself down to a winery. In 1994, he hired Eric von Krosigk as the winemaker and general manager. Infatuated with sparkling wine, von Krosigk immediately began developing the Brut Zero Dosage, a crisply dry bottle-fermented Riesling bubbly. Meanwhile, LeComte was shopping the business and in 1995 he sold the winery to a partnership led by Harry McWatters, the founder of Sumac Ridge. Vincor acquired both wineries five years later.

Hawthorne Mountain Vineyards (HMV) took some time to find its focus. To begin with, it kept the LeComte portfolio in the market for several years while developing the more premium portfolio under HMV's new name. The 11 releases from the 1995 vintage under the HMV label ranged from icewine to Meritage and from Muscat Ottonel to Pinot Meunier. Meanwhile, the LeComte label was still used for such fading varietals as Chelois. It was a clear case of a winery being all things to all markets. Secondly, a succession of winemakers moved through the poorly equipped winery, which was rebuilt only after the vineyard development was complete and after the tasting room was refurbished in 2002.

A new and more focussed era began at HMV with the launch of the See Ya Later wines. Dave Carson, formerly the assistant winemaker at Sumac Ridge, became HMV's winemaker in the summer of 2003. Everything about his career says consistency. Raised in Kelowna, he joined the crew that planted Sumac Ridge's first vineyard in 1980. Fascinated by the wine industry, he stayed there, taking a variety of cellar jobs, growing in his career through solid experience.

The HMV portfolio now is much tighter. Part of this reflects the overall Vincor philosophy of having each of its wineries develop an identity around a small number of varietals, some estate-grown, rather than compete all over the field. The flagship wines at HMV appear under the See Ya Later Ranch label. They include Chardonnay, Pinot Gris, Pinot Noir, Ehrenfelser icewine and the crisp Brut sparkling wine.

HERDER
2003
PINOT GRIS
SIMILKAMEEN VALLEY

PRODUCT OF CANADA/PRODUIT DU CANADA
WHITE WINE/VIN BLANC

13.7% alc./vol.   750ml

HERDER WINERY AND VINEYARDS

OPENED: 2004

716 Lowe Drive, Cawston, BC, V0X 1N0
Telephone: 250-498-9942
Wine shop: By appointment.

RECOMMENDED

MERLOT
PINOT GRIS
CHARDONNAY

IN 2002 CALIFORNIAN LAWRENCE HERDER, A WINEMAKER TRAINED AT FRESNO State College, planted Cabernet Sauvignon and Syrah in a .8-hectare (two-acre) vineyard near Cawston. "We have settled in the Similkameen to make big reds," he says. The Similkameen, a hot and wind-scoured valley enclosed by the mountains just west of the south Okanagan, has a history of grape growing stretching back almost 50 years. But few wineries have chosen to establish in the thinly populated valley. The winery that Herder and his Canadian-born wife, Sharon, own is only the third in the appellation. Two more small wineries are under development.

Born in 1967 in a suburb of San Diego, Herder was 14 when he tasted his aunt's homemade wine at his family's dinner table. "I was so enthused with it that I went into the attic and fired up a winemaking kit we had," he recalls. He continued to make wine from both fruit and grapes. "I was quite popular as a teenager," he laughs. Ultimately, he decided to become professionally trained. "Anybody can become a winemaker," he says. "But the advantage of having the training about chemical defects is knowing what to do when something goes wrong."

Winemaking was not his first career choice. With his wife's parents, he and Sharon, a graphic designer, founded a printing business in Burnaby in 1988.

Herder worked there for several years until the itch to make wine professionally drove him back to Fresno. The college is known as a practical, hands-on training ground, with the students making wine that is sold by the college's own winery. On graduation, Herder gained experience by working with other California wineries, including luminaries B.R. Cohn and Byron.

Always a man in a hurry, Herder found a partner and established the first Herder Vineyard on a 13-hectare (32-acre) property in the emerging Paso Robles appellation. "You get your MBA on your first project," he says ruefully. Having sunk so much capital in a large vineyard, he discovered that the winery was about to run out of cash just as the 2000 vintage was coming to market. He sold his 50 per cent interest and retreated to Burnaby again to manage the printing company, which was now thriving.

While the printing company made "tons of money," Herder's heart was not in it. When he sold in Paso Robles, he retained the Herder Vineyard brand. He moved to British Columbia with enough equipment to start another small winery. "Most of it moved through as my personal effects," he says. "It saved me thousands of dollars in taxes." He canvassed British Columbia wine regions extensively. "I looked all over Vancouver Island," he says. "I went so far as to write a paper comparing the Cowichan Valley to Burgundy, or to Paso Robles." His controversial conclusion: "You're never going to grow world-class wine on the island."

He concluded that the Okanagan Valley south of Oliver had the desirable soils and climate for growing the big wines he wanted to make. However, property with water rights was far too expensive. Herder had no intention of running short of cash a second time and settled for a small acreage in the under-exploited Similkameen. "I am much more comfortable with having a small piece of property and cranking up the winery," he says. "There are quite a lot of grapes available to purchase."

The property he bought was basically raw land. The previous owner had been restoring collector cars in a large metal-clad shed that, after a thorough cleaning, was adapted to serve as a winery. For a few months, Herder juggled this project with running the printing business until it was sold in 2002. Impatient to get back to making wine, Herder took a job at the big Jackson-Triggs winery north of Oliver.

Because he was trained, Herder was a godsend for Bruce Nicholson, the chief winemaker at Jackson-Triggs. The applicants who responded when Nicholson advertised the job included lawyers and accountants who believed that a mere love of wine qualified them. But in Herder, he got a winemaker who actually knew how to do everything, including running the new rotary fermenters that had just been installed at Jackson-Triggs. Individuals with complementary skills, Nicholson and Herder did two vintages together before Herder moved to Golden Mile Cellars late in 2003. Because Golden Mile is a much smaller winery, Herder is able to handle that winemaking job at the same time as he makes the wine for Herder.

In the 2003 vintage, Herder purchased grapes to make about 900 cases of wine for his own winery. Ultimately, he intends to take Herder to about 2,000 cases a year of premium, small-lot wines. "The first vintage is 100 per cent Similkameen," he says. "I also have contracted grapes from vineyards near Oliver. What I am trying to do is go out and find unique vineyards from which I can purchase a small quantity of grapes, one or two tons. Once I have made wine for a year or two from these vineyards, my intention is to discover the ones that are producing the best fruit and do vineyard-designated wines. I am trying to express something from the Similkameen and something from the Okanagan. I plan to find some growers that want to work with me specifically on that endeavour." The wines will be issued in both regular and reserve bottlings, depending on quality. Herder hopes that they will prove to be "unique little bottlings of something that is special."

HESTER CREEK

OPENED: 1983

13163-326th Avenue, Oliver, BC, V0H 1T0
Telephone: 250-498-4435
Web site: www.hestercreek.com
Wine shop: Open daily 10 am – 5 pm from Easter to Christmas;
    and Monday through Friday January to Easter.

RECOMMENDED

✹ TREBBIANO DRY
✹ MERLOT
✹ PINOT BLANC

DURING THE FIRST HALF OF 2004, IT WAS HARD TO FIND HESTER CREEK'S wines in the market. The reason was that Hester Creek, although it had plenty of wine in its barrels and tanks, could not afford bottles or labels after being declared bankrupt. The wines reappeared only after a Prince George trucking magnate named Curt Garland purchased the winery in a hotly contested auction. A self-made man, he started his business career as a logger at age 17. Almost half a century later, now a wine lover as well as owner of a specialized trucking company, he was shopping for a vineyard or a winery in the Okanagan, and Hester Creek was available. Now, Garland plans to build a new winery there in 2005, unlocking Hester Creek's potential. Operated properly, this could be one of the Okanagan's best wineries.

The vineyard is one of Hester Creek's advantages. It is a 28-hectare (70-acre) finger jutting out on the western side of the valley, part of a superlative stretch of vineyard land called the Golden Mile. The first grapes were planted here in 1968 by Joe Busnardo. A hard-headed Italian immigrant, he ignored advice to plant hybrid grapes and, instead, planted only vinifera, then rare in the Okanagan. When existing wineries declined to pay a premium for his grapes, he refused to sell. For a few years, he left the vineyard to its own devices. His interest revived after his vines survived a hard winter that damaged many hybrid plantings. He began selling grapes to home winemakers until he opened his own winery, called Divino, in 1983.

The wines emerging from Divino, while somewhat rustic, were unique to the Okanagan. Busnardo planted a number of varieties native to Italian vineyards, including Garganega, Malvasia and Trebbiano. Of those three, Trebbiano has succeeded as a Hester Creek exclusive. Busnardo, who preferred farming to wine-making, experimented with so many varieties that he lost track of what was in some plots. In 1996, when he sold the Okanagan vineyard and moved the Divino winery to Vancouver Island, Busnardo began similar trials in the Cowichan Valley.

The former Divino winery became Hester Creek, with winemaker Frank Supernak taking over both in the vineyard and in the cellar. Born in Nanaimo in 1961, he had been working in the Okanagan since 1987. A rising star, he was chief winemaker at Vincor's Oliver winery before joining the management group that acquired Hester Creek.

He and his partners had purchased a winery with old equipment and a vine-yard needing significant redevelopment. The vine rows, for example, were 13 feet (4 metres) apart, a third to double the distance between the rows of more efficient vineyards. It took Supernak several years to complete the infill planting, to redesign the trellising, to identify unnamed varieties and to remove unwanted varieties. To help finance all of these projects, Supernak and his partners sold the majority interest in the winery and vineyard to a company called Boltons Capital Corp., which later changed its name to Valterra Wines Ltd. A junior company that traded on the stock exchange, Valterra got the substantial bank loans needed to finish the vineyard and to build a tasting room designed by the Okanagan's best winery architect, Robert Mackenzie.

In the summer of 2002 Supernak moved from Hester Creek to Blasted Church Vineyards, once again to redevelop a vineyard, one of his strengths. "Eighty-five per cent of the winemaking starts in the vineyard for me," he said in an interview at the time. "We spend a lot of time out in the vineyard with our crews, trying to get the best product into the winery. My job is easy after that — just be a glorified babysitter." Always generous in helping colleagues, Supernak consulted for several wineries. During one of these jobs in November, 2002, he died tragically, suffocating in a wine tank while trying to rescue another wine-maker. Hester Creek had insured Supernak's life. The policy was still valid and the winery collected $500,000 on its former winemaker's life.

Hester Creek needed the money. By this time, both its banker and several private lenders were demanding to have their loans repaid (the Bank of Montreal collected most of the life insurance money). Lorrie Warwick, a former garment distributor from Winnipeg who had been running Valterra and Hester Creek since 2000, disclosed in February, 2003, that the bank was moving to foreclose on the winery.

The remainder of 2003 was a soap opera at Hester Creek. The financially strapped winery stopped paying its bills, sought new investors, even discussed merging with Saturna Island Vineyards. In the fall, securities lawyer Larry Page, the owner of Saturna, won a shareholder battle to take control of Valterra from Warwick and in November, she was dismissed as president of Hester Creek.

But at the winery that summer, it seemed business as usual (aside from the novelty of the ice cream machine that Warwick installed in the tasting room). Glenn Barry, a young Australian winemaker, was hired. Trained at Charles Sturt University, he had made wine both in Australia and Italy. He believed the Okanagan had a lot of potential after he made wines in the superb 2003 vintage. "The whole idea of getting an Australian winemaker at Hester Creek was to make Australian-style wines," he said. "We just want them clean, fruity, uncomplicated quality wines."

By mid-December, the corporate turmoil at Hester Creek got to Barry. He returned to Australia after circulating a blistering memo, contending that his salary had not been paid since September. Concerned about the state of affairs, the bank sent consultants John and Lynn Bremmer to check the winery. They were astonished to find that, among other sabotage, identifying labels had been removed from nearly every tank and barrel of wine. (Who caused this vandalism remains undetermined.) "The appearance of the operation was unkempt and con-fused," the Bremmers found. They took over maintaining the winery until the bank-ruptcy auction found new owners.

There was considerable interest in the winery and vineyard. The accoun-tants handling the auction sent out 20 information packages and received three or four firm bids in April 2004. The highest one, or so it seemed, was $5.1 million from Quails' Gate Estate Winery. At the last moment, Curt Garland emerged with a slightly better offer. It was accepted by the bankruptcy judge because it paid off not only the bank but also all trade creditors, like the label and bottle suppliers. By June, Garland had installed Eric von Krosigk as the new winemaker and Hester Creek once again was bottling and releasing wines.

Garland has only begun spending money on Hester Creek. The vineyard will see further redevelopment to increase the red varieties. The single largest planting, six hectares (15 acres), is Pinot Blanc, with which Supernak had made signature wines. The second largest block, almost the same size, is Chardonnay. Together, these blocks are larger than the total plantings of Merlot, Cabernet Franc and Cabernet Sauvignon. It is a ratio out of step with the market's prefer-ence for red wine.

Design has began on a new winery, likely a gravity-flow facility, that will give Hester Creek a presence in the south Okanagan comparable to Burrowing Owl and Tinhorn Creek. Ironically, Garland initially only wanted a small property and a hobby winery. "Hester Creek is certainly larger than we originally antici-pated," admits David Livingstone, Garland's partner who acts as the general manager at Hester Creek. "Sometimes when opportunities present themselves, you have to take advantage of them."

HILLSIDE ESTATE WINERY

OPENED: 1990

1350 Naramata Road, Penticton, BC, V2A 8T6

Telephone: 250-493-6274

Toll-free: 1-888-923-9463

Web site: www.hillsideestate.com

Wine shop: Open daily 10 am – 5.30 pm May through October and
on weekends in April; winter hours by appointment.

Restaurant: Barrel Room Bistro open for lunch daily May through October
and for dinner during the latter half of each week.

RECOMMENDED

* ❋ MERLOT RESERVE
* ❋ MOSAIC
* ❋ MUSCAT
* ❋ CABERNET FRANC
* ❋ MERLOT RESERVE
* ❋ GAMAY
* ❋ GEWÜRZTRAMINER
* ❋ RIESLING

WHEN IT OPENED IN A RAMSHACKLE LITTLE FARMHOUSE, HILLSIDE WAS
the first and the smallest winery on Naramata Road. Today, it is one of the largest.
Over those years, Hillside has transformed itself as dramatically as Naramata
Road itself, which has become the Okanagan's busiest wine route.

Before winemakers figured out this is prime terroir for grapes, there were
mostly orchards along winding Naramata Road. In 1979, Vera and Bohumir
Klokocka, who had escaped nine years earlier from Communist Czechoslovakia,
bought a postage-stamp orchard just beside the road. They had been living in

Kelowna where Bohumir, a metal worker, worked in the truck plant. Even though they had both worked for the Czech airline, they chose to become farmers, attracted by the idyllic Naramata Road setting. They struggled to make a living with their 780 fruit trees (casual outside jobs helped) before switching to vines in 1984.

They planted only vinifera grapes, including some of the Okanagan's first Cabernet Sauvignon. They also planted Auxerrois, Pinot Gris, Gamay, Merlot, a little Chardonnay — and Muscat Ottonel. The Penticton grower who provided some of the cuttings wrongly identified the Muscat as Pinot Blanc. As soon as Vera Klokocka started making wine, she realized it did not taste like Pinot Blanc. It was not until 1992 that a visiting grape expert from France identified the vines correctly. The fragrant, dry Muscat Ottonel became Hillside's flagship white wine.

Vera and Bohumir began agitating for a winery license soon after the vineyard began producing. Allied with other small growers, they lobbied the provincial government to create the farm winery license. The politicians were persuaded, so it is said, when Vera's delicious home-baked bread accompanied wines from small vintners at a tasting for the premier. The new rules followed in 1989 and Hillside opened the next year.

Hillside remained a tiny farmhouse winery until it was sold in 1996, two years after Bohumir's death. The new owners, a group of Albertan investors with an expansive vision, replaced the farmhouse (a remnant remains in the tasting room) with an imposing timber-frame building with a 22-metre (72-foot) tower. The 15,000-square-foot winery looming over Naramata Road is the epitome of "you can't miss it." Each year, it receives more than 20,000 visitors.

Initially, the expansion was over-optimistic, nearly sending Hillside into bankruptcy in 1999. But Ken Lauzon, Hillside's general manager since 1999, said in 2002: "We've turned the corner." His skills in marketing and hospitality were critical to the much-expanded Hillside finding its feet. Born in Windsor, Lauzon previously spent a decade in Alberta as a restaurant consultant and a manager of Calgary's exclusive 400 Club for business persons. He was attracted by the quality of life and by his optimistic view — in spite of Hillside's problems — of the wine industry. "I saw when I came out here that there is a lot of potential for this winery," he says. His experience as a restaurateur shows in the winery's bistro, opened in 2000. A homey room serving a wide selection of chef-prepared dishes, it has the atmosphere of a French country restaurant.

Hillside has been predominantly a white wine producer, with the signature still the Muscat Ottonel, which is released each June and snapped up by its fans. The original planting near the winery was only large enough to produce about 130 cases a year of this wine. Lauzon expanded the planting. The winery made 275 cases in 2002 and is aiming to produce as much as 900 cases a year. That includes a late harvest version; Lauzon has decided Hillside will no longer make icewine. Hillside's other white table wines include Gewürztraminer (1,100 cases in 2002), Pinot Gris and Riesling (each 800 cases in 2002), Kerner (750 cases), Pinot Blanc (600 cases) and Chardonnay (400 cases).

In 2002, Hillside planted its five-hectare (12-acre) Hidden Valley vineyard. The property, barely a stone's throw from the winery, gets its name because the north-south valley cannot be seen from Naramata Road. In addition to Gewürztraminer, Hillside put in significant plantings of Merlot and Syrah in a conscious effort to increase its volume of reds. Hillside's largest volume red in 2002, at 1,000 cases, was a peppery, refreshing Gamay. As well, the winery purchases red grapes from a vineyard on Black Sage Road south of Oliver in order to produce a full-bodied Bordeaux red and a rich Merlot reserve.

Winemaking since 1997 has been under the direction of Eric von Krosigk, one of the Okanagan's busiest consultants, and Hillside's cellar staff. The current cellar manager is Kelly Symonds. The daughter of an Abbotsford dentist, she has worked at several wineries in Australia and has an impressive dedication to making wine. "You can teach a lot of things," Lauzon observes, "but you can't teach passion."

A friendly, quick-moving man with boundless energy, Lauzon's particular passions include the winery's expanding hospitality programs and its creative marketing. In 2002, when Penticton inaugurated its Pacific Northwest Elvis Festival, a popular celebration of Elvis Presley's music, Hillside became the festival's official winery. The appropriately named wines were Graceland Gamay, Hound Dog Chardonnay and Blue Suede Blush.

Hillside is located just below the Kettle Valley trail, increasingly popular with bicycle tourists. Lauzon quickly figured out how to land significant sales to the two-wheel crowd with limited carrying capacity: Hillside delivers the wine to the cyclists' hotels in nearby Penticton.

It is not unusual to find Lauzon pitching in on the bottling line if that is the job that needs doing. He draws the line at winemaking, preferring to leave that to trained vintners. "I know enough about what I need to know but I am not a winemaker," he says. "That doesn't even appeal to me. The end result is the most appealing part."

Cassis 2004
Hornby Island Winery

HORNBY ISLAND WINERY

OPENING: PROPOSED FOR 2005

7000 Anderson Drive, Hornby Island, BC, V0R 1Z0
Telephone: 250-335-3019
Web site: www.hornbywine.com

JOHN GRAYSON DISCOVERED WINE WHILE HE WAS STUDYING MUSIC IN the late 1960s at the University of California's Berkeley campus. The defining bottle, he recalls, was Fetzer Premium Red, a budget red that over-delivered in quality. "I couldn't believe that a reasonably priced red would taste so good," he recalls. He was sufficiently impressed that, some time later, he visited the winery itself. The wine and the experience started a passion now culminating in the production of fruit wines and, ultimately, grape wines at the Hornby Island farm that Grayson has owned since 1999. Ambitiously, he hopes that this venture will be the prelude to a larger winery in the future in the Comox Valley on Vancouver Island.

Born in Windsor in 1949, Grayson set out to be a classical musician, playing with such orchestras as the National Youth Orchestra and the Montreal Philharmonic. In California, he studied contemporary composition and built exotic musical instruments with Harry Partch, an avant-garde composer on highly original instruments. Grayson brought his own instruments with him when he moved to Vancouver in 1971, where he mounted a show at the Vancouver Art Gallery on sound sculpture.

Grayson switched from music after completing a master's degree in communications. He founded, and spent 20 years running, two technology and software companies, one of which developed language translation technology. "I did a lot of travelling," he recalls. "After a while, I said enough is enough — it is time to choose a different lifestyle." That led to his move to slow-paced Hornby, where he acquired a 7.7-hectare (19-acre) farm on the southeast side of the island.

This is his second farm in British Columbia. During the 1970s, he owned a hobby beef farm near Duncan, in the Cowichan Valley and he planted a few vines here. Unsure of what grapes would succeed, he sought out John Harper, who had an experimental vineyard in the Fraser Valley and who later developed two vineyards near Duncan. Unfortunately, Harper advised that the soil on Grayson's Duncan farm was too fertile and too poorly drained to become a good vineyard.

That is not the problem on Hornby Island. A somewhat mountainous island with volcanic soils, Hornby gets very little rain during its long summer. "It has a very desert-like climate," says Grayson, who plans to capture rainwater for a large irrigation reservoir. A second, smaller rainwater reservoir will provide the winery's water supplies.

Grayson began developing the property in 2004, planting currants and gooseberries. He intends to open with fruit wines made from these berries and from blackberries. From the nearby Comox Valley, he will secure cranberries. The wines will be made by veteran enologist Ron Taylor, already the winemaker at several other fruit wineries.

Grayson, who chairs the technical committee of the Wine Islands Vintners Association, will also test several varieties of grapes on his island property. He believes that Pinot Gris and red hybrids such as Léon Millot and Agria likely will do well on Hornby. There already are several small vineyards on the island, including one which has been there for more than a decade. The island's only limitation is the late arrival of spring. To accelerate vine growth, Grayson intends to tent the plants in spring, as is done increasingly by Vancouver Island growers. Hornby has a modest legacy for agriculture, with a record of fruit growing in areas where the old forest was cleared. Today, the island is known more for the concentration of artists among its year-round population of 1,000 and a summertime deluge of tourists. Grayson, who once was president of the Vancouver New Music Society, plans to develop a series of concerts at the winery.

The winery here is expansive, somewhat by chance. When he was looking for a modest storage building, Grayson discovered a large building called Flanders at the Canadian Forces Base at Esquimalt that was being sold for one dollar to anyone who would move it. It was built around 1896 in a colonial style which survived several renovations as it became office space for the base medical personnel and the chaplain. The floors still are supported by massive, hand-sawn beams.

Grayson snapped up the bargain and found a moving company to barge Flanders to Hornby. The trip took four days but was so smooth that a cup of coffee, forgotten inside the building, was still half full when it arrived.

HOUSE OF ROSE VINEYARDS

OPENED: 1993

2270 Garner Road, Kelowna, BC, V1P 1E2
Telephone: 250-765-0802
Web site: www.winterwine.com
Wine shop: Open daily 10 am – 5 pm.

RECOMMENDED

WINTER WINE

IN THE DECADE SINCE THIS WINERY OPENED, VISITORS TO THE TASTING ROOM have come to expect value-priced wines. In the summer of 2003, the visitors got a surprise. Vern Rose, the owner, marked the winery's tenth anniversary by releasing 50 bottles of a reserve Maréchal Foch at $100 a bottle, including his signature and a special registration for collectors. It will not, however, become a regular offering. "I don't get too many millionaires out here," he acknowledges.

Rose is the most senior of Okanagan winery owners, having celebrated his seventy-sixth birthday during the 2003 vintage. He is a fixture at wine festivals and in his tasting room, always wearing one of his two white Tilley hats. The newer one is reserved for festivals; the older for the vineyard. He likes the way the manufacturer stands behind the hats, which are roughly used by Rose. Tilley has replaced two hats without charge when seams came apart.

He has been growing grapes almost since he retired from teaching at 55. He remains as passionate as ever about his second career at this winery not far from the Kelowna airport. "I love what I am doing," he says. "It has been a great fling. It is something that turned me on and I am still enjoying it." He admits he might entertain a purchase offer, but hopefully from an owner who would consider giving him another five years or so in the vineyard.

A native of Saskatchewan, Rose spent 35 years either teaching (physical education, mathematics, sciences) or administering in Edmonton schools. He moved to the Okanagan after leaving teaching, purchasing a vineyard in a neighbourhood called Belgo, near the Kelowna suburb of Rutland. With two hectares (five acres) of vines, mostly Okanagan Riesling, he settled down to learn viticulture, selling the grapes to Calona Vineyards.

In 1988 his life was changed by two events. First, vineyards were paid to pull out varieties like Okanagan Riesling; wineries, about to lose protected status with the new free trade agreement, were no longer buying grapes that did not make wines considered to be internationally competitive. Rose took the cash to pull out almost all of the Okanagan Riesling, replacing it over the next few years with Chardonnay, Merlot and Maréchal Foch. Then he regenerated some of the Okanagan Riesling, along with De Chaunac and Verdelet, two other varieties also on the pull-out hit list.

He is now almost the only producer making wines from what he calls "heritage" varieties. "I think somebody should," he argues. "They may regret it if they don't have the vines around. And some people come because they want to taste the wines. Nobody else is selling them."

Ironically, in the same year that his grape growing plans were upset by the pull-out, Rose achieved his lifetime dream of travelling to New Zealand. "From the time I was five years old, it was one of the few places that I really had a huge desire to visit." But rather than go as a simple tourist, he attended a conference on viticulture, then volunteered at a winery to lay irrigation pipes. He returned to the Okanagan, inspired to open his own winery. "I figured the only way to become a viable operation was to make your own wine out of your grapes, and sell the wine," Rose concluded.

The habits of a schoolteacher kicked in. The only winemaking previously in the Rose family had been his grandmother's saskatoon berry wine. He started taking extension courses and picking the brains of more experienced vintners around the Okanagan. "I actually learned more when I went to New Zealand and Germany and Australia for international seminars," he says. "Then there is reading material to take advantage of. My 35 years of teaching equipped me to be able to learn." The first vintage was made in 1992 and the wine shop opened in 1993 in a modest room adjoining the family farmhouse.

At the New Zealand conference, Rose met an emerging Swiss plant breeder named Valentin Blattner, some of whose early-maturing vines are now growing on Vancouver Island and the Gulf Islands. Those vineyards obtained the Blattner vines through commercial nurseries. The small but expanding plot of Blattner vines in the House of Rose vineyard got there somewhat more informally. After their meeting, the two men became friends. The wiry Rose, who enjoys hunting and fishing, took Blattner on fishing trips. Blattner, in turn, provided a handful of grape seeds of a hybrid crossing of Maréchal Foch and Cabernet Sauvignon. The variety is winter hardy and makes wines tasting like Cabernet. Rose has nurtured the resulting vines.

Having winter-hardy varieties is a priority in the Rose vineyard, set on a plateau surrounded by apple orchards and far from the moderating influence of Okanagan Lake. While the so-called Belgo Breeze, which blows across the plateau most afternoons, protects the vines from early autumn frosts, winter can be hard. One of the previous owners of the Rose property was trying to raise earthworms until a cold winter wiped out that business.

"I am pretty careful to plant mostly winter-hardy stock," Rose says, speaking from experience. "My Chardonnay went down completely in the 1996–97 winter and I had no crop at all on my Chardonnay in 1997." The vines did, however, regenerate from the roots to give Rose some very ripe grapes in the long, hot 1998 season. That fall, he turned it all into late harvest Chardonnay.

Rose makes as many as 28 different wines each year, including numerous proprietary blends. Early in his winemaking career, he succeeded in registering Winter Wine — a blend of icewine and late harvest wine — as a House of Rose trademark. Of course, there is an easy-drinking summer white and a companion that he compares with sangria, while keeping the recipe to himself. "I don't tell too much about it," he says. "It's about 50 per cent Foch, which controls a lot of the flavour and the scent. I don't want anything else printed about it."

Rose is always open to a new wine idea, however it comes about. When one of his wines refermented in the bottle, he left it alone to age into a natural sparkling wine. On another occasion, a barrel of wine developed what he thought was mould. Gary Strachan, his friend and sometime consultant, stopped him from throwing it out. Somehow, Rose had brought a natural yeast into the cellar, similar to that which creates renowned flor sherry in Spain. The House of Rose range was expanded to include a sherry-style wine. "I change all the time as the wind blows and I get the opportunity to develop something new," Rose chuckles.

Hunting Hawk
Vineyards

Red-Tailed Hawk by Allan Brooks

Merlot
Remuda Vineyard
2001

RED WINE • VIN ROUGE   13.3%
750ml   PRODUCT OF CANADA • PRODUIT DU CANADA   alc/vol

KESTREL

This is the small hawk sometimes seen hovering above the open meadows in Okanagan wine country. Maj. Allan Brooks painted this work at his Vernon-area home in 1920. A portion of the proceeds from the bottle of wine supports the creation of a gallery to house the museum's collection of Brooks's work and to further the education and wildlife conservation programs of the Allan Brooks Nature Centre Society.

ABOUT THIS WINE: Remuda Vineyard crowds a south-facing slope in the Okanagan's pocket desert near Okanagan Falls. The intensely hot summer weather brings this regal grape to its full intensity while the cool fall nights bolster the acid. The result is an avalanche of berry and a hint of cassis with a long, lingering finish. The vineyard is scrupulously tended by owners Arnie and Dwight Glash. Incredible with game, a fine roast or a good steak. Excellent now, will improve over 8 years.

HUNTING HAWK VINEYARDS

OPENED: 2002

4758 Gulch Road, Armstrong, BC, V0E 1B4
Telephone: 250-546-2164
Web site: www.huntinghawkvineyards.com
Wine shop: Open noon – 4 pm from June 15 to September 10,
and during Fall Wine Festival; or by appointment.

RECOMMENDED

MARÉCHAL FOCH
GEWÜRZTRAMINER
MERLOT

WHEN HIS OWN NEWLY PLANTED, POSTAGE-STAMP VINEYARD WAS BEING foraged by deer, Hunting Hawk owner Russ Niles bought grapes from small vineyards elsewhere in the Okanagan for his fledgling winery. One of his best discoveries was a Penticton neurologist, Dr. David Novak, who grows Gewürztraminer on a tiny, hand-cultivated vineyard on Naramata Road. In the superb 2002 vintage, Novak bargained hard for an extra $50 a ton for his grapes. After half an hour on the telephone, Niles gave in. He had no regrets later: the 2002 Gewürztraminer arguably may have been the best wine Hunting Hawk released from that vintage.

"We've found these little one- and two-acre vineyards that often are owned by retired people who can't retire," Niles says. Large wineries cannot always be bothered with small lots. Niles has the flexibility: the two-car garage he has pressed into service as a winery is jammed with tanks of various capacities, keeping batches separate through to bottling. Growers like Novak are given credit for the wines on the labels. "So they work really hard for us," Niles has found. "The quality that we get off these small vineyards is just incomparable."

It takes nimbleness like that to make it in the rough and tumble business of running a small winery, particularly when the winery is off the beaten path. Hunting Hawk is five kilometres (three miles) north of Armstrong on rural acreage that Russ Niles and Marnie, his wife, have owned for years. Gravel-topped Gulch Road, curving past the home they built for their family, is aptly named. The house, which now includes the winery, is at the bottom of a gully. The 1.2-hectare (three-acre) vineyard is on a hillside high above the house. Separating them is a ravine populated by deer and bears.

Until a high fence enclosed the vineyard, deer ate the young vegetation down to the tops of the grow tubes around each of the vines. "That just highlights one of the problems with growing grapes in essentially a wilderness area," Niles says. "In the fall of 2002, we had a bear eating grapes right out of the bins on the crushing platform. This is a natural bear highway down by the creek. We came long after the bears had staked it out, so we just have to learn to live with each other."

Niles was born in Victoria in 1957. His father was in the air force and the family moved frequently — Niles attended 14 different schools. "It really made me want to settle down," he says. "That's why I bought this piece of property." He built a career as a journalist and was the editor of the *Vernon Daily News* until that newspaper closed. He spent another five months editing an unsuccessful replacement, the failure of which triggered his decision to develop the winery. He whetted his interest as one of the minority investors in Vernon's Bella Vista winery until there was a falling-out with Bella Vista's controlling investor.

The idea to call his own winery Hunting Hawk dates from when, on assignment from the *Vernon Daily News*, he was touring a proposed Vernon area golf course. The developers considered calling it Emerald Dunes. Pointing to the hawks wheeling about the sky, Niles suggested something like Hunting Hawk would be stronger. The golf course became Predator Ridge and Niles used his idea for the winery. The labels are anchored by paintings of a red-tailed hawk and other local birds, reproductions of work by Vernon artist Allan Brooks, who had a studio there in the 1940s.

"I love wine," says Niles, a lively man who bounds around his winery as if he were on a pogo stick. "I love tasting wine, I love appreciating wine." He conceived the idea of his hillside vineyard after growing Pinot Blanc vines from cuttings taken from a neighbour's garden vineyard. Subsequently, he has planted Ortega, Perle of Csaba and Maréchal Foch, varieties that have proven themselves in north Okanagan vineyards. Niles has encouraged others in the Armstrong region to plant Foch, Hunting Hawk's bread and butter wine.

"I just happen to love the grape," he says. "It makes fabulous red wine. We are not trying to make something pretentious out of it. Foch fits in where Foch has traditionally fit in. It's an introductory red for people who are learning about wine, I think. It's a little simpler than Cabernet or Merlot or even Pinot Noir, but it has that lovely, soft, round, fruity taste and mouth feel that is not intimidating to people who are learning to drink red wine. For committed red wine drinkers, I call it pizza wine. It's casual."

Purchased grapes have enabled Hunting Hawk to make mainstream varietals such as Merlot, Pinot Noir and Chardonnay, beginning with the 2000 vintage. By the summer of 2003, he had bought barrels and was aging what he hopes will emerge as Hunting Hawk's big reds. Total winery production is about 1,000 cases and Niles intends to cap it at 1,500 cases. "My ambition is to have only one full-time employee."

In the winery's initial years, Niles has concentrated on producing value-priced wines (such as the $11.50 Maréchal Foch). In a move rare among small wineries, Hunting Hawk sells some wines in the large bag-in-box format sought by restaurants looking for wines to sell by the glass. The standard format is a 16-litre (3.5-gallon) box containing an airtight bag filled with wine. Niles happened across a large inventory of boxes that had been made, incorrectly, to 15 litres. He determined there was no rule against smaller boxes, provided the volume was disclosed. He snapped up the boxes and launched the new line, first with a blended white and later with popular varietal wines.

"It's a question of cash flow and establishing yourself in the market," he says. "There are 80 wineries all going after the same restaurants and lounges. This is something that's a little different. It's an all-B.C. bag-in-box wine at the same price as the imports that the big wineries sell. We don't make an awful lot of money from it but we do make money. It's a way of getting your foot in the door for your other products — and it works."

Hunting Hawk is the only Okanagan winery with a "white port." Again, the story shows Niles nimbly grabbing a passing chance. Beginning in 2001, he began buying grapes, including Pinot Blanc, from a small vineyard in Summerland. A delay in picking resulted in the Pinot Blanc becoming overripe. Niles asked Gary Strachan, his consultant, whether the wine should be blended away. Strachan suggested that they chaptalize it (add sugar). The result is a honeyed wine with about 16 per cent alcohol that has now joined red port (from Maréchal Foch) in Hunting Hawk's line.

"This should be fun," Niles says, gesturing around the winery. "It is obviously a serious business for me and my family. But when opportunities like white port come along, you should be open to them, and experiment with them, and see if you can create something that adds a little bit of colour to what you do and how you live your life."

INNISKILLIN OKANAGAN VINEYARDS

OPENED: 1980

Road 11 West, Oliver, BC, V0H 1T0

Telephone: 250-498-6663

Toll-free: 1-800-498-6211

Web site: www.inniskillin.com

Wine shop: Open daily 10 am – 5 pm May through October;
10 am – 3 pm weekdays only the rest of the year.

RECOMMENDED

- ✳ ZINFANDEL
- ✳ CABERNET SAUVIGNON DARK HORSE
- ✳ MERITAGE
- ✳ PINOT NOIR DARK HORSE
- ✳ VIDAL ICEWINE

THE ROMANTIC NAME GIVEN TO THIS WINERY'S NINE-HECTARE (23-ACRE) estate vineyard is Dark Horse. The inspiration came from local aboriginal pictograms that caught the attention of Donald Ziraldo, one of Inniskillin's founders. However, the name is also apt because of the winery's comparatively low profile, tucked away in one of the older Okanagan wineries. The new winery, promised shortly after Inniskillin bought this south Okanagan property in 1996, has not yet moved off the drawing board. In the current facility, Sandor Mayer, the winemaker, now jams barrels and tanks into every available corner of the 25-year-old building. The mild-mannered, uncomplaining Mayer, who planted the Dark Horse vineyard before it had a name, usually leaves the talking to his wines. These include one of the Okanagan's best Meritage red wines, and the Okanagan's first Zinfandel.

The vineyard, a hot, rock-strewn, south-facing slope on a plateau above the winery, was first planted in 1967 by a grower named Joseph Poturica. He and his sons launched Vinitera Estate Winery in 1979. In winery design, they were on the right track. The two-storey stuccoed winery's cellar is buried into the hillside for natural insulation. Eleven horizontal wine tanks were tunnelled into the earth. Quite probably the only horizontal tanks in any Canadian winery, they are still in use.

However, Vinitera's wines were rustic, in part because the vineyard was planted entirely to labrusca and hybrid vines. The struggling winery was taken over in 1982 by a Vancouver car dealer. The wines got no better. When the car dealer threw in the towel in 1987, Alan Tyabji, a former accountant at the Calona winery, took control of what he called Okanagan Vineyards. Tyabji took advantage of the 1988 government-financed program to uproot all the vines in the vineyard and then to replant entirely with premium varieties, including some of the south Okanagan's first Cabernet Sauvignon.

"Since we produced the first Cabernet Sauvignon in 1993, I don't remember a bad year," Mayer says. "Cabernet loves this place and I love Cabernet Sauvignon." Born in Hungary in 1958, he began making wine at 14 with his father before getting a university degree in winemaking and viticulture. He went to work with Hungary's major wine research institute and then moved on to a vineyard manager's job in the country's famed Lake Balaton region. When neither the salary nor the opportunities were adequate, he and his wife, Andrea (also a winemaker), slipped out of Hungary. After a year in Austria, an uncle in the Okanagan sponsored their immigration to Canada.

The timing was bad. There were almost no jobs in British Columbia's depressed wine industry. Mayer took what he could get. Tyabji hired him in the summer of 1990 to replant the vineyard. It was then an ugly tangle of wires, posts and dead vines. "Many times, I went up to the vineyard, looked at the big mess, scratched my head and went home," Mayer recounted later.

Typical of vineyard development at the time, a varietal smorgasbord was planted. Half the vineyard was dedicated to the three major Bordeaux reds, now blended in the Meritage, and Pinot Noir. The other half consisted of five different whites: Chardonnay, Riesling (now mostly for icewine), Pinot Blanc, Muscat Ottonel and just over half a hectare (1.5 acres) of Gewürztraminer. "In 1990, nobody had experience in what varieties could grow here," Mayer notes. "I know what I would plant if it were bare land now. But Alan Tyabji in 1990 had a very good idea to put all these big reds into the soil. Few people planted Cabernet Sauvignon in those days." In 1999 the Muscat was replaced with Merlot. "In the near future, I would like to replace the Gewürztraminer," Mayer adds. "It actually grows very well but we have this unique site to grow better reds. It almost seems to be a waste of acreage if we can grow Cabernet Sauvignon."

Mayer would consider replacing the Chardonnay and the Pinot Blanc in the vineyard with reds like Shiraz, although the Vincor group has given Inniskillin Okanagan a mandate to make Pinot Blanc. "It's hard to give up anything here, based on quality," Mayer laments. "It is hard to give up any variety."

The Okanagan Vineyards winery has been known as Inniskillin Okanagan since 1996, when it was acquired by Inniskillin Wines, Ontario's pioneering estate winery. Located near Niagara-on-the-Lake, Inniskillin was founded in 1975 by Donald Ziraldo and his Austrian-born winemaking partner, Karl Kaiser. A charismatic promoter of Canadian wines generally, Ziraldo wanted to establish Inniskillin as a producer in both major wine regions. After merging Inniskillin with what has become Vincor, Ziraldo made his Okanagan move. The first wines were made in the 1994 vintage with grapes from Inkameep Vineyards; Ziraldo's conception at the time was to develop a joint venture winery with the owners of Inkameep. That was shelved when Vincor, on behalf of Inniskillin, was able to buy Okanagan Vineyards.

Today, the Inniskillin Okanagan winery relies on nearby Vincor vineyards for the grapes to produce about two-thirds of Inniskillin Okanagan's annual output of 25,000 cases of wine. Dark Horse, a rugged property with so much sharply broken rock that it is difficult to cultivate the lean soil, accounts for the other third. Mayer maintains that it produces premium quality. "This vineyard is very significant," Mayer says with a certain paternal pride. "This is the cream of all the wines we make."

While the new winery promised by Inniskillin has not materialized so far, the existing winery has been updated. That includes temperature-controlled tanks, including temperature control on the famous horizontal tanks. "We learned how to use them," Mayer says. "You try to find the advantage in everything." One of the biggest changes has been in the barrel program. Where he formerly had 25 to 30 barrels, Mayer now has an inventory of about 400 barrels. Seventy per cent are American oak barrels built by a French barrel maker and used chiefly for aging the Meritage, the other Bordeaux reds and the Zinfandel. The latter variety was first made at Inniskillin Okanagan in the 2002 vintage from grapes grown on a Vincor vineyard on the Osoyoos Lake Bench.

Typically modest, Mayer says his first Zinfandel, only 250 cases, is "promising" when the quality, in fact, is a match for premium California Zinfandels. He is not trying to duplicate the California style but rather to capture the spice and vivid fruit reflecting the Okanagan's climate. It will take more than one vintage to work out how to grow the grape and how to finish the wine. "It is more difficult than Pinot Noir," he suggests. It is a variety that tends to produce too heavily and, when this happens, ripens the bunches unevenly. As a result, the quantity of fruit on vines must be thinned continually through the growing season. In the winery, Mayer still is figuring out what kind of barrels to use and for how long.

The marvel of it all, he chuckles, is that Zinfandel, a variety that thrives in long Mediterranean seasons, is growing in the Okanagan. He still remembers being told, when he was planting the Dark Horse Vineyard, that Cabernet Sauvignon would never ripen properly. "How life changes!" Mayer says. "The mentality and the thinking have changed. Never say never. Never say that anything is impossible."

JACKSON-TRIGGS VINTNERS

OPENED: 1981

38691 Highway 97 North, Oliver, BC, VOH 1T0

Telephone: 250-498-4961

Web site: www.jacksontriggswinery.com

Wine shop: Open 9 am – 4:30 pm Monday through Friday;
   closed weekends and holidays.

RECOMMENDED

* ICEWINES
  (INCLUDING SPARKLING ICEWINE)
* MERITAGE PROPRIETORS' GRAND RESERVE
* SHIRAZ PROPRIETORS' GRAND RESERVE
* MERLOT
* CHARDONNAY PROPRIETORS' GRAND RESERVE
* VIOGNIER
* DRY RIESLING
* SAUVIGNON BLANC

UNTIL 2000, WHEN JACKSON-TRIGGS CHIEF WINEMAKER BRUCE NICHOLSON made one of British Columbia's first Viognier wines, he favoured Chardonnay when he wanted to relax with a glass of wine. He still regards versatile Chardonnay as the world's greatest grape variety but the characters of Viognier — "orange blossoms, apricots and peaches" — have seduced his palate. "I try every Viognier I can find," he says of this exotic French white grape now being grown by Jackson-Triggs and only a few other Okanagan vintners.

It is likely that Nicholson is the envy of his peers, and not just because he has Viognier. He works with some of the Okanagan's best grapes. Jackson-Triggs, through parent Vincor International Inc., owns or leases about 405 hectares

(1,000 acres) of professionally managed vineyards, planted primarily since 1998 with an intelligent range of desirable varieties. When the sites were chosen, Australian vineyard expert Richard Smart, retained as an advisor, said that the vineyards would enjoy Canada's "most favourable" climate for growing grapes. In the 2003 harvest, those vineyards delivered the grapes that enabled Jackson-Triggs to make about 150,000 cases of wine. The major varieties include Merlot, Shiraz, Cabernet Sauvignon, Chardonnay and Sauvignon Blanc. (The Viognier vines yield only 1,100 cases of wine each year.)

Nicholson has some of the best winemaking tools in the Okanagan in this sprawling winery that was quadrupled in size in 2002. "It has all the bells and whistles of any of the top estate wineries in the world," says Donald Triggs, the chief executive of Vincor. Public tours of what is now one of Canada's largest wineries are not offered. That may be just as well, given the risk of losing visitors among the towering stainless steel tanks or in the cellar with about 3,500 barrels.

The Jackson-Triggs winery has evolved from the original winery built on this site in 1981 by T.G. Bright and Co., a predecessor company now folded into Vincor, Canada's largest wine producer. The Brights winery initially was controversial. The site was (and still is) leased from the Osoyoos Indian Band. In 1981, critics — including other First Nations bands — were incredulous at an alcohol-producing facility on reserve land. Sam Baptiste, the Osoyoos chief at the time and now manager of the band's Inkameep Vineyards, resisted the protests. The winery has become a leading employer on the reserve. Jackson-Triggs is also a partner at Nk'Mip Cellars, the band-owned winery that opened in 2002 at Osoyoos.

The largest Jackson-Triggs vineyards are on the Osoyoos Band's land as well. The 97-hectare (240-acre) Bull Pine vineyard on the sandy bench east of Osoyoos Lake is named for the region's native conifers. The winery's largest plantings of Merlot and Cabernet Sauvignon, done in 1998 and 1999, are in sun-baked Bull Pine. Nicholson also gets his Viognier from a three-hectare (7.5-acre) planting here. When a nearby 66 hectares (163 acres) were being planted in 1999, the crew encountered a family of bears that had wandered down from the mountains. Now called the Bear Cub vineyard, this includes Shiraz and the Okanagan's first Zinfandel. Some of the largest plantings of such white varieties as Sauvignon Blanc and Riesling are in new vineyards just southeast of Oliver: the 53-hectare (130-acre) Hayfields vineyard planted in 2001 and the 69-hectare (168-acre) Cherry Grove vineyard planted in 2002. The names reflect previous crops on these sites.

"Merlot is where we started to make our name in the red wine industry," Nicholson believes. This is the wine (although it is being pushed hard by his juicy Shiraz wines) that he is most likely to pour for himself when he is not relaxing with Viognier. Born in 1958 in Niagara Falls, he is a chemical engineer who, after making wine at home, offered to work without salary at Inniskillin just to get his foot in the door. Before Inniskillin responded, he was hired in 1986 to work in the laboratory at the Château-Gai winery in Niagara Falls. The following year, he was transferred to Casabello, Château-Gai's sister winery in Penticton. Both wineries disappeared into the merger that produced Vincor; and when Casabello closed in 1994, Nicholson moved to the Jackson-Triggs winery.

With good grapes and an experienced cellar team, Jackson-Triggs has begun to release wines that are consistent award winners. This is especially so for Nicholson's icewines, which have taken the top trophies both in Canada and at international events in London and in Bordeaux. "More [awards] have come out of this building than anywhere else in Canada," Nicholson believes. He attributes that to using only Riesling grapes, to paying close attention to the balance of sweetness and acidity — and to his personal winemaking technique, kept close to his vest. "I don't usually disclose it," he says quietly.

For all the awards he has won, Nicholson remains a winemaker who pushes himself in the pursuit of perfection. "Somebody asked me what my goal is," he says. "When I go into competitions, I want that wine to stand out and I want it better the next year. I keep setting the bar higher for myself. And if the *Wine Spectator* gives me 100 on every wine, I'm going to look for 105. It may not be realistic but I am going to do that."

KETTLE VALLEY WINERY

OPENED: 1996

2988 Hayman Road, Naramata, BC, V0H 1N0

Telephone: 250-496-5898

E-mail: kettlevalleywinery@telus.net

Wine shop: Open daily 11 am – 5 pm May through mid-October, or by appointment.
Groups of more than eight should book an appointment.

RECOMMENDED

* ✹ MALBEC
* ✹ PINOT NOIR RESERVE
* ✹ OLD MAIN RED
* ✳ CABERNET SAUVIGNON
* ✳ MERLOT
* ✳ PINOT NOIR HAYMAN VINEYARD
* ✳ ROCK OVEN RED
* ✳ SCHÖNBURGER
* ✳ SHIRAZ
* ✳ PINOT GRIS
* ✸ GEWURZTRAMINER
* CHARDONNAY

EXCEPT FOR ICEWINE PRODUCERS, FEW WINERIES HARVEST GRAPES LATER than Kettle Valley. In several recent vintages, the Bordeaux reds in the winery's Old Main Vineyard just south of Naramata were not picked until November. By leaving its grapes on the vines so long, Kettle Valley is squeezing every last calorie from the season to make big, bold wines. That is the house style of this boutique producer whose name is taken from the storied rail line that operated in the British Columbia Interior between 1910 and 1973.

"Our wines certainly reflect our taste in the wines we enjoy drinking," says Bob Ferguson who operates the winery with brother-in-law, Tim Watts. "Our style has always been bigger, robust, ripe, full-bodied wines because that is the style we enjoy. The luxury of being small is that you can afford to do that. We have certainly tried to make wines that are very intense and full-bodied. That's our style and our mark."

They came to winemaking in 1980 as amateurs. Ferguson was born in Scotland in 1950, grew up in Canada and became a chartered accountant in Vancouver. Watts, eight years younger, was born in Victoria and became a geologist. After marrying sisters, they discovered a shared interest in winemaking and started buying Okanagan grapes. In 1985 Watts and his wife bought a home near Naramata and put in a test block of Chardonnay and Pinot Noir, ignoring warnings that these varieties could not be ripened there. The grapes did ripen and, starting in 1989, the partners began acquiring vineyard acreage and phasing down their former careers. The Old Main Vineyard was planted in 1990 to Cabernet Sauvignon, Cabernet Franc and Merlot, one of the earliest plantings of Bordeaux varieties on the Naramata Bench. Today, Ferguson and Watts own or manage about eight hectares (20 acres) near the winery and would buy more if they could.

The Naramata Bench, influenced by the proximity of the lake, has proven itself for growing fine grapes. "Our Old Main Vineyard ripens Cabernet Sauvignon on a north-facing slope before Pinot Noir on a south-facing slope here," Watts says. "Here" is the vineyard at the winery, a short walk away from Old Main. "It comes down to the lake," Ferguson explains. Old Main is on a picturesque bench overlooking Okanagan Lake. Most of Kettle Valley's other vineyards are also close to the lake; one planting of Gewürztraminer is so close that one can stand among the vines and toss stones into the water.

Ferguson and Watts grow grapes to demanding standards. The average yield from their vines is perhaps half of what could be grown because that is what must be done to grow bold wines. "We are prepared to take less crop," Ferguson explains. "We are not farming to make money. We're farming to grow grapes to make wine and we're going to make our money from winemaking." His shrewd accountant's reckoning tells him that Kettle Valley's smaller volumes of interesting wines can be sold at premium prices. "It's a lot easier to sell a limited quantity of wine at $25 than an extensive quantity at that same price," he maintains.

The signature wines here have been the reds. The winery opened its tasting room in 1996 (in what formerly was a three-car garage) with a Pinot Noir from 1992 and a Chardonnay from 1994. Boldly Burgundian, that Pinot Noir remained vibrantly alive a decade later, displaying the long-lived style of Kettle Valley wines. The reds are seldom released until they have spent at least two years in barrels and bottles. As an example, the winery's 2000 Merlot spent 21 months in barrels before being bottled for release early in 2003.

The winery released 264 cases of that Merlot. That is a typically small volume of individual wines. Kettle Valley's total production reached 4,000 cases in 2001 and is not planned to exceed 5,000 cases, the maximum the partners believe they can make without taking on staff. "We want to be hands-on," Ferguson says. "We want to be involved in the process. The whole idea of being involved in the wine business was to *do it*, not to give the good jobs to someone else while you turn out to be the management."

They make numerous small lots of highly individual wines with labels drawing on the railway heritage. The partners once released a Chardonnay as Caboose. An occasional blend of red varieties is called Brakeman's Select. A late harvest dessert wine from Pinot Noir, also made only occasionally, is called Derailer. Since the 1997 vintage, the winery's reserve blend of Cabernet Sauvignon, Cabernet Franc and Merlot has been called Old Main Red. The partners, who like blending wines, have recently included Petit Verdot and Malbec in the blend.

Ferguson and Watts also keep wines separate to show off the qualities of individual vineyards. Small wineries have this flexibility, Watts says. "You can take a very small batch and isolate it and have something really wonderful. In a large winery, you don't have the ability to do that." As an example, the winery's Hayman Vineyard Pinot Noir can be dark, brooding and long-lived, whereas Pinot Noir from the nearby Foxtrot Vineyard, under contract to Kettle Valley, yields a lively wine with bright notes of cherries and raspberry.

Besides being flexible, they are fast on their feet when opportunity knocks. "The 2000 Malbec went straight into our Old Main Red, along with Petit Verdot," Ferguson says "But in 2001 we held a little Malbec out because a lot of restaurants in Vancouver were quite keen to see a Malbec from British Columbia. It was never our intention to release a Malbec — it was always intended that it be blended. But there's been a lot of interest in the variety."

This same pragmatism has led Kettle Valley to expand its range of whites beyond Chardonnay, taking advantage of their own grapes and grapes from contracted growers. The winery makes an intense Pinot Gris, a rich Gewürztraminer and a unique dry Schönburger. "One of the vineyards [with Gewürztraminer] is right on the lake," Watts says. "We're hoping that will give us a lot of fruit character." The result is a powerful wine made in the style of Kettle Valley's reds. "The style we are doing it in is pretty consistent with the style in which we do all of our wines. Gewürztraminer, Chardonnay, Sauvignon Blanc, Sémillon — they all have a lot of skin contact. In the vineyard, we make sure there is lots of sun on the fruit. We make sure those skins have a lot of flavour and a lot of colour as well. We give it some skin contact time. Essentially, all the flavour we can get into those grapes comes out in the wine. They are not crisp and fruity, they are great big complex whites."

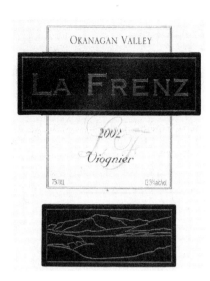

LA FRENZ WINERY

OPENED: 2000

740 Naramata Road, Penticton, BC, V2A 8T5
Telephone: 250-492-6690
Web site: www.lafrenzwinery.com
Wine shop: Open daily 11 am – 5 pm May through October; or by appointment.

RECOMMENDED

* ❋ CHARDONNAY
* ❋ SHIRAZ
* ❋ SÉMILLON
* ❋ PINOT GRIS
* ❋ VIOGNIER
* ❋ ALEXANDRIA
    MONTAGE

ONCE WHILE INTERVIEWING WINEMAKER JEFF MARTIN, I REPEATED THE CLICHÉ, good wine is grown in the vineyard. With a touch of impatience, he snapped: "Winemakers also make wine!" During his decade in the Okanagan, the Australian-trained Martin has often produced good wines in situations where he had little to do with the vineyard. In several vintages, he made the icewine for Paradise Ranch, including that winery's acclaimed 2000 wines. From time to time, he consulted for other wineries, including Stag's Hollow Vineyards before the owners there employed a full-time winemaker in 2001. Sometimes it is hard for his employers to define Martin's contribution. "The wine just gets better when he arrives," suggests Linda Pruegger, one of the owners of Stag's Hollow.

At La Frenz, Martin applies the winemaker's art to purchased grapes for a significant portion of La Frenz's annual production, now more than 3,600 cases. And he runs his own vineyard. In 2002, Jeff and Niva, his wife, planted the 2.5-hectare (six-acre) vineyard, converting a former apple orchard that fronts strategically on busy Naramata Road. The varieties are Merlot, Shiraz and Viognier.

In 1977, when he was 20, Martin began working as a winemaker trainee at the big McWilliams winery in his hometown of Griffith in New South Wales. The winery helped finance their promising recruit's degree in science at Charles Sturt University. By 1989, Martin was the chief winemaker at the McWilliams premium winery. He came to the Okanagan in 1994, where he did five vintages at Quails' Gate Estate Winery before going back to Australia to start his own winery. "I'd reached the point where I figured it was time to do something for myself," he says.

He and Niva were going to risk their life's savings on a winery. "If I was going to put all those dollars into something, where was I going to do it?" he asked himself. "Where was I going to be likely to succeed?" The surprising answer was not in Australia's overheated wine industry. With 1,800 wineries already open, it was not likely another one would attract much notice. "In my 20-some years in the industry," Martin admitted to himself, "it would have been the worst time to start a winery back there." It was not only that. He did not like the way the Australian wine industry had developed. "It's all business … wine made to a price point," he says. "There's no passion in it."

Jeff and Niva returned to the Okanagan, purchasing grapes in 1999 to make the wines that were released under the La Frenz label the following year. To husband their finances, the Martins made several vintages at the nearby Poplar Grove winery, marketing them under the Poplar Grove license. "My resources have to go as far as possible," Martin says. "I keep it pretty lean." La Frenz opened its own tasting room in the summer of 2002 after the winery was built.

There is a story behind the winery's name. It is not, as is sometimes thought, that it was inspired by a bibulous evening drinking Foster's with "la friends." It is, in fact, the surname of Martin's paternal grandfather, an old family name from the Schleswig-Holstein region of northern Germany. But his parents divorced when he was a teenager and Martin grew up using his mother's maiden name.

Martin's winemaking repertoire is broad. He is adept, for example, in the use of barrels, fermenting such varieties as Chardonnay in barrels and often letting reds do their final "fizz" in the barrel. The gentle aeration that wine undergoes in barrels is important to the development of texture as well as taste. Australian wineries often use chips or blocks of wood to impart oak flavours to inexpensive wines. "You can use bags of oak chips," he says. "But you really can't replicate barrels yet." Martin has even learned some of the cooper's trade. He knows how to refresh used barrels by taking them apart and shaving the inner sides of the staves to expose fresh oak.

That the winemaker is pivotal, as Martin will remind you, was evident when he made his first vintage at Quails' Gate and created that winery's Old Vines Foch. The vineyard at Quails' Gate was being replanted with premium varieties when

Martin arrived. However, there were still a few blocks of 25-year-old vines, including the workhorse red hybrid Maréchal Foch. Most Okanagan vineyards had removed the variety in favour of Bordeaux reds. Martin suggested treating the Foch as he would an old block of Shiraz in Australia, sharply reducing the crop on the vines to achieve superbly ripe and intensely flavoured fruit. The wine, dense and plummy, was aged in American oak, like much Australian Shiraz. Released at double the usual price for Foch, it became an instant cult wine. Other Canadian wineries copied the style and the reputation of Foch was salvaged.

There could also be a cult wine in the future at La Frenz. In their vineyard, the Martins planted Schönburger, an aromatic German white. It seems an odd choice since La Frenz already has a solid following for Chardonnay, Sémillon and Pinot Gris. Martin's intent is to make a fortified wine with Schönburger, somewhat in the style of the intriguing fortified Muscat made in Australia. In other words, a wine to show off the artistry of the winemaker.

LAKE BREEZE VINEYARDS

OPENED: 1996

930 Sammet Road, Naramata, BC, V0H 1N0

Telephone: 250-496-5659

Web site: www.lakebreezewinery.ca

Wine shop: Open daily 10 am – 5 pm except weekends only in April.

Restaurant: The Patio serves lunch on weekends in June, daily July through
  mid-September.

RECOMMENDED

* PINOT BLANC
* SÉMILLON
* PINOTAGE
* PINOT GRIS
* MERLOT
* EHRENFELSER
* LATE HARVEST PINOT NOIR
  MERLOT
  CABERNET FRANC
  ZEPHYR BRUT

BEFORE THEY GOT INTO THE BUSINESS, THE OWNERS OF LAKE BREEZE WERE
financial executives in Alberta who enjoyed touring wineries on their time off.
There has not been much time for such recreation since they took over Lake
Breeze in the fall of 2001.

"It's hard work," Gary Reynolds, the managing partner, has found. "When
you get into something that is both your love and your hobby, you don't have
a lot of time left to enjoy your hobby anymore!" Most people who have
changed careers to follow the wine passion have made the same discovery. The

two previous owners of Lake Breeze moved on. The current owners see themselves here for the long haul because, as Reynolds puts it, "we get to be part of a dynamic and interesting industry, and to live in a beautiful place. We are not in it for the money."

Even though ownership at Lake Breeze changed three times in the winery's first six years, the wines have been reliable. The explanation: from the beginning, the winemaker has been Garron Elmes, a professionally trained young vintner from South Africa. "He is creative and consistent," Reynolds believes.

The winery was opened in 1996 by Paul and Vereena Moser, a Swiss-born couple who bought a Naramata Bench vineyard in 1994 after leaving South Africa, where Paul had run several manufacturing businesses. He built a white stucco winery among the vines in a design mirroring the style of South Africa's small Cape wineries. Elmes, born in 1972 in Capetown, was a recent graduate from an agricultural college at Stellenbosch when he was recruited to make the initial vintage at Lake Breeze in 1995.

The winery was sold in 1998. "I am an entrepreneur," Moser explained to one journalist. "Once business becomes administration, I become bored with it." However, two years before selling, Moser made a decision that left the imprint of South Africa on Lake Breeze. He planted about 40 vines of Pinotage, the red grape that was created in South Africa in 1925 and, even today, is seldom grown anywhere else. Reynolds has found some room in the vineyard to increase the planting slightly but, even at full production, Lake Breeze never expects to make more than 100 cases of Pinotage each year.

The new owners of Lake Breeze, Wayne and Joanne Finn, had been running a helicopter company on Vancouver Island. They were drawn to the wine business after numerous vacations in California's wine country. But after operating Lake Breeze for a couple of years, the Finns put the winery into the hands of a real estate agent in the spring of 2001. That coincided with another vacation in wine country by Gary Reynolds and his partners. They had vineyard property in mind and found the picturesque Lake Breeze winery irresistible.

"We're all financial folks," says Reynolds. A chartered accountant who was born in Montreal in 1955, Reynolds was handling finances for Edmonton's public schools. Tracey Ball, his wife, is the chief financial officer of the Canadian Western Bank. Drew MacIntyre is an investment banker in Calgary and his wife, Barbara, is also an accountant. "We should be able to figure things out," laughs Reynolds. He is the only one of the partners to have quit his former career because Lake Breeze, at an annual production of 4,000 cases, is not yet large enough to support two families. "I think we know this is not a get-rich adventure," he says.

Since taking over in the fall of 2001, Reynolds and his partners set out to double the winery's capacity, beginning with adding a good-sized tank cellar with high ceilings and a well-equipped laboratory. The original cellar, now the barrel room, was so compact that custom-made square stainless steel tanks, not the usual round ones, had been installed so that more could be jammed into the tight space. When the partners first looked at the winery, Elmes told them what was obvious even to a layperson. "We were at our absolute peak here," Reynolds says. Elmes had had to set up his laboratory in the owners' house and wine was being stored in the garage. Now, there are two cellars and a tasting room around a shaded patio, all still in the original Cape style.

At any time, Lake Breeze offers at least a dozen different wines. Reynolds wonders whether Lake Breeze has too many varietals for a small winery. However, he is not about to get rid of any. "In a small winery with a lot of its sales from the walk-in trade, when there are many varieties, someone always walks away with something because there is something for everybody," he says. The white wines here include Chardonnay, Pinot Gris, Pinot Blanc, Gewürztraminer and Ehrenfelser.

Lake Breeze also makes one of the few examples of Sémillon in the Okanagan, a Bordeaux white variety not as well known as it should be because it is usually blended with Sauvignon Blanc. On its own, Sémillon can be full-textured with a refreshing grapefruit tang. "Some people find it over the top" Reynolds says. "There are some really robust fruit flavours in there. We continue to make it. It's got a great place in the vineyard. But there is only so much call for it. Who knows? Maybe in the future, it will be the rage." Like Gewürztraminer, a current rage. "We can't make enough of it."

The Lake Breeze reds include Merlot, Cabernet Franc, Pinot Noir and Pinotage, all of them barrel-aged. Garron Elmes argues that good reds cannot be made without the use of oak barrels. He was not entirely pleased with his 1995 reds, which were not oak-aged because barrels had not arrived for that vintage. Now, with a dedicated cellar for barrels, Elmes has begun working on what Reynolds calls a "serious" red wine. "Not that we don't make one now," Reynolds adds quickly. "Our Merlot is popular but we don't make enough of it."

By "serious" he means a Bordeaux blend that would incorporate some Cabernet Sauvignon from purchased grapes, complementing the Merlot and Cabernet Franc already grown at Lake Breeze. "Once we see the fruit, we'll decide," Reynolds says. "It wouldn't be a straight Cabernet Sauvignon, nor a Cabernet-Merlot, but something more interesting. And aged longer. Right now we can only really afford to keep the red wine for two years and release it in its second year because of barrel space and other economics."

LANG VINEYARDS

OPENED: 1990

2493 Gammon Road, Naramata, BC, V0H 1N0

Telephone: 250-496-5987

Web site: www.langvineyards.com

Wine shop: Open 10 am – 5 pm from May 1 to October 15; and by appointment.

RECOMMENDED

- ❁ SELECT LATE HARVEST RIESLING
- ❋ LATE HARVEST RIESLING
- ❋ LIMITED EDITION VIOGNIER
- ❋ LATE HARVEST PINOT BLANC
- ❋ PINOT AUXERROIS BRUT "LD"
  GRAND PINOT WHITE
  GRAND PINOT RED
  GEWÜRZTRAMINER
  MARÉCHAL FOCH

EARLY IN HIS CAREER AS A WINERY OWNER, GÜNTHER LANG LED ME through a tasting that ended with an unusual Pinot Auxerrois. Made from very ripe grapes and fermented on the skins, it was a honeyed, bronze-tinted wine. "I'd like to make a wine that nobody else has," he confided. He realized his ambition in 1998 when Lang Vineyards launched its Original Canadian Maple wines, a trademarked range of red, white and sparkling wines that now comprise half of this winery's sales — and most of its exports to Asia. All the wines are flavoured with maple syrup.

Lang grew up far from the sugar maple trees of eastern Canada. Born in 1951 in Stuttgart, he was training as a manager with Mercedes-Benz when he and his wife, Kristina, were charmed by the Okanagan during a 1979 vacation. A decisive man, Lang bought a small vineyard near Naramata. In short order, his entire family — including his parents, his brother and Kristina's parents — also immigrated to Canada.

Lang had not grown up on a vineyard and he had not really planned to open a winery. "I looked at everything that was for sale in the Okanagan," he recalls. "I just bought the vineyard because I fell in love with the place. It was an older vineyard, on the market for two years. Nobody was interested in it at all. It was the best buy: we got two lots and a great view. I paid $129,000 at the time for nine and a half acres together. The house I designed and built."

The Langs discovered they liked growing grapes but, with a European palate, they concluded that there was little prospect of making good wine with hybrid grapes. They quickly replanted more than half of the vineyard with Riesling, Bacchus and Pinot Meunier and grafted some hybrid vines to Pinot Noir. A little bit of Maréchal Foch was retained. Lang teamed up with several other growers in 1985, pressing the provincial government to grant licenses to small vineyards. Lang Vineyards opened in 1990, one of the first of what were called farmgate wineries because it was intended they would sell wines mostly from their farms.

Modern and well-equipped, the Lang winery has the fingerprints of the Mercedes mentality all over it. The sterile cleanliness of the bottling line would compare with a hospital. Throughout the winery, the equipment is gleaming stainless steel. "No small winery has equipment like this place has," says Ross Mirko, who took over as winemaker in 2002. The tasting room, if somewhat modest in size when a tour bus unloads its passengers, is neatly organized and invitingly cool during hot Okanagan summers.

In the initial years, Lang made the wines himself, having used the decade before the winery opened to educate himself. To give himself more time to create and sell products unique to the winery, Lang employed German-trained Petra Koeller in 1997 as winemaker. When she went on maternity leave five years later, Mirko took over. Trained in New Zealand, Mirko has worked at or consulted with several Okanagan wineries as well as creating wines under his own Calliope label. Mirko has been careful to protect the Lang style, which typically means no oak and, in many wines, a touch of sweetness. For example, the winery produces about 700 cases of off-dry Maréchal Foch each year, quite distinct from any other Okanagan example of this varietal. It is always the fastest-selling wine in the tasting room. Lang has a strong following for its style and there is no reason to change what works.

Lang is always quick to jump on opportunity. He scored a big success when he began putting icewine, first made in 1992, in cobalt blue bottles so popular that customers even bought empty bottles. Icewine led to the Original Canadian Maple wines. "I asked myself how we would serve the Asian markets in years when we could not make icewine," he recalls. His idea was to sweeten wines with maple syrup, an iconic Canadian confection better known than icewine.

This product line was launched in 1998. The red is a blend of three varieties: Merlot, Pinot Noir and Pinot Meunier. The base wine is first fully fermented to about 12 per cent alcohol before being diluted with enough maple syrup to achieve the desired flavour and sweetness. The alcohol in the final wines is around 9 to 10 per cent. The amount of maple syrup in each bottle "is a little bit of a secret." It is roughly between 13 and 17 per cent pure maple syrup, he confides.

The white version is slightly sweeter than the red. "With the same content as the red, it would not be good enough," he has found. "It needs more maple syrup." The base for the white usually is Auxerrois because the variety is more neutral than either Riesling or Pinot Gris. "We tried with Riesling but the combination was like diesel," Lang says.

The Canadian Maple Brut was conceived when Lang made a cuvée of sparkling Auxerrois as a millennium wine and used maple syrup as the dosage. It continued to sell after the turn of the century. "We have a high number of people buying the Maple Brut or the maple wine because they are so different," Lang says. "They cannot find something similar."

It seems that whenever Günter Lang has an idea, it stays in his line. In 2002, the winery had 34 wines on its sales list. "We have many products for a small winery but that big list of products shows our optimism," he suggests. "It means we are very active. We are not just trying to make the money with four or five products. We always try to find something new again." One development resulted in a luxury white blend, the winery's 2000 Grand Pinot. It is a full-bodied white combining four grapes: Pinot Auxerrois, Pinot Blanc, Pinot Gris and Pinot Meunier. "This was my own idea," he says of the Grand Pinot. "First, you start out as a very conservative thinker — you make only varietal wines. After a certain time, you think 'I'm limited — why should I not break out and make a blend?'" His objective was to make a wine so versatile it can accompany almost any food. "It is what you give someone who does not want red wine," he explains. A red Grand Pinot, a blend of Pinot Noir and Pinot Meunier, was released from the 2002 vintage.

There is, however, a limit to his ambition. With a production of about 8,000 cases, Lang Vineyards has reached a comfortable size for the owner. "We have no plans to go too big because we are limited with our property," he says. "To become very large — that is really not our goal."

LARCH HILLS VINEYARD AND WINERY

OPENED: 1997

110 Timms Road, Salmon Arm, BC, V1E 2W5
Telephone: 250-832-0155
Web site: www.larchhillswinery.com
Wine shop: Open daily noon – 5 pm from April 1 to October 31; or by appointment.

RECOMMENDED

- ❋ ORTEGA DRY
- ❋ ORTEGA LATE HARVEST
- ❋ TAMARACK ROSÉ
- ❋ SIEGERREBE DRY
- ❋ SIEGERREBE LATE HARVEST
- ✸ GEWÜRZTRAMINER
- ✸ MADELEINE ANGEVINE

ANYONE LESS OBSTINATE THAT HANS NEVRKLA WOULD NEVER HAVE planted grapes here. Larch Hills is one of the most northern, and certainly British Columbia's highest, vineyard at 700 metres (2,300 feet) above sea level. The Salmon Arm district was never included in the landmark 1984 atlas of British Columbia grape-growing areas. After buying the forested property in 1987, Nevrkla sought professional advice about developing a vineyard. The provincial grape expert just shook his head. "Everybody thought it was such a totally lost, hopeless case," Nevrkla found when he sought additional opinions.

"But I already had the land and it was something I was going to do, regardless," Nevrkla recalls. In a test plot, he planted a few example of many varieties and figured out by 1992 what would grow and what would not. The biggest disappointment was Riesling; the fruit persisted in ripening only to "green bullets" and the vines were yanked. He determined that three whites, Ortega, Madeleine Angevine and Siegerrebe, would ripen on his mountainside slope. Nevrkla gradually developed a 2.6-hectare (6.5-acre) vineyard and began making wine commercially in 1995. He and Hazel, his wife, opened the winery in 1997, soon confounding the sceptics by succeeding. "After that, all kinds of people told me they always knew it would work here," Nevrkla chuckles over a spicy glass of Ortega, the winery's signature white.

Born in Vienna in 1946, the ruddy-cheeked Nevrkla — pronounced *never claw* — began making wine at home after he and Hazel, who is British, moved to Canada in 1970. In Calgary, where they lived then, he became a winemaking instructor at the local school board. The Nevrklas came to know the Okanagan from buying grapes there, moving in 1987 to a 29.5-hectare (73-acre) property south of Salmon Arm. The site is not in the Okanagan Valley but, from the upper part of the Larch Hills vineyard, one can see the northern beginning of the valley.

For several years, Larch Hills was the only winery in the Salmon Arm area. Nevrkla discovered that he barely registered on the industry's radar screen. "You know those wine route signs with the clusters of grapes?" he asks. "Well, when I joined the [British Columbia] Wine Institute, the first thing I thought would happen is that they'd put some signs up for me. They said there was no money in the budget for a sign for me. Things went downhill from there." He dropped out of the institute in 1999, becoming a founding member of the rival Association of British Columbia Winegrowers. The decision meant the removal of the VQA symbol from his wines. He says it never hurt his sales, 70 per cent of which are made right in the cozy Larch Hills wine shop. "If I get five serious inquiries about VQA in one season, it's a lot!" he says. "People either already know the story and don't ask, or they don't care one way or the other." The highways department has erected a sign on Highway 97A, south of Salmon Arm, directing visitors to Larch Hills's otherwise secluded location.

The northern location of this vineyard determines the style of its wines: crisp and fresh, with piquant acidity and moderate alcohol levels. "Alcohol is not everything," Nevrkla says. "The 1997 Ortega was only 9.4 per cent alcohol and it was a beautiful wine. The 2000 Ortega is only 10 per cent. We find that we can make very nice wines in that range. That way, you can drink another half a bottle without having to worry." Only Siegerrebe, a variety that was bred to be a sugar factory, provides the exception. The dry version that Nevrkla made in 2001 reached almost 14 per cent. In most vintages, however, Larch Hills makes a plump, moderate-alcohol late harvest Siegerrebe rather than fermenting it to dryness.

The wines of Larch Hills also include Pinot Noir, Merlot and Gewürztraminer, all made with grapes contracted from growers near Westbank. "They won't work here, or work very poorly," Nevrkla says of those varieties. "If it got really hot here, you could grow a Pinot Noir, but I'd rather grow a grape that works great here."

Nevrkla is counting on Agria to become the estate-grown red at Larch Hills. He started slowly with a test planting in the mid-1990s of less than 100 vines. He was not being excessively cautious; rather, vine material was difficult to find. "We almost had to beg on our knees for the cuttings," he recalls. Some were obtained from Cherry Point Vineyards on Vancouver Island, the first winery in British Columbia to release an Agria (from the 1998 vintage). Other cuttings came from the plant health centre at Saanich and from a small nursery in Salmon Arm. Once the vines were established, however, they provided all the additional cuttings he needed for extending the rows of Agria in his vineyard.

Developed in Hungary, early-ripening Agria produces intensely dark-coloured grapes. "When we pick it, I can tell who has been eating the grapes because their teeth are blue," Nevrkla says. He started making trial wines, typically in 50-litre (11-gallon) lots, in 2000, to determine the best style for what can be a robust red. The vineyard's first significant harvest is expected in 2005. "I know I have three more years to come up with the perfect Agria," he said in 2002.

While there is room on his sun-drenched slope for more vines, Larch Hills is about as big as Hans and Hazel want it to be. The winery was designed to produce between 2,000 and 2,500 cases of wine a year. "We have basically reached that point now," he says. "It makes us a living. We sell out virtually every year, so marketing is not a major headache. I would hate to sit on 10,000 cases and see them get older every year and have to really think of how to get rid of them. But 2,500 cases almost sell themselves. Once you get much beyond that, you have to hire more people. I kind of like to actually get my hands dirty with the stuff rather than tell somebody else to do it."

LAUGHING STOCK VINEYARDS

OPENING: PROPOSED FOR 2006

1548 Naramata Road, Penticton, BC, V2A 8T7
Telephone: 250-493-8466

WHEN DAVID ENNS DECIDED TO MAKE WINE, HE JUMPED IN WITH BOTH feet, buying expensive equipment and the best Cabernet Sauvignon he could find in Washington. Of course, he did not jump into the grapes literally, having bought a pricey Italian crusher for the job. His total commitment, beginning with the very first wine he made in 2001, suggests that interesting wines should be expected from his vineyard on Naramata Road.

Born in Edmonton in 1957, Enns is the son of a peripatetic air force officer. The Enns family experienced a typically nomadic military career, with postings across Canada and in Europe. "I got to see the world before I was a teenager," Enns says.

In the 1970s, his family finally set down roots in Kelowna, where Enns went to high school. Ironically, when Enns and his wife, Cynthia, were looking for a place to establish a winery, they considered Europe before the Okanagan. He remembered the mediocrity of the wines of the Okanagan when he was growing up there. "We did not take the wines seriously," he admits.

Having left Kelowna after high school, Enns had not tasted the dramatic improvement in the Okanagan's wine quality in the 1990s. In any event, he was building a career in the investment business. He started in retail banking and moved into the mutual fund business. In 1999 he set up Credo Consulting Inc. in Vancouver, to provide research and advice to financial institutions on packaging and selling mutual funds and other financial instruments. Cynthia Enns, who has a master's degree in business administration and expertise in marketing and advertising, is his partner, as she is in the winery. They decided to call the winery

Laughing Stock in riposte to stock market friends who have teased them about their second career in wine.

"She has always been passionate about wine," Enns says about his wife. "When we first met, our wine cellar totalled half a dozen or 10 bottles. And we built it over the last few years to seven or eight hundred." They collected primarily wines from Europe or from the west coast of the United States, including Washington. Enns often took advice from John Clerides, the operator of an independent wine shop in Vancouver called Marquis Wine Cellars.

In 2000, David Enns accompanied the wine merchant on a tasting and buying tour of Washington wineries. He was thoroughly smitten by the passion and commitment of the boutique winery operators. "That sort of opened my eyes," he recalls. "Anybody with some passion can get into the business. You don't need to have a winery that's been passed down six generations."

Enns also discovered that Clerides did not dabble at winemaking. "So I challenged him: 'How could you ever be polished and finished and a master of wine if you have never made wine yourself?'" Enns remembers. In the vintage of 2001, they bought 454 kilograms (1,000 pounds) of Cabernet Sauvignon from the Seven Hills Vineyard at Walla Walla, a renowned appellation producing some of Washington's greatest red wines. As Enns tells the story, Clerides lost interest in making wine by the time they had driven to Walla Walla, loaded the grapes and returned to Vancouver in one extremely long day.

But Enns was fully engaged now, calling on his contacts in the wine business for some basic advice on what to do with the grapes. "After I picked up the grapes from Washington, I went home and, much to the chagrin of my wife, I bought a small Italian crusher-destemmer with a little motor. I bought a brand-new French oak barrel for $1,300. I bought a 300-litre stainless steel floating top fermenter. I set up a mini-level winery in my friend's garage. I wanted to see if you bought the best, could you make the best?" The wine was promising enough that Enns, who took a couple of years of science in college, purchased Washington-grown Syrah in 2002 and began jetting to the University of California at Davis for winemaking courses.

Enns and his wife began looking at wineries in France and Portugal. "My goal was a small, family-run winery making handcrafted, age worthy, premium and super premium wines, with a 5,000-case capacity," he says. Then at wine festivals, they discovered how much Okanagan wines had improved since the 1970s. They gave themselves two years to find a suitable vineyard in the valley. Three months into the two-year plan, they found 2.2 hectares (5.4 acres) on Naramata Road in March 2003. It was already planted to 1.2 hectares (three acres) of Merlot that yielded its first crop that fall. A warm site with a southwestern exposure, the vineyard, which they call Hobo Bluff, is sandwiched between the Naramata Road and former Kettle Valley Railway line. The spot is called Hobo Bluff because, in the 1930s, it was a campsite used by the transients that the police had chased from Penticton.

A portable business, Credo Consulting quickly moved to the Okanagan once Enns had a vineyard to manage. A consultant himself, he retained consultant

Valerie Tait for viticultural guidance. She quickly disabused him of the notion that good wine is made primarily in the winery, a fairly common misconception among home winemakers. "Val taught us very early on that there are more decisions made in the vineyard than there are in the winery," Enns said late in 2003. "I challenged her at first, but having gone through a growing season, I understand."

It was through Tait that Enns established a mentoring relationship with Ian Sutherland, whose highly regarded Poplar Grove winery is near Laughing Stock. Under Sutherland's able tutelage, Enns made about 500 cases in 2003. In effect, Enns arranged to apprentice for at least three vintages with one of the Okanagan's best self-taught winemakers. "I didn't want to hire a fly-in consultant," Enns says. "I really wanted to learn the industry from the ground up." The 2003 wines, a Merlot and a promising blend of Cabernet and Merlot, are planned for the winery's first release in 2006. Enns intends to keep his wines tightly focussed: a few reds from Bordeaux grape varieties and whites from Pinot Gris and Chardonnay.

"We've learned so much so quickly," Enns summed up his first season as a commercial vintner. "You can't learn unless you do it. You can't read winemaking — you need to do winemaking and grape growing. You can learn lots from a textbook but you cannot master it. I don't need to know everything about winemaking and grape growing. I just need to know everything about winemaking and grape growing in Naramata."

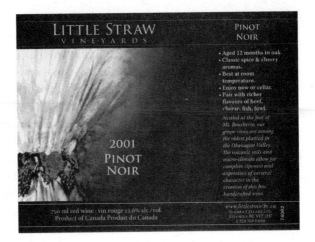

LITTLE STRAW VINEYARDS

OPENED: 1996

2815 Ourtoland Road, Kelowna, BC, V1Z 2H5

Telephone: 250-769-0404.

Web: www.slamka.bc.ca

Wine shop: Open daily 10 am – 5.30 pm April through October.

No charge for tastings; $5 per person fee for tours.

RECOMMENDED

※ OLD VINES AUXERROIS
✹ SAUVIGNON BLANC
PINOT NOIR
TAPESTRY

IT IS HARD TO MISS THIS WINERY'S PROMINENT SIGN EVER SINCE IT was moved farther south on Boucherie Road, away from a distracting intersection. Peter Slamka, the winemaker, jokes that it must be the world's most expensive sign at $500,000. That is about what it cost the Slamka family in 2000 to buy the vineyard and orchard property to which the sign was moved. They acquired a vineyard adjacent to the family's long-established vineyard, doubling their total holdings to nine hectares (23 acres). The improved visibility for the winery's sign was an important bonus because Little Straw Vineyards, as the winery began to call itself in 2004, tries to sell nearly all of the 2,000 cases it makes each year entirely from the winery's tasting room. The name change (from Slamka Cellars) is not as dramatic as it seems: in the family's native Slovak language, Slamka means "little straw."

The folksy new name may also extend the winery's market. Along with several other small wineries, Little Straw has not cracked many restaurant wine lists. "As a small winery, you are overlooked in all kinds of things," the winemaker complains. The VQA stores provide the winery's main retail outlet but, with the proliferation of new wineries in the last decade, shelf space is limited. Of course, the most profitable sales are those made at the winery. "We have a good little machine that makes money," he says. "We just want to fine-tune it a little more."

Peter Slamka likes dealing with his customers. He tries to give them what he calls "the winery experience" that comes from meeting actual winery owners. A winemaker who does not work the tasting room, he argues, misses the chance to sound out consumer reactions. "To me, that's the best part of the business," he says. "I like being out front, selling wine. For me, it's a challenge, seeing how many bottles of wine I can sell, and getting people excited. You have about 15 seconds to connect with them. You know, you can be as nice as you want, but even if you are just off a little bit, they notice. I had people come in and I spent 20 minutes with them. They bought nothing, they left. I could hear one of them through the window, saying, 'He was nicer last time.'" He sighs at the memory. "It's valuable experience. You get to know your customers and you see what they like."

The Slamka family has been growing grapes since 1969 when Joe Slamka, Peter's father, converted an orchard. The elder Slamka had left his native Czechoslovakia in 1948 and, after a decade as a machinist in Edmonton, moved to an orchard near Westbank. Poor returns from tree fruits triggered his subsequent switch to grapes. He was one of the earliest to plant Auxerrois, the fruity white from Alsace that is one of the winery's flagship wines. Peter Slamka underlines the maturity of the vines by producing what he calls an Old Vines Auxerrois.

When the government allowed small farm wineries in 1989, the Slamka family decided to make wine rather than sell grapes. Peter Slamka, born in 1954, began making wine in small volumes for family consumption. In 1993, he took off with his wife on a seven-month world tour that included visits with winemaking cousins in Austria, and to wineries in Australia's Barossa Valley. He made what he calls his first "official" vintage for the winery in 1994, opening to the public two years later.

"I've had consultants in, but in the end, it's my palate and what I think," he says. "I've learned to keep the wines as safe as possible. I don't have any razzle-dazzle formula. Winemaking's been around for thousands of years. I just keep it simple. And I call other winemakers once in a while and say, 'Taste this, what do you think?' Sometimes, you get your palate sensitized to your own wines. It's nice to get another opinion."

The Auxerrois is made in two styles. The version called Old Vines, rich and full, is perhaps aimed at Chardonnay palates. About a third of the wine in the blend is aged in French oak and spends time on the lees; the remainder of the wine is done in stainless steel, retaining fruitiness. Peter Slamka's second version is called Pinot Auxerrois; fruity and off-dry, it is aimed at palates attuned to Germanic wines. Little Straw is among only a handful of wineries in British Columbia that still make Auxerrois. The variety has an undeservedly low profile among consumers. When Slamka released the winery's first Sauvignon Blanc in 2002, he exulted that, at last, he had a white "that I don't have to explain."

"Auxerrois is a good hand sell here," Slamka adds, gesturing around his compact tasting room. "It doesn't sell anywhere else. Everybody else seems to be getting out of Auxerrois. We decided we are not going to, because we have these old vines and because I think it makes a nice wine. We even make the icewine from it, which is unique."

The winery's best-selling white is Tapestry, an off-dry blend of Auxerrois, Riesling, Siegerrebe, Schönburger and Traminer. (The small planting of Traminer, rarely seen in the Okanagan, was developed from 10 plants that Peter Slamka's grandmother had in her luggage on returning from a 1970s visit to Austria. While the provenance was unorthodox, Peter assures that the vines came from a nursery certified free of disease.) Tapestry's creative blend yields a lively wine with spicy flavours.

Slamka's primary red is Pinot Noir. In recent years, Merlot and Maréchal Foch also have been planted so that the winery might be able to offer its clients the more full-bodied wines. "If all you have is Pinot Noir, then you have missed out on a sale with half the people, because they are looking for something bigger," the winemaker says. "By having Foch and Merlot, there has got to be something there that they like."

However, Pinot Noir seems a variety suited to the Slamka vineyard, a site that could be described as cool because of its southeastern exposure. Like so many Pinot Noir producers, Peter Slamka regards his award-winning wine as a work in progress. "I notice the Pinots are all very delicate and very smooth, where ours has a little more meat and potatoes," he says. Making that elusive Pinot Noir he has in mind will involve more expensive barrels and lower yields from the expanded plantings of the variety.

"It gives us the opportunity to thin out the Pinot Noir crop and get really good flavours instead of tonnage," he says of the additional acreage. "We didn't have enough tonnage. Now that the new vines are coming into production, we'll be able to thin down to one cluster and get some intense flavours. No sense making 400 cases of mediocre Pinot Noir. You've got to make 200 cases of the best you can make."

LOTUSLAND VINEYARDS

OPENED: 2002

28450 King Road, Abbotsford, BC, V4X 1B1
Telephone: 604-857-4188
Web site: www.averyfinewine.ca, www.lotuslandvineyards.com
Wine shop: 11 am – 6 pm Tuesday through Sunday May through October;
   11 am – 5 pm Thursday through Sunday November through April.

RECOMMENDED

❈ GEWÜRZTRAMINER
PINOT GRIGIO
MERLOT

BEING CLEVER DOES NOT WORK EVERY TIME. DAVID AND LIESBETH Avery launched their Fraser Valley winery in December, 2002, with a name and a label that was a play on words: A'Very Fine Winery. A year later, it became Lotusland Vineyards. "Our old name was kind of cutesy but it required too much explanation," David explains. "Plus, it made us look like a 30-year-old winery."

Creating a new brand for the winery was the work of Bernie Hadley-Beauregard, the Vancouver marketing consultant who created the colourful caricature labels for both Blasted Church Vineyards in the Okanagan and for Salt Spring Vineyards. The Okanagan winery was known formerly as Prpich Hills; more accurately, it was unknown in the market. But the winery achieved profile and sales immediately after relaunching as Blasted Church. David Avery's banker, having noted that remarkable transformation, suggested a similar strategy to lift A'Very's sales. It was the first time, Hadley-Beauregard laughs, that business has been referred to him by a banker.

The consultant had run through 437 names to find Blasted Church. Lotusland sprang to his mind quickly when he realized that Avery's vineyard, eight and a half acres (3.4 hectares) of reclaimed gravel pit just west of Abbotsford, is within Greater Vancouver. "Why don't we just take the approach of having a vineyard in the city?" Hadley-Beauregard asked. Lotusland, which had not been used for any products, is a common term encapsulating the Vancouver lifestyle. The winery has turned its labels into what David Avery calls "a celebration of Vancouver." The 2001 Merlot label, for example, has photographs of 21 individuals who have made a difference in the city. They now are making a difference for the wine sales. "Their old brand was just not working," Hadley-Beauregard said.

Lotusland's owners came to wine through David's amateur winemaking and through Liz Avery's gardening. Born in Toronto in 1955, David was managing an office supply company until the winery demanded his full-time attention. Liz was born in Paraguay, the daughter of a farmer who moved to Canada in 1973. The roadside property near Abbotsford was just a hayfield when the Averys bought it in 1996. They concluded that vines would thrive on the sandy soil, with its precise south-facing slope.

Before ordering vines from an Ontario nursery in 1997, they sought advice from experienced growers in the Okanagan and nearby in the Fraser Valley. Claude Violet, the owner of Domaine de Chaberton, had been growing grapes near Langley since 1982. Most of Violet's vines are white varieties suited to the comparatively cool climate of the valley and to what consumers were drinking in the 1980s. But the trend had changed. "Plant red," Violet advised. Almost half the vineyard is planted to early-ripening clones of Pinot Noir, supplemented with several rows each of Pinot Meunier, Merlot, Cabernet Franc, Gamay and Zweigelt. More recently, Avery has added a small plot of early-ripening red varieties from Switzerland.

David and Liz manage their vineyard organically. It is a matter of principle, perhaps with a potential commercial benefit if there are consumers demanding organic wines. "I've always been a gardener and I've always done it without poisons and herbicides and insecticides," Liz Avery says. "If I can do it on a small scale, we figured we could do it on a larger scale." They are more at ease with the environment in their chemical-free vineyard. "We've walked around vineyards that use heavy herbicides and pesticides and walked around in our own," David says. "Our own is full of butterflies and bees and ladybugs. We've got a really nice balance in the vineyard."

David made the first wines from the vineyard in 1999, producing a mere 25 litres (5.5 gallons) after losing most of his small first harvest to birds. With adequate nets in place, he harvested enough in 2000 for 2,800 litres (615 gallons) and then, with the addition of grapes from the Okanagan, he made a big jump in 2001 to 54,000 litres (11,900 gallons).

Subsequently, he scaled production back, making smaller lots of more individual wines and discovering that small is beautiful. In the 2003 vintage, when the winery made about 16,000 litres of wine, he consciously limited himself to the fruit of his vineyard and from that of a nearby Fraser Valley grower. "I am having way more fun making wine," he says.

Avery completed the re-invention of the winery and its brand by switching from cork closures to screw caps, one of the first British Columbia wineries to do so. This also should prove to be a plus for the winery. In earlier times, the screw cap was associated with wines of indifferent quality. That has changed rapidly, with the arrival of expensive whites from New Zealand and Australia in bottles closed with screw caps. It is undeniable that this is one of the best means of preserving the natural freshness of wines. Lotusland's leading 2002 white wines, a Pinot Grigio and two Gewürztraminers, are crisp and fresh. "We raised the bar," David Avery believes.

MALAHAT ESTATE VINEYARD

OPENING: PROPOSED FOR 2004/2005

1197 Aspen Road, Malahat, BC, V0R 2L0
Telephone: 250-474-5129

THE STEEPLY PITCHED VINEYARD ON THIS PROPERTY SHOULD BE ENOUGH to discourage a person half his age. But when the vines need spraying, Lorne Tomalty, who was born in 1923, straps the spray pack on his back and sets out. It takes two and a half days to cover the two hectares (five acres), planted on terraces on a southeastern slope, with the top of the vineyard 26 metres (86 feet) higher than the bottom. The determined Tomalty is a vivid illustration of the passion that many find in wine growing.

Even without this small winery, Tomalty can say he has had a lifetime fuller than most. Born in Ottawa, he spent World War II as an armoured corps officer. After being discharged, he enrolled in economics and political science at the University of British Columbia. When he tried to enter the job market in 1949, his education attracted two offers: one as an airline ticket agent and the other as an insurance salesman. So he worked for a while as a miner in the Yukon until he could afford to return to university for a master's degree in public administration.

Upon graduation in 1952, he joined the British Columbia government as a personnel assistant. By the time he retired in 1985, he had become what he calls the government's "czar of manpower." He and his wife, Peggy, a nurse, bought a 4.6-hectare (11.5-acre) property near the scenic summit of the Malahat, north of Victoria. After clearing some trees, he decided to plant grapes. With an elevation of 192 metres (630 feet), this is one of Vancouver Island's highest vineyards.

Tomalty's interest in wine arose from years of making wine at home with friends of Italian heritage. When he began planting vines in 1995, he sought advice (and cuttings) from the vineyard manager at the Newton Ridge vineyard on the Saanich Peninsula. As a result, the Malahat vineyard reflects the choices made at Newton Ridge, which is also on a mountainside, but not as high. Ortega and Pinot Noir account for about 80 per cent of the plantings, with the remainder of the terraces planted to Pinot Gris. Planting on the remaining terraces, at the top of the vineyard, is scheduled for 2005, with Pinot Noir dominating Tomalty's choice.

His initial winery application was filed in 1997. Ironically, the civil service he had once worked with managed to lose the paperwork. Later, he concluded that was good fortune because his preparations then were still premature. "I'm an Irishman," he chuckles. His forebears came from Ireland five generations ago. "The luck must still be there."

Six years later, when the second application was filed, Tomalty was much more prepared. He had begun to make wine, with Glenterra's John Kelly as his mentor, and he had converted a large double garage on the property to accommodate the winery and the tasting room. His début wines included one barrel of 2002 Pinot Noir good enough that the discriminating Kelly reserved a case for himself.

Malahat Vineyard's whites are likely to be crisp, reflecting the cool site that gets the morning sun but not the evening sun. The grapes certainly ripen adequately, especially in a warm year like 2003 when the Ortega in particular delivered good sugars and moderate acidity. As well, the Pinot Noir has surprised Tomalty with good colour to match the fruitiness. With more vines coming into production, he was able to make three barrels of Pinot Noir in 2003.

Perhaps the main challenge of the vineyard arises from its location on a mountain abundant with birds and deer. The solution to the bird problem is to net the vines, even if that is not easy to do in a terraced vineyard. The deer are kept at bay with a solid fence and guard dogs. As for all the manual labour in the vineyard, Tomalty also relies on hired help and on assistance from his son, David, the operator of an excavation business.

The tasting room is just a short distance from the well-travelled Malahat Highway and the luxurious Aerie resort. Tomalty is confident about patronage, if only because of the loyalty that Vancouver Island residents have toward what is grown on the island. "Vancouver Island is a unique place," he says. "A large percentage of the people buy local products."

MARLEY FARM WINERY

OPENED: 2003

1831D Mount Newton Crossroads, Saanichton, BC, V8M 1L1

Telephone: 250-652-8667

Web site: www.marleyfarm.ca

Wine shop: Open daily 11 am – 6 pm in summer; call for spring and fall hours; closed in January.

RECOMMENDED

PINOT GRIGIO

NOVINÉ

KIWI

LOGANBERRY

BLACKBERRY

BEVERLY MARLEY, AN AMATEUR VINTNER OF FRUIT WINES FOR MORE THAN 15 years, says she does not drink because it depresses her. And then, with a light-hearted peal of laughter, she launches into yet another self-deprecating anecdote about her introduction to grape growing as she and Michael, her husband, developed this eclectic winery.

There was, for example, the assignment to inventory the vines in an abandoned two-hectare (five-acre) vineyard north of the Victoria International Airport. The Marleys already have a vineyard that large on their own farm, but a family friend had alerted them to this property, neglected ever since the failure of a nearby plant nursery several years earlier.

The vineyard, a tangled mess of wild blackberries and broken posts, had been someone's experimental block with several rows each of about 18 varieties. "I went up there in the rain one day to see what kinds of grapes they had," Beverly

Marley recounts. "At the end of each row, there is a little metal tag that tells you. So I wrote everything down. At home, I got out all the books, because I had never heard of some of these varieties. By the end of the afternoon, I was frustrated. Not for anything could I find Novine. It wasn't in any book. And then it dawned on me: 'It isn't Novine — it's No Vines!'" As soon as they got over their mirth at this, the Marleys decided that the blended house wines at Marley Farm would be labelled Noviné Red and Noviné White. "With an accent," Michael chuckles.

The Marleys have a fund of stories like that. They are having more than the usual amount of fun in the wine business. They have more types of wines than many others (ever heard of sparkling elderflower?). And for visitors to the winery who, like Bev, do not drink, there might be one of her mincemeat tarts or a taste of mango chutney, made with an old recipe that the Marley family brought to Victoria in 1975 when they left Jamaica.

Marley is a famous name in Jamaica and, yes, Michael is a second cousin of the late Bob Marley, the famous reggae artist. After a degree in structural engineering from a university in London, Michael Marley created a construction business in Jamaica. When he got fed up with the politics there, he started fresh as a house builder in Victoria, ultimately flourishing as a commercial property developer both in western Canada and in Arizona.

In 1995, the Marleys, who preferred rural acreages because Bev keeps horses, purchased a good-sized farm on Mount Newton Crossroads, on the Saanich Peninsula north of Victoria. Fraser Smith, a nearby neighbour and the founder of the Vancouver Island Grape Growers Association, convinced Marley that the farm was suited to viticulture. Over two seasons, beginning in 2000, the Marleys planted Pinot Gris and Ortega. Michael Marley figured that Ortega was his "insurance crop" and that Pinot Gris was also likely to do well. He planted Pinot Noir because he wanted a red variety. "Pinot Noir can also make some excellent sparkling wine. If that is my downside, I can put up with it." Of course, sparkling wine is the overwhelming passion of the consulting winemaker Marley retained, the ubiquitous Eric von Krosigk.

Von Krosigk soon found that the winemaking needs of Marley Farm would challenge all of his Geisenheim training, and then some. As soon as Michael Marley decided to get into the wine business, he bought the necessary tanks and a bottling line. "To leave it to sit there for nine months doing nothing, I found unacceptable," Marley says. "So Bev decided to do some fruit wines."

Von Krosigk was enlisted as the professional support. "It's very new territory for me," he admits. "I've tried a lot of fruit wines but had never made them. I took fruit wines at Geisenheim, a couple of courses. The concept was that, unlike grapes that have a very good balance, fruits have to be managed differently. You have to build the wine around the fruit."

By the time the winery opened in 2003, he had "built wines" with an array of fruits, berries and even ginger. From blackberries, which grow abundantly on the four kilometres (2.5 miles) of riding trails on the farm. From loganberries, which have almost vanished from the Saanich Peninsula. From raspberries, blueberries, apples, pears, rhubarb. The kiwi fruit wine was Beverly's idea to provide a bit of a market for struggling local kiwi farmers. Physically, it is one of the more difficult wines to make because the fuzzy hide is unwanted in the fermentation vat. So, unless the Marleys find a suitable tool, the acidic fruit all must skinned by hand. The first serious batch of kiwi wine was made using two tonnes (2.2 tons) of fruit; Beverly and friends who volunteered to help took nearly a week to deal with the kiwis.

The elderflower wine was von Krosigk's idea, with Beverly researching country wine books for recipes. "A friend of mine in Austria made a sparkling elderflower and I just loved it," von Krosigk says. The white elderberry flowers, after being separated laboriously from the stalks by more of Beverly's friends, are immersed in a base of sugar water and fermented. It is meant to be a light, refreshing wine with only three per cent alcohol and with a dramatically aromatic nose. "It is just a delightful drink," the winemaker says. It is also a difficult wine to pull off. Not yet satisfied with the result, the winery in the spring of 2004 was still debating whether to release what will be a Canadian first.

The Marleys have elevated the image of fruit wines with sharp packaging. They sought out expensive frosted wine bottles from an Italian supplier. The bottles flatter the natural colours of the fruit wines. "It also makes the wine look cold and yummy," Beverly suggests.

The attractive tasting room at Marley Farm, which looks across the vineyard toward Mount Newton to the north, also offers what von Krosigk no doubt views as conventional wines. The vines at Marley Farm are young and, because the soils are still being brought into nutritive balance, are struggling. However, von Krosigk has located a vineyard in Kaleden that grows organic Pinot Noir for Marley Farm, along with a south Okanagan source of Pinot Gris.

A regulatory hassle detracted somewhat from the fun the Marleys have had with the winery. Michael Marley owns two pubs and a golf course. That was a significant impediment to Marley Farm getting its license because there is an ancient regulation preventing a winery owner from selling his wines at any other licensed premise he owns. Marley had to provide notarized statements from his entire family, his Arizona business partners and even the landlords from which the pubs are leased, that he would not sells his wines in his pubs.

"I have a friend who owns a restaurant," says Marley, who now laughs bitterly about the experience. "He said, 'You are trying to make the best wine on Vancouver Island, and if you are successful and people want to drink your wine, they have to come to my restaurant!'"

MARSHWOOD ESTATE WINERY

OPENING: PROPOSED FOR 2004

548 Jade Road, Heriot Bay, Quadra Island, BC, V0P 1H0
Telephone: 250-285-2068
E-mail: marshwd@connected.bc.ca
Wine shop: Call for hours.

UNLESS SOMEONE PLANTS GRAPES AT SOINTULA, THIS WINERY WILL BE the most northerly on British Columbia's coastal islands, placing it off the beaten path for wine touring. But Martina and Kerry Kowalchuk, the owners, are not people who duck challenge. For instance, feisty Martina recently worked toward a black belt in karate, taking lessons in the same class as her teenage son. "I don't know if working in the vineyard helps with karate, or if I couldn't do all of the knee bends required in the vineyard without karate," she laughs.

A 10-minute ferry ride from Campbell River, Quadra Island, with nearly 3,000 year-round residents, is known for superb tourist amenities, including internationally known fishing resorts and hotels, sea kayaking, cycling, extensive hiking trails and Village Bay Lakes, the largest lake system on any Gulf Island. Some tourists come to enjoy Rebecca Spit provincial park. Others experience the native heritage of the Cape Mudge Indian Band, including historic petroglyphs. "It's an interesting island," Martina says.

The aboriginal name for the island was Tsa-Kwa-Luten, meaning gathering place. The First Nations have kept the name alive as the name of a 30-room lodge operated each summer at Cape Mudge. When the Canadian government named the island in 1903, it was the history of Spanish exploration on the west coast that was honoured. Juan Francisco de la Bodega y Quadra was the Spanish naval commander who, in 1792, negotiated with Captain Vancouver to return coastal properties that the Spanish had taken from the British in an earlier war.

The Kowalchuks have lived on Quadra since 1985, having been attracted there after a visit to the island. Born in Kenora, Ontario, in 1955, Kerry grew up in Alberta before moving to the west coast. Martina was born in Prince Rupert, the daughter of a policeman, and grew up in the succession of British Columbia communities to which her father was posted. Ultimately, she attended the leading fine arts school in Vancouver, now known as Emily Carr. There, during a drawing class, she met Haida artist Bill Reid and worked for him one summer, making jewellery. She continues to paint and sell her works, but on a sporadic schedule resulting from running various businesses and tending the 1.6-hectare (four-acre) vineyard. Her studio serves as the winery's tasting room, where they also sell her art and the wooden bowls that Kerry carves.

Living on an island involves hustling for a livelihood, something the Kowalchuks are good at. "Initially, we had a diving company," she says. "My husband is a commercial diver. We had a boat. We started by diving for octopus and then moved on to sea cucumbers. That worked well [until] they got fished out. We had to invent another job for ourselves." They bought the island's only gas station, adding to the business until they owned a small shopping mall called Village Square.

Since they no longer worked on the ocean, they sold their waterfront home, purchasing 65 hectares (160 acres) in one of the island's inland valleys. "It dawned on us that we were not really ocean people, we were dirt people," she says. "We like to grow things." A long, south-facing glacial moraine rises from the property's picturesque marsh and pond. On the toe of this slope, they built a long, low rancher hugging the land, designed by Martina in the style of Frank Lloyd Wright. Higher up the slope, they planted a trial plot of 80 Ortega vines. "We were just trying to see if it would work," she says.

With Kerry as winemaker, they have been making their own wines for more than 10 years. That led them, in the summer of 2001, to open Fermentations, a wine-making shop in Village Square, where wines were made for other customers on the island. Because of Kerry's considerable experience with fruit wines, island residents were soon bringing their own fruits to Fermentations to be vinified alongside products of wine kits. Meanwhile, the Kowalchucks expanded their Ortega planting, making both grape wines and fruit wines for themselves.

The winemaking store, a good place to learn the craft of wine production, influenced equipment decisions for the Marshwood winery. For example, the tanks they installed are costly stainless steel, not polyethylene. Even when equip- ping the winemaking store, they used glass containers for wine storage after noting that some plastic containers retain flavours. "We thought that can't be good," Martina says. "It gets down to that passion thing. We want to do it as well as we can." The winemaking store, which had become quite successful, was sold 18 months after they opened it. Liquor licensing regulations prevented them from getting a winery license while they still had the license for the winemaking store.

The vineyard, growing on what once was a forested slope, is planted primarily to Ortega. The Kowalchuks, taking advice from several Cowichan Valley wineries, have also planted Pinot Gris, Dornfelder, Agria and Pinot Noir. All varieties took hold successfully, particularly the Ortega and the Agria. Quadra's growing season is not much different from the other Gulf Islands, with the moderating effect of the ocean and a growing season that extends from March to the end of October. The marsh that inspired the winery name is one of the property's features, attracting abundant wild fowl for bird watching. The population of colourful dragonflies inspired Martina to feature their image on the winery's labels.

The Kowalchuks have developed a palate for the dry, even tart, table wines that their vineyard gives them, even if some of their wines are expected to be finished off-dry as the market might demand. "You can't manipulate where you live," she says of the vineyard. "So if the product is leaning in that direction, we want to go with it and work with that uniqueness. Because of this terroir and the microclimate, we want eventually to produce sparkling wine by the classic Champagne method." In addition to the estate-grown grapes, Marshwood also plans to make fruit wines with its own strawberries, raspberries and wild cranberries, supplemented with commercial cranberries from a farm near Campbell River.

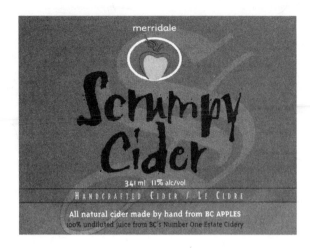

MERRIDALE CIDERWORKS

OPENED: 1992

1230 Merridale Road, Cobble Hill, BC, V0R 1L0

Telephone: 250-743-4293

Toll-free: 1-800-998-9908

Web: www.merridalecider.com

Wine shop: Open 10:30 am – 6 pm Sunday through Thursday;
until 7 pm, Friday and Saturday.

Restaurant: CiderHouse offers the choice of booked lunches or platters of
prepared local cheese and sausage. Picnic facilities also available.

RECOMMENDED

* SCRUMPY
* SOMERSET CIDER
* WINTER APPLE
  TRADITIONAL CIDER
  CIDRE NORMANDIE
  CYSER

THE GRASS UNDER THE APPLE TREES IN MERRIDALE'S 5.6-HECTARE (14-acre) orchard is manicured to putting perfection, enhancing the self-guided tours. The tour is especially enticing when ripening apples dangle temptingly within reach. But if the apple at hand is a Tremlett's Bitter, temptation will vanish with the first bite.

"The English call it a spitter," chuckles Rick Pipes, Merridale's co-owner and cider maker. "Nobody swallows a bite of Tremlett's Bitter." It is one of about 16 varieties of cider apples grown here — apples with strange names such as Michelin, Yarlington Mill, Dabinett, Chisel Jersey, Kermerien, Julienne, Judaine, Frequin Rouge, and Hauxapfel. Some taste bitter, some are sweet, some are acidic. Blended together, they produce ciders that compare well to the classic ciders of Britain and France — because Albert Piggott, who founded Merridale, planted authentic European cider apple trees.

Born in Scotland in 1925, Piggott was a teacher with a passion for cider, realized only after he retired at 56 to southern Vancouver Island. He planted an orchard here because the climate and the soils compare well to England's best cider regions. Merridale was incorporated in 1987 and, after getting the equivalent of an estate winery license, began selling its products in 1992.

The authentic personality of Piggott's ciders was expressed particularly by a bitter cider called Scrumpy, a traditional farmhouse cider drawing its name from English slang: to *scrump* an apple was to steal it. An educated palate is required to appreciate traditional ciders and that is particularly so with Scrumpy. When Rick Pipes and Janet Docherty, his wife, purchased Merridale in 2000, their first instinct was to ditch Scrumpy.

"Neither of us could drink it," Pipes admits. "But some people said they really liked the Scrumpy and were very loyal to the product. They would phone us up here and say, 'Ma's Beer and Wine Store is out of Scrumpy.' These were people who would go in every day and pick up their bottle of Scrumpy." Rather than dropping it, Pipes adjusted the blend to make the robust beverage less rough and more appealing. "They complained a little bit when I reformulated it but they are drinking it," he reports. "We gained more sales than we lost." And Merridale's improved Scrumpy won both gold and silver medals at a major American competition in 2002.

Pipes and Docherty took over Merridale in a career-changing move. Docherty, a petite mother of three, is a commercial realtor with a sure touch as a marketer. Pipes has a commercial law practice in Victoria, where he grew up. Prudently, he continued to practice law as he and his wife worked to turn Merridale into a business standing on its own feet. Central to their strategy is making Merridale a destination for wine tourists in the Cowichan Valley. That is one reason for the manicured orchard and the comfortable hospitality building overlooking the orchard, completed in 2003. Piggott had only been able to sell about 10 per cent of Merridale's ciders at the farm. Pipes and Docherty intend that farm sales will reach 60 per cent, even after expanding cider output significantly since taking over.

At the outset, Pipes knew little about making cider. He planned to rely on Piggott's expertise and on help from an experienced cellar hand at Merridale. But just as the cidery was changing hands, the cellar hand died in a car crash and Piggott went to New Zealand for six weeks "while we fermented our first batch," Pipes remembers. "People bought it and I thank them for that, but compared to the cider we are putting out now, it was awful." Pipes, who once considered becoming a doctor, relied on his university knowledge of science to grasp the technical aspects of making cider. He called on his lawyer's research skills to dig out information and find the top English cider consultants. "Without them, it would have taken way longer for me to learn," Pipes says. "I don't think we could have done what we've done to this point without the Internet."

Scrumpy was not the only Merridale product that was reworked. "We've tinkered with all the formulas," Pipe says. He completed work that Piggott had begun on a crisply dry sparkling cider called Somerset, which is packed in a Champagne bottle. He reworked Normandy, a dry French-style cider now barrel-aged and vintage-dated, called Cidre Normandie. With 12 per cent alcohol, this cider is in a full-sized wine bottle and is aimed at getting Merridale onto the dinner table throughout the year. That will take Merridale beyond bread and butter pub ciders and refreshment ciders. "We're trying to get out of that traditional, spritzer-like, fizzy image," he says. "Our sales are twice as much in the summer months as they are the rest of the year. We need to get on the fall dinner table. We need to expand the way people think of drinking ciders." Indeed, Merridale even encourages pairing its Cyser, a well-balanced honey-sweetened cider, with spicy Asian cuisine.

At the same time, Pipes has developed additional products, including Winter Apple (a dessert-style cider), another Champagne-style cider, cider vinegar and a varietal cider. He believes that one of the French cider apples in the Merridale orchard, Frequin Rouge, has the balance, the flavour and the aroma to yield an attractive single-variety cider. He also hopes to attract a premium price for it. "My cider is costing me the same amount to make as wine and yet my margins are half as much," Pipes complains.

Packaging is a challenge that Pipes is still confronting. Most of the Merridale ciders are released in plastic containers. The image of those bottles gets in the way of selling the ciders for what they are really worth but the plastic bottles are a matter of safety. Except for the very driest products, Merridale ciders contain unfermented sugar and there are no chemical preservatives except for a minimal amount of sulphur. The ciders are refrigerated from the bottling line to the consumer to stop fermentation from starting again. Refermentation in glass bottles could cause some to explode. That means that some plastic bottles are here to stay until there is a way of sterilizing cider while retaining the crisp, fresh flavours. Meanwhile, a group of craft cider producers in Britain and North America, including Merridale, is developing a new bottle specifically for ciders.

MIDDLE MOUNTAIN MEAD

OPENING: PROPOSED FOR 2004

3505 Euston Road, Hornby Island, BC, V0R 1Z0
Telephone: 250-335-1392
Web site: www.middlemountainmead.com

THE COLORADO SCHOOL OF MINES IS ONE OF THE WORLD'S TOP SCHOOLS for geologists. Apparently, it is also one of the most civilized. Meadmaker Campbell Graham traces his interest in wine and other fermented beverages to a liberal arts course on wine tasting that he remembers as a "refreshing break" from courses required for his master's degree in geophysical engineering. He became an enthusiastic home winemaker, as did his wife, Helen Grond, also a geologist with a master's degree from the University of British Columbia. Now, they have combined their science and their passion in British Columbia's second meadery or, in the medieval usage they prefer, a mead-house.

Graham was born in 1956 and grew up in Ottawa. Grond was born a year later in Newmarket, Ontario, and grew up on a family farm. They have both enjoyed international careers. Grond, whose master's thesis was on the platinum group metals, formed her own junior exploration company while still at university. Later, she worked on projects from the Yukon to Argentina. Graham worked on geophysical exploration projects around the world, including recent searches for World War II–era Japanese treasure believed to have been buried in the Philippines.

They moved from Vancouver to Hornby Island in 1992 in order to raise their two children in a country setting. Except in summer, when perhaps 50,000 tourists visit the island, Hornby is a quiet, charming island off the sheltered east coast of Vancouver Island. They settled on a five-hectare (13-acre) property near the south end of the island. The property is on a well-drained gravelly hillside.

About a third is forest but the rest has been cleared and fenced. Of that, about 1.6 hectares (four acres) was planted. "Helen is a passionate gardener," Graham says. "She chose herbs in general and lavender in particular for our site."

"As Helen researched and developed her herb business, she began noticing intriguing references to metheglin, which is herb-infused mead" Graham says. "It's the Welsh word for medicine. She suggested that it was an obvious complement to herb production. After quite a bit of research, we both agreed that we'd like to embark on a commercial meadmaking venture."

They decided that a small-scale, artisan winery was appealing on a number of levels. The decision was cemented when Graham and Grond began researching the romantic history of mead, a beverage basically made by fermenting a mixture of honey and water. "We fell in love with the language of mead: cysers, melomels, pyment, metheglin," Graham says. "These are various types of meads based on whether the mead is flavoured with herbs, spices, fruit, flower blossoms — whatever. Beautiful language is part of meadmaking. We also discovered that mead was of central importance in pagan rituals and Celtic spirituality, which appeals to us personally. Its importance can be seen in the word honeymoon, which comes from the custom of giving the newlyweds a month's worth of mead to ensure a fertile beginning to the marriage. Each discovery made us feel more and more that we were being inducted into mysterious realms."

British Columbia's other meadmaker, Robert Liptrot at Tugwell Creek Farm, came to making mead through a lifetime of keeping bees (Liptrot regards mead as the "pinnacle of beekeeping"). Graham and Grond, on the other hand, had no experience with bees until they launched this venture. Initially, they planned to buy the honey needed for meadmaking. However, evolving rules of land-based wineries in British Columbia, under which they fall, require that at least a quarter of the raw material be produced on the farm. Graham and Grond satisfied the regulators by placing twenty beehives on their land, producing honey from the herbs and other flowers there.

"We'd always intended to keep bees," Graham says. "It really fits in with our vision of what we wanted to create here — but we'd planned to leave that venture to a little later." The bees should produce intriguing honey from the various plants grown on the property, including lavender. "One of the special varietal honeys will definitely be lavender, since we have about 3,000 plants," Graham says. "I expect that will make a lovely mead. I've made mead with salal honey, which is lovely. And we are sowing our meadow areas with fireweed, and I know the fireweed honey will make a great mead."

For the meadery, Graham and Grond converted a compact cabin on their property. Production is on the ground floor, where Graham has equipped the meadery with stainless steel tanks and oak barrels used for aging. The second-floor tasting room has a panoramic view over the herb fields and beyond that, to the ocean and the mountains. The products being offered include traditional mead (just fermented honey and water) as well as meads flavoured with herbs or with fruits such as blackberry. The styles range from dry to sweet.

Given his experience with making wine, Graham plunged into meadmaking with gusto. "I've become an intense autodidact on the subject of meadmaking and all things fermenting," he says. "I've developed a lot of respect for the mead-makers' art, but at the same time, I feel more and more that I can be good at this." He credits the large number of meadmakers on the Internet that are willing, and even eager, to help another devotee of one of man's oldest fermented beverages. "It is astounding, the number of very informed people who take time to share their knowledge. We're all building on a tradition that goes back for millennia. It's both reassuring and humbling," he says.

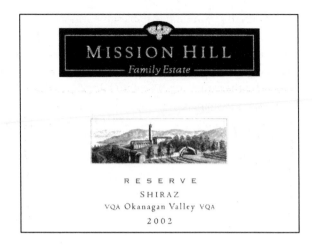

RESERVE
SHIRAZ
VQA Okanagan Valley VQA
2002

MISSION HILL FAMILY ESTATE WINERY

OPENED: 1966

1730 Mission Hill, Westbank, BC, V4T 2E4

Telephone: 250-768-7611

Web site: www.missionhillwinery.com

Wine shop: open daily. Tour program includes deluxe tours and
private tastings. Charges apply; check Web site for details.

Restaurant: Terrace open daily for lunch May through October; for dinner from
June 14 to Labour Day weekend.

RECOMMENDED

* OCULUS
* SELECT LOT COLLECTION CHARDONNAY
* SELECT LOT COLLECTION SYRAH
* RESERVE SHIRAZ
* RESERVE PINOT BLANC
* RESERVE PINOT GRIS
* PINOT BLANC
* RIESLING ICEWINE
* RESERVE PINOT NOIR
* CABERNET-MERLOT

SHORTLY AFTER ONE INTERVIEW WITH ANTHONY VON MANDL, THE OWNER OF
Mission Hill, I happened to meet his father, Martin. I commented on how fiercely
determined his son seemed to be. "Yes," agreed the elder von Mandl. "He has all
the ambition I never had."

The father certainly was too self-deprecating (he had been a successful textile
manufacturer in Czechoslovakia until fleeing the Nazi threat just before World
War II). But he had put his finger on the special drive possessed by his son. That

incandescent ambition has turned the Mission Hill winery, which had dirt floors when von Mandl bought it in 1981, into a breathtaking structure of quiet dignity. Von Mandl's goal is that Mission Hill should become one of the 10 leading wineries in the world, both for the experience offered to visitors and for the wines created by John Simes, a winemaker with fairy dust on his fingers.

The winery perches on Mount Boucherie near Westbank like a monastery on a Tuscan hilltop, its pastel concrete purposely tinted to the earth hue of the mountain. The ambiance is so reverential that visitors to the cathedral-like under ground cellar tend to whisper. During the six years of construction, completed in the summer of 2002, every significant feature of the design was tested first with scale models. No expense was spared because von Mandl was building for the ages. "I wanted to create a winery and a structure that would be enduring, that would be as relevant in 200 years, 300 years, as it is today," he says. "To me, a sense of timelessness was absolutely essential."

In its day, the original Mission Hill winery was also the talk of the Okanagan. A dynamic individual named Tiny Walrod (who died before the winery opened) led a syndicate of local businessmen to build the mountaintop winery modelled on the architecture of California's Spanish missions. They reasoned that an attractive winery with a stunning view would draw many wine tourists. They were correct: Mission Hill today attracts about 150,000 visitors a year. But it could not do that in 1966 because wineries were not permitted to have tasting rooms until the mid-1970s.

The winery soon was close to bankruptcy and the original investors sold it to Ben Ginter, a rough-mannered Prince George brewer who had made a fortune in heavy construction and squandered it on making wines like Hot Goose and Fuddle Duck. Ginter changed the winery's name to Uncle Ben's Gourmet Wines and later, after another brush with failure, to Golden Valley, before selling it in 1981 to von Mandl, who reverted to the fine original name.

The desire for an Okanagan winery had been with von Mandl since, as a young wine merchant, he prepared a report on such a venture for Josef Milz AG, a German winery whose wines von Mandl sold in Canada. (Milz decided against investing in the Okanagan.) Von Mandl had grand objectives in his mind when he took control of Mission Hill. In a speech that October to the Kelowna Chamber of Commerce, he predicted the day when the Okanagan would have "world-class vinifera vineyards" and wine tourism like California's Napa Valley.

The forecast was ahead of its time. In 1981, the 13 wineries then in the Okanagan relied primarily on hybrid grapes. Mission Hill owned no vineyards, nor was there much acreage of "world-class vinifera" planted before 1992. Mission Hill's best wines during the 1980s were made with vinifera grapes pur-chased from Washington State vineyards. As Okanagan vinifera became avail-able, Mission Hill bought them. Ultimately, the winery did buy vineyards and is now the Okanagan's largest vineyard owner.

The grape that established Mission Hill's reputation was Chardonnay grown in an Oliver vineyard in 1992. John Simes, formerly chief winemaker for New Zealand's largest winery, took over Mission Hill's winemaking in September,

1992. He was so impressed with the quality of the Oliver Chardonnay — "the fruit was brilliant," he said — that he had new barrels rushed to the winery so that he could barrel-ferment the wine. If it was not the Okanagan's first barrel-fermented Chardonnay, it was one of the first. Early in 1994 the wine took the top trophy at the annual International Wine and Spirits Competition in London. A first for a British Columbia winery, it was promoted as the "world's best Chardonnay."

Taking the wine quality to the next level required that Mission Hill buy its own vineyards, an assignment that Simes executed aggressively. By 2004, Mission Hill owned or controlled about 380 hectares (940 acres) of what are "world-class vinifera vineyards" in five different areas of the Okanagan. As a result, Simes controls the quality of the wines from the vineyard right through to the completely rebuilt winery.

In 1996 von Mandl had hired Tom Kundig, a renowned Seattle architect, to redevelop the tired, 30-year-old winery. "It was clear to me that a landmark showcase winery was absolutely essential to the future of the Okanagan," von Mandl said later. "It certainly is now bringing visitors from many countries, and not only to Mission Hill Family Estate. People that have never heard of the Okanagan are reading about Mission Hill and are coming here."

The early plans for a rebuilt Mission Hill were not nearly as grand as the final result. "The winery turned out to be more spectacular than I could ever have imagined," von Mandl says. "I had a very clear vision but it started off far more modest, as initially I never could imagine there would be a way to finance this kind of a winery here in the Okanagan Valley." The cash, an estimated $40 million, came from the market success of a vodka-based beverage called Mike's Hard Lemonade, sold by Mark Anthony, von Mandl's imported wine and beverage company.

Von Mandl's nose for hot-selling beverages is legendary. Two imported wine brands he helped create in 1978, St. Jovian and Magic Flute, were Canadian best-sellers in their day. He got the Canadian license for California Cooler, the 1980s mega-hit alcoholic cooler. In the mid-1990s in Australia, he came across a vodka-laced fruit drink called Two Dogs and relaunched it here in 1995 as Mike's. It succeeded beyond expectations.

With a river of cash flowing in, Kundig, the architect, was encouraged to think big. "We built full-scale models of virtually everything," von Mandl says. "We modelled everything out of plywood, just to make sure it was right. Because if you are building something to be around for generations, there is only one way to do it — you have to do it right."

Mission Hill was not rebuilt just for the show. The investment gave Simes the tools to make great wine. "John has been critical," von Mandl says of his winemaker. "His arrival was a turning point for winemaking in the valley. John is not only passionate but is so incredibly excited about the potential. He, like I am, is never ever satisfied with anything we produce. It really does not matter what award we win anywhere in the world, we always believe we can do better."

Mission Hill has the capacity to produce about 350,000 cases of wine a year, with 80 per cent of that coming from its own vineyards. The very best are released as Select Lot Collection wines. Simes found many of the properties and advised on what grape varieties should be planted. It was clear from von Mandl's earlier research for Milz that good white wines could be grown in the Okanagan. "We did not know at the time that we could be so successful with Bordeaux reds and with Syrah," von Mandl says. "That has been one of the most exciting discoveries." Accordingly, Simes has extended the Mission Hill repertoire of wines very considerably. Oculus, the winery's Bordeaux-style red, is one of the Okanagan's premium reds.

By coincidence, Simes and von Mandl are both in their early 50s, with long careers in wine ahead of them. Von Mandl has focussed his famous ambition almost exclusively on Mission Hill. "Really, I firmly believe it is going to take my lifetime and beyond to realize the full potential of this incredible region and this incredible valley." he says. "My ambition is not about size; it's not about scale; it's not about being the biggest. It truly is about quality."

MISTRAL VINEYARD

OPENING: PROPOSED FOR 2008

1865 Naramata Road, Penticton, BC, V2A 8T9

THIS VINEYARD IS ALL ABOUT AARON AND PATRICIA ANDERSON'S LONG infatuation with the Naramata Bench. Patricia grew up in Penticton, where her father owned the sawmill in which Aaron, in 1972, began his career in lumber sales. At various times, the Andersons have lived on properties north of Naramata, with great views over Okanagan Lake. At times, Aaron arranged his career so that he could work in Vancouver three or four days a week and commute to his country office. The commute became too onerous in 1997 and they moved to Vancouver, selling a large hillside property where they had stabled horses. Unable to stay away, the Andersons began looking for another country home on the Naramata Bench in 2001. When they came across four hectares (10 acres) with a derelict orchard, they closed the purchase within an hour.

Aaron Anderson was born in 1951 in Fort McMurray, Alberta, and grew up in Vancouver when his father, an airline mechanic, was transferred in 1953. After high school and a stint at the British Columbia Institute of Technology, he headed north again, this time to Fort St. James, where he met Patricia. A Vancouver native, she was a professional figure skater and was teaching in the north. The Andersons then teamed up to run a business that combined groceries, a restaurant and a small hotel. But after a few years, they moved to the Okanagan; while his work took them away from the valley, they returned each time they could. In more than three decades in lumber sales, Aaron Anderson rose to become the vice-president of marketing for Lignum Ltd., a major independent producer (now Riverside Forest Products).

Aaron admits he has no practical experience at winemaking, other than minor experience as a home winemaker. "I know how to drink it," he smiles. More than just a casual consumer, he has belonged to such wine clubs as the Opimian Society and has collected wines. "I've got about a 2,000-bottle cellar."

The thought of planting grapes had already occurred to the Andersons when they owned their Naramata property with its horse stables. A previous owner had prepared 2.4 hectares (six acres) for a vineyard before discovering that his well provided insufficient irrigation water.

They snapped up their latest Naramata Road property in 2001 in part because the price was right. The property was so neglected that Aaron compared it to an abandoned trailer court. "It took us about six months to clean it up," he recalls. The aspect of the site — most of it has an excellent southwest slope toward the lake — led them to rip out the fruit trees and prepare a vineyard. There is adequate water and the Andersons also invested in a sophisticated computer-controlled irrigation system that conserves water by delivering it to the plants with the utmost precision.

They made their planting decisions carefully, after first immersing themselves in literature and courses about viticulture and then retaining consultant Val Tait to advise on the vineyard. Beginning in 2003, about 3.2 hectares (eight acres) has been planted. The varieties mainly are reds: Merlot, Cabernet Franc, Malbec and Syrah. In most instances, there are at least two clones of each variety. "We're trying to grow as much complexity as possible," Aaron says.

There also is a modest planting of Dunkelfelder, a neutral grape with an inky dark colour that is useful in touching up the colour intensity in wines. It seems unlikely that Anderson would need it with the varieties he is growing but there apparently is demand for the variety from other wineries. One winery asked him to plant his entire vineyard to Dunkelfelder. The white varieties at Mistral are Pinot Gris and Viognier.

Because Aaron Anderson figures his lumber sales career still has a few years to run, Mistral — with Patricia managing the vineyard — expects to sell most of its grapes to other wineries for some time. However, Anderson also plans to work with a wine-making consultant, acquiring the skills needed to make the wines himself in time. The first wines to be released by Mistral likely will be blends incorporating the Syrah.

"I am a big blended wine fan," Aaron says. "I am thinking of getting away from the varietal way of describing wine in favour of more of a field blend, which is what I like."

MORNING BAY FARM

OPENING: PROPOSED FOR 2005

6621 Harbour Hill Road, North Pender Island, BC, V0N 2M1
Telephone: 250-629-8350
E-mail: mrngby@netscape.net

NEW ZEALAND'S BRILLIANT WINE INDUSTRY SERVES AS AN INSPIRATION TO a significant number of British Columbia vintners. Keith Watt, who owns Morning Bay Farm, is one more example. "I'm in admiration of New Zealanders because they are not selling to themselves," he said after spending a month there in 2002. "They are selling to British and French and California consumers. We have an easy time of it. We are selling to British Columbians." A novice in the wine business, Watt came back from New Zealand with insights into viticulture and the concept for the simple gravity-flow winery designed for Morning Bay, the first winery on the Pender Islands.

The Pender Islands, two contiguous islands joined since 1903 by a bridge, are the second most populous of the Gulf Islands, with about 2,000 permanent residents and a great many tourists in summer. Watt is counting on those visitors to be among the customers for a winery that has the capacity to make 4,500 cases of wine a year. "I see Morning Bay wines as being small-lot, handmade wines."

The plan is ambitious for a winery on an island. Watt believes he is realistic about agriculture, given his background. The son of a farm equipment company manager, Watt was born in Winnipeg in 1951. Pursuing journalism, he became a producer of radio documentaries for the Canadian Broadcasting Corporation. His work won three Jack Webster awards for excellence in British Columbia journalism and a University of Iowa award for a documentary on Prairies soil degradation. He continues to consult in radio and to write.

"When I was going to university, we lived on a farm outside of Peterborough," Watt recounts. "I worked for the farmer in the summertime. We were building a barn because his barn had burned down. He was spending the evenings in his basement straightening enough nails for us to pound in the next day. So I came to the business of agriculture with my eyes open. The level of commitment and work; the level of expertise in really diverse, complicated areas; that's the staggering thing about any type of agriculture."

In 1992 he bought his property on North Pender. It was then a steep, forested slope on the flank of Mt. Menzies, with a view across Plumper Sound to Saturna Island. Watt conceived the idea of a vineyard and a winery while watching, through a telescope, planting at Saturna Island Vineyards. When he got serious about his own project, he gained some experience by volunteering to work at Saturna Island.

Not everyone on Pender welcomed the new vineyard. "There's been some contention about the winery, or the vineyard," Watt admits. "It represents a land use that is different from the prevailing land use philosophy, which says you don't cut trees down, you conserve them. Well, we cut trees down." Watt had to reshape the land after clearing trees. Half of the 5,000 vines are planted on 20 terraces cut along the steep slope, with a substantial irrigation pond created at the bottom. The vineyard, he says, is appropriate use for agricultural land. The two-level winery with a partially buried barrel cellar is set discreetly among the trees. The vineyard itself backs against a national park. Watt calculates that hikers in the park might very well satisfy their thirst in Morning Bay's tasting room.

Watt planted two hectares (five acres) in the fall of 2002. The varieties included Pinot Noir, Pinot Gris, Gewürztraminer, Maréchal Foch and Schönburger, along with a small number of Léon Millot vines and about 400 Riesling. Most did well in their initial seasons, although Watt also learned it is challenging to turn an acidic former forest floor into a vineyard. "I am confident that now it is a farming problem — one of fertility, soil analysis and soil balance," Watt said at the end of the first year. "Of course, this is all new to me but I have good help."

His consultant both for the vineyard and for making wine is Eric von Krosigk, who has had a number of clients on Vancouver Island and the Gulf Islands, including Saturna Island Vineyards. Watt adopted the von Krosigk model of making wine with Okanagan grapes. In 2002, about 750 cases were made in the Okanagan for Morning Bay; in 2003, a further 1,200 cases were made. The varieties include Pinot Gris, Pinot Noir, Riesling, Merlot and Cabernet Sauvignon.

Even when the Morning Bay vineyard is in production, Watt intends to keep wines from Okanagan fruit in his range. "What we are trying to do is find individual vineyards and then try to really feature their product," he says. "We are trying to do distinctive, small-batch wines, normally from single vineyards if we can."

The desired style, however, is meant to reflect an interpretation of island life. "We are not going to make a big Cabernet, for instance, or a big Merlot," Watt promises. "Our feeling is that our winery is associated with summertime and the Gulf Islands and sunshine. It is really not the time when you want those heavy, brambly, oaky red wines. You want something a little bit lighter and a little bit fruitier, like a Merlot you would not be afraid to serve with salmon."

MT. BOUCHERIE ESTATE WINERY

OPENED: 2001

> 829 Douglas Road, Kelowna, BC, V1Z 1N9
> Telephone: 250-769-8803
> Toll-free: 1-877-684-2748
> Web site: www.mtboucherie.bc.ca
> Wine shop: Open daily 10 am – 6 pm in summer; 11 am – 5 pm in winter.

RECOMMENDED

- ❋ PINOT GRIS
- ❋ GEWÜRZTRAMINER
- ✸ SUMMIT RESERVE
- ✸ PINOT NOIR

WITH REFRESHING CANDOUR, SARWAN GIDDA EXPLAINS WHY HIS family remained grape growers when they bought a vineyard in 1975 with the intention of replacing the vines with apple trees. "It was better money than the apples," he says. Since that discovery, this Punjabi-born family has acquired about 71 hectares (175 acres) of vineyards, growing both for their modern estate winery near Westbank as well as for several other wineries. It is probable that the Gidda brothers grow more varieties of grapes — including an obscure Russian variety called Michurinetz — than any commercial Okanagan grower.

The Gidda brothers have farming in their blood. Mehtad Gidda, their father, had been a farmer in India until, at the age of 29, he brought his family to British Columbia in 1958. A very hard worker, he laboured at sawmills while investing his savings in orchard property. "Dad wouldn't let us get into farming until we got educated," Sarwan remembers. "He thought farming was too hard." The eldest of the three brothers, he studied business administration. Nirmal earned a science degree and Kaldep, the youngest brother, trained as a mechanic. Now, all are partners in Mt. Boucherie and the vineyards.

Sarwan was still in school in 1975 when his father, who had been growing apples for six years, bought the family's first vineyard near Westbank. Grapes were sold at that time through a powerful marketing board. The varieties even included Bath, a red labrusca with a prodigious yield. "We could grow 15 tons to the acre and sell it for $200 bucks a ton," Sarwan recalls. "That was darn good. It was real money." The Gidda family had begun converting the vineyard to better wine grapes, including Gewürztraminer, before the 1988 vintage. That fall, many growers accepted government payments and purged mediocre grape varieties then grown in two-thirds of the Okanagan.

"We wanted to stay in the business, so we didn't take the money," Sarwan Gidda says. It was a mistake. They subsequently bore the costs of replanting themselves. But they were so committed to growing grapes that they plunged in more deeply at a time when others questioned whether the British Columbia wine industry would even survive. Their Westbank vineyards were expanded to 22 hectares (55 acres). In 1991, they looked at several properties farther south, including acreage on Black Sage Road that had been fallow since the 1988 pull-out. Finally, they acquired what was called the Sunrise Vineyard near Okanagan Falls. The big attraction was a two-year-old house on the vineyard because Kaldep's home had just been razed in a fire. But it also came with 16 hectares (40 acres) planted largely to desirable wine grapes, including some of the Okanagan's first Merlot.

The brothers lined up wineries for this fruit and remained alert for other opportunities. They were not satisfied that they could grow a full range of red wine grapes at either Okanagan Falls or Westbank. In 1998, they were able to buy a 36-hectare (89-acre) producing vineyard near Cawston in the Similkameen Valley. "Beautiful vineyard," Sarwan enthuses. "I think it is the best growing area in the world! I've seen the Napa Valley and I think we can grow just as good as them. We're growing everything: Riesling, Gewürztraminer, Lemberger, Kerner, Pinot Gris, Chardonnay, Merlot, a little bit of Bacchus. The new variety, Syrah. A little bit of Cabernet Sauvignon. Pinot Noir. Lots of Pinot Noir there. And Gamay. It's a good-sized piece."

It was natural that, as growers, they would develop a taste for wine. "I didn't like wine at the beginning," Sarwan says in another candid moment. "But the winemakers would come by at Christmas time. We'd get all this wine and we'd start drinking it. Then we'd start tasting tank samples and they'd tell us why this wine is better than that wine." Ultimately, the conversion was complete. "I'm a wine drinker now," he says. "I'd rather drink wine than anything else but it took time."

The "ultimate," he adds, "is owning your own winery." The decision to build the Mt. Boucherie winery, currently making 10,000 cases a year, involved a bit of defensive calculation on the part of the family. "We could see the writing," Sarwan says. "There was an oversupply of grapes." With grape prices under pressure, the family concluded it would be more lucrative to start putting their own grapes through their own winery.

Mt. Boucherie attracted notice first for its Gewürztraminer. That is because the variety does well in their vineyards. It is often recommended as the wine to serve with East Indian dishes. "With spicy foods, we usually have a Gewürztraminer or a Pinot Gris," Sarwan says. "With heavier foods, like pork chops or steaks, heavier red goes better." And the winery's Pinot Noir, with some grapes grown in the Similkameen, is full-bodied in style. Even fuller-bodied wines may be possible in the future. Mt. Boucherie has one of the Okanagan's largest plantings of Zweigelt, an Austrian red capable of producing both table wine and icewine.

And then there is Michurinetz which, on its own, yields an inky red. In 2002, Alan Marks, the consulting winemaker for Mt. Boucherie's early vintages, used it in a blend modelled on his concept of an "old-style Italian red." The wine was blended with Maréchal Foch, Gamay and Merlot. However, it was then sold to a small Kelowna wine marketing company called Bumble Bee Wines. That company released the wine as Stinger Red Reserve.

When Marks returned to manage the Summerhill winery in 2003, he was succeeded in the Mt. Boucherie cellar by his protégé, Graham Pierce. Born in Vancouver in 1971, Pierce came into wine through an early career in food service. He came to the Okanagan in time to join Summerhill just as that winery was developing its first restaurant. When an interest in wine took precedence, Pierce became a Mt. Boucherie cellar hand under Marks and immersed himself in winemaking courses at Okanagan University College. The style that Marks set for Mt. Boucherie wines continues with Pierce. "We're just staying the course," he says.

NEWTON RIDGE VINEYARDS

OPENED: 1998

1595 Newton Heights Road, Saanichton, BC, V8M 1T6
Telephone: 250-652-8810; 250-652-1644
Wine shop: By appointment only.

RECOMMENDED

☀ ORTEGA
☀ PINOT GRIS

NEWTON RIDGE IS THE SMALLEST WINERY IN BRITISH COLUMBIA — IF NOT IN the entire universe. The production from the winery's mountainside vineyard north of Victoria has been averaging less than 250 cases a year, handcrafted wines that obviously are hard to find. Four varieties are grown in the 1.2-hectare (3-acre) vineyard: Pinot Noir, Pinot Gris, Pinot Blanc and Ortega. Perhaps because of the unique site, Newton Ridge's Ortega arguably is the best Ortega on Vancouver Island.

How does a winery this small flourish? Newton Ridge has been owned by a succession of millionaires who developed the property as a luxurious country residence and then took pride in the wines. The property is high on the south-facing slope of Mount Newton, about half an hour north of Victoria. On a clear day, the incomparable view sweeps from the San Juan islands on the east to the mountains of the Olympic Peninsula to the south. Other fine country homes dot the slope, including that of John Brickett, the Saanich Peninsula's most experienced grape grower, whose substantial vineyard has an exposure similar to Newton Ridge. Brickett has supplied grapes at one time or another to most of the Saanich Peninsula wineries, including Newton Ridge.

The first owner to plant vines at Newton Ridge was Peter Longcroft, a wealthy entrepreneur who fully intended that the postcard-sized vineyard would support small-scale wine production. However, before that happened, he sold the property in 1996 to Peter Sou, a native of Holland who had retired to Victoria after a career with Bechtel Corp. as an engineering executive. He secured the winery license and Newton Ridge, initially supplementing its own grapes with purchased Okanagan fruit, began selling wine in 1998.

Sou was an unlikely owner because he does not drink. However, he and Debbie, his wife (who does enjoy wine), often entertained in their rambling home. Sou came to appreciate what a gem he owned at one dinner party in 1999 where the guest was Sinclair Philip, the owner of Sooke Harbour House. This elegant restaurant and country hotel has British Columbia's most extensive wine list.

On the afternoon of the dinner, Bob Bentham, the winemaker at Newton Ridge, was doing routine analysis of the wines. He was particularly impressed with the Ortega. "I pulled off a little flask and took it up to the house about four o'clock," Bentham recalls. "I said, Debbie, how would you like to try a first taste of our Ortega? She took a sip of it, put some in another glass and put it in the fridge. When Philip came for dinner about seven o'clock, she gave it to him. That did it. He said, 'I'll buy it all.'" And all of the 1998 Ortega, less than 25 cases, ended up on the Sooke Harbour House wine list, conferring instant credibility on Newton Ridge. "It helped us sell our other wine," Bentham says.

After that, Sou took considerable pride in the winery until he sold the property in the fall of 2002. The moneyed new owners, Tom Shoults and Niki Suvan, soon picked up the special feeling for the vineyard and winery.

Newton Ridge is a labour of love for the individuals associated with it. "I don't look on it as a job," Bentham says. "It is just what I want to do in my spare time." For Bentham, who was born in Victoria in 1944, winemaking is an accidental second career. Trained as an electrician, Bentham for many years looked after security alarm systems for Canadian military and police facilities across western Canada before becoming the electrical superintendent for the Esquimalt naval base. In 1998 he retired to spend more time on his passion for sailing and the sloop on which he and his family once lived. Then Peter Sou asked him to move into the apartment above Newton Ridge's small winery and keep an eye on the property when the owners were away.

The consulting winemaker at Newton Ridge is Todd Moore, who juggles contracts at several wineries while working as a fireman in the Okanagan. "We get along quite well," says Bentham, a self-described meticulous person who has acquired the basics of winemaking. "I respect his knowledge and expertise. He respects my commitment to do a good job." In between periodic visits to Newton Ridge, Moore is only a phone call away when Bentham needs help.

Given Newton Ridge's limited production, being meticulous is essential. "One mistake is a costly one," Bentham says. "That's just part of the business. The smaller you are, the more crucial it becomes." The wines are made with careful restraint. Pinot Noir, Pinot Gris and Pinot Blanc are aged in oak barrels but never long enough to overwhelm the characteristically lively fruit flavours typical of island vineyards. The Ortega, where fruit is paramount, is aged only in stainless steel tanks.

"I think our flagship wine here, and this is my personal opinion, is our Ortega," Bentham suggests. "I've heard from other people that ours has really got a distinct taste and nose. Why does our Ortega taste so good? It has to be absolutely nothing but what is in the soil."

The Ortega grape, an early-maturing cross developed in Germany, is widely and successfully grown on Vancouver Island. Generally, the varietal has struggled to achieve the prestige that the market confers on varieties such as Pinot Gris. Indeed, before Sinclair Philip bestowed his blessing on Newton Ridge, four rows of Ortega had been grafted over to Pinot Gris as a trial to see whether the whole vineyard might be converted. "In retrospect, it was a mistake," Bentham says. "If I was planting a vineyard here on the island, I'd make sure Ortega was one of the varieties."

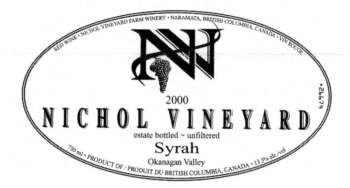

NICHOL VINEYARD

OPENED: 1993

1285 Smethurst Road, Naramata, BC, V0H 1N0

Telephone: 250-496-5962

Web site: www.nicholvineyard.com

Wine shop: Open 11 am – 5 pm Tuesday through Sunday from late June
to Thanksgiving and during festivals; by appointment at other times.

RECOMMENDED

* ✹ SYRAH
* ✸ PINOT GRIS
* ✸ CABERNET FRANC

DURING THE SUMMER, KATHLEEN AND ALEX NICHOL OFTEN HEAD INTO their vineyard at dawn because the heat can be too blistering by midday. One reason for this is the south-facing granite cliff towering 91 metres (300 feet) above the vineyard, radiating the heat of the day. Before they planted the 1.8-hectare (4.5-acre) vineyard, the Nichols took careful readings of what are called heat summation units. They discovered that their patch on the Naramata Bench, an abandoned pear orchard they had purchased the year before, was hotter than the south of France. That is why their initial grape order included 1,350 Syrah vines from a nursery on the Rhone, which they planted in 1991.

The Nichols were ahead of the curve, being the first in the Okanagan to plant Syrah. By 1996, when they gave cuttings to Paul Wickland, their former dentist, for a new vineyard at Okanagan Falls, others in the Okanagan had identified warm sites for Syrah. By 2002, this was the sixth most widely planted red in the Okanagan. A decade after Nichol harvested its first full-bodied Syrah, the variety has been recognized as one of the Okanagan's most promising reds.

Given their backgrounds, one would hardly have expected the Nichols to be pioneering grape varieties. In his first career, Alex Nichol, who was born in Calgary in 1945, played the double bass in the Vancouver Symphony Orchestra; Kathleen worked as a corporate librarian. His mother-in-law, who had surplus plums from trees in her Vancouver yard, introduced him to home winemaking in 1973. (He returned the favour by attaching her name, Maxine, to one of the artful blends he makes each year, often with differing varieties.) In 1979, while taking master classes with his instrument in London, he took a challenging wine course during his free time. He confirmed a growing ambition to make wine by writing a book on British Columbia wineries in 1983 and starting to search for a vineyard.

By the time the Nichols figured out how to finance a winery, the industry was awash with pessimism that any winery would survive free trade. They pushed ahead anyway in 1990. In addition to Syrah, they planted primarily Pinot Noir, Cabernet Franc and Pinot Gris. They added St. Laurent vines that were being removed from a provincial government test plot. A red grape now grown primarily in Austria, the vines were free to any grower prepared to give cuttings to anyone else in Canada who wanted them. Alex has provided cuttings to others each year since 1994. He has made a modest volume of wine from his St. Laurent grapes, formerly selling it exclusively to Kelowna's Grand Okanagan Resort.

As a musician (who still plays with local orchestras and relaxes by practicing Bach suites), Nichol had a few things to learn about growing grapes. "More heat is not necessarily better," he says of one lesson. He discovered (as did others in the Okanagan) in the extraordinarily hot 1998 vintage that excessive temperatures retarded his Cabernet Franc and, to a lesser degree, his Syrah. To conserve water during extreme heat, the vines shut down. Nichol's solution is simple: the irrigation system has been augmented with overhead sprinklers. The winery's newsletter in 2002 called this "our automatic cooling system ... When the temperature hits 31 degrees C, our overhead cooling system comes on, cooling down those plants for five minutes out of every 30 minutes. Working in the vineyard in that temperature, we have found that about the time the human beings are about to shut down, the water comes on. The spray feels wonderful to us, and we now know exactly how the plants feel."

Not only was 1998 a hot vintage; it also was a big one. That year, Nichol Vineyard produced 1,500 cases of wine. That, Alex said, "is the maximum the two of us can handle, given our approach to grape growing and winemaking." Too much winemaking, he says ruefully, translates into too many months of treatments from a physiotherapist. In subsequent vintages, production has averaged 1,200 cases, limited to a small but disciplined number of wines, almost all of them red. Usually, the only white is Pinot Gris, made in a style reflecting Nichol's taste for intense, full-flavoured wines. The variety works so well in this vineyard that Nichol sometimes wishes he had planted only Pinot Gris. "It would be a piece of cake," he chuckles.

This is a winery dedicated to estate production, with the exception of two bins (barely enough to make a barrel of wine) of Michurinetz each year from

Wickland's Knollvine Vineyard. (Alex had once encouraged Wickland to plant this rustic Russian red and, feeling some guilt for giving that advice, has taken the grapes to make eclectic red blends.) Kathleen had argued for an estate-only focus from the start, but it took Alex the best part of the decade to come around to the view that he should not be purchasing grapes. In the initial years, of course, the vineyard was not producing enough fruit to keep the wolf from the door. When Nichol opened its tasting room in the fall of 1993, the winery's portfolio included Verdelet and Maréchal Foch, with some Chancellor in the barrels. These were dropped quickly, especially after the fine 1994 vintage. It was the Syrah from that vintage — fat, rich and spicy — that put Nichol Vineyard on the map. And perhaps more importantly, onto the wine lists of some of British Columbia's best restaurants.

The credit for the quality of the wines needs to be shared between the owners, with a particular nod to Kathleen Nichol's ruthlessness in thinning the crop, especially the vigorous Syrah. Whether it is because he is soft-hearted or just parsimonious, Alex acknowledges that he is reluctant to hack away at excess fruit. "I just count the bunches and chop, and I tell Alex, 'Go away if you don't like it, go somewhere else,'" Kathleen says. The point is that a high-quality wine can only be made when the vine's natural productivity is curbed, even when that means cutting off bunches of healthy grapes to concentrate flavours in what is left. "I'd rather have 100 cases of fabulous wine than 400 cases of not very exciting wine," Kathleen says firmly.

NK'MIP CELLARS

OPENED: 2002

1400 Rancher Creek Road, Osoyoos, BC, V0H 1V0

Telephone: 250-495-2985

Web site: www.nkmipcellars.com

Wine shop: Open 10 am – 7 pm in summer; 10 am – 5 pm in spring and fall.
Inquire for winter hours. Picnic facilities.

RECOMMENDED

* ☀ RIESLING ICEWINE
* ☀ MERITAGE QᵂAM QᵂMT
* ☀ PINOT BLANC
* ☀ MERLOT QᵂAM QᵂMT
* ☀ CHARDONNAY QᵂAM QᵂMT
* ☀ RIESLING

THE ENTREPRENEURIAL OSOYOOS INDIAN BAND, ALREADY OPERATING nine other businesses, cut no corners in developing Nk'Mip Cellars, the first winery in North America owned by Aboriginals. Robert Mackenzie, the Okanagan's leading winery architect, designed the 16,000-case winery, an elegant Santa Fe–styled structure surrounded by vineyards on a hill overlooking Osoyoos Lake. Vincor International Inc., Canada's largest wine group, was enlisted as a 49 per cent partner for its powerful marketing skills. Winemaker Randy Picton, a rising star as Tom DiBello's understudy at CedarCreek, was recruited for the Nk'Mip Cellar and promptly made a gold medal Chardonnay in his debut 2002 vintage. The grapes he used were grown at Inkameep Vineyards, the Band's oldest business (established 1968).

Clarence Louie, the youthful elected chief of the 370-member Osoyoos Band, says the winery is the culmination of "30 years of talk" that began soon after the Inkameep Vineyard was started just north of Oliver. Now about 97 hectares (240 acres) in size, it was for years the south Okanagan's largest planting of premium vinifera grapes. "I imagine most vineyard producers have dreams and ideas about opening up their own wineries," the chief says. "The Osoyoos Indian Band is no different."

The first step was taken in 1980 when the Band put up a building near the vineyard and leased it as a winery to T.G. Bright & Co., a predecessor to Vincor. It was controversial at the time, opposed both within the Band and in the broader community by those who feared it would add to alcohol abuse among Band members. Inkameep manager Sam Baptiste, then the chief, argued that responsible winery jobs would resolve social problems. Chief Louie says that is precisely what happened. Band members became long-service winery employees in some of the most coveted jobs on the reserve. That winery, still leased from the Band, is now the Jackson-Triggs winery, one of the largest in the Okanagan.

The Nk'Mip Cellars project evolved from a casino application. In response to a provincial government tender, the Band proposed a luxury resort with a casino at Osoyoos, a village that goes to sleep after the summer tourist season. When the idea was rejected, the Band deftly substituted a winery as the resort's anchor. By the time Nk'Mip opened, the Band had also created a nearby cultural interpretation centre and begun working toward building a lakeside hotel.

Recognizing the value of an experienced winery partner, the Band approached Vincor, a company already closely aligned with them. As well as the Jackson-Triggs winery, Vincor leases 400 hectares (1,000 acres) on the Osoyoos Reserve for vineyards. Vincor offered the Band capital to build a winery. "What we really wanted was a joint venture," says Chris Scott, the Band's economic development officer. "I wanted a partner that would assure us that when that winery starts up, it has the expertise of a management team behind it, specifically in the marketing." The Vincor contribution included technical services: the first two vintages for Nk'Mip Cellars were made by Bruce Nicholson, the veteran winemaker at Jackson-Triggs.

Nk'Mip Cellars is a very focussed winery, as its portfolio shows. The winery opened with two whites, Chardonnay and Pinot Blanc, and two reds, Merlot and Pinot Noir. The style can be called international mainstream. The Pinot Blanc is fermented in stainless steel to underline the fruit flavours. The Chardonnay gets a light six-month touch of oak, again leaving the fruit dominant on the palate. Both the Pinot Noir and the Merlot are aged as long as a year in oak, adding a touch of complexity to these popular varietals.

Since Picton took command of the cellar just before the 2002 harvest, the Nk'Mip portfolio has added a Riesling and several reserve-grade wines. The term *reserve* would have been ambiguous on the Nk'Mip label. The solution was clever: the winery dipped into the Band's Okanagan language and came up with

QʷAM QʷMT as the designation for its premium wines. The term, pronounced *kw-em kw-empt,* means "achieving excellence."

Picton has the choice of grapes to support that objective. The eight hectares (20 acres) around the Nk'Mip winery give him Shiraz and other reds. The Cabernet Sauvignon that anchors the winery's Meritage comes from a fine block he identified in a Vincor vineyard. The Riesling comes from old vines at Inkameep. The award-winning 2002 QʷAM QʷMT Chardonnay resulted, in part, from special treatment accorded Nk'Mip's block of Chardonnay at the Inkameep vineyard. When that vineyard was developed originally, the vines were planted in east-west rows. As a result, the grapes hanging on the north side of the rows typically ripen about 10 days later than those on the sun-drenched south. In 2002, Picton asked Inkameep to pick the north side of several Chardonnay rows later than the south side. The jump in quality of the finished wine was so significant that the practice was extended in 2003 to more Chardonnay and to other varieties. "There are probably not a lot of vineyards that would go to that length for you," Picton says. "It is nice to be working with a vineyard that will."

Picton took a circuitous route to winemaking. Born in Yorkton, Saskatchewan, in 1958, he has a business administration diploma from Calgary's Mount Royal College. After an industry recession derailed his first job in the purchasing department of a lumber company, Picton and his wife ran a Penticton campground and motel. When that business was sold, Picton spent 10 years as a tree planter. "It was extremely physically demanding work," he says. "I decided I should start looking at other options."

He enrolled in the inaugural winery assistant program at Okanagan University College in 1995. "At the time what I knew about wine was that it was either white or red." In April, 1996, he joined CedarCreek as a cellar man. Within five years, he was the associate winemaker. On several occasions, he filled in as interim winemaker during staff changes. "We didn't have anybody else in the cellar," Picton recalls. "I had to go down and put my boots on and do all that, and then come up and make sure we were getting things done properly in the lab and that the paperwork was being done. It was a good learning experience." By 2001, Picton had been given responsibility for several of CedarCreek's varietals. When Nk'Mip needed a winemaker, Picton was ready.

The attraction of Nk'Mip includes working in a well-designed new winery. "Working in a facility that is well-equipped and maintained is not only efficient from a labour standpoint," Picton says. "It can add to the quality of the wines that are produced here as well, just because things don't get missed."

NOBLE RIDGE WINERY

OPENING: PROPOSED FOR 2005/06

2320 Oliver Rand Road, Okanagan Falls, BC, V0H 1R0
Telephone: 250-497-7945

DURING A 1998 FAMILY SABBATICAL TO EUROPE, CALGARY LAWYER JAMES D'Andrea was instructed by several colleagues to look for wineries in which, as partners, they could invest. He found two properties in the south of France but his partners backed away. D'Andrea remained interested, even more so after a subsequent hiking holiday in Tuscany with Leslie, his wife. On returning to his practice, he began looking for vineyards both in Ontario and in the Okanagan. In 2001 he purchased a 10-hectare (24-acre) property south of Okanagan Falls. "We loved the beauty of it," he says. "It overlooks Vaseux Lake." More to the point, wineries nearby, such as Blue Mountain and Stag's Hollow, were making the sort of wines that D'Andrea admired. Now, he hopes to join their league.

Born in Welland, Ontario, in 1954, D'Andrea moved to Calgary in 1982 after graduating from law school. His entire career has been with Bennett Jones, the firm founded in 1897 by the future prime minister, R.B. Bennett, and which employs about 250 lawyers today. D'Andrea heads the firm's employment practice group and has written several books on this field of law. In his spare time, he referees minor league hockey.

"Leslie and I have always liked wine," D'Andrea says, explaining the decision to launch a winery. He and his wife had come to know the Okanagan during family vacations. They were soon adding an increasing number of British Columbia products to a wine cellar reflecting their catholic tastes for both New World and Old World wine. Leslie, born in Toronto in 1958, has a master's degree in health administration. Recently, however, she has switched her interest to viticulture through courses at Okanagan University College. Her husband found himself putting aside his law books to read her texts. "It's contagious, once you get the bug," he admits.

The property they purchased had 1.4 hectares (3.5 acres) of grapes that had been planted in 1986, but the total plantable area was five times that large. The defining feature on the vineyard is a ridge with two slopes, one to the south and one to the north. The name of the winery was inspired by the ridge and by the intention to grow only noble varieties. The original planting included Cabernet Sauvignon, Merlot and Chardonnay. Shortly after taking over the vineyard, the D'Andreas added another 1.6 hectares (four acres), split evenly between Pinot Noir and Pinot Gris. Encouraged by the quality of the first crop of Pinot Noir in 2003, they have decided to fill most of the remaining area with that variety and with Chardonnay. They are considering a little Pinot Meunier as a base for sparkling wine.

With the help of a consulting winemaker, Noble Ridge produced a modest volume in 2003, most of it red wines unlikely to be ready for release until 2005. The small quantities likely will be available only in the wine shop. For now, existing buildings on the property are being pressed into service as the wine cellar and the tasting room. "The winery, that is still a work in progress," he says.

As a lawyer with a very busy practice, D'Andrea employs a vineyard manager and expects to use consulting winemakers for some time. But he seizes every chance to spend time working at Noble Ridge. "When I get out there, it is so different from what I do that I just love it," he says. He has even thought about learning to be a winemaker. "At this point it is not in the cards, because of the career," he admits. "Some day I would like to."

OROFINO VINEYARDS

OPENING: PROPOSED FOR 2005

2152 Barcello Road, Cawston, BC, V0X 1C0
Telephone: 250-499-0068

SCHOOLTEACHER JOHN WEBER STARTED HIS EDUCATION IN VITICULTURE at the sharp end. He and his wife, Virginia, a nurse, were both working at their professions in the small town of Vanguard, Saskatchewan, when they decided in 2000 to do something different. First they tried to buy a greenhouse in Swift Current, their home city. Shortly after that transaction fell through, they found a 2.4-hectare (six-acre) vineyard near Cawston, most of it with mature grape vines. Weber, who had never worked in vineyards, took over in March, 2001, and spent the next month pruning the vines.

"We spent that first year on a huge learning curve, trying to do our best," he says. And they did well enough to deliver good grapes to the vineyard's winery clients. "We got lucky," he suggests. "Some people call it a pretty ballsy move." Some might consider opening a winery even more audacious for these enthusiastic newcomers to the industry.

Both were born in Swift Current in 1969. John got an English degree from the University of Saskatchewan while Virginia, his high school sweetheart, became a registered nurse at the University of Calgary. They spent much of 1991 travelling and working in Europe. They were introduced to wine in the vineyards of Bordeaux and Burgundy. John returned to university to qualify as a high school teacher, interrupting that course to spend four months in Brazil, working with street kids. On graduating as a teacher, he returned to Brazil, spending another four months on agricultural development projects. Meanwhile, Virginia took a nursing project in India. Once they got travel out of their systems, they returned home. John spent five years teaching at Vanguard, a community just south of Swift Current, while Virginia took a nursing position in that city.

While they were in Europe they had absorbed the "romance," as John calls it, of vineyards. The vineyard in the Similkameen Valley has rekindled the feeling, with a dash of realism. "I guess there is a certain amount of romance in growing grapes," he says. "That's maybe before you sit on the tractor for hours and hours, and do all your pruning." Located on a flat bench near the Crowsnest winery, the vineyard was developed in the early 1990s by Sandor Mayer, now the winemaker at Inniskillin Okanagan, who sold it when Inniskillin's Dark Horse Vineyard required his full attention. Both Mayer and Matt Leak, the subsequent owner from whom the Webers bought the property, planted a substantial number of varieties. These include Pinot Noir, Merlot, Cabernet Franc, Pinot Blanc, Chardonnay, Riesling, three different varieties of Muscat and small numbers of other vines obviously under trial. "We have 13 Gewürztraminer plants on the property," John says. "We're going to ferment some of it and if we like it, we'll keep it. If not, we'll graft them over."

In the Similkameen, Virginia resumed her nursing career but John, determined to master grape growing quickly, has sought only substitute teaching jobs. The flexibility of that arrangement has given him time to enrol in Okanagan University College's programs for viticulture, wine marketing and cellar technology.

Orofino Vineyards — Spanish for fine gold and also the name of the mountain overlooking the vineyard — made its first wine in the 2003 vintage, a total of 10 barrels of Merlot, Pinot Noir and Cabernet Franc. For the 2004 vintage, the Webers plan to make a slightly larger volume of red wine plus some Riesling and a late harvest wine with the Muscat grapes. The winery expects to have about 500 cases on hand when the tasting room opens, growing carefully to about 1,200 cases a year as Orofino develops a market and a reputation for its wines.

In the initial years, the Webers are relying on consulting winemakers. The first vintage was made at nearby Herder Vineyard by Lawrence Herder, the Fresno-trained winemaker who is also in charge of the cellar at Golden Mile. "The idea is to hire a winemaker and apprentice right here, on our property, but wean ourselves off, so that eventually Virginia and I, but mainly myself, will be the winemaker," John says.

For the winery building, the Webers chose an energy-efficient design, the first of its kind among British Columbia's wineries, that employs straw bales. They also have considered solar energy and other environmentally friendly technologies for the winery. "We'd like to promote ourselves as a green technology winery," John says.

OSOYOOS LAROSE

OPENED: 2004

Jackson-Triggs Winery, Oliver, BC, V0N 1T0.
Telephone: 250-498-4981

RECOMMENDED

✹ OSOYOOS LAROSE

ABOUT 80,000 VINES FLOURISH IN THE OSOYOOS LAROSE VINEYARD AND IT IS not an exaggeration to suggest that winery manager Pascal Madevon is on first-name terms with each vine. He has mapped the vineyard in tiny blocks and put the details onto his computer. During the long summers, he spends more time in the vineyard than in the winery, "controlling" the vines, as he puts it. In winter, he leads the pruning crew. This obsessive attention to detail is the reason why he is producing what he believes (many agree) is the best red wine in the Okanagan. He says that the wine — the first release from Osoyoos Larose was its 2001 vintage — is better than he ever expected it would be when he arrived from France to make that vintage.

Vineyard planting began in 1999 on a sandy bench on the west side of the Okanagan Valley overlooking Osoyoos Lake. The vineyard and the winery are a joint venture between Vincor International, Canada's largest wine producer, and Groupe Taillan, a French giant that owns at least seven top estates in France. The winery's name neatly melds Osoyoos with Taillan's most distinguished estate, Château-Gruaud Larose. Madevon has made the initial vintages in a self-contained section of Vincor's Jackson-Triggs winery just north of Oliver. Osoyoos Larose is expected to get its own winery on the vineyard about 2010.

When the partners announced the joint venture in the summer of 2000, they projected that the first Osoyoos Larose wines would not be released for five years. Premium wine producers in Bordeaux always sell wines from young vines under second labels, never under an estate's first label. "At the beginning, we intended to have two labels and the first release of the 2001 would be under the second label," Madevon says. "But the wine is so good, we decided to put Osoyoos Larose on the '01 label and we put 95 per cent of the 2001 wine into the blend. Incredible!" (Only six or seven barrels, made from the tannic hard-pressed juice, was excluded.) This is just one of the surprises that have Madevon pumped about "creating new wine in a new land, with a new language."

Born in Paris in 1963, Madevon specialized in mathematics in high school. While his classmates went on to qualify for professions, he chose agriculture because he likes outdoor work. His city upbringing placed him at a disadvantage when studying viticulture and enology in Bordeaux, in classrooms filled with wine growers' sons. "I didn't even know how to drive a tractor," he remembers. But he had an early passion for wine, acquired while tasting with his grandfather who had a small vineyard in Burgundy. Most of his winemaking career in France was spent at Château La Tour-Blanche, a cru bourgeois of Médoc. In addition to making wine, Madevon has also written two wine books, one of which has gone through several editions and sold 25,000 copies.

Volatile and energetic, Madevon is not an elitist. He likes to drink Beaujolais because the wine is inexpensive and reflects its terroir so well. A man with a farmer's muscular build, he is at home working in the vineyard. Except for the fractured syntax of his English, he has adapted quickly to the Okanagan and to the egalitarian way of doing things here compared with France. "I have a very nice friend here," he says. "He was one of my workers in the cellar. In France, it is impossible that a manager would have a friend who is a worker. I like this sort of spirit in the work place. I want to stay a long time here. I want to share two countries in my life — France and here."

That also has something to do with the wines he found in the Okanagan. "I am very surprised by the quality of the wine here because it is a very young industry," he says. "If I compare it to the Médoc, except for the classified growths, there is very nice wine here."

The Osoyoos Larose vineyard, the location of which was chosen by Groupe Taillan's viticulturist, is planted exclusively with the five chief varieties grown for red wine in Bordeaux. The largest area is planted to Merlot, accounting for the rich plummy fruit in the finished wine. When fully planted, the vineyard will be about 40 hectares (100 acres), enough to produce 25,000 cases of wine, 10 times the quantity of the first release. The French deliberately chose a vineyard on the west side of the valley. When the sun drops behind the nearby mountains, the vines end the day considerably cooler than they would on the sun-baked eastern flank of the valley. Alain Sutre, the viticulture consultant from Groupe Taillan, says that the grapes at Osoyoos Larose mature more slowly and develop more intense flavours.

The vineyard is farmed with surgical detail. The stylized map of the vineyard on Madevon's computer resembles a crossword puzzle, except that each square represents a block of five vines. The winemaker has entered data on the vigour of the soils and the productivity of the individual vines so that each block, or each group of blocks, can be farmed according to its vigour. Ultimately, he hopes to balance the soils in each block so that the grapes develop as uniformly as possible. "We try, after five or six years, to have exactly the same vigour every-where," he says. "But we never forget that we are not making a car. It is a vine. There is nature behind it."

Madevon was somewhat surprised at the good health of the grapes in the dry, disease-free Okanagan climate. In one vintage, a basket of grapes forgotten by the pickers remained in the vineyard for almost a month before Madevon found it. "They were exactly as they were when they were picked," he marvels. "If you did that in France, in three days, there would be nothing [but rotten fruit]."

Madevon's penchant for detail — "the amount of detail makes the difference, all the time" — extends into the superbly equipped winery. His French-made fermentation tanks are unlike any others in the Okanagan: squat steel tanks shaped like the historic wooden vats of Bordeaux that provide superior contact between the skins and the fermenting wine. His pump is deliberately slow and gentle, and he avoids pumping wine at all if he can. When a barrel of wine needs to be emptied, it is raised by the forklift and gravity moves the wine. When Osoyoos Larose finally builds its winery (in 2008 or 2009), the building will be set into the side of the hill, again harnessing gravity.

Even the hand-operated corker Madevon uses when he bottles samples is the most expensive corker he can find so that finished samples look professional. "I consider when people want to taste the wine, it is important they have a nice sample, with a nice cork," he says. The corks are as long as those in wines from top Bordeaux wineries.

"I try to progress all the time," he says. "I try to get better. We did not arrive from France believing we know everything." While the style of Osoyoos Larose might well be compared with wines from the commune of Margaux, Madevon is firm that he is not making French wine. "The grapes come from Canada. This is a Canadian wine."

PARADISE RANCH WINES

OPENED: 1998

901 525 Seymour Street, Vancouver, BC, V6B 3H7

Telephone: 604-683-6040

Web site: www.icewines.com

RECOMMENDED

* ✳ CHARDONNAY ICEWINE
* ✳ MERLOT ICEWINE
* ✳ RIESLING ICEWINE
* ✲ LATE HARVEST MERLOT

A NUMBER OF THINGS SET PARADISE RANCH APART FROM ITS PEERS. It is one of only two wineries in the world making icewine and late harvest wine exclusively (the other one is Ontario's Royal Demaria). It is one of the Okanagan's largest producers of icewine. Paradise has operated without a winery of its own (other wineries have made the wines under Paradise's direction) and, more recently, the winery has not even had its own vineyard. Obviously, there is a story here.

How far do you want to go back? Let's start at 1904 when Matthew Wilson arrived in the Okanagan to homestead a property that came to be known as Paradise Ranch because of its great beauty. A short drive north of Naramata, the 257-hectare (635-acre) property is perched on a series of plateaus between Okanagan Mountain Provincial Park and the lake. The Wilson family raised Black Angus beef cattle and planted orchards. In 1975, Edmonton economist Hu Harries and his family bought the property and began developing vineyards there four years later. After Harries died in 1986, his son, Jeffrey, took over management of the property, ultimately expanding the vineyard to about 40 hectares (100 acres).

Both Jeff Harries and his wife, Leona, are busy Okanagan physicians who, remarkably, found time to convert the vineyard to vinifera from the original hybrids, selling the fruit to various wineries. Looking to generate more value from the grapes, Jeff Harries decided to dedicate a portion of the harvest for icewine. He enlisted Jim Stewart, a Vancouver lawyer and businessman, as his partner in Paradise Ranch Wines, which was licensed in 1998.

"When Jeff suggested we get into this business, he told me that demand exceeded supply," Stewart recalls. Paradise tested the waters with two icewines in the 1996 vintage, a Chardonnay and a Pinot Gris, and then plunged ahead to make eight in 1997 — including a rare Viognier — six in 1998 and three in 1999. Stewart recalls that his favourite was a Gewürztraminer icewine. With no production facility and no winemaker of its own, Paradise had its wines made at various wineries, including Red Rooster, Calona Vineyards and Hester Creek, by a succession of consultants. In the 2000 vintage, consulting winemaker Jeff Martin was in charge when Paradise Ranch made an astonishing 40,000 litres (8,800 gallons) of icewine. After Martin got busy with his own winery, Alan Marks, Summerhill's director of winery operations, took over as the Paradise winemaker.

By that time, Jim Stewart had learned that the demand for icewine does not, in fact, exceed the supply. "Competition was greater than I had been led to believe," he discovered. "There had been a widespread assumption that if you make it, the consumers will come to you. That is not the case. It has taken countless hours on airplanes and in airports to make this business work."

Fortunately, Harries had chosen a business-savvy partner. Stewart, after practicing business law, had become a director of a bottled water company. As well, he founded and was chief executive of a successful software company (which sold animation software to clients like the British Broadcasting Corporation). In almost a decade of selling software and water prior to the wine company, Stewart had developed personal credibility in Asia, the key market for icewine. "I had a lot of business contacts," he said. "Asia is very relationship-based."

There are reasons why few wineries make only icewine. Icewine is not an everyday buy and therefore the market is limited. A luxury wine, it appeals to gift buyers, to tourists and to consumers with expensive tastes. By using visually appealing bottles for its wines, Paradise Ranch set itself apart in the crowded icewine market. Made in Italy and printed in the United States, the frosted bottles feature a window on one side that reveals an image of a bear eating grapes in a vineyard. The liquid in the bottle magnifies the picture. It depicts what happened one early winter night when Harries came upon a bear in the vineyard, gorging on sweet grapes prior to hibernating. The cost of these elaborate bottles (nearly 10 per cent of the selling price of the wine) caused Paradise Ranch to settle on making only three varietals, Riesling, Chardonnay and Merlot. It would be impractical to order pre-printed bottles for a larger array of varietals.

The uncertainty of climate is the second reason few wineries focus only on icewine. The rules for icewine require that the grapes be picked at -8°C (18°F) or lower, at a minimum sugar concentration of 35° Brix. The winters of 2001 and

2002 were unusually mild in the Okanagan. The required freezing temperature came so late that Paradise Ranch was only able to make late harvest wines. Even very good late harvest wines, which they were, command only half the price of icewine. The substantial quantities of icewine made in the previous years kept Paradise Ranch in business. Winter returned to normal in 2003, with sharp cold spells before and after Christmas that enabled Paradise Ranch to rebuild its icewine inventory.

Stewart and Harries were considering building a winery at Paradise Ranch, an idyllic lakeside vineyard with two kilometres (just over a mile) of waterfront. However, in the summer of 2002, the Harries family sold the entire property to Mission Hill. Stewart acquired the Harries interest in the wine company and, with Mission Hill taking all of the grapes, bought grapes from independent growers throughout the Okanagan.

Ultimately, Paradise Ranch — Stewart kept the name — is destined to have a home of its own and to broaden its range of wines. "There is a certain lack of convenience until we get a winery surrounded by vineyards. I see Paradise having a facility where we can sell table wines in the domestic market; and to have a destination-type winery where we can sell our dessert wines and our table wines," Stewart said in 2003. "I like the idea of selling from a cellar door. I have to find the right location."

PELLER ESTATES

OPENED: 1961

2120 Vintner Street, Port Moody, BC, V3H 1W8
Telephone: 604-937-3411
Web site: www.andreswines.com

RECOMMENDED

- ✹ **PRIVATE RESERVE MERLOT**
- ✹ **TRINITY ICEWINE**
- **PRIVATE RESERVE CABERNET FRANC**
- **HERITAGE RIESLING**

THE STYLE OF THE WINES MADE UNDER THE PELLER ESTATES LABEL IN British Columbia began to change significantly in 2003. During the year, the company's sales team grumbled that the Peller red wines were more tannic and astringent than wines from competitors. In response, Robert Summers, the chief winemaker, set up a blind tasting that compared Peller's 2002 reds with similar wines from other wineries. The result was what Summers expected: the 2002 Peller wines scored better than the sales team expected. The perception that the wines are too firm was based on some previous vintages. Since taking over the direction of Peller winemaking in the Okanagan in early 2002, Summers has begun crafting wines in which the fruit is more forward and the tannins are softer. They have become, in short, approachable New World wines, departing from the winery's previous Old World bent.

It marks a rejuvenation in British Columbia for a company that began making wine here in 1961 as Andrés Wines Ltd. before growing to become an Ontario-focussed national producer. Peller, the family name, has gradually taken over from Andrés (still the corporate name) on the labels of premium wines made from

Canadian grapes. In the current decade, the company has invested about $5 million in better winemaking equipment in British Columbia, cemented relations with its nine premium growers in the Okanagan and Similkameen valleys, and edged ever closer to building a boutique winery in the Okanagan. The pieces are being put in place to enable Summers to craft the super-premium Peller wines that, unlike the situation in Ontario, have been missing amid the focus on value priced British Columbia wines.

Hungarian-born Andrew Peller, whose grandson, John, now runs the company, established a winery after a successful stint as a brewer in Hamilton. He came to British Columbia because the Ontario government would not give him a viable license. (He had infuriated the regulators by flaunting a ban on beer advertising.) The winery was built in the Vancouver suburb of Port Moody because, as Peller recounted in his autobiography, the city "almost gave me the three and a half acres I had my eye on." It made sense in that era, before wine tours were allowed in British Columbia, to build the winery close to the market, not close to the grapes.

In the decade before Andrés acquired an Ontario winery, its Port Moody winemakers created the products that fuelled the company's early growth. None is more famous than Baby Duck, a pink sparkling wine that was cheaper than other sparkling wines because the low alcohol content attracted less tax. Andrew Peller scored a home run with the 1971 release of Baby Duck. "Within five years it had put us in a league we never anticipated joining," he wrote of a wine that was once the best-selling Canadian wine. It is still being made.

By the time Summers began to supervise the winemaking, the Port Moody winery was showing its age. But since 2002, the cracked floors have been replaced and the old stainless steel tanks have been rebuilt and new small ones added for small-lot winemaking. There is better climate control in the barrel cellar. The entire winery has been wired so that it can be controlled by computer. Resident winemaker Philip Soo can monitor tanks of wine from his home computer. Summers can look at the data from Ontario, where he is based.

A University of Guelph graduate in food sciences, Summers has been a winemaker since 1987, except for a year in a distillery, a job he found too methodical compared to winemaking. After working at Henry of Pelham and Cave Spring, two Ontario boutique wineries, he joined Peller in 1997, becoming chief winemaker two years later.

The son of immigrants from Hong Kong, Soo was born in Vancouver in 1969. He began making wine and beer to supply his dormitory roommates when he was taking a degree in microbiology at the University of British Columbia. "I was known as the liquor guy, always supplying the booze for the parties," he laughs. His passion ignited, he added a technical diploma in food sciences to his degree and went to work for Brew King, a maker of wine kits. Andrés bought Brew King in 1997 and moved Soo to Port Moody three years later as a junior winemaker.

Over the past decade, several young winemakers at Port Moody have worked under the eye of such senior Peller winemakers as J.-L. Groux, a French winemaker who spent more than a decade at Hillebrand, an Ontario boutique winery owned by Andrés. (Groux left in 2004 to help start an independent winery near Niagara-on-the-Lake.) Summers took over supervising Port Moody from Groux. "There is no right or wrong but J.-L. and I definitely have two different styles of winemaking," Summers says, by way of explaining the shift in the style of the Peller wines. "I have no traditional heritage." For example, Summers, in his pursuit of fruit-forward wines, allows red wines only half the time on skins that Groux might do. Summers believes that prolonged maceration extracts astringency from the grape seeds.

Summers also embraces the new techniques and the technology employed by other New World wine regions to yield softer, fruitier wines. However, the most important influence on the new style has been taking place in the vineyards. Until recently, Peller owned no vineyards in British Columbia since the early 1960s but did foster initial planting at the Inkameep Vineyard, owned by the Osoyoos Indian Band. The company still buys grapes there today, processing these (and fruit from its other growers) at its own crushing plant at Inkameep. In 1998, the winery entered into a joint venture with Similkameen landowner Roger Hol. Andrés has since invested $1 million to develop the 26-hectare (65-acre) Rocky Ridge Vineyard near Cawston.

Like other wineries, Peller now is spending far more time on managing the vineyards with its growers so that its winemakers have superior quality grapes to work with. "Once I got involved in B.C., I researched when we were picking in prior years and I think we were picking too early," Summers says. The Okanagan's long, dry, frost-free autumn, compared with Ontario vineyards, permits grapes to hang until fully ripe. "In Ontario, we don't see that level of ripeness on the Bordeaux grapes that we get out here," Summers concluded after going through the 2003 vintage. "We picked later that year than we had in the past."

The entire range of Peller VQA wines — whether the basic Heritage line, the mid-range Private Reserve wines or the top-end Andrew Peller Signature wines — have begun to reflect the new bag of tricks that Summers can now employ. "I love to make the high-end wines, but I also love to make the $10 and $12 wines that offer great value to the consumer," he says. "But don't get me wrong. I love to make the premium stuff, too. If we can't make great wine in B.C., then we've got a problem."

PEMBERTON VALLEY VINEYARD AND INN

OPENED: 2000

1427 Collins Road, Pemberton, BC, V0N 2L0
Telephone: 604-894-5857
Toll-free: 1-877-444-5857
Web site: www.whistlerwine.com

RECOMMENDED

MARÉCHAL FOCH

BEARS OCCASIONALLY FORAGE IN OKANAGAN VINEYARDS WHERE THERE are plenty of grapevines from which to choose. For the bears of the Pemberton Valley, the only game in town is the 1.2-hectare (three-acre) vineyard in the front yard at Patrick and Heather Bradner's winery and country inn. An electric fence might be an effective deterrent but Patrick is not certain about even that. To be sure, he tempted fate in the fall of 2003 by leaving the vineyard's Chardonnay unpicked. Then an early November frost snapped across the vines, giving him his first chance ever to make icewine. He succeeded even though he was competing for frozen grapes with two bears.

Fortunately, the bear population usually keeps to itself in the forested hills surrounding Pemberton. This sleepy village is less than half an hour's drive north of bustling Whistler, where Patrick Bradner still sells real estate while his winery and inn become established. "The vineyard-winery is not a money-making thing yet," he conceded, interrupting the making of his 2003 icewine for an interview. "It's kind of a hobby out of control."

Born in Vancouver in 1957, Bradner is the son of a land developer who bought property in Whistler early in the 1960s, primarily so that the family could ski when it wanted to. Bradner, who has a business degree from Simon Fraser

University, followed his father into real estate. He also learned to enjoy wine at the family table.

"My dad always really liked wine," Patrick recalls. "Even when we were 12 or 13, he would let us have a glass of wine with our roast beef dinners on Sunday nights. I started to develop a palate for wine fairly young." By the time he was a teenager, Bradner was making beer with his friends. Subsequently, he became an avid home winemaker. In Whistler, where he and his wife moved in 1987, Patrick Bradner was part of a quartet that made an average of about 1,000 bottles of wine a year with purchased grapes. By the time Pemberton Vineyard made its first commercial vintage in 1999, Bradner had accumulated almost a decade and a half of experience.

The Bradners purchased their property on the northern edge of Pemberton in 1995. Because Patrick wanted to grow grapes, they first took a hard look at various locations in the Okanagan, including Naramata Road, where property prices had just spiked. Wearing his realtor's hat, Bradner chose the Pemberton Valley. Land prices were lower and he could continue his lucrative work selling Whistler real estate. And there was plenty of room for vines on the 2.8-hectare (seven-acre) property. In 1995, he planted about 3,500 vines of Chardonnay and Pinot Gris with vines obtained from the Okanagan. A few years later, after being impressed by a bottle of Quails' Gate Old Vines Foch, he planted about 500 Maréchal Foch plants.

While the Pemberton Valley has a renowned seed potato industry, this is believed to be the valley's first vineyard. Bradner compares the climate for grape growing to that of the Cowichan Valley on Vancouver Island, with greater heat in summer. "The Pemberton Valley is kind of an east-west valley," Bradner explains. "It has a bit of an arc in it, bending out to the south. We are right in the arc, so we get really good sun. In midsummer, the sun is on our property from 6:30 in the morning to eight o'clock at night. That's one reason why this valley gets so hot. The sun doesn't cross it — it goes the length of it."

The growing season, however, is shorter than on Vancouver Island. There is a risk of frost in early May that can damage the young buds on the vine. As well, late September frosts are occasionally sharp enough to kill the leaves, putting an end to the vine's ability to ripen the grapes. Bradner soon discovered that Chardonnay needs longer seasons than the Pemberton Valley affords. In his initial vintages, he took to blending somewhat acidic Pemberton Chardonnay with fully ripe Okanagan Chardonnay. By 2003, he decided that the Okanagan fruit was better on its own. That is why unpicked Chardonnay was still on the vines for icewine that November.

Chardonnay and Pinot Gris (which requires a shorter season than Chardonnay) were planted because the varieties are commercially popular. When Bradner rethought his strategy in 2003, he decided to replace much of the Chardonnay with some early-ripening Muscat varieties. As well, he decided to plant more Maréchal Foch.

A robust French hybrid, Maréchal Foch matures reliably in the Pemberton Valley, producing red wines potentially so big that Bradner likes to add as much as 20 per cent Pinot Noir into the final blend. It "tames" the wine, in his view. "The Foch on its own can be a little too black," he finds. Of course, part of the reason is that Bradner supplements his own vineyard with grapes purchased from a Kelowna grower who has a block of "old vines" Foch.

This has been one of the most popular wines at the cellar door. Restaurants, which sell the winery's Chardonnay and its Cabernet-Merlot, have not been as receptive. Bradner notes that Maréchal Foch is seldom found on any restaurant wine lists, with a few rare exceptions. The solution, he believes, is to create a proprietary name for the wine (as Vancouver Island's Alderlea Vineyards has done by dubbing its Foch "Clarinet.")

With his tiny vineyard still trialling successful varieties, Bradner expects to rely on Okanagan grapes for some time. In its initial years, Pemberton Vineyard limited production to the minimum required of wineries, about 4,500 litres (almost 1,000 gallons) a year. The objective is to double that over the next several years, to the point where the wines and ancillary activities provide a living beyond real estate. In addition to being a winery, Pemberton Valley also offers a three-unit bed and breakfast. (Each room is named for a wine region; naturally, the Champagne Room is the most luxurious.)

The Bradners also plan to develop a cooking school here, replacing one that closed in Whistler. "If it works," Patrick says, "we'll sell a lot of wine that way."

PENTÂGE WINERY

OPENED: 2003

4400 Lakeside Road, Penticton, BC, V2A 8W3
Telephone: 250-493-4008
Web site: www.pentage.com
Wine shop: Call for hours.

RECOMMENDED

* SYRAH
* SAUVIGNON BLANC
* PINOT GRIS

THE POWERFUL MAGIC OF THIS WINERY'S LOCATION IS BEST EXPERIENCED as Paul Gardner and spouse Julie Rennie initially felt it: standing on the rock outcrop at the upper edge of the vineyard. In the still morning air, Skaha Lake sparkles to the west. There are songbirds in the trees and snatches of conversation floating from Penticton's nearby beach. When they saw it in the spring of 1996, Vista Ridge, as the vineyard is called, was a derelict orchard with possibilities.

They were then living in an affluent Vancouver neighbourhood and had come to the Okanagan to take a work break. Julie has long been the executive assistant to a financier while Paul worked as a marine engineer. Born in Singapore in 1961 and raised in Canada, he had spent most of the previous 20 years at sea and was a master engineer on an ocean-going towboat. He had begun making wine at home and enjoying wines with friends who had good cellars. But until he stood on this picturesque property at the southern edge of Penticton's city limits, the idea of developing a winery had not occurred to him. "I came up here and, within the space of a weekend, decided that there was absolutely no reason not do this," he remembers.

As he acquired a new set of skills, there were times when his wide romantic streak was challenged. The nine-hectare (23-acre) property rises steeply from Lakeside Road, first to an undulating plateau with nearly three hectares (six and a half acres) of vines, before resuming its ascent toward the Okanagan's most famous rock-climbing cliffs above Valleyview Road. Gardner spent much of the 1996 summer contouring the property with a bulldozer. He tried to stabilize the slopes with grass but it was not fully rooted before a heavy snow was followed by a sudden thaw.

"New Year's Day in 1997 turned almost into a beautiful spring day," Gardner recalls. "By noon the water running off the area had brown dirt in it, turning my driveway into a little river. And the city had a backhoe down on the road, dumping *my property* into trucks. I'll tell you that was about the peak of depression. The boats at that point looked pretty good." Subsequently, he installed a drainage system to prevent further erosion. The worry, however, has not left him. "My biggest fear here is that I am going to have a pipe break and I'll wake up in the morning and see my land down on the road — and a portion of my vineyard with it."

It is a risk worth managing, given the qualities of the site. Drenched by the sun and the reflected heat from the lake, the vineyard delivers mature fruit. Gardner has packed seven varieties into the space, some on terraces, and most exposed optimally to the sun on open lyre trellises. Not one to cut corners, Gardner imported metal trellises from California because he believes they last much longer than conventional wooden ones. He even considered having them galvanized against rust until he was told that would be unnecessary in the dry Okanagan; in fact, shiny metal would attract birds to his grapes.

An open-minded novice, Gardner took advice where he could find it. "I found in the summer of 1996, when I was going through the valley talking to wine growers, that the information is available if you are willing to ask the questions and listen," he says. "I talked to all the people I could to get a good idea of what I should be planting based on what the public wanted and what would grow in the area."

His whites are Sauvignon Blanc and Gewürztraminer. Norman Gardner, his father, grows Pinot Gris on a new .8-hectare (two-acre) vineyard on the hillside behind the winery. The reds at Pentâge are Syrah, Cabernet Sauvignon, Cabernet Franc, Merlot and Gamay. The winery's name arose from the fact that Gardner grows five reds and the Latin for five is *penta*. "I've always thought I would like to make a blend of five reds," he says. "It won't be a Meritage, it will be a Pentage. I didn't want the winery name to be another creek; I just wanted to use a single word."

Since the first vintage of 2000, Gardner relied on consulting help from Ross Mirko and from Sumac Ridge winemaker Mark Wendenburg, who owns a small vineyard to the north of Pentâge. "If the grapes are good and you follow advice, it does seem easy at times," maintains Gardner. He is never happier than when he is working among his vines. "I am lucky because it is a pleasurable place to work; it doesn't seem like the drudgery that it could be," he says. "I also like machinery and I have got to say that I have always felt that grapes are a logical engineering machine. They follow this genetic pattern. Basically all the species and varietals are different, but once you learn what a varietal will do, it will duplicate that time and time again."

Gardner's parents moved from Vancouver in 1997. "They fell in love with the Okanagan by babysitting my house over the first winter," Paul says. His British-born father, trained in aeronautical and mechanical engineering, had retired after a career as a trade development officer with both the federal and British Columbia governments. The elder Gardner's home included a four-car garage in which the first two Pentâge vintages were made. Subsequently, an equipment shed on Paul Gardner's property was turned into a winery. The target is a total production of 2,000 cases a year.

In a massive outcrop at the top of the vineyard, Gardner sliced a huge wedge from the rock for a naturally cooled winery some time in the future that will include a tasting room with a panoramic lake view. "It is as close to a cave as I can get without rock boring," he says. "It amazes people to come up here throughout the year and see the amount of labour that goes into a winery. They sometimes shake their head and say 'Where is the romance?'" Gardner's reply is to savour Pentâge's Syrah, a full-bodied red, or its oak-matured Sauvignon Blanc.

"This has been anything but boring, working with things that grow, right from the fruit to the finished wine," he says. "Ships were always waiting to sink or to be scrapped. I was maintaining things for a short period. Here, I can create something that can last for years."

PINOT REACH CELLARS

OPENED: 1997 (NAME TO BE CHANGED)

1670 Dehart Road, Kelowna, BC, V1W 4N6
Telephone: 250-764-0078
Wine shop: Open noon – 5 pm Tuesday through Saturday and long-weekend Sundays.

RECOMMENDED

OLD VINES RIESLING

WHEN SUSAN DULIK LAUNCHED THIS WINERY, THE INTENTION WAS TO FOCUS on wines from the Pinot family, and to reach for quality. That explains this Kelowna winery's initial name, Pinot Reach Cellars. In 2004, Eira Thomas and Eric Savics, the new owners, changed the name to Diamond Hunter Vineyards. The irony, which also had occurred to Dulik, is that the 2,500-case winery made its name with its Old Vines Riesling, which accounted for 18 per cent of its production and almost 100 per cent of its reputation.

With the winery, Susan Dulik had realized her dream to make wine on the family vineyard. The dream lasted until her father's ill health triggered the sale of both the winery and the vineyard. The highlights of Dulik's career as a winery owner included winning a gold medal at an international Riesling competition, and having her wine singled out for praise by the renowned British wine writer, Jancis Robinson. Thomas and Savics, who took over the property in the spring of 2004, intend to specialize in Riesling.

"We think the strength [of the property] is these old vines that we have," Thomas says. "We want to try and produce a very high-quality product. In order to do that well, we figure we should focus on one or two things, rather than try to re-establish Pinot Reach as something that it hasn't been in the past."

There are at least two reasons why the Riesling is special here. The block that supports the Old Vines Riesling was planted in 1978, making it one of the Okanagan's most mature plantings of Riesling. It is axiomatic that older vines, with roots reaching deep into this clay-loam soil, yield grapes in which the fruit and mineral flavours are concentrated. "We get berries on the Riesling that are smaller than peas," winemaker Roger Wong says. "When you have that much surface area, with that little juice inside, there is so much concentration. The flavour is in the small berries."

Secondly, vineyards in East Kelowna seem well adapted for Riesling. This particular vineyard is situated at elevation on a hillside, a considerable distance from the lake. The vineyard pitches, sometimes steeply, to the southwest and is bathed by sun throughout the day. The aspect almost eliminates the risk of frost because the air flows from the hills above down toward the city in the valley. Late-ripening Riesling is safe here.

This is one of the oldest vineyards in the Okanagan. Labrusca grapes may have been planted as early as 1915. That is why the property was called Pioneer Vineyard by J.W. Hughes, a legendary Kelowna horticulturist who acquired it (and several other Kelowna area vineyards) in the 1920s. Hughes was the first Okanagan grower contracted to a winery, Growers' Wines of Victoria, then the only winery in British Columbia. Undoubtedly, he planted labrusca; these were the only grape vines available and the fruit certainly was adequate for the sweet port and sherry-style wines being made at that time.

Susan Dulik's grandfather, Martin, an immigrant from Czechoslovakia by way of Saskatchewan, went to work in the Pioneer Vineyard in 1934. Ten years later, Hughes agreed to sell the property to Dulik. By the 1960s, Susan's father, Daniel, began working at Pioneer, influencing its subsequent development. Den Dulik, as everyone calls him, refused to replant the vineyard to hybrid grapes — except for a small plot of Maréchal Foch — because he did not think they made much better wine than labrusca. He was persuaded by the German-born wine-makers at Growers and by Dr. Helmut Becker of Geisenheim to switch to vinifera, planting two hectares (five acres) of Riesling in 1978. The first wine from those grapes, a 1981 Jordan & Ste-Michelle Riesling, won a gold medal.

The vineyard, now with 15 hectares (37 acres) under vine, was expanded to include Bacchus, Optima, Pinot Noir, Pinot Blanc, Chardonnay and Pinot Meunier. In 1997, Den Dulik filled the last vacant spot with Gewürztraminer and a small block of Cabernet Sauvignon. The latter variety is not ideal for the north Okanagan but, well-grown by Den Dulik, produced several good vintages for the winery.

In contrast to the Duliks, neither Savics nor Thomas have experience at growing grapes. However, they have the financial resources to buy experience. Wong, who joined Pinot Reach two years after it opened, remains the winemaker. The new owners took their first season easing into the business, with little wine to sell. No wine could be made at Pinot Reach in 2003 because three weeks of fire in the nearby forest saturated the grapes with smoke. "It was horrible," Wong discovered when he fermented a trial batch of wine. For his own Focus label, which is exclusively Riesling, he had to buy grapes elsewhere in the Okanagan.

Savics was born in Latvia in 1943 into a family of war refugees. He grew up in Vancouver and, after getting an economics degree, moved to Toronto to become a stockbroker and a founding partner of First Marathon Securities Inc. His wine knowledge — "I've always enjoyed wine," he says — started when he helped a chef finance a successful Toronto restaurant.

Thomas, a geologist, grew up in a mining family. She graduated from the University of Toronto in 1990 just as the diamond discovery boom began in Canada's north. Thomas had intended to do a master's degree in gold exploration until her father insisted she was needed at Aber Diamond Corporation, his exploration company. In 1994, when she was only 26, she was managing the exploration team when Aber discovered what would become Canada's second diamond mine. Since then, Thomas has helped launch two other companies searching for diamonds in the Canadian north.

It was her younger sister, Lyndsay, who convinced Savics and Thomas to acquire the Dulik property. Lyndsay Thomas has now begun a course of studies toward becoming a winemaker herself. "It started from the idea that the real estate would be worthwhile," Savics says. The vineyard, with a splendid view of the city and Lake Okanagan, is only a ten-minute drive from the heart of Kelowna. "I'm very much a rookie here," he admits. "The question is what would be the potential of this property if we do it right. What could we do if one were patient?" The answer to that question should be world-class Riesling.

POPLAR GROVE WINERY

OPENED: 1997

1060 Poplar Grove Road, Penticton, BC, V2A 8T6
Telephone: 250-492-4575
Web site: www.poplargrove.ca
Wine shop: Check the Web site for summer hours.

RECOMMENDED

* **RESERVE**
* **MERLOT**
* **CABERNET FRANC**
* **PINOT GRIS**

THE WINES THAT PRAGMATIC IAN SUTHERLAND MAKES AT POPLAR GROVE are not tasted by the Vintners Quality Alliance panel. He has no quarrel with VQA, unlike several other wineries on the Naramata Road. He is just saving the cost of the tasting fees.

"In 1997, our first year, we were required to be VQA," Sutherland recalls. "We never put the VQA stickers on our bottles and nobody noticed. So the next year, we didn't have to be VQA and we didn't have to pay them the money. We'd sold out the first year and, sure enough, we sold out within five weeks in the second year. We quickly realized that VQA was essentially a marketing plan ... hand-holding for a timid public. And the people who are buying our wines are not that demographic. The whole concept of VQA makes perfect sense, but it makes no sense to us. It's a marketing tool that doesn't apply to us. So we don't enter."

Sutherland has always marched to his own drummer. Born in Montreal in 1952, he left university when marine biology bored him to backpack around the world. While trekking in Nepal, he met Gitta, his Danish-born wife, a nurse and a kindred free spirit (they climbed most of the way up Mount Everest). To earn a living after moving to the Okanagan in 1975, Sutherland learned the demanding trade of high-pressure welding and boilermaking. The lucrative trade supported both home winemaking and a passion for collecting fine wines. By the time he and Gitta opened the winery, their palate was attuned to the best reds of Bordeaux. They had learned well. The first Cabernet Franc and the first Merlot, both from 1995, that Poplar Grove released won gold and silver medals at the 1997 Okanagan Wine Festival.

Getting there, however, involved trial and error. What is now Poplar Grove's vineyard was an apple orchard beside Okanagan Lake when the Sutherlands bought it in 1991. The apple trees were replaced with Merlot and Cabernet Franc vines from France. Echoes of a hippie commune in Nepal can be detected as Sutherland recounts how the first hectare of vineyard was planted.

"We did things like invite 20 friends over, bought 20 $6 shovels and made the mistake of feeding them wine before we went to work," Ian Sutherland laughs. "I think they each planted one grape vine and then we proceeded to go back on the deck where the beer was and called it an evening." The planting was completed the next day, but when the irrigation was turned on, nothing happened. Sutherland reamed out the dealer who, on examining the system, pointed out that all 2,500 water emitters had been installed backwards.

Always eager to improve his skills — whether from his own mistakes or the expertise of others — Sutherland often travels to wineries in Australia or New Zealand to help with the crush. His terms for picking the brains of other wine-makers are simple. "I'll work for nothing," he says. "I'll work for food." And occa-sionally for other pleasures. In 2003 he sought out a winery experience in Western Australia's Margaret River because he regards this as one of the world's top regions for Cabernet Sauvignon — and because Western Australia's beaches offer superb surfing. Among others, Sutherland has worked at Seresin Estate, a small winery in New Zealand's Marlborough district that, like Poplar Grove, crushed its first grapes in 1996 and, as a sideline, makes olive oil. He also has had the large winery experience with a season at Miranda, an Australian winery producing well over a million cases a year.

"The biggest thing I brought back [from Australia] was pride in what we're doing." Sutherland says. "I always thought, 'Oh God, Australia — we can never be as good as them'. And I went down there and we made a million litres of plonk — and it was from their premium area. They would kill for the structure we have. I was literally standing there with a pallet of tartaric acid and a bin of tannins — enological tannin from Italy, ground-up grape skins — pounding them into every bin of grapes I put into that crusher. It's very much a chemistry game down there. They do volume exquisitely. They do clean exquisitely but, you know what? They don't really have very many good grapes."

He was inspired to learn cheese production in 2001 during a working vacation at a winery just outside Melbourne, Australia. There was a small cheese factory nearby. "After watching these guys, I thought 'How hard is this?'" he says. "These guys are making fabulous cheese. I already have a lab. We already know about buying cultures. I already know about stainless steel." He returned to the Okanagan and enlisted a partner, Sandra Chalmers, who had worked in the Poplar Grove vineyard. "Just like the wine, we both started from ground zero, knowing nothing, and we found people in Australia who make fabulous cheese — and got them drunk until they gave up their techniques," Sutherland says. The Poplar Grove Cheese Company released a blue cheese and a Camembert-style soft cheese in May 2002 to much the same acclaim won earlier by the wines. "It's all in the quality of the industrial espionage," he chuckles.

In keeping with Sutherland's artisanal view of life, both ventures are small. Poplar Grove produces between 1,500 and 2,000 cases a year, primarily Merlot, Cabernet Franc, Pinot Gris and Viognier (with a small quantity of Chardonnay). In 2002, Sutherland added some Malbec to his vineyard, primarily to blend into his reserve red wines. He also contracted grapes from a small neighbouring vineyard. The Sutherlands are not driven to be larger. "At the end of the day, one of the hardest things to recognize is when you've arrived at where you want to be — and stop," Ian says. "Empire building is not in the cards for us. There's no appreciable increase in the quality of your life just because you have more employees and more headaches. Gitta and I essentially run this whole show. She does the accounting and the laundry [and manages the vineyard]. I do the spraying, the winemaking and most of the cooking. We make a small amount of wine. Our last release sold in six days. And the rest of the time, our time is ours."

Poplar Grove's reds are dark, plummy wines structured to develop with moderate aging, while the white wines show understated elegance. The quality arises in the vineyard, on a sun-bathed plateau facing westward toward the lake. Even in a cool year like 1996, the Poplar Grove wines showed finely concentrated fruit. "I would attribute it to Gitta's rigorous pruning and our light crop," Sutherland says. "The other thing in our favour is this lake. It is such a huge influence on our weather, through the amount of heat the lake stores, which we then get to use in the fall." He calculates that his vines have green leaves — and thus the ability to keep maturing the grapes — as much as a month later than vines in the Oliver area.

Sutherland's benchmark continues to be Bordeaux. Beginning with Poplar Grove's 1998 Reserve (a blend of 80 per cent Merlot and 20 per cent Cabernet Franc), he has been retaining his bottled reds in the winery's cellar for release three years after vintage. "Look at the French," he expounds. "Their Bordeaux releases happen in September, three years after harvest. If you are building big wines, designed for aging, they are really not approachable until that mark. It is definitely worthwhile."

QUAILS' GATE ESTATE WINERY

OPENED: 1989

3303 Boucherie Road, Kelowna, BC, V1Z 2H3
Telephone: 250-769-4451
Toll-free: 1-800-420-9463
Web site: www.quailsgate.com
Wine shop: Open daily; call for hours and tour information.
Restaurant: Old Vines Patio offers lunch and dinner May through October.

RECOMMENDED

* FAMILY RESERVE WINES
  (INCLUDING PINOT NOIR, CHARDONNAY, CHENIN BLANC, RIESLING, GAMAY)
* RIESLING ICEWINE
* OPTIMA BOTRYTIS AFFECTED
* LIMITED RELEASE WINES (ESPECIALLY MERLOT)
* OVF RESERVE
  ALLISON RANCH WINES

IF BEN AND TONY STEWART, THE BROTHERS WHO RUN QUAILS' GATE, CREATED a winery flag, it would surely feature the Southern Cross, the constellation above Australia and New Zealand. Every Quails' Gate winemaker in the past decade learned his trade under the Southern Cross, even Vancouver-born Grant Stanley, the winemaker since the 2003 vintage. He learned to make wine in New Zealand, most recently with a top Pinot Noir producer. With that on his résumé, he fits well at Quails' Gate where Pinot Noir and Chardonnay are the flagship wines among the 40,000 cases produced annually.

The Stewarts are one of the Okanagan's pioneer horticultural families. Richard John Stewart, Ben's grandfather, arrived from Ireland in 1906 and soon was followed by two brothers. First, the Stewarts established nurseries. Then

Richard Stewart, Ben's father, bought the Allison ranch near Westbank and in 1963 began planting what has become the Quails' Gate vineyard. Meanwhile, Richard John's two brothers were among the founders of the Mission Hill winery in 1966. Perhaps because that winery struggled for years, Ben's side of the Stewart family did not open its own winery until 1989.

Ben Stewart, who was born in 1957, initially became a banker; his brother, Tony, born in 1966, became a stockbroker. Ben returned in 1979 to manage the family vineyard and later to launch a small farm winery. Tony joined the partnership in 1992. Ben had learned how to make wine: his passion for Pinot Noir began in 1980 when he made the first of several home vintages with Don Allen, a veteran Okanagan winemaker (who died in 2000). Fully engaged with the vineyard, Ben retained consulting winemaker Elias Phiniotis to make Quails' Gate's first five vintages.

When he relaunched Quails' Gate as a larger estate winery, Ben Stewart hired his first Southern Cross winemaker. Jeff Martin, a confident graduate of Australia's best wine school, came from the big McWilliams winery in the summer of 1994. He had a profound impact on Quails' Gate, making big, appealing wines, often with bold oak supporting the fruit. In one of his more inspired creations, Martin turned the grapes from the vineyard's mature Maréchal Foch into an Australian Shiraz look-alike called Old Vines Foch. Formerly a pariah French hybrid, Maréchal Foch was rescued from obscurity. It is now a staple full-bodied red with wineries across Canada, including Quails' Gate, which makes a port-style Foch as well as two grades of Old Vines, both rich and plummy.

Martin's winemaking led Quails' Gate to release its wines in three quality tiers, with Family Reserve at the top. The excellent 1994 vintage, Martin's first, yielded reserve quality wines. At Quails' Gate, the best Pinot Noir and the best Chardonnay became the Family Reserve wines. They won awards and sold for premium prices. That reflected prestige on the winery's standard Limited Release range and on the value-priced Allison Ranch wines. The challenge of every winemaker since Martin has been to craft more wines worthy of being Family Reserve. Martin left Quails' Gate after the 1998 vintage and now operates his own winery, La Frenz, on Naramata Road.

Martin was succeeded by an Australian Pinot Noir specialist named Peter Draper. Unhappily, Draper died suddenly in November 1999, midway through a difficult Okanagan vintage. The wines were finished by a team of winemakers volunteered to Quails' Gate by Thomas Hardy & Sons of Australia in a unique gesture of international support. (The link is that Hardy and Quails' Gate share the same wine marketing agent in British Columbia.)

Once again, Quails' Gate dipped into the gene pool of Australian winemakers, coming up with a swaggering rugby player named Ashley Hooper. Like Martin, he was a graduate of Roseworthy Agricultural College. He arrived in the summer of 2000 and stayed for three vintages before the pull of his family took him back to Australia. Unquestionably, the wines got better at Quails' Gate during his tenure, partly because of continual improvements in the vineyards owned by or controlled by Quails' Gate. Hooper was proud to show off his wines back in Australia. "I think the wines we have made here are quite comparable on an international level," he said before leaving the Okanagan.

A friendship that Hooper and Grant Stanley struck up in 2001 paved the way for Stanley to take over at Quails' Gate. Stanley was born in Vancouver in 1967 to parents who immigrated from New Zealand. There was no wine back ground: his father was a printer and his mother a dental technician. Stanley developed his passion for wine in the hotel and restaurant trade, including two years running a large restaurant in London and another two with a caterer at the Whistler ski resort.

Excited by the wines being made in New Zealand, he and his wife, Annabelle, moved there in 1991. A horticulturalist, she began propagating vines at the storied Cloudy Bay winery while Grant went to work at Montana Wines, one of New Zealand's largest producers. Montana made it possible for him to take a two-year diploma course in winemaking. From there, Stanley sought out smaller wineries, eventually spending six vintages at Ata Rangi, one of New Zealand's leading producers of Pinot Noir. In the fall of 2001, he was sent to Oregon to make Pinot Noir with two wineries there. Before returning to New Zealand, Stanley did a quick tour of the Okanagan, tasting with Hooper at Quails' Gate. Stanley was astounded by how vastly Okanagan wines had improved in the years he had been away. He did not hesitate to return to Canada when Quails' Gate, at Hooper's urging, offered Stanley the winemaking job just before the 2003 vintage.

Stanley has the tools to take Quails' Gate to the next level in wine quality. He was involved in making Ata Rangi wines that won the top Pinot Noir trophy three times at the International Wine and Spirit Competition in London. Hooper had never made Pinot Noir before arriving in British Columbia; his preparation for the 2000 vintage was three days in Oregon, picking the brains of winemakers there. Fortunately, he was a quick learner: he made solid Pinot Noir. And he did such a good job with the rest of the winery's extensive portfolio that Riesling and Chenin Blanc have joined the elite Family Reserve range.

Stanley's winemaking style is more subtle but also more daring. On the subtle side, he does not let oak dominate the wines. "I feel that I would like to show more fruit," he says. "We have fantastic fruit and I would like to let the fruit speak a little clearer in the wines." The white wines made at Quails' Gate in 2003, consequently, are bursting with fruit flavours. On the daring side, he espouses long periods of fermentation, as long as 28 days for the Pinot Noir, at very warm temperatures, a rather Burgundian method. As a result, the Quails' Gate Pinot Noirs from 2003 are darker in colour, fuller in body and more intense in flavour than earlier vintages.

The Okanagan, he maintains, is "God-given" for growing grapes and thus for growing great wine. "Canada is not yet in the higher echelons of winemaking countries in the world," Stanley says. "I know we're good. But how good can we be? I wouldn't be here if I didn't think we can be right up there with some of the great producers."

RAVEN RIDGE CIDERY INC.

OPENED: 2003

3002 Dunster Road, Kelowna, BC, V1W 4A6

Telephone: 250-763-1091

Web site: www.k-l-o.com

Wine shop: Open seasonally.

Restaurant: The Teahouse is open daily from 11:30 am (10:30 am on Sunday)
mid-April through October.

RECOMMENDED

* ✹ BRAEBURN ICED CIDER
* ✹ AMBROSIA
* ✸ FUJI ICED CIDER
* GRANNY SMITH ICED CIDER
* FUJI APPLE WINE
* SPARKLING CIDER

ALWAYS READY TO DIVERSIFY HIS APPLE BUSINESS, RICHARD BULLOCK IS open to new ideas. The technique for growing apples with logos on them was adapted from a practice he spotted during a 1990s business trip to Japan. Japanese orchardists put opaque bags over selected apples on the trees early each summer. The apples grow to full size without colouring. The bags are removed a few weeks before harvest. A decal is applied to each apple and the fruit, now exposed to the sun, acquires its normal colour — except for the decal, which is peeled off at harvest, leaving behind a vivid white image.

Each year now, corporate clients order significant quantities of apples with logos from the Kelowna Land & Orchard Company, the historic farm that the Bullock family has operated in East Kelowna since 1942. Richard Bullock figured, correctly, that some clients would find crisp, fresh apples with a corporate message more novel as gifts than baseball caps or pens. Most of the apples grown on this 61-hectare (150-acre) farm near the city of Kelowna are sold conventionally to fruit packers. But the logoed apples give Bullock's company a point of difference. "It is value added," says Nicole Bullock, Richard's daughter. "We're not making a ton of money on it. It is something different. It is too labour-intensive to be a money-maker."

Nicole Bullock runs the family's Raven Ridge Cidery, which sells its products — iced apple cider and apple wine — from the farm's fruit shop and gift store. It is the latest in the growing range of businesses that the Bullock family has developed on its farm. Born in Kelowna in 1968, Nicole Bullock has a degree in agriculture from Lakeland College in Vermilion, Alberta, where she specialized in livestock.

Nicole credits her father with spotting the idea for cider. "My father was in Quebec a few years ago and saw the ice cider being produced there," she says. The idea sat on the back burner until the fall of 2002, when an unexpected October cold snap settled on the orchard while the three latest-maturing varieties — Fuji, Braeburn and Granny Smith — remained on the trees. The Bullocks seized the opportunity to salvage apples no longer suitable for the fresh market and the Raven Ridge Cidery was conceived. "My mom, Jacqui, was the one who put up the money," Nicole says. "My brother, John, is the one that grows the fruit and I do the rest."

There is a long tradition of entrepreneurship here. The original Kelowna Land & Orchard Co. was established in 1904, one of five land companies that developed Kelowna. The company that carries the name today was acquired in 1942 by Romanian immigrant John Bullock, Richard's father. It is still one of the largest apple producers in the Okanagan. However, to counter cycles in the orchard trade, the Bullocks have exploited the tourist potential of their site. The farm occupies a plateau commanding a postcard-perfect view over the city and Okanagan Lake to the southwest. Tourists trek here every season for orchard tours, visits to the petting zoo and elegant lunches and dinners at The Teahouse restaurant. The ravens swooping across the skyline inspired the cidery name.

To take advantage of the October 2002 freeze, the Bullocks had to move fast. Not having a winery or a winemaker at the farm, they struck a deal with nearby Pinot Reach Cellars to ferment and bottle the ciders and the apple wine. It took some persuading before the provincial government's liquor regulators would agree to this, since land-based wineries are supposed to have their own processing facilities. Nicole Bullock finally convinced them that it would be imprudent to sink money into a winery until she determined the winery's viability. The regulators grudgingly agreed to give Raven Ridge a "grace period."

Pinot Reach winemaker Roger Wong makes the ciders and the apple wine. Born in Vancouver, Wong is another of those winemakers who started a totally different career before falling passionately into wine. His 1987 degree from the University of British Columbia is in urban and economic geography. He became a cartographer and then a technical records keeper with the federal Department of

Energy, Mines and Resources. But in 1995, chafing at his nine-to-five routine, he left the civil service and volunteered to help Tinhorn Creek pick its grapes that fall.

Wong had been making wine as an amateur for a number of years. He augmented what he had learned as a hobbyist in 1996, when he started working in Tinhorn Creek's cellar. He has since taken technical courses at the University of California at Davis. He moved to Pinot Reach in 1998 as an assistant winemaker, becoming the chief winemaker the following year. There, he makes all styles of wine, from still to sparkling, except for fruit wines.

With Raven Ridge, Wong showed he also has a sure hand with apple wines. The concept of iced cider is inspired by icewine. Unlike icewine, there are no stringent production rules for processing apples. Most producers of ice cider in eastern Canada simply freeze the apples commercially. Nicole Bullock says she would prefer to wait for nature to do the job, if only because "it makes a better story."

Raven Ridge, which produced 4,500 litres (1,000 gallons) in its first vintage, chose not to blend the three apples into a single cider. "We thought of it but I don't think it would fly," Nicole says. "People like varietals." However, the cidery released a blended iced cider, Ambrosia, in 2004 to mark the centenary of Kelowna Land & Orchard Company. There is a significant difference among the three varieties made in the initial year. The product made with Granny Smith apples, notable for their natural acidity, is so tart and crisp that it has been served in The Teahouse as a palate cleanser between courses. The cider made with the juice of Fuji apples, which are high in sugar, has a softness and sweetness appropriate to an after-dinner drink.

The most popular of the trio, Nicole says, is the iced cider made from the juice of Braeburn apples, a variety with good sugar and balancing acidity. "You can serve this instead of sherry before dinner," she says. It has flavours of caramel and baked apples, finishing with notes of spice and smoke. "To me, it's the way a good hand-rolled cigar finishes," she says. How would such a surprising simile occur to her? "I used to work in a fishing lodge," she laughs.

RECLINE RIDGE VINEYARDS AND WINERY

OPENED: 1999

2640 Skimikin Road, Tappan, BC, V0E 2X0

Telephone: 250-835-2212

Web site: www.recline-ridge.bc.ca

Wine shop: Open daily 10 am – 5 pm July through September; noon – 5 pm
    April through June and in October; or by appointment.

RECOMMENDED

* ✵ OPTIMA
* ✳ ORTEGA
* ✳ PERLE DESSERT WINE
* ✳ SIEGERREBE
* MARÉCHAL FOCH

MICHAEL AND SUSAN SMITH BEGAN ERECTING THE RECLINE RIDGE WINERY,
a gingerbread-style log house, in 1998 during the blistering summer that no one
in Salmon Arm has forgotten. A huge forest fire in August forced the evacuation
of half this city, which is on the TransCanada Highway beside Shuswap Lake. The
Recline Ridge property, 14 kilometres (8.7 miles) west of Salmon Arm, was not
threatened. Even so, the Smiths were thrown off schedule after transport trucks
refused to deliver winery equipment while the fire raged. This has just been one
of the unexpected challenges this couple has met in developing one of British
Columbia's most northern land-based wineries, a three-hour drive from Oliver,
the self-described wine capital of Canada.

Born in Ottawa, Michael Smith had been a serious home winemaker for
more than 20 years before launching Recline Ridge. He took to the hobby with
ease. When he gave samples of his early wines to his parents, his father accused

him of steaming labels from commercial wines. "I was incensed until I realized what a compliment he was paying me," Smith laughs now. The winery name, originally the label for his home wines, was inspired by a ridge in northern British Columbia where he once relaxed in the sun while hunting elk.

However, the winery decision was impulsive. Michael was then managing Salmon Arm's cable television company while Susan is a clerk in the town's planning department. They already had a busy life. Michael, whose brother is a commercial pilot in the United States, had taken up flying ultralight aircraft and Susan had an interest in horses. They had planted pasture grass after clearing the trees from their country property. "We left an acre on the side unseeded," Susan says. "We were going to put in vines for our personal use." When they started to put in a pasture fence that fall, the ground was frozen. By spring, they had changed their minds and began turning the pasture into about 2.2 hectares (5.5 acres) of vineyard. The varieties chosen included Ortega, Optima, Siegerrebe, Madeleine Sylvaner, Madeleine Angevine and Maréchal Foch, most of which already grew successfully at the Larch Hills winery south of Salmon Arm.

They planted Foch and what they were told was Gewürztraminer in the hot spring of 1998 without the benefit of irrigation. The Smiths tried to secure irrigation water from a nearby creek but the application stalled terminally in aboriginal land claims. They went ahead with the vineyard anyway. The Foch struggled for a few years to become established. Not the so-called Gewürztraminer. "These vines were happier than anything," Susan said. But they soon learned they had been supplied the wrong vines: the robust grapes were Concord. They grafted them to Siegerrebe and, when that failed, they replaced the Concord entirely with actual Siegerrebe vines.

The winery opened on July 19, 1999 — fortunately, a Friday when government offices in Victoria were open. "It was an open and closed day," Michael remembers. When a local health inspector discovered that the winery's water supply was the local creek, he ordered the winery closed and threatened to confiscate all the wine. He thought that the water was used in manufacturing the wine. After a few quick phone calls to the Victoria regulator who had approved the winery in the first place, Recline Ridge re-opened by mid-afternoon. But the Smiths were required to put bottled water in the tasting room, to warn guests not to drink tap water, and, ultimately, to install their own chlorination system. For the record, Michael Smith would not add water to his wines.

To a degree, these episodes all arose because of Recline Ridge's comparative remoteness from all other wineries in British Columbia except Larch Hills. The local regulators did not understand winemaking and the local vine supplier had limited knowledge of vines. It is not easy for Michael and Susan to get away for industry meetings in the Okanagan. Yet by persevering, they have developed the profile that brings customers into the wine shop in the peak summer season when the Shuswap swarms with vacationers. Before he ran a winery, Michael Smith admitted to mild irritation with the traffic congestion during his summertime commuting into Salmon Arm. "And now," he chuckles, "when the highways are full, I love it."

Two of the best varieties in his vineyard have been Siegerrebe and Ortega. Both ripen early to sugar levels that produce just over 11 per cent alcohol, which is quite enough for the light, fruity style of the wines. The Siegerrebe has been one of Recline Ridge's most popular whites. The debut 1999 vintage of that varietal was especially remarkable in its vivid aromas and flavours.

To supplement his own vineyard, Michael purchased fruit from some of the other small vineyards in the Shuswap area as well as from the Okanagan. At times, that has resulted in artful blends. In 1998, Madeleine Sylvaner and Madeleine Angevine were blended into a light wine called Cuvée Madeleine. While the wine sold well, Michael figured it needed a bit more substance. He added Chardonnay from purchased grapes in subsequent years, producing a summer white now called Shuswap Serenade.

In their tasting room, they soon found there is a strong demand for red wines. "We started off with two reds in the first year, the 1998 Maréchal Foch and the 1998 Chancellor, and we didn't have any trouble selling those at all," Michael says. Both were made from purchased grapes. He could get no Chancellor in 1999 but then found a source for the next several vintages. In 2001, he was able to buy Pinot Noir from a vineyard near Osoyoos. He made the wine in what he considers a Burgundian style and also had no difficulty selling it.

The challenge, however, is that Recline Ridge has been reluctant to sign long-term grape contracts until the winery develops certainty about its markets, what Michael calls "our point of equilibrium." The winery makes between 1,500 and 2,000 cases of wine a year, selling most it from the winery. Until the Smiths have more time to devote to marketing, they are comfortable with that volume.

The wines are well distributed through private wine stores in the British Columbia Interior and through the network of stores handling products from wineries belonging to the Vintners Quality Alliance. Unlike many of the newer small wineries, the Smiths have chosen to get VQA approval for their wines. The comments from the VQA's professional tasting panel provide, for the most part, helpful feedback.

VQA also helps to sell the wines. "It's a bonus for us," Michael has found. "The people who recognize the VQA walk into the tasting room and say, 'Oh, the wines are all VQA!' It is having an impact on the marketing of the products. That was part of our business plan."

RED ROOSTER WINERY

OPENED: 1997

891 Naramata Road, Penticton, BC, V2A 8T5
Telephone: 250-492-2424
Web site: www.redroosterwinery.com
Wine shop: Open daily 10 am – 6 pm April through October; and by appointment.
Restaurant: Light lunches on the shaded patio.

RECOMMENDED

- ✴ GOLDEN EGG
- ✴ GEWÜRZTRAMINER
- ✴ PINOT BLANC
- ✴ VIN SANTO
- ✴ MERITAGE RED
  MERITAGE WHITE
  PINOT GRIS
  PINOT NOIR

WHEN THIS WINERY FIRST OPENED, BEAT AND PRUDENCE MAHRER announced that Prince Charles would be there to celebrate the opening. To no one's surprise, he declined the invitation. Standing in for him was the winery's rooster, also named Prince Charles (another of their chickens was called Prince Edward). The bird was the star of a practical joke typical of the self-described "fun-loving" owners of Red Rooster.

Before they emigrated from Switzerland to the Okanagan in 1990, Beat and Prudence ran a fitness centre in Basel. Too busy to have conventional pets, they kept a few chickens. They acquired another small flock soon after buying an orchard just outside Naramata in December of 1990. Their unusual affection for birds subsequently inspired the winery's memorable name. The rooster motif continues to weave itself through this winery's story, from the Web site to the wine list. Red Rooster's super-premium red, first crafted from grapes in the 2001 vintage, is called The Golden Egg.

In Portugal, the rooster is thought to bring good luck. It certainly has worked for the Mahrers. They outgrew their original winery within five years of its opening. In 2003, they invested more than $1 million in a new Naramata Road winery capable of making 20,000 cases of wine a year, or double their current production. "We also take luck into our own hands," says Beat. "We have an excellent business sense." Born in Switzerland in 1959, he is a man of flexible skills. A carpenter by trade, he built the couple's comfortable house, and has now supervised the construction of two wineries. Since arriving in the Okanagan, he and Prudence both have become pilots (she has a commercial license), using their Piper Super Cub for recreation when they can get away from the busy winery.

They knew very little about wine growing in 1991 when they decided to replace the mature apple trees on their property with vines imported from France. "We had a gut feeling that grapes would do well here," Beat says. "Our neighbours thought we were crazy because the market for Jonagold apples was hot." Their business sense was serving them well. While the wine business has flourished, many struggling apple growers either joined the conversion to vineyards or sold to someone else who did. The Naramata Bench, bathed by reflected warmth from Okanagan Lake, is one of the best vineyard regions in the Okanagan.

The Mahrers sold grapes from their initial six-hectare (15-acre) vineyard for a few years. They decided in 1996 to expand into a winery, retaining Eric von Krosigk as the consultant to design the 279-square-metre (3,000 square-foot) winery and to guide the ever flexible Beat through the first four vintages. In time, the work at Red Rooster grew to the point where a full-time winemaker was needed. Beat and Prudence, who pilots the farm's tractor as easily as an airplane, now own or have farming control over about 14 hectares (35 acres) of vines, mostly on Naramata Bench, and buy from other growers farther south in the Okanagan.

The current winemaker, Craig Larson, joined Red Rooster in time for the 2002 vintage, making an immediate impact. The winery's Alsace-style Gewürztraminer from that vintage, when entered in its first competition the following spring, was given one of the eight prestigious awards of excellence from British Columbia's Lieutenant-Governor, patron of the competition. Born in Wadena, Saskatchewan in 1956, Larson spent more than a dozen years as a printer in Saskatoon with a developing passion for wine.

In 1996, he enrolled in a training program at the Covey Run winery in Washington State. By 1999, he was the assistant to Tom DiBello at the Washington Hills winery. Now the winemaker at CedarCreek, DiBello alerted Larson in the summer of 2002 to the job at Red Rooster. Larson has just completed a year away from winemaking, as a sommelier with a luxury hotel in southern California. He left the job because of the skimpy salary, but for Larson, who is gifted with an acute palate, the experience was a cram course in tasting great wines.

Larson's winemaking is marked by a meticulous attention to detail. "I do all the cellar work myself," he says. "Everything has to be sanitized and sterilized." He also has a particular enthusiasm for French wines. "I love Old World wines," he says. "Of course, I was trained with New World techniques. So I try to make wines in an Old World style with, of course, the fruit of the New World." The finesse of this style is demonstrated with both Red Rooster's Pinot Noir and its Bordeaux blends, including the refined Golden Egg.

The move to the new winery gave Larson equipment and space that was lacking in the original winery. The new winery's tasting room alone is the same size as the former winery and the new winery is six times as big as the old one. The Mahrers tried first to expand close to the original site, offering to buy a neighbour's farm. In the end, their business sense told them that sales would be far better if Red Rooster were highly visible on Naramata Road rather than tucked away on a side street.

"We feel privileged that we had the opportunity to build one more time," Prudence says. "The first building was very, very good, but we still had a few things we could do better. It's like people say — your *third* house is the dream house."

SALT SPRING VINEYARDS

OPENED: 2003

151 Lee Road at 1700 block Fulford Ganges Road, Salt Spring Island, BC, V8K 2A5
Telephone: 250-653-9463
Web site: www.saltspringvineyards.com
Wine shop: Open daily noon – 5 pm May, June and early September; 11 am – 5 pm
    July and August; noon – 5 pm Saturdays from September 20 to May 8;
    or by appointment. Bed and breakfast available.

RECOMMENDED

- ❁ PINOT BLANC
- ❁ MERLOT BIN 537
- ✳ GEWÜRZTRAMINER
- ✳ BLANC DE NOIRS
- ✳ LÉON MILLOT
- ✳ MARÉCHAL FOCH
- BLACKBERRY PORT
- CHARDONNAY

AS SEASONED BED AND BREAKFAST OPERATORS AS WELL AS NEW WINERY
owners, Bill and Jan Harkley like to provide memorable breakfasts to their
guests. But on some early summer mornings, spraying the vineyard before the
wind rises may take precedence. The Harkleys resolve this conflict quite practically by offering a buffet breakfast and a compensating discount. Juggling a
multitude of tasks is nothing new to this high-energy couple.

Salt Spring Vineyards can claim to be the first winery licensed on Salt Spring
Island. The paperwork was delivered to the Harkleys in September 2002 a mere
30 minutes before their neighbour, Garry Oaks Estate Winery, received its license.
Both wineries opened their tasting rooms the following spring, keenly aware of

the special expectations placed on any of the island's producers — whether the product is art, poetry, cheese or wine. The largest of the Gulf Islands, Salt Spring Island has a year-round population of about 10,000 high achievers. "Salt Spring has developed a reputation for doing everything nicely and properly," Bill Harkley believes. "Even the bed and breakfasts on the island, we've noted, are really quality. So we wanted to maintain that standard and produce a quality wine on the island. There is something pretty special about Salt Spring."

The Harkleys fit right into the Salt Spring demographic. Born in Vancouver in 1940, Bill Harkley was an airline pilot, continuing to help train other pilots after he reached the mandatory retirement age of 60. Jan Harkley, who was born in Calgary in 1953, is a chartered accountant. More recently, she has taken courses at Royal Roads University to qualify as an executive coach. Before moving to Salt Spring Island, they had run a successful bed and breakfast in a floating home on the Fraser River in Ladner.

They looked at several properties on Salt Spring, rejecting those offering only ocean views. "We thought, waterfront is nice — but when you build such a place, what else are you going to do but sit and enjoy it?" Bill Harkley says. "There is nothing wrong with that but we like to be more active." They decided to grow grapes and researched the soil maps for suitable property. When they bought on the slope of Lee Hill in 1997, they reasoned that its accessible location on the Ganges-Fulford Road, the island's main thoroughfare, would be an advantage for the future winery. "The CA side of me said that we needed to be on the main road," Jan explains. "It's nice to make wine, but it would also be nice to sell it."

Their interest in wine growing was born in the vineyards of Germany and California. In the latter part of his career as a pilot, Harkley frequently flew into Frankfurt and often relaxed among the nearby vineyards along the Rhine. "That was one of my biggest inspirations," he says. "The way they can cover the hills with vines there in Germany is just amazing." As their interest in wine grew, the couple enrolled in extension courses at the University of California at Davis. While he focussed on viticulture, Jan studied the chemistry of winemaking. She has continued taking Davis courses even as she calls herself the "junior" wine-maker. The "senior" winemaker is Paul Troop, who is also working on his own winery project across the road from Salt Spring Vineyards.

Their property on Salt Spring Island is on a part of the island that was renowned for apples before Okanagan orchards took over the market. By the time the Harkleys bought their farm, it had become an unruly tangle of black-berry bushes with a recent history of automobile wrecking on it. Cleaning this up was exactly the kind of challenge they relished. "Bill and I both like making things better," Jan says. "It gives us a lot of pleasure and we are both prepared to work hard and do it. And we like working together."

The island's climate for growing grapes is comparable to the Cowichan Valley on Vancouver Island. Thus, when the Harkleys planted the 1.2 hectares (three acres) of vineyard in 2000 and 2001, they chose the varieties found around Duncan: Pinot Gris, Pinot Noir and Chardonnay, along with a French hybrid called Léon Millot.

They were encouraged to plant the red hybrid after a Swiss plant breeder named Valentin Blattner stayed in their bed and breakfast in 2000. Blattner, who has a vineyard and small winery near Basel, does ground-breaking research on varieties suitable for cool climates and has vineyard clients on Vancouver Island. "He said 'Oh, come stay with us.' He said it enough times that we took him up on it," Jan recalls. "We went in October and picked grapes for him." They drank, and admired, his Léon Millot wine and decided to include the grape in their vineyard. Léon Millot was developed by the same breeder who created Maréchal Foch. It has a similar ability to ripen early and to yield big red wines.

In their own vineyard, the Harkleys began picking their first harvest on October 24, 2002, having the great fortune of a fine warm vintage. Of course, the young vines provided only a modest yield in their first harvest, so this fledgling winery augmented the production with purchased grapes. That included Pinot Blanc from another vineyard on Salt Spring, Pinot Noir from a small grower on the Saanich Peninsula and Merlot from a grower in the Okanagan. "Our business plan has always been to purchase Merlot from the Oliver area," Jan says. The winery opened in the spring of 2003 with about 500 cases of wine. The Harkleys do not plan to produce more than 700 or 800 cases a year at full production, although the initial positive market response to the wines may change those plans somewhat.

Jan Harkley was somewhat surprised when sales ran ahead of her projections. There could be several reasons for that, one of which has to be the winery's cheeky labels, designed by Bernie Hadley-Beauregard, the Vancouver marketer who had previously created highly visible caricature labels for Blasted Church Vineyards in the Okanagan. His labels for the Harkleys are lively sketches that mirror the Salt Spring Island lifestyle. The 2002 Bin 653 Merlot (the bin numbers are drawn from island telephone exchanges!) features a flying female form clad only in a diaphanous veil and red gumboots. Jan describes the figure as "Eartha," the earth goddess. It recalls an island resident who once protested against proposed logging by riding down a Vancouver street dressed as Lady Godiva.

2001 VINTAGE

SANDHILL

cabernet – merlot

BURROWING OWL VINEYARD

VQA OKANAGAN VALLEY VQA

SANDHILL

OPENED: 1999

1125 Richter Street, Kelowna, BC, V1Y 2K6
Telephone: 250-762-9144
Toll-free: 1-888-246-4472
Web site: www.sandhillwines.ca

RECOMMENDED

- ✹ SANDHILL ONE
- ✹ SANDHILL TWO
- ✺ SANDHILL THREE
- ✺ SYRAH SMALL LOTS
- ✺ MALBEC SMALL LOTS
- ✺ PETITE VERDOT SMALL LOTS
- ✺ CHARDONNAY
- ✹ SÉMILLON SMALL LOTS
- ✹ SAUVIGNON BLANC
- ✹ PINOT BLANC
- SANGIOVESE SMALL LOTS

SANDHILL WAS LAUNCHED IN 1999 AS A PRESTIGE LABEL OF CALONA VINEYARDS. The wines were so well received that Sandhill simply evolved into a stand-alone winery. In 2004, plans were made to move from the cavernous Calona winery on Richter Street in Kelowna to a new winery at the Burrowing Owl Vineyard on Black Sage Road. The decision sets the winery down at the source of most of the grapes for its refined and exciting wines.

In the interest of clarity, let me unravel the distinction between Burrowing Owl Vineyard and the Burrowing Owl Estate Winery. Today, the winery owns one-third of the vineyard while Sandhill, through Cascadia Brands, the parent company of both Sandhill and Calona Vineyards, owns the other two-thirds. The vineyard was begun in 1993 by Jim Wyse, five years before he opened the Burrowing Owl Estate Winery. The vineyard was expanded and the Wyse winery launched after Cascadia Brands invested in both in 1996. The Wyse family and Cascadia dissolved their partnership six years later. Now Sandhill, which makes only single vineyard wines, gets grapes from its part of Burrowing Owl Vineyard and the Wyse family rely on grapes from their part of the vineyard. That is why two competing wineries both have the Burrowing Owl Vineyard designation on their labels.

The irony is that Calona, the Okanagan's oldest winery, recognized the vineyard potential of Black Sage Road in the 1960s. Then owned by Kelowna's Capozzi family, the winery invested in one of the initial vineyard developments on this sun-drenched sand south of Oliver. Calona's subsequent corporate owners sold the vineyard in the 1970s. However, the winery continued to buy the grapes, mostly French hybrids, until the vines were removed in the great pull-out after the 1988 harvest.

In 1993, Wyse, a Vancouver real estate developer, began assembling land and planting the Burrowing Owl Vineyard. Familiar with the terroir, Calona began buying grapes again from the area and then, in 1996, invested in the project. In 1997, both Burrowing Owl and Sandhill made wines, both using the facilities on Richter Street (Burrowing Owl's own winery was not completed until 1998). The immediate acclaim won by the Wyse winery spilled over onto Sandhill. The wines from the two wineries are distinct from each other. Consumers tended to regard them as interchangeable because both wineries had a similar sketch of an owl on the labels.

By the time Calona and Wyse restructured their partnership in 2002, the Wyse winery was producing about 16,000 cases of wine and Sandhill was only a few thousand cases smaller. Under the revised ownership, Wyse retained 46 hectares (114 acres), including the Burrowing Owl winery, while Cascadia Brands got 70 hectares (174 acres) of vineyard.

One key to Sandhill's success is the way that vineyard manager Richard Cleave and winemaker Howard Soon work together. A graduate of a British agricultural college, Cleave has managed vineyards on Black Sage Road since 1975. He and partner Robert Goltz have supervised up to 526 hectares (1,300 acres) for several producers, including his own Phantom Creek Vineyard. For years, Cleave argued that British Columbia would not be taken seriously as a wine region until good red wines were being made. He thought so little of the red hybrids, even though he was growing them in former years, that he almost never drank British Columbia reds until Sandhill came along. Today, Cleave co-signs the Sandhill bottles with Soon, keeps cases of the reds in his personal cellar and enjoys them with friends and guests at his house in the vineyard.

The Sandhill wines turned Soon into a late-blooming star winemaker. The grandson of a shopkeeper who emigrated from China in the 1880s, Soon was born in Vancouver in 1952. A University of British Columbia biochemistry graduate, he spent several years as a brewer before joining Calona in 1980. There, he moved through the ranks from quality control to the master winemaker. Witty and engaging, Soon also emerged as one of the Okanagan Valley's most popular wine educators.

Sandhill makes only single vineyard wines. So far, Soon has limited Sandhill to three different vineyards. The winery's 2001 Pinot Gris came from a Naramata vineyard that Rod and Don King converted from apples in the early 1990s. Cleave's low-yielding Phantom Creek vineyard is planted to Cabernet Sauvignon, Malbec, Petite Verdot and Syrah.

Most of Sandhill's fruit, of course, comes from the large Burrowing Owl vineyard, from blocks planted between 1994 and 2000. Merlot, Cabernet Sauvignon, Cabernet Franc and Syrah are the major reds; Chardonnay, Pinot Gris, Pinot Blanc, Sauvignon Blanc and Sémillon are the primary whites. Two small blocks are planted with Sangiovese and Barbera, two Italian reds that Cleave has championed for the Okanagan.

The selection of premium grapes from vineyards that once produced hybrids or apples is enviable and Soon is making the most of his options. The mainstream varietals, such as Chardonnay and Merlot, are produced in quantity and, with their affordable pricing, sell quickly. Where appropriate, Soon ages and sometimes ferments wines in French oak. He handles oak with a delicate touch. "Oak should not be the dominant factor in the aroma or taste of a wine," he maintains. "The core flavour of the wine comes from the vine, not from the barrel." In their first several vintages, the Sandhill reds have been firmly structured in a style designed to express the fruit best after several years of bottle aging.

Beginning with the 1999 vintage, Sandhill also inaugurated its "Small Lots" program. Made in small quantities, these wines fall somewhere between experimental and reserve. "The Small Lots editions are an indication of what our winemaking future might hold," Soon says. Wines under this program include the only Sangiovese made in British Columbia (191 cases made in 2001); a Barbera (250 cases in 2000); and a Sémillon (155 cases in 2002). The small quantity of Syrah made for this program in both 2000 and 2001 was snapped up as soon as it was released.

Sandhill's single vineyard approach has not stopped Soon from making complex blended reds because each vineyard grows enough varieties to support such blends. From the Phantom Creek vineyard in 2000, Soon blended Cabernet Sauvignon, Malbec and Petit Verdot and called the wine (only 75 cases) Sandhill one. He put together a second blend that vintage from Burrowing Owl Cabernet Sauvignon, Merlot and Cabernet Franc, and this wine (263 cases in 2001) was called Sandhill two. Following that, he assembled a blend of Sangiovese, Barbera, Merlot and Cabernet Sauvignon, calling it Sandhill three (398 cases in 2001). Richard Cleave, who once could not be bothered with wines from the grapes he had to grow, now shows off these wines like a proud father.

SATURNA ISLAND VINEYARDS AND WINERY

OPENED: 1998

8 Quarry Trail, Saturna Island, BC, V0N 2Y0

Telephone: 250-539-5139

Toll-free: 1-877-918-3388

Web site: www.saturnavineyards.com

Wine shop and bistro: Open daily 11:30 am – 4:30 pm
May through September and on weekends in October.

RECOMMENDED

CHARDONNAY ROBYN'S VINEYARD

RIESLING

AS THE STORY GOES, THIS VINEYARD AND WINERY, THE FIRST ON THE Gulf Islands, was conceived in 1995 when Vancouver securities lawyer Larry Page was lunching in Le Gavroche, a classically French restaurant then owned by Jean-Luc Bertrand, who had just returned from a two-year sabbatical in Burgundy. Page's former son-in-law, when interviewed by a lifestyles magazine, sourly pegged the inspiration to the second bottle of wine.

Page (and some partners) owned a tract of waterfront land on Saturna with 30 large lots overlooking Plumper Sound. Page built a rambling home on one and, over several years, sold the others. His conversation with Bertrand involved what to do with the 31.5 hectares (78 acres) of dormant farmland on a sunny bench uphill from the lots. Bertrand not only advised Page to plant grapes, he left the restaurant to live on Saturna and develop the vineyard. Sadly, he died in 1997, the year before the vines he had planted produced enough grapes for the island's first crush. Once Page got over the shock of his friend's death, he enlisted Okanagan winemaker Eric von Krosigk to continue developing the vineyard.

With about 24 hectares (60 acres) under vines, this is by far the largest vineyard on the Gulf Islands.

Saturna's rich history adds colour to this winery. The island was named in 1791 after the seven-gun Spanish schooner *Saturnina*, one of the Spanish ships exploring the British Columbia coast. Saturna is one of the least-populated of the Gulf Islands (about 300 residents). Before the winery was developed, the major activity was Saturna Lodge, a comfortably rustic seven-room accommodation now also owned by Page and his family.

When Page bought the farm that has become the vineyard, he discovered that the question of the farm's beach access once triggered considerable litigation. The individual who purchased the farm in 1936 turned it over a decade later to his daughter and son. The property was divided after the two had a falling out, with Robert Thomson, the son, settling in a beachfront cottage and leasing his farm acreage to his sister and her husband. He agreed to let them use a road across his land when they needed to send their sheep to market or to bring in materials.

Some of those sheep were destined for the renowned Saturna Beach Lamb Barbecue which became an annual tradition after the first one in 1950. When Thomson decided to sell his property, including the leased acreage, in 1987, he said there would be no more beach barbecues. His sister went to British Columbia Supreme Court, demanding beach access along the road, called Quarry Trail. She won there, and again at the Appeal Court, but she could not persuade her brother to sell her the farm. In 1990, he sold it to Page — who allowed the annual lamb barbecue to resume.

The south-facing vineyards back against a soaring granite cliff that stores the heat of the day, releasing it to the vineyard during the cool evenings. The initial block, which takes its name, Rebecca's Vineyard, from Page's daughter, was planted in 1995 with Gewürztraminer, Pinot Gris, Pinot Noir and Merlot. Robyn's Vineyard, named for Page's wife, was planted in 1996 with Pinot Noir, Chardonnay and Pinot Meunier (Bertrand's model was Champagne). In 1998 and 1999, the five-hectare (12-acre) Longfield Vineyard was planted exclusively to Pinot Gris on a plot that had been called the long field in its previous farming history. The final block that was planted, beginning in 2000, has been called Falconridge because of the abundant population of falcons on the cliff above.

In the winery's first five years, Saturna purchased Okanagan grapes to support wine production until its nascent vineyard was ready. When the winery began selling wine in 1998, it had 4,400 cases, all from Okanagan grapes. Several of the wines, including two made from Inkameep Vineyard grapes, won medals in subsequent competitions. Whether using Okanagan fruit was a good strategy is debatable. There has been sales resistance from purist-minded consumers (and this is true for all the island wineries) who believe that wineries with island place names should limit themselves to their own grapes. Whether the complaint is fair is beside the point. Saturna Island Vineyards, which opened a new winery in 2001 with capacity to make 17,000 cases a year, stopped bringing in Okanagan grapes in 2003. The winery's own vineyard can grow enough grapes to satisfy the winery's current sales.

It has not been an easy project. Persistent labour shortages on the under-populated island make it difficult to have sufficient vineyard workers on hand for what is, after all, a large vineyard. Saturna Island Vineyards has brought in a mechanical harvester to help with the harvest. In 2004, Page, recognizing the vineyard's cool climate attributes, went to New Zealand (his wife's birthplace) in search of a winemaker with appropriate experience.

When the winery began selling its products, Page assumed that the wines would join the rather good list of British Columbia wines at the lodge. That has not been possible because of the provincial regulation that forbids the owner of a winery from selling through another licensed establishment he owns. There would be an exception if the lodge were in the middle of the vineyard. Unfortunately, it is on the other side of the island. Page hired another lawyer to lobby for a regulatory change, to no avail. More recently, the winery has been looking for a partner to develop a resort right at the vineyard.

SCHERZINGER VINEYARDS

OPENED: 1995

7311 Fiske Street, Summerland, BC, V0H 1Z0

Telephone: 250-494-8815

Web: www.scherzingervineyards.com

Wine shop: Open daily 10 am – 5.30 pm from April 1 to October 31;
and by appointment.

RECOMMENDED

❋ GEWÜRZTRAMINER SELECT
❋ SWEET CAROLINE
❋ AMY'S RIESLING
SUSAN'S SENSATION
PINOT NOIR

THE SIGNATURE WINES AT SCHERZINGER VINEYARDS HAVE ALWAYS BEEN made from the spicy Gewürztraminer grape. The vines were planted in this Summerland vineyard as early as 1978, when that variety was very much a contrarian choice for the Okanagan. Today at wineries across British Columbia, popular Gewürztraminer wines fly off the shelves. "They call it the G wine," laughs owner Ron Watkins. "Young people who don't know how to pronounce it just ask, 'Have you got any G wine?'" The variety takes up about two-thirds of the three-hectare (7.4-acre) vineyard.

Watkins and his wife, Cher, acquired this winery in 2001 when Edgar and Elisabeth Scherzinger decided to retire. Edgar chose Gewürztraminer for the vineyard, a southward-facing slope of sand and rock, when he converted what had been a money-losing cherry orchard. Along with most of his peers in the fledging wine industry of the 1970s, Scherzinger was flying blind. He was a third-generation woodcarver from Germany's Black Forest who had been making a living in Canada since 1961 as a fine carpenter. He knew a little bit about wine, making it at home, but not much about viticulture. By the time he retired, Edgar was one of the Okanagan's most assured growers of Gewürztraminer and passed on his knowledge to Watkins.

The view from the compact tasting room at the winery makes it obvious why the Scherzingers were attracted to this quiet rural property on Fiske Road. It is at the foot of Giant's Head, the extinct volcano that looms over Summerland. To the east of the vineyard is the spectacular Trout Creek Canyon. The vineyard itself backs onto the only stretch of the Kettle Valley Railway still with rails. During tourist season, a vintage steam train puffs by the vineyard on a short but romantic ride between Trout Creek and Summerland. Some day, Watkins hopes, he will be able to establish a stop for the train at the vineyard for casual wine tastings. "A lot of people have never been close to grapevines," Watkins asserts.

Few grape growers in the Okanagan had experience with Gewürztraminer when the Scherzingers were planning their vineyard. They had moved in 1974 to Summerland from Vancouver. When the unprofitable cherry orchard ate into their savings, Elisabeth opened what became a flourishing delicatessen in the town and her husband began growing grapes. The few vines already growing there were labrusca which, Scherzinger discovered, produced poor wine. Other growers in the Okanagan advised him to plant hybrid varieties. While he did plant a bit of Okanagan Riesling (which was pulled out in 1988), Scherzinger really wanted to grow Gewürztraminer, an aromatic, fruity white popular in Baden and in Alsace, wine regions near the Black Forest where Scherzinger grew up. He imported plants from Yakima, Washington, after being assured that the variety was thriving there in conditions comparable to the Okanagan.

As Watkins sees it, that decision continues to benefit the winery. "We've got an advantage," he says. "We have some Gewürztraminer vines that are 24 years old. We have some of the oldest vinifera in the valley here. You get the bold flavours that way, and the varietal character."

Watkins is a disciple of Scherzinger. Born in Winnipeg in 1950, Watkins grew up in California. He moved to the Okanagan after high school, working several years in orchards before becoming a house builder. Cher Watkins, a banker, is a native of Summerland, where the couple settled after marrying. A close friendship with the Scherzingers fired such an interest in wine that Ron Watkins took the Okanagan University College course in viticulture before ever thinking about running a winery.

In the late 1990s, Watkins moved his construction business to the Kootenays. His specialty is building homes and commercial buildings with bales of straw. It is an economical style of building practiced in the United States for 80 years. "Once it's built, it can't catch on fire," Watkins contends. "There's no air in the walls. It is much safer than a regular frame house. And probably 10 times the hurricane strength." When a new winery is built at Scherzinger — and the current one is at its full capacity of 2,400 cases a year — Watkins plans to use bales for part of it.

When Watkins lived in eastern British Columbia (not far from Nelson), he thought seriously about planting a vineyard there until he was invited back to Summerland to take over the Scherzinger winery. To learn how to grow grapes and make wine, he spent three years working closely with Edgar prior to purchasing the property.

As a consequence, the wines at Scherzinger remain close to the style set by the winery's founder and admired by its clientele. To be sure, Watkins has tweaked the selection slightly. "I've added a few more reds," he says "I've added a Merlot. And I've gone a little tinge drier. Not a lot drier but a little drier. We have a lot of off-dry wines, because our style is going to stay the same. It's a fruit-forward style. And to get that fruit intensity while getting the [impression] of dryness, an off-dry seems to fit our style really well. So five of our nine wines are off-dry."

The vineyard also grows Pinot Noir and Chardonnay but Gewürztraminer rules the tasting room list. The selection includes a dry version, another that is off-dry and a third that is slightly sweet. The grape is also blended with Pinot Noir in an award-winning rosé called Sweet Caroline (named for a Scherzinger daughter who died in a car crash in 1992). In a dessert wine called Opus 2000, Gewürztraminer is combined with Riesling and Chardonnay.

"Young people really enjoy Gewürztraminer because of its diverse flavours and spiciness," Watkins says. "It's different from any other grape. They can drink it with spicy food and foods with a lot of flavour — it can keep up with those foods."

SILVER SAGE WINERY

OPENED: 2001

32032 87th Street, Oliver, BC, V0H 1T0
Telephone: 250-498-0319
E-mail: silversagewinery@hotmail.com
Wine shop: Open daily 10 am – 9 pm.

RECOMMENDED

❋ FLAME
❋ RASPBERRY
❋ CHERRY
✸ BLUEBERRY
✸ PINOT BLANC DESSERT WINE
✸ SAGE GRAND RESERVE

ANNA MANOLA ALWAYS CLOSES HER WINERY ON NOVEMBER 10 AS A MEMORIAL to that tragic Sunday in 2002 when a winery accident claimed the lives of her husband, Victor, and consulting winemaker Frank Supernak.

During the rest of the year, the baronial winery's expansive tasting room is a restful oasis with a warm welcome. Restful, that is, unless you taste Flame, the fiery dessert wine infused with red pepper, one of the most original wines in the Okanagan. This is the only winery in the Okanagan with a full dance floor and with guest accommodation within the building. Designed as a destination winery, it was still under construction when Victor died (overcome by carbon dioxide in a tank of fermenting wine). Fiercely determined, Anna completed the building. With its riverfront setting, it is one of the Okanagan's most attractive wineries.

"It was a dream I couldn't let down," she says. "It would have been much easier for me to just sell it. Silver Sage would not be the same because nobody else had our vision." The Manolas had purchased the property in 1996 because they found the Okanagan irresistible. The object was to create "a piece of paradise" and entertain people. Even now, after all she has been through, Anna Manola still says that V0H, the first three letters of the Oliver postal code, stand for Valley of Heaven.

Victor and Anna grew up in wine country in Romania. "My father was a winemaker," says Anna, who was born in 1954. "I grew up in the winery, actually. I worked as a student for five years in the winery with my father. Being in the wine business in Romania was not considered a job for a woman, so I became a teacher." Both her family and Victor's family owned substantial vineyards that were taken over by the state. While her father continued to work in the state winery, Victor was an independent spirit who chafed under Communist rule. In 1975, when he was 20, he smuggled himself out of Romania, at considerable personal risk. After six months in an Austrian refugee camp, he came to Edmonton. Once he established himself, he brought Anna to Canada in 1980.

Victor Manola became a successful construction contractor in Vancouver (the detailed workmanship of the Silver Sage winery reflects his skill). Anna returned to teaching, specializing in mathematics, having written texts in Romania to teach the subject with games. "Math has to be fun," she maintains. A creative woman with an eye for colour, she also painted and created elegant needlepoint, examples of which hang in the Silver Sage tasting room. "Wine goes with beautiful things, with elegance, with nice ambiance, with companions," she says. "Me, I don't just drink wine because I am thirsty."

The valley-bottom property south of Oliver that they bought in 1996 was a former vineyard that had lain fallow since 1988. It was a tangle of roots, posts and wires, enveloped with the sage that grows wild throughout the valley. "Such a beautiful smell," Anna remembers. "That's where the winery name comes from." Later, one of Victor's more unusual creations — and he was a very resourceful winemaker — involved infusing fermenting Gewürztraminer with sage plants to produce the winery's Sage Grand Reserve.

"We planted the vineyard in 1997," Anna says. Ultimately, nine hectares (23 acres) were planted to Pinot Blanc, Merlot, Pinot Noir, Gewürztraminer and Schönburger. "It was just a labour of love. We were commuting from Vancouver every single Friday. I had a job, Victor had a company. And the boys, my sister, Victor's sister, his father ... all the family came here. We were working seven days a week, without a day of holiday."

Their riverside location is more prone to frost than higher-elevation vineyards. In 1999, their first harvest, a sharp frost at the beginning of September snapped through their Pinot Blanc. They salvaged the grapes, pressing them and blending the finished wine with commercially frozen peaches. Yet another of Silver Sage's inventive wines was born. "We always turned a bad thing into a good thing," Anna smiles. "Victor was a very spontaneous person."

They had already begun to make fruit wines in 1996, initially for export. They only began to sell the fruit wines (along with grape wines) domestically in

2001 after the collapse of an export deal with a Japanese purchaser. The fruit wines give Silver Sage a deliberate point of difference among the other wineries. "Before we went into this business, we visited quite a few vineyards and wineries," Anna says. "Not just in the Okanagan. We did the Napa Valley, Sonoma and Europe." In this way, they refined their vision for what they wanted to do. "I always said that Silver Sage would not have a chance, coming with just three or four more grape wines into such a well-established region like the Okanagan."

Anna's knowledge of fruit wines goes back to her youth, at her father's side. Working with such fruits as raspberries, blueberries, cherries, peaches, apricots, pears and quince, she makes wines that are remarkable for their intensity of colour, aroma and taste. She freezes the fruit to reduce the water content and thus concentrate the sweetness and flavour, then ferments the must slowly at cool temperatures. The wines are finished by fortifying them to 20 per cent. Only the fruit wines that are blended with grape wine are finished lower, about 14 per cent.

"I never produced a dry fruit wine," Anna says. "It's juicy, it's full of aroma, it's sweet. It's got that natural, natural fruit. It's a different style I am making. That's what makes each winery so original. I never see another fruit winery or another grape winery being my competition. We are in this business to complement each other."

Anna Manola has a special relationship with her peers in the wine industry, who rallied around as she endured personal tragedy in 2002. Sandra Oldfield, the winemaker at nearby Tinhorn Creek, led the team to finish the 2002 wines for Silver Sage after Victor's death and helped Anna find a qualified cellar worker for the 2003 vintage. Full of gritty courage and helped by her family, Anna completed work on the elegant winery and immersed herself in the business.

"I need to be busy," she says, a husky catch in voice. "I cannot sit and really acknowledge the damage that was done to my life. I know that for today, I have so many things to do. The pain comes at the end of the day when Victor is not there to say how much we accomplished."

SKIMMERHORN WINERY AND VINEYARD

OPENING: PROPOSED FOR 2006

1218 27th Avenue South Creston, BC, V0B 1G1
Telephone: 250-428-7421

THE SKIMMERHORN VINEYARD, PLANTED IN 2003, OCCUPIES A PLATEAU just south of Creston, overlooking the canyon of the Goat River. The view is breathtaking. The vines are on a steep slope with an ideal southern exposure. In the canyon beyond the vineyard, the emerald-hued river, a tributary of the Kootenay River, bends like a horseshoe around the Skimmerhorn property. This scenic spot is not well known, even to local residents, because the canyon is not readily visible from Highway 3 as it crosses the Creston Valley. Allen and Marleen Hoag, who own this vineyard, will need to devise excellent signs to attract visitors until their winery has established a profile.

The winery's name is prominent in Creston, where it is found on everything from a motel to a mountain. Hoag has just begun to research the person behind the name. It is believed to refer to Frank Skimmerhorn, an American who moved to the Creston area in the nineteenth century, a possible fugitive from justice who became a pillar of the community north of the border.

This will be British Columbia's most eastern winery, and the second one in the Kootenays. The groundbreaker was Columbia Gardens, which opened in 2001 near Trail. When Hoag was considering a vineyard, one of the first persons he consulted was Tom Bryden, one of the founders of Columbia Gardens. There is no reason why vineyards should not flourish in the Creston Valley, provided appropriate varieties are planted, since apples and other fruit have grown in the valley since 1901. A community named Wynndel trumpeted in the 1920s that it was the world's strawberry capital.

Born in Alberta in 1958, Hoag grew up in Victoria and became a millwright. His father had worked with a department store in contract sales and then moved to a fruit farm near Creston. Hoag took over the farm in 1984 and still operates it, growing cherries and apples. In some years, the market value of the produce has been degraded by hailstorms. Looking to salvage value from hail-damaged fruit, the Hoags began researching the production of apple and cherry ciders.

Hoag was well down the road to establishing a cidery when he had second thoughts. "The reality is that cider is a fairly small and specific market," he says. "It might be easier to get experience in a market that is a little more active. That's why we decided to do a grape winery. It may be a path of less resistance."

The Hoags came to that conclusion at the same time that the vineyard property came onto the market. The property had been an orchard until, in an acrimonious dispute with his tenant, the former owner bulldozed the trees into a bonfire and planted barley for one season. "It was perfect," Hoag chuckles. He bought the property in the fall, with nothing to clear away but barley stubble. The scenic values of the site clinched the decision to develop a vineyard.

The 5.6-hectare (14-acre) vineyard is planted primarily to four varieties. Maréchal Foch and Gewürztraminer vines are planted on the site's richer clay soils, while Pinot Noir and Pinot Gris are on the lighter sandy loam. "I put the Pinots on the very best sites, our absolute best spots, hoping that we can do a good Pinot Noir," Hoag says. "We want to do more than just an acceptable red."

An assortment of other varieties, including Riesling, Schönburger and Auxerrois, have also been planted here and at a .8-hectare (2-acre) site on the Hoag fruit farm. These are being tested for possible icewine production. Hoag believes that the Creston Valley, which can get sharp freezes in mid-November, could produce some excellent icewines.

Hoag's plan for building a winery depends on when the vines begin bearing sufficient grapes. He is not pushing for production, knowing, as an experienced farmer, that this is how quality wine grapes are grown. "It is our goal to have relatively small crops," he says. "That way, we will be able to achieve earlier ripening and get good-quality fruit. Since our market is relatively unknown, and we presume it to be small, there is no need to run to huge volumes right away." In the meantime, Hoag will be schooling himself in viticulture and winemaking, since there is not much chance of enticing a consulting winemaker from the Okanagan. There is so little chance of that, in fact, that he is even making inquiries in the southern hemisphere for winemakers interested in the challenge of doing a few vintages in Creston.

SPILLER ESTATE WINERY

OPENED: 2003

475 Upper Bench Road North, Penticton, BC, V2A 8T4
Telephone: 250-490-4162
Web site: www.spillerestates.com
Wine shop: Open daily spring through late fall. Lunch available during summer.

RECOMMENDED

✴ CHERRY
  PEACH
  APRICOT
  PEACH DESSERT WINE

KEITH AND LYNN HOLMAN OPENED THIS WINERY, ALONG WITH THE comfortable bed and breakfast next door, partly in a defensive move against the eroding economics of the orchard business. "It happened mainly because you can't make a living fruit farming," Lynn Holman says bluntly.

The Holmans are among the Okanagan's most experienced orchardists. Lynn Holman's family has grown fruit for three generations, beginning with Cedric Sworder, her grandfather. She and Keith have managed more than 40 hectares (100 acres) of fruit trees near Penticton for more than 25 years. As the profitability in apples declined, they have diversified, adding lucrative late-season cherries.

Their most visible diversification has turned the Spiller's Corner fruit stand, one of the Okanagan's oldest, into a destination with a winery and an elegant inn in a 1930s-era home built by the late Elbert Spiller. He was another of the early orchardists in the region. No doubt to the chagrin of his heirs, the Spiller name also gained notoriety in Penticton because Elbert's daughter was convicted of embezzling a substantial sum from the bank where she worked. Perhaps this bit of local lore might one day find its way onto a whimsical wine label.

When the Holmans bought the Spiller house from the estate in the late 1990s, it had fallen into genteel disrepair. It has been carefully restored as a four-unit bed and breakfast inn commanding a 360-degree view of surrounding orchards and vineyards. With its bright green roof and period architecture, the inn could be a neat farmhouse transported from the Swiss Alps. The winery tasting room, with a similar green roof, is across the patio in a renovated garage.

Fully occupied with their orchards, the Holmans have retained experienced individuals to manage the inn and to make the wine. The initial innkeeper, Joe Chan, a family friend of the Holmans, is a veteran Victoria hotel food and beverage manager (the storied Empress is one of the hotels on his résumé). A friendly individual with an open mind when it comes to wine, Chan had a taste for Bordeaux red wines. He was sceptical about fruit wines. "When Keith asked me to come up and do fruit wines, I said, do I have to drink the stuff?" When he left after the first season, he was a convert to fruit wines and left behind many good ideas for pairing the wines with food. "This is fun stuff," he said of the wines. "Let's have a good time and let's laugh. I know a lot of people bought wine because they had a good time [in the wine shop]."

The wines are crafted by Ron Taylor. A microbiologist with a University of British Columbia degree, Taylor spent the first 25 years of his winemaking career at the Andrés winery in Port Moody. After a brief diversion into the bottled water industry, Taylor has a flourishing second career making fruit wines. He has consulted with most of British Columbia's fruit wineries, currently making the wine at Spiller in the Okanagan and at the Westham Island winery in Delta. At Spiller, grape wines are returning to his repertoire. In 2004, the Holmans purchased a 6.8-hectare (17-acre) vineyard next to the nearby Benchland winery. The varieties planted include Zweigelt, Gewürztraminer, Chardonnay, Riesling and Pinot Gris.

All the fruit wines are made from fruit grown in the Holman orchard. The Spiller apple wine, crisply fresh and dry, is blended from the juice of five varieties of dessert apples: Fuji, Gala, McIntosh, Red Delicious and Golden Delicious. The Spiller pear wine, made with Bartlett and Anjou pears, is dry, with concentrated flavours of spicy fruit. Joe Chan drew on his background in restaurant kitchens for food-pairing ideas. "You know what I do with my pear wine?" he asked rhetorically. "I finish off my pork tenderloin with it and I do a sauce with it. I use the apple wine to make a sabayon sauce with my salmon. Lemon juice and apple wine and egg yolks. It is slightly different from hollandaise, which everybody has. Also, apple wine is great with smoked salmon."

For the peach wine, which is soft and off-dry, Taylor uses Red Haven. The winery also offers a sweeter, dessert-style peach wine, made from the ripest of peaches. The ripe, lingering flavours of the port-style cherry dessert wine reflect Taylor's skill at balancing fruit wines so they appeal to consumers who prefer sweetness and also to those who want a drier finish so the wine will go with food. Chan recommends pairing the cherry wine with duck breast as well as with chocolate pâté. The tangy apricot wine, made from the Tilton variety, shows similar balance. Chan uses it to create apricot and banana breakfast crêpes, sautéing the fruit in the apricot wine and a dash of dark rum.

ST. HUBERTUS ESTATE WINERY

OPENED: 1992

5225 Lakeshore Road, Kelowna, BC, V1W 4J1

Telephone: 250-764-7888

Toll-free: 1-800-989-WINE

Web site: www.st-hubertus.bc.ca

Wine shop: Open daily 10 am – 5.30 pm May through October;
noon – 5 pm Tuesday through Saturday November through April.

RECOMMENDED

- ✳ OAK BAY PINOT NOIR ICEWINE
- ✳ CHASSELAS
- ✳ ICEWINE
- ✳ OAK BAY GAMAY NOIR
- OAK BAY PINOT MEUNIER
- MARÉCHAL FOCH
- SUMMER SYMPHONY

IT WOULD BE HARD TO FIND MORE RESILIENT PEOPLE THAN LEO AND Andy Gebert, the owners of St. Hubertus. Their winery and Leo's heritage home (circa 1932) were razed by a forest fire in late August, 2003. They had a temporary wine shop open within a week. A permanent new shop opened for the Okanagan Wine Festival at the beginning of October. They introduced two new labels, Glowing Amber and Fireman's Red, with profits going to a local relief fund. And work had begun to replace both the winery and the home.

Theirs was the only winery destroyed that summer when a forest fire burned the Okanagan Mountain Provincial Park from Naramata to Kelowna. The dense smoke hanging over the vineyards east and southeast of Kelowna impregnated the skins of the grapes, making many unsuitable for table wine. The Gebert brothers did not bother to pick their vineyard, making wine instead from grapes purchased elsewhere in the Okanagan. Remarkably, St. Hubertus was able to make all of its usual varieties in 2003, even Chasselas. Quails' Gate, the only other winery with Chasselas, allowed St. Hubertus to buy some of its wine.

Both luck and good planning explain why St. Hubertus, a 10,000-case producer, hardly missed a beat. When the winery burned, the only wine lost was 2,000 litres (440 gallons) of port. All other wine from the previous vintage, including the 2002 icewine, was already bottled and stored in the new warehouse a short distance from the winery. The warehouse, a corner of which became the new tasting room, was untouched by the fire. An older storage building nearby was turned into the new winery. And everything had been insured. "Leo is very religious about that," Andy says of his brother. "Whenever new equipment arrives, it is always fully insured."

You would expect nothing less, since the brothers are Swiss. Leo was born in 1958 at Rapperswil, a picturesque agricultural community in the German-speaking part of Switzerland. He trained as a banker and then worked in the United States with a plastics fabricator. But as a student, he spent his summers in small Swiss vineyards and that fired his desire to be a farmer.

With Barbara, his wife, he came to Canada in 1984 to farm. He chose British Columbia because of the mountains. "Paradise," as Gebert likes to call it. In Switzerland, land holdings are small, tightly controlled and very costly. Here, he could buy a substantial vineyard in a single parcel.

"When we bought the vineyard, my parents were involved in it," Leo says. "But my Dad passed away shortly after we got the vineyard, so it basically went into the estate. And then it was subdivided into two properties. I kept St. Hubertus on one side [of a ravine] and Andy got the other side." Andy's vineyard is called Oak Bay, a name now also on reserve-level St. Hubertus wines. The brothers have a seamless relationship. "We are brothers, we married sisters, we are neighbours, we are business partners and that's as close as any family ever should get together," Andy smiles. "We are very different from each other — I guess that's one of the reasons why it works." Andy, who was born in 1965, came to Canada in 1990 after a few years skippering yachts in the Caribbean. He has been an active winery partner since 1994.

The brothers grow grapes on one of the oldest vineyards in the Kelowna area. It is believed it was planted in 1928 by J.W. Hughes, the Kelowna horticulturist who established commercial vineyards in the Okanagan at this time. The vineyard, when Leo took over, was a mixed bag of varieties. Diamond, a white labrusca cross, came out as soon as Leo tasted the wine. Verdelet, a white French hybrid planted in the 1960s, was used for a value-priced white until it was removed in 2001 to make way for more profitable grapes. "There is one Verdelet plant still there," Leo says. "Even the birds don't get too wild about it. I'm sure that's not a good sign." However, a Riesling block planted in 1978, now one of the Okanagan's oldest, still makes full-flavoured wines.

Leo was cheered when he found the vineyard had a plot of Chasselas, the major white in Switzerland. The delicate wine made from these grapes has become the signature wine for St. Hubertus, even selling to Switzerland. "If it weren't a Swiss variety, I wouldn't plant it," Leo says. "It ripens well in the summer, no problem. It is not very winter hardy. It is so easily damaged by late frost."

Leo Gebert learned early about frost in the vineyard. "In 1984, on October 31, it went to 13 below Fahrenheit," he recalls. "Everything was green. The harvest wasn't even done at that time. It caused tremendous damage to the vineyard. Then in 1985, at the beginning of November, it dropped. Out here, it was 28 below Fahrenheit. And for five weeks, the warmest we had was minus 18. That was basically our first year here. It was a little bit on the devastating side. The first cheques I got were from crop insurance."

Yet he found that Riesling and Pinot Blanc had survived the brutal cold. Gebert proceeded with additional plantings with his crop insurance and later with government adjustment payments. With the exception of Maréchal Foch, the entire vineyard has been converted to premium vinifera grapes, including Pinot Meunier, Pinot Noir, Gamay, Bacchus and Merlot. Subsequent experience has brought some changes. Bacchus, for example, is prone to disease and Merlot ripens too late. Even though the vanity plates on two of Leo's vehicles read Merlot and Bacchus, both varieties have come out, replaced chiefly by Gewürztraminer. But for the smoke damage in 2003, the Okanagan's first Chambourcin would have been made. The variety is similar to Foch, but darker and more full-bodied. "They say it's the Rolls Royce of the Foch and we are very successful with the Foch, so we figured this is a logical extension to it," Andy explains.

To consumers, it seems there are two wineries here because of the two labels: St. Hubertus and Oak Bay. "We consider the Oak Bay as the Grand Reserve," Leo says. "All Oak Bay wines are either barrel-fermented and/or barrel-aged." The use of oak is Andy's influence. "He likes oak barrel-aged wines and I don't," Leo admits. But then he backs away from such a categorical rejection of oak. "The way we use it in the Oak Bay wines, I don't have a problem with it. But I quite often have a problem with heavy oak. I prefer the fruitier-style wine. When you look at the trends of the wines, people are going back to the fruitier, natural-style wines. In the Okanagan, that's what we're really strong in."

ST. LASZLO VINEYARDS

OPENED: 1984

Highway 3, Keremeos, BC, V0X 1N0
Telephone: 250-499-2856
Wine shop: Open daily 9 am – 5 pm and later if necessary.

RECOMMENDED

ROSE PETAL
RASPBERRY
PINOT GRIS LATE HARVEST

AS WINEMAKER JOE RITLOP JR. PUTS IT, "WE SING AND DANCE TO OUR OWN MUSIC here." He could be speaking of the winery's substantial range of grape and fruit wines, which is as numerous as the players in a small orchestra. This selection runs all the way from rose petal wine to a varietal, the only one made in British Columbia, from Clinton grapes. Generous and informal, the Ritlop family usually has most of the wines available for tasting in this modest Similkameen Valley winery.

The winemaker's comment also reflects the Ritlop family's stubborn streak. His father, also named Joe, launched the winery in 1984 after he could not get other wineries to buy all of his grapes. In a 1985 interview with me, he recalled telling wineries: "If you don't want all of them, I won't sell you any."

"We are not the go-with-the-flow crowd," Joe Jr. acknowledges. Winemaking here is resolutely traditional, eschewing the use of sulphur as a wine preservative and using only the wild yeasts that come naturally from the vineyard. Joe Jr. is inclined to think of the certified enologists employed at some other wineries as chemists. "We are vintners," he says. "We are from the old school of thought." His father once refused a wine writer's request for an interview, saying he was not going to give away the secret of his wines.

The elder Ritlop was born in Slovenia in 1933, into a family that had been making wine for at least three generations. He came to Canada in 1954 and made a living where he could find it. "In this country, you work at what you can get," he told me in an interview the year after he opened the winery, initially called Keremeos Vineyards. He and Mary, his Saskatchewan-born wife, came to British Columbia in 1963 and, seven years later, bought an eight-hectare (20-acre) property at the outskirts of Keremeos. "I find this to be the most favourable climate," he explained later. "I can grow better-quality grapes here than in the Okanagan Valley."

He began planting grapes in 1976. The initial choices reflected an era when vinifera varieties had few champions. Like everybody else, Joe Ritlop planted hardy hybrids, including Verdelet (still in production), Interlaken and Clinton. The latter is an old American hybrid seldom seen today although it was grown once even in northern Italy because it could withstand the *Phylloxera* that killed traditional European vines in the late nineteenth century. *Phylloxera*, an insect that sucks sap from vine roots, is not a significant threat in the sandy Similkameen, but cold winters are.

"I tried to select the hardiest I could," Joe Ritlop said in 1985. "We have cold winters — a dry cold. So far most of my plants have survived." But while he chose winter-hardy varieties, Ritlop also took an early gamble on vinifera, including Chardonnay and Gewürztraminer. Among his first plantings was Riesling, which then was just being introduced to the Okanagan and Similkameen valleys. The proliferation at St. Laszlo occurred because Ritlop planted small test plots of numerous varieties. "Always," he vowed, "I am going to keep many varieties."

One of those freezing winters early in the 1980s snapped across the vineyard when there were still unpicked grapes. Jumping at the opportunity, the Ritlops made icewine. This style of wine was so unfamiliar in Canada at the time that St. Laszlo was prevented from entering it in the Pacific National Exhibition's 1985 wine competition because there was no icewine category. Credit for Canada's first icewine generally is given to Walter Hainle who made a hobby-sized batch in 1973. When Hainle and his son, Tilman, opened Hainle Vineyards in 1988, they were able to offer icewines from vintages as early as 1978. Technically, St. Laszlo could argue that it was the first British Columbia winery to commercialize icewine since the Similkameen winery opened three years earlier than Hainle. Today, Joe Jr. just shrugs. Who was first is not an argument that interests him so long after the fact.

With the perception, or perhaps the reality, that winters have become milder, Joe Jr., who was born in 1957, has added or plans to add some mainstream vinifera to the vineyard. The varieties include Merlot, Pinot Noir, Pinot Gris and Gamay. "We are evolving," Joe Jr. explains. "We're coming out with a whole new generation of products."

It makes for crowded shelves in the tasting room because, some years ago, Joe Jr. also began introducing fruit wines at St. Laszlo. "I am the guy that resurrected the fruit wine idea," he maintains. Tourists coming into the tasting room asked for such wines. "So I accessed some raspberries and made a trial batch. It proved to be very popular." Since that inaugural wine, he has added products made from cherries, strawberries, pears, peaches, blackberries, blueberries, saskatoons and elderberries.

His most intriguing non-grape wine came about in 2001 when he was asked if he would make a wine from rose petals. When he agreed, he was surprised to get 22.7 kilograms (50 pounds) of rose petals of assorted hues. The result was a wine that was light pink in colour and exotically spicy in aroma and flavour. Now, it has become part of the St. Laszlo repertoire whenever Joe Jr. gets his hands on rose petals. As for the recipe, it is a brave person who will ask.

ST. URBAN WINERY

OPENING: PROPOSED FOR 2004

47189 Bailey Road, Chilliwack, BC, V2R 4S8
Telephone: 604-858-7652
Wine shop: Call for hours.

CHRISTMAS, 2003, BEFORE THIS WINERY OPENED, PAUL KOMPAUER'S GIFT FROM his wife, Kathy, was a framed copy of his family tree. It shows winemakers were in the family in Europe at least since 1740. Kompauer was a 19-year-old university student when he fled Czechoslovakia in 1968, just after Soviet tanks rolled in to subjugate the Czechs. While he became a successful civil engineer in Canada, the passion for making wine never left him. Now he is re-creating his heritage in a most unlikely place, a flat, four-hectare (10-acre) farm east of Chilliwack, where the Fraser delta runs up against the mountains.

He grew up in the village of Rača, a suburb of Bratislava, the capital of Slovakia, the country that emerged in 1993 when Czechoslovakia split. The Slovak wine route runs along the Danube here, through communities with small vineyards. Paul Kompauer's older brother, Otto, runs the vineyard that was returned to the family when state-owned farms were disbanded. The brother also looks after a house and an acre of vines that Paul and Winnipeg-born Kathy bought in Rača a few years ago. Paul had grown up across the street, remembered good times in the home's wine cellar, and could not resist the nostalgic bargain when he saw the house for sale.

"I am a seventh-generation winemaker from Slovakia," he says. "I made my first wine when I was 12, 13 years old — independently. And it was drinkable, too." He had just finished a year at college when the Soviet tanks invaded. Kompauer, too independent to live under Communism, was already planning to leave the country for the West. The invasion accelerated that plan. "The Russians invaded on the twentieth of August and I left on the fourth of September," he remembers. "I was in Canada on the tenth of October."

After getting his engineering degree from the University of Alberta, Kompauer moved to British Columbia in 1976 because the milder climate reminded him of home. His first Canadian winter, months of snow in Thunder Bay, had been a shock after Bratislava.

In 1989, three years after starting his own consulting engineering firm, Kompauer began searching for a place to grow grapes and make wine. He and Kathy planted a tiny vineyard in Surrey, where they then lived, to grow Bacchus and Ortega. Kompauer crafted a blended white that he called Alzbeta Sonata, in tribute to his mother (Alzbeta is the Slovak equivalent of Elizabeth). He found a desirable vineyard in the Similkameen Valley but, in a flat real estate market, failed to sell his Surrey home to raise the necessary cash.

He continued his engineering business while making wine at home. Finally, in 2001, the Kompauers acquired what was then known as the Back in Thyme Vineyard, just east of Chilliwack and four kilometres (2.5 miles) south of the Trans-Canada Highway. A previous owner, a dairy farmer, had planted table grapes about 15 years earlier. The vineyard was taken over by Dennis Sept, who came up with its poetic name. He put in three hectares (seven acres) of wine grapes, including Madeleine Angevine, Ortega, Kerner, Siegerrebe and Agria, selling the fruit to wineries and to amateurs who often won awards with the spicy Siegerrebe.

Sept's plans for a winery were abandoned when a marriage breakdown led to the sale of the property. By the time the Kompauers took over the vineyard in the summer of 2001, it had been neglected for two years. "We had no idea how much we were going to harvest," Kathy says. "We had no idea about the quality. We were taking a big risk. But it was the location. It was an established vineyard on a busy corner."

That fall, they were only able to harvest 800 kilograms (1,800 pounds) of Agria, an early ripening Hungarian vine capable of producing dark, full-bodied and somewhat rustic reds. Agria takes well, however, to oak-aging. Kompauer, who has a taste for moderately oaked reds, has most of it in French oak barrels. They were also able to pick white grapes in 2002, making wines that are crisply fresh and unoaked.

The vineyard should allow the winery to produce as much as 2,000 cases of wine a year when Kompauer, who is winding down the engineering company, has restructured it to suit his plans. Concluding he has too much of both Ortega and Siegerrebe, he is replacing some of those vines with Zweigelt, Pinot Noir and Gamay Noir.

His farm is one of the hottest locations in the Fraser Valley for growing grapes. In a hot, dry year like 2003, the early-ripening whites achieved enough sugar to yield bold, dry wines with 13 per cent or more alcohol. The most significant challenge, however, is the risk of rain in October when grapes still are on the vines. The heavy October downpour in 2003 forced the Kompauers to abandon some unpicked grapes. When fully in production, the winery will reduce this risk by buying some grapes from the Okanagan.

Chilliwack is a long way from the Slovakian wine trail. However, the Kompauers are determined to re-create some of that ambiance here. The tasting room décor, including the bright floral entrance and decorative glass in the windows, is inspired by Slovakia's cozy wine cellars. The Kompauers are reviving the religious tradition of celebrating one's name day — the feast day of the saint after whom one is christened (if, indeed, one has a saint's name). Customers will be able to buy wines at a discount on their name days.

The winery's name is that of the patron saint of vineyards. Many wine towns in Slovakia have statues of St. Urban, protecting the vines from frost. It is not entirely clear how an individual who was Pope for eight years in the third century achieved this distinction, but tradition has it that spring frost never occurs after May 25, St. Urban's day. "We were once visiting in this little town outside of Bratislava, called Pezinor," Kompauer remembers. "It's an old wine town with a museum of wine and grapes. We went there and found a big party in the little courtyard. They were celebrating St. Urban's day." By the end of the merry party, the idea had been born of naming his new winery after the saint.

STAG'S HOLLOW WINERY

OPENED: 1996

12 Sun Valley Way, Okanagan Falls, BC, V0H 1R0
Telephone: 250-497-6162
Toll-free: 1-877-746 5569
Web site: www.stagshollowwinery.com
Wine shop: Open daily 10 am – 5 pm May through October, or by appointment.

RECOMMENDED

- ✸ RENAISSANCE CHARDONNAY
- ✸ RENAISSANCE MERLOT
- ✸ RENAISSANCE PINOT NOIR
- ✸ SAUVIGNON BLANC
- SIMPLY CHARDONNAY
- TRAGICALLY VIDAL

THE WINERY NEXT DOOR WAS NAMED WILD GOOSE BECAUSE FOUNDER Adolf Kruger found a flock on his property one day. At Stag's Hollow, the name was inspired when the owners, Larry Gerelus and Linda Pruegger, encountered a deer in their vineyard. That is where the similarity ends between the wineries. Where the Kruger family makes Riesling and Gewürztraminer, Stag's Hollow has pinned its flag to Merlot, Pinot Noir and Chardonnay. It is the paradox of the Okanagan that the grapes of far-flung European appellations are growing side by side here. For wine touring, however, this is extremely convenient. Wine varieties of Germany, Alsace, Burgundy and Bordeaux can be sampled in tasting rooms only a short stroll from each other.

Gerelus and Pruegger bought their four-hectare (10-acre) property near Okanagan Falls in 1992. Born in Winnipeg in 1952, Gerelus trained to become an insurance actuary. He was an independent financial consultant in Calgary who had long dreamt of growing grapes and making wine. Pruegger, who worked in the marketing department of a major oil company, admits to being less drawn to the vineyard lifestyle. "I left a job I really enjoyed," she said during an interview in 2000. "What I would enjoy now is having an eight-to-six job and a paycheque every two weeks." Winery owners can only dream of regular hours. However, with steadily more impressive wines, Stag's Hollow's fortunes have looked up since that interview.

The pair took over a vineyard then planted entirely to Chasselas and Vidal. When a grape contract with Mission Hill expired in 1994, Gerelus grafted all of the Chasselas to Merlot and Pinot Noir, and most of the Vidal to Chardonnay. Some 85 per cent of the grafts succeeded and the vineyard was back in production in the 1995 vintage, producing wines with which Stag's Hollow opened the following year. Gerelus retained a small plot of Vidal, one-seventh of the vineyard, making both dry and dessert wines from this full-flavoured white grape. He called a recent release Tragically Vidal because the variety is, as the back label put it, "tragically on the verge of extinction."

Initially, Stag's Hollow began making its mark with Chardonnay, particularly after employing consultants like Jeff Martin, who has a sure touch with that grape. "I have my limits when it comes to making wine," Gerelus admits. "The wines that we made in the past had only been good because they had okay winemaking from excellent grapes. But the potential is huge to make superb wines. The 1999 vintage was a turnaround for me." In a year more challenging for reds than either 1998 or 2000, Gerelus teased superb Merlot from his vineyard to make wines, under Martin's tutelage, that won gold and silver medals at subsequent wine competitions. This established Stag's Hollow as one of the Okanagan's solid Merlot producers.

In 2002, Michael Bartier, the former assistant winemaker at Hawthorne Mountain Vineyards, joined Stag's Hollow as winemaker. Bartier is a master of Chardonnay and, like most winemakers, enjoys the challenge of Pinot Noir. He did both effectively at Stag's Hollow.

Bartier moved on in 2003 to start his own winery but his stamp remains because Bradley Cooper, his successor, learned winemaking at Hawthorne Mountain Vineyards with Bartier. Born in New Westminster in 1958, Cooper is a journalism graduate from Langara College. After several years as a writer and photographer with community newspapers, he switched careers to work in restaurants, where he developed an interest in wine. Cooper moved to the Okanagan in 1997 to work in the wine shop at Hawthorne Mountain, soon moving into the cellar. He honed his experience by working the 1999 vintage at Vidal Estate in New Zealand and the 2000 icewine harvest at Stonechurch in Ontario. In 2002, he left Hawthorne Mountain for the winemaking team at Mt. Baker Vineyards in Washington State but returned to the Okanagan in time for the 2003 vintage at Stag's Hollow.

Stag's Hollow has been scaling up its annual production, now about 1,500 cases of wine, with grapes purchased from two small vineyards — one nearby and one at Keremeos — whose owners grow to the exacting standards set out by Gerelus. The repertoire grew in the 2002 vintage, with Stag's Hollow producing its first Sauvignon Blanc and its first Gamay Noir. The winery's reserve wines are issued under the Renaissance label, while the easy-drinking wines come out under labels such as Simply Merlot and Simply Pinot. At full capacity, the compact cellar at Stag's Hollow has room to make about 3,000 cases a year.

SUMAC RIDGE ESTATE WINERY

OPENED: 1980

17403 Highway 97, Summerland, BC, V0H 1Z0
Telephone: 250-494-0451
Web site: www.sumacridge.com
Wine shop: Open daily 9 am – 9 pm March through December;
   9am – 5 pm January and February.
Restaurant: Cellar Door Bistro open daily for lunch and dinner.

RECOMMENDED

- ✷ STELLER'S JAY
- ✷ PINNACLE
- ✷ WHITE MERITAGE
- ✷ RED MERITAGE
- ✸ MERLOT BLACK SAGE VINEYARD
- ✸ SAUVIGNON BLANC PRIVATE RESERVE
- ✸ CHARDONNAY PRIVATE RESERVE
- ✸ GEWÜRZTRAMINER PRIVATE RESERVE
- ✺ CABERNET SAUVIGNON
- ✺ CABERNET FRANC
- ✺ PIPE
- ✺ PINOT BLANC ICEWINE
- ✺ BLANC DE NOIRS

IN THE SPRING OF 1992, A FEW MONTHS BEFORE JOINING SUMAC RIDGE to make wine, Mark Wendenburg planted a test plot of Pinot Noir in his family's vineyard south of Penticton. "At that time, I thought Pinot Noir was going to be the red wine of the Okanagan valley," the gently spoken, German-trained winemaker says. "I don't think it is. I think Merlot is it right now."

No doubt he changed his mind after having great success with Merlot at Sumac Ridge. It was the major variety that Sumac Ridge planted in its 46.5-hectare (115-acre) Black Sage Road vineyard in 1993. Fruit from those young vines in its 1995 Merlot powered Sumac Ridge to the "winery of the year" award in a national competition. Merlot is the leading component in the winery's Pinnacle, the ultra-premium $50-a-bottle red created in 1997 and released only from top vintages. The Black Sage Road vineyard initially also included a 5-hectare (13-acre) block of Pinot Noir. When the site proved to be too hot for that finicky red, it was replaced with Merlot and Sauvignon Blanc.

If anyone assessed grape varieties in the Okanagan, it is Sumac Ridge. Over the years, it has made wine from so many varieties that a full restaurant wine list, from sparkling wine to port-style wine, can be assembled from Sumac Ridge's portfolio. The portfolio has been reduced slightly since 2000, when Vincor International Inc. purchased Sumac Ridge. For example, Riesling was dropped because Hawthorne Mountain Vineyards, a sister winery, has a better source of Riesling grapes. "We drop something but we also seem to gain something," Wendenburg says. The winery's unoaked Chardonnay, launched from the 2001 vintage, is a bigger success than Riesling.

Sumac Ridge was founded in 1979, one of the Okanagan's first estate wineries. The estate winery regulations, released three years earlier by the government, required these new wineries to have vineyards of their own. Commercial wineries — such as Casabello in Penticton where Harry McWatters, Sumac Ridge's president, began his wine sales career in 1968 when he was only 23 — bought all their grapes from growers. The government believed that estate wineries would grow better-quality grapes and thus raise wine quality.

As McWatters likes to tell the story, he made his first wine from potatoes when he was a teenager. Born in Toronto and raised in Vancouver, he was intending, like his father, to become a salesman for a scale company until Casabello sought him out. The winery was then only two years old but McWatters was so enthralled by the industry that he neglected to establish the terms of his salary. When he got his first cheque, he found he had taken a pay cut. He stayed the course to become one of the most important figures in the Okanagan. In addition to establishing Sumac Ridge as a leader among the estate wineries, McWatters was a founder of the Okanagan Wine Festival and of the British Columbia Wine Institute.

McWatters and Lloyd Schmidt, the viticulturist who was his initial partner in Sumac Ridge, bought a golf course at Summerland, in a highly visible location right beside the highway. It was a brilliant choice, readily accessible to visitors and offering food service. At the time, winery restaurants were not allowed in British Columbia. McWatters got around the rules by keeping the clubhouse restaurant open as the place where tourists could enjoy Sumac Ridge wine with food. In stickhandling around pointless restrictions, McWatters has always held that "forgiveness is easier than permission." A decade after the winery opened, the golf course was turned over to other owners who built a new clubhouse. The original clubhouse, enlarged several times, includes a large wine shop and the winery's own Cellar Door Bistro restaurant.

Sumac Ridge relocated a few holes of the golf course to create a 2.8-hectare (seven-acre) vineyard, extending now from the winery parking lot east toward the lake. Riesling and Gewürztraminer were planted. The signature wine at Sumac Ridge became its Gewürztraminer, still one of its best-sellers. McWatters is proud that Sumac Ridge never planted any hybrids, even if it made wine from them because there was a shortage of vinifera. "I didn't like them," he says of hybrids. The winery bought Verdelet, Okanagan Riesling and Chancellor and even made award-winning wines. The winery was into its second decade before it acquired a good supply of vinifera by developing the Black Sage Road vineyard.

Before 1993, few growers in the Okanagan had much experience with French grape varieties. McWatters believed he was taking a risk, but a necessary one, in the Black Sage vineyard with winter-sensitive vines such as Merlot and Sauvignon Blanc. Both have succeeded. "The best fruit for that comes off the Black Sage vineyards," says Wendenburg.

Most of Black Sage is planted to the Bordeaux reds: Merlot, Cabernet Sauvignon and Cabernet Franc (with a little Malbec and Petite Verdot added recently). The single varietal reds have won their share of awards. But Wendenburg's most impressive wines are the blends of the Bordeaux varieties, Meritage and Pinnacle. Meritage (rhymes with heritage) is a California-developed trade name for blends, both red and white, with Bordeaux varietals; Sumac Ridge was the first Canadian winery to adopt the term.

Sumac Ridge's white Meritage is primarily Sauvignon Blanc, some of it barrel-fermented, enriched with a dash of Sémillon, yielding a remarkably elegant wine with great persistence. The red Meritage is a polished blend of Cabernet Sauvignon (50 per cent), with equal parts of Merlot and Cabernet Sauvignon. Pinnacle, the luxuriously big Sumac Ridge red, is at least 60 per cent Merlot, with other Bordeaux varietals and a touch of Syrah. "A masculine wine, I would call it," Wendenburg says, describing the red's leathery, cigar box character. "It's the kind of wine you'd have with a stogie." Both Meritage and Pinnacle are aged a full 25 months in small oak barrels.

One of the most expensive table wines in British Columbia, Pinnacle is produced in limited volume (less than 500 cases) only in those years when Wendenburg believes he has exceptional wines for the blend. "When it's $50 a bottle, we are certainly trying to make a statement," he says. Since the inaugural 1997 Pinnacle was released in 2000, it has had an impact on how the winery's other reds are perceived. "You know what it's done?" McWatters chuckles. "It has taken all the resistance away from the $25 Meritage! Meritage is now, in people's eyes, a great buy. I always thought it was a great buy. People say the Pinnacle is wonderful but they would just as soon have two bottles of the Meritage."

When it comes to selling wine, McWatters, who remained the winery's president after its sale to Vincor, is an incomparable showman. The first winery owner in 1989 to release a premium sparkling wine, Steller's Jay, he taught himself the explosive trick of sabering, a thespian technique of cracking chilled necks from the bottles by rapping them sharply with a sabre or a heavy knife. The neck blows harmlessly away, leaving McWatters dispensing the foaming beverage to an impressed audience.

Sumac Ridge pioneered sparkling wine in the Okanagan. "We did our first trials with sparkling wine in 1985," McWatters recalls. This involved extensive work at the Summerland research stations with different yeast strains and grape varieties before settling on Pinot Blanc as the backbone varietal. The first commercial vintage was made in 1987, the year in which the raucous Steller's jay was chosen as British Columbia's official bird, inspiring the name of the wine. It was released in July 1989.

The winery has had other sparkling wines in its range, retaining only a Blanc de Noirs as a partner to Steller's Jay. Sumac Ridge now is producing about 5,500 cases of Champagne-method Steller's Jay annually, about one-twelfth of its total wine production. "I can see us ramping up the production of sparkling wine to 10,000 cases," McWatters says. "We haven't sold much to other parts of Canada yet."

SUMMERHILL PYRAMID WINERY

OPENED: 1992

4870 Chute Lake Road, Kelowna, BC, V1W 4M3

Telephone: 250-764-8000

Toll-free: 1-800-667-3538

Web site: www.summerhill.bc.ca

Wine shop: Open daily 9 am – 9 pm.

Solstice meditations in the pyramid at 7 pm on each of the solstice days.

Restaurant: Sunset Bistro open daily for lunch and dinner.

RECOMMENDED

- ✷ CIPES GABRIEL CHARDONNAY CUVÉE
- ✷ CIPES BRUT
- ✷ CIPES GABRIEL
- ✷ PINOT NOIR ICEWINE
- ✷ ZWEIGELT ICEWINE
- ✷ PLATINUM PINOT GRIS
- ✷ MERITAGE
- ✷ CABERNET SAUVIGNON
- ✷ LADY OF THE HARVEST RIESLING
- EHRENFELSER
- BACO NOIR
- BLAUFRANKISH
- CHALICE

THE MOMENT WAS PROFOUNDLY UPSETTING. SUMMERHILL FOUNDER STEPHEN Cipes, surrounded by a group of wine writers, was well into an impassioned discussion of the positive ions and negative ions within the winery's candle-lit pyramid. Soon, the writers would be asked to hold hands, standing silently to feel the energy. Then a cell phone began to chirp. One of the writers had not turned it off, as Cipes had requested, before entering the hallowed chamber. The spell of a pyramid tour drained away after the unwelcome intrusion.

Whether or not one understands pyramid power, tours of the pyramid (on the hour between 12 pm and 4 pm) are not to be missed. Like every other winery in the world, Summerhill can show its visitors the usual accoutrements, from bottling lines to barrels, before concluding comfortably in one of the largest tasting rooms in the Okanagan. (Summerhill needs the room because, as a favourite stop for tour buses, this is one of the valley's most visited wineries.) But no other winery — *perhaps no other winery in the world* — has a scale model of the Great Pyramid of Egypt in which all of its wines are aged. Cipes believes that pyramid aging makes good wines taste better. He recites three years of trials in which tasters compared wines from a pyramid to similar wines stored elsewhere. In most cases, he says, the pyramid wines were preferred. There is something to be said for his views. Many old wine cellars in Europe, with their Roman arches, share some of the geometry of pyramids. "There is a definite correlation between liquids and perfect geometry," Cipes maintains.

The gleaming white pyramid, built in 1997 on the hillside above the winery, certainly sets Summerhill apart, reflecting the mercurial nature of its elfin owner. The individuality is everywhere — in the wines, in the marketing, even in the grand piano in the wood-panelled tasting room. The winery set out to be an important producer of sparkling wine, referring to itself as "British Columbia's First Champagne House." Today, it makes every major style of wine, even including a sherry-styled wine called Chalice. Table wines and icewine now are about three-quarters of Summerhill's production, even as it maintains its image as a sparkling wine house.

Summerhill has become the largest organic wine producer in the Okanagan, operating the single largest organic vineyard. This is driven by the owner's environmental idealism: he adopted organic practices in the Summerhill vineyard soon after buying the property. Recently, he has encouraged Summerhill's growers to become organic. There is a practical reason for this. "Flawless sparkling wine can only be made from organic grapes," he believes. The wines are not labelled organic, which is an involved certification process. Many Summerhill wines, and all of those in its Enchanted Vines series, are organic.

Born in New York in 1944, Cipes (the name rhymes with stripes) was a successful real estate developer in that state until a quality-of-life decision brought him and his family to the Okanagan in 1987. He purchased a rambling house on a 26-hectare (65-acre) property overlooking Okanagan Lake, near Kelowna. Because grapes were already growing there, he decided to open a winery after taking part in the sparkling wine trial conducted in the Okanagan in 1990 and 1991 by Schramsberg Cellars, a renowned California producer. The Californians thought the Okanagan had ideal conditions for making sparkling wine, just not enough Chardonnay and Pinot Noir grapes.

The Summerhill vineyard has a lot of Riesling. Winemaker Eric von Krosigk, who helped launch Summerland, persuaded Cipes to make sparkling Riesling. Von Krosigk, a native of Vernon, had just completed six years of wine studies in Germany, where he specialized in sparkling Rieslings. Working under a blue tarpaulin beside the three-car garage at the Cipes house, Summerhill's first winery, von Krosigk created several bubblies, including Cipes Brut, still the flagship sparkler at Summerhill. In his first vintage there, 1991, he also made a sparkling Chardonnay, about 2,000 bottles of which remained on the lees for at least six years. When the wine was released in time for the Millennium, Summerhill put it in a distinctive pyramid-shaped bottle, called it Gabriel and asked $100 a bottle. Only 2,000 bottles were made of a wine that won a gold medal in 2000 at the Chardonnay du Monde competition in France.

Since opening, Summerhill has had several winemakers, each with experience in making sparkling wines. In 1994, when von Krosigk went to another Okanagan winery, Missouri native Alan Marks, with a doctorate in the chemistry of sparkling wines, took over. (He is now director of winery operations.) Bruce Ewert, who became winemaker in 2002, came from Hawthorne Mountain, where he had been making the Riesling Brut that competed directly with Cipes Brut. "I didn't miss a beat," Ewert chuckles. Born in Prince George in 1963 and an engineering graduate of the University of British Columbia, Ewert began his career in 1986 at Andrés. He took a winemaking sabbatical to Australia in 1994 and, for some years, has been a member of the British Columbia Wine Institute's research and development committee.

Ewert accepted the unsolicited offer from Summerhill because Hawthorne Mountain seemed in no hurry to rebuild its antique winery while Cipes had replaced his three-car garage in 1995 with a new winery. In fact, the Summerhill cellar was already becoming overcrowded. "It is a 20,000-case winery but we are producing 40,000 cases," Ewert said in the spring of 2003. "So I am finding where the weak links are and dealing with them." Expansions proposed over several years should result in a separate barrel room, more riddling racks for the sparkling wines and gravity-flow production that takes advantage of the property's contours. Ewert will not be around for these upgrades; in mid-2004, he left to start his own winery in Nova Scotia.

Initially, Summerhill's table wine production was biased toward white varieties, including Riesling and Ehrenfelser. That range has grown to include Pinot Gris, Gewürztraminer and Chardonnay. Both Alan Marks and Bruce Ewert broadened Summerhill's scope to include such reds as Maréchal Foch, Baco Noir, Merlot, Cabernet Franc, Cabernet Sauvignon, Syrah and Pinot Noir. "Pinot Noir is one of my passions," Ewert says. "I worked for five years at Hawthorne Mountain to achieve what I planned to achieve with the grape. My style is now set in stone. I vary it based on what the grapes are like, but it is pretty much Burgundian."

Summerhill defies the perceived trend to warmer winters by striving to be one of the Okanagan's most significant icewine producers. The winery has even opened a sales office in Japan, an important icewine market. In the vintage of 2002, almost the entire vineyard fanning out on the slope below the winery was left for icewine. The varieties included Riesling, Chardonnay, Gewürztraminer and Pinot Noir. About 200 tonnes (220 tons) of fruit remained on the vines at the end of October, when the normal vintage is over. It was the end of February before it was cold enough to freeze the grapes for icewine. Cipes had seen this before. In 1991, he and von Krosigk left Riesling hanging for icewine through an El Niño winter until the following April, when the surviving grapes were salvaged for a late harvest wine.

"It paid off in 2002," Ewert says. While the quantity of grapes had been reduced by two-thirds (mostly by dehydration), he was able to make excellent icewines. It paid off again in 2003. Many of the grapes growing around the winery, including all the reds, had developed smoke-saturated skins when the summer's forest fires raged nearby. The grapes were unsuitable for making table wines involving skin contact — but they were fine for icewine, which is not fermented on the skins. A sharp cold snap just after Christmas yielded a good icewine harvest at Summerhill.

Stephen Cipes has never hesitated to price his wines aggressively if he believed that was justified. Summerhill's Pinot Noir icewine, at $108 a half-bottle, was for some time Canada's most expensive table wine. The price reflected the fact that red icewines are comparatively rare. Then in 2002, Summerhill released Canada's first Zweigelt icewine at $148 a half-bottle. Even so, visitors should not be deterred from going to Summerhill's grand tasting room, where wine prices start at $10 and do not often exceed $25.

Thetis Island
Vineyards
2004
Pinot Gris

White Wine — THETIS ISLAND VINEYARDS — Vin Blanc
11% alcvol — Thetis Island, British Columbia V0R 2Y0 — 750 ml
Product of Canada — Produit du Canada

THETIS ISLAND VINEYARDS

OPENING: PROPOSED FOR 2004

90 Pilkey Point Road, Thetis Island, BC, V0R 2Y0
Telephone: 250-246-2258
Web site: www.cedar-beach.com
Tasting room: Seasonal hours or by appointment.

DURING THEIR WINE TRAVELS, COLIN AND CAROLA SPARKES HAD COME across European vineyards that used sheep to "manage" the weeds and grass between the vines. So when they established their Thetis Island vineyard in 2000 they bought nine sheep. The charming idea turned into a headache. The sheep population tripled, beyond the vineyard's capacity to feed them, especially during the dry summer of 2003, and they began chewing young vines. Colin Sparkes finally replaced the cuddly flock with a riding mower. "They certainly did a good job on ground cover management but, to be honest, they were more hassle than they were worth," he conceded.

The sheep were a step in this couple's learning curve as they took on a new career running a vineyard and a resort. Theirs is the first winery on this bucolic little island, which was named for a Royal Navy frigate that patrolled these coastal waters between 1851 and 1853. Today, the 350 permanent residents live quietly either with magnificent seascapes or in homes hidden away among the island's forests. It is a delicate matter to disturb the routine with something new, like a winery. Any Okanagan winery that wants to offer picnic facilities need only get a simple license. On Thetis Island, Colin Sparkes was surprised to find that he might need commercial zoning for his rural property, a clearing in the middle of the forest, unless he can convince regulators that a picnic area is not a restaurant. However, hiccups like that seem unlikely to deflect the dream that he and his wife formed in the wine regions of Europe and California.

Growing grapes and tending sheep takes Sparkes back to his first job as an English farmhand. Born in London in 1957, he eventually took a degree in agricultural engineering. At the age of 30, now with a master's degree in artificial intelligence, he moved to Heidelberg in Germany to join SAP AG, an international German software company. Here, he met his wife, Carola, another SAP consultant, who grew up amid German vineyards.

In Heidelberg, Sparkes recalls, "we lived about 20 minutes from a famous white wine producing area in the Rhine." However, a two-year San Francisco assignment for the couple, with side trips to British Columbia, fostered the idea of a winery in a locale where one also could pursue adventure tourism, including sea kayaking and sailing.

"We really liked the lifestyle out here," Colin says. "When we returned to Germany, we wanted to go into something quieter, more agricultural. We looked at hundreds of properties in France, old vineyards near Bordeaux and Provence, but we could never find the potential for starting an adventure business. So we decided to come to Canada." On Thetis Island, they bought a waterfront property called Cedar Beach, now a small resort. Carola has continued to work with SAP while Colin manages the resort and develops the vineyard, which also has a guest cottage.

The vineyard is on a warmer, four-hectare (10-acre) site inland from the resort. After clearing the forest, Sparkes planted about 1.6 hectares (four acres) in the fall of 2000. He hedged his bets, planting a range of varieties, including Pinot Noir, Pinot Gris, Gewürztraminer, Chardonnay, Agria and Merlot. There also were a few vines of Cabernet Sauvignon, included by error in his order, that are growing quite successfully. After a two-year search for the variety he calls his "Holy Grail," he found and planted 200 vines of Pinotage. This is only the second planting of this South African variety in British Columbia (the other is at Lake Breeze in the Okanagan).

There is scepticism about any new vineyard on the Gulf Islands. Indeed, nearby Overbury Farm, one of the oldest resorts on Thetis Island, has had some challenge ripening grapes on its 1.2 hectares (three acres) on a cooler site closer to the sea. Sparkes is confident in his south-facing vineyard, some of which is terraced.

"The pilots that fly here say Thetis Island has a climatic hole," Sparkes says. "There is always blue sky over Thetis when the rest of the area is grey. I must say that is not an old wives' tale. I have observed that myself. It has often been blue and sunny here and raining elsewhere, which has been frustrating because we wanted the water."

Sensitive to the limited water on the Gulf Islands, Sparkes built a large pond at the top of the vineyard for irrigation water. "Many people tried to persuade us to dig wells," he recalls. "An equal number tried to dissuade us from doing that, because we could be using someone's else's domestic water to irrigate our grapes. Which would not make us too popular."

He began acquiring the art of winemaking first by fermenting cider from apples gathered among old orchards on the island. In 2002, he purchased blackberries from the First Nations people on Kuper Island (just south of Thetis) and was encouraged by the outcome. Complimentary tastings were well received by guests at the resort. "We also took a couple of cases back to Europe," he says. "I've had numerous requests to buy blackberry port by the caseload. Of course, I was unable to do that because I didn't have a license."

While the licensing application moved through the bureaucracy, Sparkes gained more experience by making trial lots of wine for his own use at several Vancouver Island wineries. His primary mentors have been Dave Godfrey of Godfrey-Brownell and Jim Moody of Vigneti Zanatta, from whom Sparkes also purchased Pinot Gris in one vintage.

The Thetis Island vineyard is expected to start producing modest quantities of fruit in 2004. "We have four acres planted and no plans to expand our vineyard beyond five acres until we have the winery and the picnic patio up and running," Sparkes said late in 2003. "From our business plan, we are looking at reaching about 5,000 litres of our own production a year and keeping that steady for the next four or five years."

THORNHAVEN ESTATE WINERY

OPENED: 2001

6816 Andrew Avenue, Summerland, BC, V0H 1Z0
Telephone: 250-494-7778
Web site: www.thornhaven.com
Wine shop: Open daily 10 am – 5 pm from May 1 to October 14; or by appointment.
Restaurant: Patio offers wine by the glass and deli food. Picnics welcome.

RECOMMENDED

- ❊ SAUVIGNON BLANC/CHARDONNAY
- ❊ DULCE MIA
- ❊ DIOSA
- ❊ PINOT MEUNIER
- ❊ PINOT NOIR

EXCEPT FOR FIVE YEARS WHEN HE RAN THE ONLY BOOKSTORE IN Dawson Creek, his hometown, Dennis Fraser has been a farmer. It is just that the scale has changed, he explains, looking over the neat vineyard spread out below the tasting room windows at Thornhaven.

Once, Fraser owned a 971-hectare (2,400-acre) farm near Dawson Creek. "You just went and went and went," he says, describing how he piloted his mammoth Steiger tractor around the endless fields of grain. It certainly is different in Thornhaven's 3.6-hectare (nine-acre) vineyard. "That Steiger tractor held half as much fuel in its tank as I use here *all year long*! Here, you know every vine. Growing grapes seems personal."

The grain farm was sold in 1989. "I got tired of it," he says. Pamala Fraser, his wife, went to university three years later in southern British Columbia, triggering a family decision to leave Dawson Creek for the Okanagan Valley. "Vancouver was too big," Fraser recalls. He bought an apple orchard on a south-facing slope below Giant's Head, the extinct volcano that towers over Summerland. At first, he was only going to plant a small plot of vines. He eventually converted it all to vines because, to a farmer who had operated a huge grain farm, the small vineyard seemed deceptively easy work.

In 1996, Dennis Fraser asked his son, Alex, to come from Dawson Creek to Summerland to help with contouring the steeply sloped property and plant half the vineyard. Farming was not the independent-minded young man's avocation. When he was 14, he went to work in a Mr. Mike's restaurant in Dawson Creek. Five years and three restaurants later, he found himself in charge of the kitchen at Dawson Creek's biggest hotel and planning a career as a chef. "I couldn't do that," Alex said about farming. "I like to make something that you can actually sit down and eat or drink. If you make something as a chef, you know someone's going to enjoy that. If you are farming canola, there is not an end person that says, 'This is really good, you did a really good job on this.'"

Alex went back north after the vineyard was planted, figuring on picking up his career. He was called back to Summerland the next summer to discover that his father's plans had now gone beyond growing a few grapes. "Over the winter, he'd had too much time to think, I guess, and he got the whole idea of a winery," Alex said later. "And that appealed to me because once again, it was producing something." The remainder of the vineyard was planted over the next several years. In 1999, the first 700 cases of Thornhaven wine were made in Dennis Fraser's garage.

Like the vineyard, the winery grew beyond Dennis Fraser's initial modest idea of a tasting room on the ground floor of his home. Instead, he had an architect design a sandy-hued Santa Fe pueblo, one of the most picturesque wineries in the Okanagan. The winery is set into a hillside, with the cellars cooled by the earth on three sides. The patio and wine shop on the top floor command panoramic views over the vineyards behind Giant's Head. "We went a little overboard," Alex suggested.

To fill the gaps in his experience, Dennis Fraser has relied on consultants. Valerie Tait, one of the Okanagan's leading viticulturists, has advised in the vineyard and Christine Leroux supervises the winemaking. The choices that Dennis Fraser made for the vineyard have given Thornhaven a tight varietal focus — primarily Pinot Noir, Chardonnay, Sauvignon Blanc and Gewürztraminer. In style, the white wines are crisply fresh with a dry finish. The emphasis with both the reds and the whites is on the fruit. The use of oak is sensibly moderate.

Thornhaven is one of the few Okanagan wineries that makes Pinot Meunier, a red grape related to Pinot Noir but typically used to make Champagne. "We did not choose to plant Pinot Meunier," Alex said. "The former owner of the grape nursery down the street there slipped that into our shipment of Pinot Noir. We have four rows." The shipping error, as it happens, yields a light, lively red that sells well in the tasting room.

Thornhaven's production rose to 950 cases in 2000 and to 1,800 cases in 2001. The vineyard at full production will produce 2,200 cases. The winery itself has a capacity of about 4,000 cases but seems in no hurry to get there, perhaps because Dennis Fraser's plans for a family winery suffered unfortunate setbacks in 2003. His wife succumbed to cancer, and Alex left to become an electrician. "Alex tells me that it was always my dream, not his," Dennis says.

TINHORN CREEK VINEYARDS

OPENED: 1995

32830 Tinhorn Creek Road, Oliver, BC, V0H 1T0
Telephone: 250-498-3743
Toll-free: 1-888-4-TINHORN
Web site: www.tinhorn.com
Wine shop: Open daily 10 am – 5 pm. Picnic facilities.

RECOMMENDED

* ✳ MERLOT RESERVE
* ✳ MERLOT
* ✳ CABERNET FRANC
* ✳ PINOT GRIS
* ✳ CHARDONNAY
* ✳ GEWÜRZTRAMINER
* ✳ KERNER ICEWINE

THE OKANAGAN VINTAGE OF 2002, LEGENDARY FOR ITS QUALITY, TESTED the resolve of growers. After a mild spring resulted in an explosion of healthy buds, the vines set out to produce record yields. Tinhorn Creek picked 589 tonnes (649 tons) of grapes from its vineyards and made 41,000 cases of wine, the largest quantity since the winery opened. More could have been made if the vines had been left to their own devices — but at the risk of diluting the quality. In fact, Tinhorn Creek reined in the exuberant vines by dropping about 250 tonnes (275 tons) of grapes onto the ground earlier in the season. The result: "The wines look wonderful," Sandra Oldfield, the winemaker, reported after the harvest. "We have huge red wines this year and in particular the 2002 Merlot is more extracted than ever before."

Dropping excess bunches of grapes — called the green harvest because it is done before clusters turn colour — is the standard way to grow good wines. It is among the lessons that Sandra Oldfield and her husband, Kenn, Tinhorn's general manager, learned a decade earlier at the University of California's renowned wine school at Davis.

The influence of California has left its mark on Tinhorn Creek. It began when Bob Shaunessy, a Calgary oilman, developed a passion for wine while touring California vineyards. In 1992 he enlisted Kenn Oldfield in a partnership to develop an Okanagan winery that would be every bit as fine as those he had admired in California. Born in Orillia, Ontario, in 1955, Oldfield, a chemical engineer, had his own consulting business in Alberta but was ready for a new career. He went to Davis for a master's degree in viticulture. That was where he met Sandra, a Californian who had progressed from the tasting room at the Rodney Strong winery in 1989 to a master's degree in winemaking.

As Kenn Oldfield was completing his studies in 1993, Shaunessy bought vineyards. South of Oliver, on the west, or Golden Mile, side of the valley, he acquired 12 hectares (30 acres) that included adjoining vineyards and the site for the winery. On Black Sage Road, on the east side of the valley, he acquired 53 hectares (130 acres) of fallow land, a former vineyard that had been pulled out after the 1988 harvest. With these substantial holdings, Tinhorn Creek is self-sufficient in grapes. In fact, Tinhorn sold 10 hectares (25 acres) of vineyard in 2004 to Burrowing Owl Winery.

Of the many decisions that Shaunessy and the Oldfields faced, naming the winery was the easiest since Tinhorn Creek (usually dry) runs through the Golden Mile property. One of the vineyards Shaunessy bought already operated under the creek's name. In the past, that creek also shared its name with the Tin Horn Quartz Mining Co. Remains of the exhausted mine are visible just beyond the Gewürztraminer vines at the top of the vineyard.

The vineyards were developed so that 60 per cent of Tinhorn's wines would be reds — Merlot, Cabernet Franc and Pinot Noir — and 40 per cent white. In addition to Chardonnay, Tinhorn planted Pinot Gris and was considering Pinot Blanc until Sandra pointed out that it is too similar to Chardonnay and suggested aromatic Gewürztraminer instead. The vines were planted in a cool six-hectare (15-acre) section of the vineyard at the west end of the property, where it rises to an elevation of 480 metres (1,575 feet) and is in shade by late afternoon. The resulting wine, fresh and spicy, has been one of Tinhorn Creek's best-sellers.

Tinhorn Creek's Pinot Noir has been good enough to get the winery invited to the elite Pinot Noir Symposium, held annually in Oregon. However, the winery is best known for its Merlot and its Cabernet Franc. Most of the Merlot is grown on Black Sage Road, in what the winery calls its Diamondback and Rushmere vineyards. There is also two hectares (five acres) of Merlot on Golden Mile, already planted when Tinhorn Creek bought the vineyard. "If the Merlot had not already been here, we probably wouldn't plant it here," Kenn Oldfield says. "We would have put it all on Black Sage Road." The winery's 1994 Merlot, grown on

Golden Mile, won a silver medal in the Okanagan Wine Festival, but the 1998, which now included fruit from the second harvest at Black Sage Road, was the Canadian wine of the year in a 2001 national competition. "Merlot is very nice over here," Oldfield says of Golden Mile. "If we only had land on this side, I wouldn't hesitate to put Merlot in again. But given the land we have got, if we were to rejuggle, I think I would put all the Merlot on Black Sage."

Initially, Shaunessy and Kenn Oldfield were going to plant Cabernet Sauvignon in the Diamondback Vineyard. Then they discovered that Cabernet Sauvignon's average growing season is 186 days, six days longer than the average frost-free period on Black Sage Road. "Oops!" Oldfield recounted. "We did not feel comfortable that we would be able to ripen Cabernet Sauvignon frequently enough that we were willing to bet the farm on it." Then he discovered that Cabernet Franc's growing season is 176 days. "Bingo!" That is how this variety became one of Tinhorn Creek's major reds.

The disadvantage of Cabernet Franc is the variety's tendency to yield wines that taste green and herbaceous when the grapes are not fully mature. With careful vineyard work, Tinhorn Creek produces wines from this variety that are, as they should be, generous in body and ripe in flavour. Part of the secret is having the discipline, as the winery did in 2002, to green harvest aggressively and let the remaining grapes ripen properly.

Part of Tinhorn Creek's California feel is the winery itself, which could easily have been transplanted from a hillside in Napa. Spectacularly perched at the tip of a plateau, the ochre-toned building, which opened in 1996, was designed by Calgary architect Richard Lindseth. The viewing deck adjoining the spacious tasting room is a breathtaking 100 metres (328 feet) above the floor of the valley. A new cellar for 800 barrels, completed in 2002, was designed by Lindseth in the same style. Between the buildings, Tinhorn Creek has a 350-seat amphitheatre for summer concerts.

In the manner of a Napa winery, Tinhorn Creek works at making itself a destination, keeping its wine shop open daily through the year even when neighbouring wineries are not open except on weekends or by appointment. Perhaps Tinhorn Creek's most unusual inducement is its "WineLovers' Club." A guest house not far from the winery, with similar views over the valley, offers some of the most luxurious wine country weekends this side of Napa.

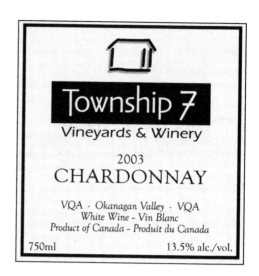

TOWNSHIP 7 OKANAGAN WINERY

OPENED: 2004

1450 McMillan Ave, Penticton, V2A 8T4
Telephone: 250-770-1743
Web site: www.township7.com

WHEN WINEMAKER MICHAEL BARTIER SET OUT TO DEVELOP A WINERY and vineyard on the Naramata Bench, Township 7 owners Gwen and Corey Coleman agreed to back him. They wanted a second outlet on one of the Okanagan's busiest wine tour routes. They also saw it as an opportunity to cement their relationship with Bartier, a rising star among Okanagan vintners. Bartier and the Colemans spent months looking for a winery name. After they were refused registration for three of their choices, they decided they need look no further than Township 7, capitalizing on the solid reputation they had established already. "Why re-invent the wheel?" Corey Coleman asked.

Wherever Bartier has worked, Chardonnay has been the queen of varieties. The grape became one of his passions in 1998 when he did a vintage in Australia with the Thomas Hardy winery. "I was working with the best maker of white wine in the southern hemisphere," he says, referring to a winemaker named Tom Newton. "He had a passion for Chardonnay and his excitement passed on to me." After coming back to the Okanagan, Bartier made award-winning Chardonnay in several cellars. Township 7 Okanagan opens with two wines: one is a Merlot and the other, naturally, is a Chardonnay.

The son of an accountant, Bartier was born in Kelowna in 1967 and grew up in Summerland. A lean mountaineer, Bartier has a degree from the University of Victoria in recreational administration. However, on graduating in 1990, he took a job with a wine marketing agency then owned by Labatt Breweries. "I wasn't interested in the recreational field," he says now. "By the time I realized that, I was too far along in my degree to stop those studies."

The job with the wine agency provided the opportunity to visit wineries in France and in the United States. "It gave me the interest and the passion for wine," Bartier remembers. One side of the business that did not appeal to him, however, was selling wine. "I am not a salesperson," he admits.

He left the agency in 1995 to return to the Okanagan, intending to pick up his original interest in the outdoors. "My dream was to become a professional climbing guide. I came out to the Okanagan to boost my résumé on difficult climbing routes." Those include the Skaha Bluffs just south of Penticton, one of the world's more challenging rock-climbing venues. Ultimately, Bartier decided this was definitely not for him. While he considered himself a capable ice climber and mountaineer, he concluded he was "a mediocre rock climber."

While working on his climbing skills, Bartier took a job as a cellar hand at Hawthorne Mountain Vineyards. By the end of a season, he had been promoted to assistant winemaker, leading him to abandon professional climbing. "I realized it was just too dangerous an occupation," he says. "And I was having too much fun in the wine cellar." He applied himself to this new job with gusto, taking extension courses from various American winemaking schools to underpin his career with professional skills. By the time he left Hawthorne Mountain after the 2001 vintage, he was crafting some of the Okanagan's best Chardonnay wines.

"Like a lot of careers, I got into this quite by accident," he says. "I feel really privileged. I was at the right place at the right time. I can't see anyone now coming into the wine industry as wet behind the ears as I was, and rising so fast."

He left Hawthorne Mountain because he wanted to develop his own winery; Vincor International Inc., which owns Hawthorne Mountain, does not permit its winemakers to operate wineries on the side. Bartier has no problem with that policy. "Vincor is an outstanding employer that treats its people very well," he says. "I had just been there a long time. I always knew I wanted to do my own winery."

As an interim measure, he became a consulting winemaker for small Okanagan wineries, including Stag's Hollow for the 2002 vintage. He has been the winemaker for Township 7 from this winery's inception in 2001. In the 2003 Canadian Wine Awards competition, Township 7's 2002 Chardonnay was judged not only the best Chardonnay but the year's best Canadian white wine. Two years earlier, the Hawthorne Mountain 2000 Gold Label Chardonnay, also made by Bartier, was the top Chardonnay in the competition. "A winemaker can really put his fingerprint on Chardonnay," Bartier says. "I find that appealing."

For the Township 7 Winery, a 2.8 hectare (seven-acre) orchard on Naramata Road, just outside Penticton, was purchased in 2003. The property, with a good southwestern exposure, has views of both Okanagan Lake and Skaha Lake. With the exception of some pear trees retained for ambiance, the fruit trees have been replaced with Chardonnay vines and two other Bartier favourites, Gewürztraminer and Syrah. "I am also toying with the idea of some Pinot Gris," he says.

Township 7 is making a big bet on Syrah. "It has become a big interest of mine," Bartier says. "It is impressive what Syrah can do in this valley." Besides planting the variety on the Naramata Bench property, the winery has long-term contracts with three independent growers on Black Sage Road whose vineyards include Syrah. Bartier also is making wines from Sémillon, Sauvignon Blanc and the big Bordeaux reds, Merlot and Cabernet Sauvignon, with wine in barrels for a potential Meritage red.

Township 7's modest Langley winery is now dedicated to making sparkling wine while the new winery just at the edge of Penticton makes the table wines for both of the Township 7 facilities. The Okanagan winery is larger but not much more elaborate than the one in Langley. "You will not see a lot of lipstick," Bartier laughs. "My priorities are, number one, the grapes; number two, the barrels — you need good barrels for Chardonnay and the reds — and number three, the equipment."

That is the same order one would get from any winemaker. "I just want to respect the fruit that comes from the vineyard," Bartier says. "Quality is all in the fruit. That is such a pat answer among winemakers, but it is the essence of it."

TOWNSHIP 7 VINEYARDS & WINERY

OPENED: 2001

21152 16th Avenue, Langley, BC, V2Z 1K3

Telephone: 604-532-1766

Web site: www.township7.com

Wine shop: Open daily 11 am – 6 pm July, August and December; noon – 6 pm
    Thursday through Sunday the rest of the year; closed in January.

RECOMMENDED

* ☀ MERLOT
* ☀ SYRAH
* ☀ CHARDONNAY
* ☀ CABERNET SAUVIGNON
* ☀ SEVEN STARS
* ☀ SAUVIGNON BLANC

THE OWNERS OF THIS WINERY AND ITS SISTER WINERY IN THE OKANAGAN, Gwen and Corey Coleman, both have university degrees in commerce — she in marketing and he in finance. It shows in their savvy approach. Township 7 focusses on the best-selling varietals for premier restaurants and for a growing list of private customers. Keeping their award-winning wines exclusive has created a remarkable buzz around this winery. Operating one winery near the Vancouver market raised the winery's profile among restaurateurs; the second winery in the Okanagan places Township 7 before a growing number of wine tourists. In college, this business plan would receive an A.

Corey Coleman was born in Saskatoon in 1964. Gwen, a farmer's daughter, was born in Melville a year later. They met at the University of Saskatchewan and, on graduation, pursued commercial careers. At one point, Gwen was a national production manager, based in Montreal, for a drug company.

"We got our first appreciation of wine and the wine industry on a trip to the Napa Valley and Sonoma Valley of California in 1989," Corey recalls. "If you don't come from a long tradition, you need some kind of outside source to influence you. I don't think it was a conscious revelation at that time. It was just something we really enjoyed. As we went on holidays subsequently, we always ended up visiting the wine growing regions wherever we could. Washington State, France. We even did the Eastern Townships [in Quebec]."

When they left Montreal in 1995 to return west, they headed straight for the Okanagan Valley. "We decided it was an opportunity for us to try something different, something new," Corey says. "I sent out résumés to 23 wineries and stopped in at each one and introduced myself. I said, I have a business background but I am very interested in wine and would like to learn the business." He started by helping Tinhorn Creek plant its Black Sage Road vineyard, then moved into the winery's cellars and subsequently joined Hawthorne Mountain Vineyards in 1997, working with growers and understudying the winemakers for three vintages. After working as an independent consultant, Gwen Coleman took a marketing job for Hawthorne and Sumac Ridge, associated wineries. All the while, they were preparing for their own winery.

The Colemans purchased some Merlot grapes in 1999 to make Township 7's initial wine — some 312 cases. They declassified another 105 cases of 1999 Merlot into a lower-priced product blandly called Red Table Wine. This was one of the few times when their marketing instincts let them down. Even though Township 7's wine quickly won acclaim, few restaurants wanted to list Red Table Wine. Consumers even steered away from it in the wine shop. Lesson learned. The next time the Colemans need a second label, they will find a smart name.

They searched the Okanagan for a vineyard site before buying, in November, 1999, their two-hectare (five-acre) property on 16th Avenue, one of the busiest through streets in the Fraser Valley south of the river. It is a market-driven decision, for they could have purchased four times the acreage in the Okanagan, where vineyard prices then were lower. "The real key was to be closer to our customers, the Lower Mainland being the main market for B.C. wines," Corey explains. "We felt it was easier to move the grapes here than it was to try to get the people out to the Okanagan. We felt we could also have more direct contact with our customers. We wouldn't need to rely on agents as much and we would have that personal contact to both enhance our image and assist our business." They renovated a 1929 farmhouse for themselves and rebuilt a 1959 farm building for the winery and tasting room. The farm's hayfield became a vineyard, planted primarily to Pinot Noir and Chardonnay, now used in the winery's sparkling wine, and Optima, for a dessert wine.

The Township 7 property was previously part of a larger farm owned by a Langley pioneer named Norman Wilson. The Colemans have preserved history in the winery's evocative name. "When we were purchasing the land, we were sitting in our lawyer's office and reading the legal description and that name jumped out," Corey says. It was what the area was called before it was Langley.

Cautiously, the Colemans put another five names on a list and polled their friends. Township 7 won. The additional appeal was the number seven, to which the Colemans are partial. The winery opening took place on the seventh day of the seventh month in 2001. The sparkling wine, which began with the opportunistic purchase of Pinot Noir and Chardonnay in 1999, is called Seven Stars.

Township 7's flagship wines, made with grapes from two leased South Okanagan vineyards, are Merlot, Chardonnay and Syrah, with Pinot Gris and Sauvignon Blanc rounding out the early offerings. Recognizing that he is a graduate in commerce, not enology, Corey Coleman has employed consulting winemakers. Vancouver-born Glen Fukuyama, now working in Washington State, helped with the 1999 vintage. Michael Bartier, formerly the assistant wine-maker at Hawthorne Mountain and the initiator of Township 7's Okanagan winery, has supervised subsequent vintages.

Township 7's wines have scored well in competition. For example, in the 2002 All-Canada Wine Championships in Windsor, the winery entered four wines and won four medals, including gold for both Seven Stars and the 2000 Merlot, of which 1,117 cases were made. The Colemans intend to keep Township 7's size to that of a boutique winery, making a combined total of 4,000 to 5,000 cases a year at the two wineries. "Our goal is to make the best wine out of the best British Columbia grapes that we can get," Corey says.

TUGWELL CREEK HONEY FARM & MEADERY

OPENED: 2003

8750 West Coast Road, Sooke, BC, V0S 1N0

Telephone: 250-642-1956

Web site: www.tugwellcreekfarm.com

Wine shop: Open noon – 4 pm **Wednesday through Sunday, May through September;**
open weekends during the rest of the year.

RECOMMENDED

✳ VINTAGE MEAD

SUMMER MELOMEL

SOLSTICE

SACK

IN THE ARCANE WORLD OF MEAD BREWING, ONE OF THE CLASSIC references is a 1669 book of recipes entitled *The Closet of the Eminently Learned Sir Kenelme Digby, Knight.* But as mead texts go, that is a modern work (even if hard to get). Robert Liptrot and Dana LeComte, the proprietors of British Columbia's first meadery, have gone much further back to research ancient fermentation techniques. "We've gone back to interpretations of the cuneiform tablets, going back to Mesopotamia," Liptrot says. "And to Egyptian recipes." That scholarship is a measure of how seriously Liptrot approaches mead. A beekeeper since childhood, he regards mead as the ultimate result of beekeeping.

Technically, mead is fermented honey wine. Mead makers have their own medieval language to describe the various beverages that can be made. Traditional or vintage mead is made by fermenting just honey and water. When spices or herbs are added, the mead is called metheglin, said to be a transliteration of *meddyglyn,* a Welsh word meaning medicine, presumably because medicinal herbs were made palatable by mixing in mead. When fruit or fruit juice is added, the mead is called melomel. There are abundant sub-categories of this style. Mead made with rose petals is called rhodomel. When the fruit is apple or apple cider, the mead is called cyser. When grapes or wine are added, the mead is called pyment. All of these styles are made into beverages that are either dry or slightly off-dry. As Liptrot says, it is a myth that mead is necessarily sweet. However, those meads made to be rich and sweet are called sack.

The revival of mead making evident elsewhere in the world has just begun to stir in British Columbia, with the opening of Tugwell Creek on Vancouver Island and Middle Mountain Mead on Hornby Island. These pioneering mead-eries have not had an easy time. With no regulations in place for meaderies, the provincial bureaucrats have struggled with how to approve these operators and their products. Liptrot has run into regulatory barriers against making both pyment and cyser. A man with low tolerance for bureaucracy, he has wisely left it to Dana, his wife, to deal with this issue. "I tend to go out there and get stung by bees, and look at that as being a much better day than writing letters to people in Victoria," he says.

"I have been keeping bees since I was seven years old," says Liptrot, who holds a master's degree in entomology. Born in 1956 and raised in East Vancouver, he juggled beekeeping with other jobs until deciding in the late 1990s to make it his career. He and Dana had been living in New Westminster. He had managed to keep as many as 20 hives, taking them out to clear-cuts in the forest each summer and wintering the hives in his city home. Timely gifts of honey kept their neighbours relaxed with his hobby.

In 1996, searching for a more rural home, the couple found a five-hectare (12-acre) property in Sooke, about 10 minutes north of Sooke Harbour House, one of Vancouver Island's most luxurious resorts. Liptrot now enlarged his bee-keeping business considerably. Soon, he was deploying about 100 hives each season in the forested mountainsides beyond Sooke. The bees gather nectar from plants flourishing in the clear-cuts, including wild salal and fireweed. Depending on how generous nature is, Liptrot harvests between 1,800 and 2,700 kilograms (4,000 to 6,000 pounds) of honey each season. Most is sold directly from the Tugwell Creek farm, with enough kept for the production of about 5,000 litres (1,100 gallons) of mead annually.

"We need to determine whether or not there is an actual market for the mead or whether people are buying it because it is novel," Liptrot says. "We want to start out small and not get over-capitalized and just see where it goes from there."

After a quarter-century of experimentation, Liptrot got serious about making mead around 1994, making four barrels of what he now calls vintage mead. His approach was patterned on how he understood flor sherry is made: the wine was left to age and oxidize in the barrels. "I walked on eggshells for about three years," he recalls. "We were not sure if we could pull it off, but we did. It produced a product very similar to sherry. It was very dry. It was an apéritif. It was exceedingly dry, with about 14.5 per cent alcohol, and with really nice honey and blossom overtones to it." Initially, all the mead was for personal consumption or for gifts. When the meadery opened, however, a portion of this mead was bottled, selling out in a matter of months. Vintage mead now has a regular place in the Tugwell Creek range, along with spiced metheglin (called Solstice), fruity melomel and sweet sack.

Liptrot ages most of the meads in French oak barrels; some also finish fermentation in the oak. The time in oak typically is shorter than would be the case with wine, to prevent the wood flavours from dominating the complex taste of mead. The fruit mead, or melomel, spends almost no time in oak. "Melomel is quite a delicate wine," he explains. "We are trying to bring forward the flavours of the fruit as well as the honey and marry them in such a way that they won't be overpowering each other." The fruit comes from Tugwell Creek's own heritage bushes of marionberry, loganberry and gooseberry. The wine, slightly off-dry, has only 11 per cent alcohol, enhancing its ability to be paired with foods. Liptrot recommends pairing this mead with salmon or serving it at picnics.

Liptrot acknowledges that mead is still a beverage that needs to be explained to consumers. As a result, Tugwell Creek is marketing it selectively through restaurants — such as the Sooke Harbour House — that have good wine lists and knowledgeable wine servers prepared to "spend some time with their clientele to explain mead," Liptrot says. "I don't think it does well unless someone sells it a little bit."

Consequently, he was delighted when he learned that the province's second meadery, Middle Mountain Mead, was under development. "I'd like to see some more meaderies starting up," he says. "It will lend credibility to what we are trying to do." And it will give Tugwell Creek an ally in defining the regulations for meaderies.

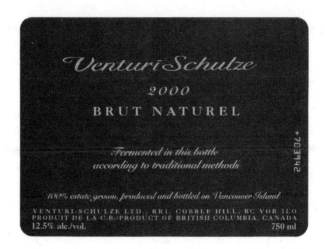

VENTURI-SCHULZE VINEYARDS

OPENED: 1993

> 4235 Trans-Canada Highway, Cobble Hill, BC, V0R 1L0
> Telephone: 250-743-5630
> Web site: www.venturischulze.com
> Wine shop: By appointment.

RECOMMENDED

* ✹ BRUT NATUREL
* ✹ BALSAMIC VINEGAR
* ✹ PRIMAVERA
* ✹ BRANDENBURG NO. 3
* ✸ MILLECOLORI/MILLEFIORI
* ✸ HARPER'S ROW
* ✸ PINOT NOIR
* ✦ ANGEVINE
* ✦ ORTEGA

SOON AFTER THIS WINERY OPENED IN 1993, A TASTING WAS HOSTED FOR a group including a senior provincial bureaucrat who regarded himself as a wine expert. "Take my advice," he told Giordano Venturi. "Sweeten your wines and you will have no problems selling them!" Venturi kept right on making wines in a crisply dry style that has been compared to Champagne without the bubbles. "We all evolve," Venturi believes. A decade later, the same person, by now retired, participated in another Venturi-Schulze tasting. "What he liked best was our Madeleine Angevine," Venturi recounts triumphantly. "It is so dry that it is mouth-puckering."

Far from having problems selling, the winery routinely sells its wines at prices higher, on average, than any other Vancouver Island winery. Production is limited, with only 800 cases made in 2002 and a potential of perhaps 2,000 cases in a few years when a new vineyard is in full growth. "I think we are on the right track," Venturi says. "We've maintained our reputation. We are considered the best."

Now that the public's palate has caught up with Venturi's star-bright style, he is on a crusade — backed by Marilyn Schulze, his spouse, and her winemaking daughter, Michelle — about the individuality of Vancouver Island wines. Unlike Venturi-Schulze, most island wineries supplement their vineyard production with Okanagan grapes. Venturi-Schulze argues that wineries using only island-grown grapes should fix a unique sticker on the bottles, as well as ask restaurants to segregate estate-grown island wines from the rest on their wine lists.

"We just have this idea," Marilyn Schulze says. "I guess it is a purist attitude, but we truly believe that Vancouver Island can have an incredible identity that will end up being marketable elsewhere, too." Venturi believes that island wines should be celebrated for their uniqueness. "You can't get this wine anywhere else," he points out. "I would really like to develop this area as a destination — that people would come here to get the wines they cannot get anywhere else."

Certainly, few wineries anywhere have wines as individualistic as those at Venturi-Schulze. It is by no means easy to grow quality wines in the changeable climate of Vancouver Island. The vineyard practices that Venturi-Schulze uses to get fully ripe fruit each fall drive his costs, according to Venturi's estimates, to three or four times what it costs to grow grapes in the Okanagan. That may explain why some other island wineries rely on Okanagan grapes for a portion of their output. "I think it is a really bad mistake in this area to have allowed wineries to start up with Okanagan grapes," Venturi insists.

To understand what drives Venturi-Schulze, one starts with the fact that Venturi was born into a poor family in Italy in 1941. "We knew our place and our dreams had to be constrained within these boundaries," Venturi wrote later in a short memoir explaining Brandenburg No. 3, Venturi-Schulze's singular dessert wine. One Sunday morning during his adolescence, he was among a group invited to listen to a new recording of that Bach concerto. In his memoir, he recalls the host's luxurious villa, the music "leaping from wall to wall in an enchanting game" and the taste of an unnamed liqueur served as the recording played. Years later, he created a wine originally called La Rocca until its taste recalled that morning in the villa and what then seemed like an "unreachable something." The amber wine, a lively medley of black currant, caramel and honey flavours, was renamed for the concerto.

The elusive somethings in Venturi's adolescence also included balsamic vinegar, another luxury beyond his reach. Authentic Modena balsamic vinegar is made from wine grape juice that is first concentrated to half its volume through prolonged simmering, then inoculated with vinegar bacteria and finally aged for many years in small barrels. Giordano Venturi, who came to Canada in 1967 and worked first as an electrician before becoming an electronics teacher, made himself a small barrel of balsamic vinegar in 1970 to live the tradition that once eluded him.

When he and Marilyn Schulze began growing grapes on Vancouver Island in 1988, a portion of each year's vintage, beginning with 1990, was reserved for vinegar. Today, the fragrant cellar of vinegar barrels (including the 1970 barrel) is slowly aging more than $1 million-worth of balsamic vinegar. Each year, about 2,000 precious bottles, each containing only one cup, are sold for about $50 each. "It took me 30 years to reach this production," Venturi says. "By the time I am ready to leave either this earth or this vineyard, whichever comes first, the maximum [annual] production I see is about 4,000 bottles."

Marilyn Schulze matches her husband when it comes to single-minded determination. Born in Australia in 1951, the daughter of a doctor who immigrated to Canada in 1970, she brings to the winery a highly useful degree in microbiology. She met Venturi when both were teachers, a stressful profession they were happy to leave behind for the heritage farm beside the highway, near Cobble Hill, where they initially planted 1.2 hectares (three acres) of vines.

They were encouraged to grow grapes when they discovered that John Harper, a pioneer research grower, had a nearby vineyard. In 1973, Venturi, living in suburban Vancouver at the time, purchased some vines from a nursery Harper then had in the Fraser Valley. "He used to call me son," Venturi recalls. Besides renewing the friendship on Vancouver Island, Venturi purchased Pinot Gris vines from him. "How's my row?" Harper would ask whenever they met. When Harper died in 2001, Venturi-Schulze paid him tribute with a superb dry white, an artful blend of Pinot Gris and Schönburger, called Harper's Row.

At first, Venturi and Schulze struggled with their vineyard. Their 1991 crop was consumed by birds. Deer, rabbits and raccoons munched either on the vines or on the fruit. Periodically, wasps sucked the juice from aromatic grapes (in 1991 they tried to salvage some fruit by vacuuming the wasps from the grapes). And when those challenges were overcome by the mid-1990s, weather patterns changed. "The first eight years here, we didn't get an April frost, let alone a May frost," Schulze says. She recalls picnicking in the vineyard in March; in recent years, bud-killing frosts have struck into early May.

Always ingenious, Venturi and Schulze began tenting the late-ripening varieties such as Pinot Noir, Kerner and Pinot Gris. Plastic tents deployed over the rows in the spring not only protect the vines from frost but, acting as small greenhouses, accelerate growth by two or three weeks. This has now become common in many other island vineyards. As Venturi discovered in 2002, the improvement in grape maturity can be spectacular. He was able to pick Pinot Noir in late September rather than October and the fruit was so ripe that the wine fermented to a robust 14 per cent alcohol. Venturi smacks his lips as he remembers the fruit. "I'll tell you, that Pinot Noir, I had problems putting it in the crusher, I was so busy eating it."

The original vineyard, two hectares (five acres) after being fully planted, was too small to support both wine and vinegar production. In 1999, they were able to buy an adjoining pasture, making room for an additional 5.2 hectares (13 acres) of vineyard. It was part of a $2.5 million expansion that also included a new winery. "With the expansion now, we have a comfort corner," Venturi says. "No matter what the weather, we will still have enough grapes." Many of the vines in the new vineyard were created, at $5 a vine, in a laboratory with tissue taken from the very best disease-free vines in the original Venturi-Schulze planting. A portion of the new vineyard was set aside for the future planting of experimental varieties. Venturi-Schulze is evaluating five promising early-ripening reds from a Swiss nursery (as are several other island producers). "Vancouver Island is white wine country, with the exception of Pinot Noir, really," Marilyn Schulze says. "But people want a big red. Everyone is looking for the promising big red for the island."

Labels such as Brandenburg No. 3 and Harper's Row illustrate the Venturi-Schulze strategy of creating proprietary labels, even for wines made from single varietals. To begin with, some of the varieties — Kerner, Madeleine Angevine, Schönburger — are not the fashionable ones that command the prices Venturi-Schulze needs to cover the cost of growing grapes here. Schönburger, thus, becomes Primavera; another fine dry white called Millecolori (or Millefiori) is made from Madeleine Angevine, Siegerrebe and Ortega. "We decided to create our own identity around our proprietary names," Marilyn Schulze says. The identity extends even to the packaging. Except for the No. 3, the wines all go into Champagne bottles that can be closed with crown caps, an effective way of ensuring none of the wines suffer from cork taint.

VICTORIA ESTATE WINERY

OPENED: 2002

1445 Benvenuto Avenue, Brentwood Bay, BC, V8M 1R3
Telephone: 250-652-2671
Web site: www.victoriaestatewinery.com
Wine shop: Open daily 11 am – 8 pm.
Restaurant: Madeleine's Bistro open daily 11 am – 8 pm.

RECOMMENDED

✳ MERLOT
✳ RIESLING
  MARÉCHAL FOCH
  CHARDONNAY
  PINOT GRIS

IN REAL ESTATE, IT IS THE LOCATION THAT COUNTS. FOLLOWING THAT principle, the investors behind Victoria Estate Winery opened their 1,951-square-metre (21,000 square-foot) winery in 2003 near Butterfly World and the Butchart Gardens, unquestionably the premier tourist attractions on the Saanich Peninsula. "I don't think there is a winery in North America that has 1.3 million people going by its door," general manager Edd Moyes said just before the opening. "Sure, we're on the coattails of Butchart Gardens, but we're hoping that we're going to draw enough people out here that it will also help them. We're going to do whatever it takes to get people out to this area. It is definitely going to be a tourist winery."

And that is how it turned out. The winery, just a half-hour's drive north of downtown Victoria, opened in May and by the end of the year had welcomed an estimated 52,000 visitors, some of whom then continued on to other of the island's wineries. Wine sales at Victoria Estate were so brisk that, according to founding winemaker Eric von Krosigk, "we went through a couple of vintages very, very fast." The winery quickly vaulted to the front as the largest of Vancouver Island's wineries, with ambitious plans to be even larger.

Victoria Estate Winery was conceived initially by Fraser Smith, a Saanich-area financial planner who had a hobby Chardonnay vineyard on nearby rural acreage he has since sold. Smith is the sort of guy who attacks ventures like an evangelist seeking converts. His discovery of grape growing turned him into the Saanich Peninsula's leading proselytizer of vineyards. He took the lead in forming the Vancouver Island Grape Growers Association. Now called the Wine Islands Vintners Association, it practically includes everyone on the island or the Gulf Islands who is growing grapes or would like to. Smith enlisted von Krosigk, one of the busiest winemakers in British Columbia, and then, beginning in 2000, raised about $3 million for the winery.

One needs cash to do anything substantial on the Saanich Peninsula. For a long time this fertile peninsula, with a moderately Mediterranean climate, has been Victoria's garden. Loganberries once grew here in such abundance that two of British Columbia's earliest wineries were founded to make wine from surplus berries: Growers' Wine Company in 1923 and Brentwood Products in 1927. The latter firm, which renamed itself Victoria Wineries, soon was taken over by Growers'. The fields that once grew loganberries (the berries were decimated by plant disease) have become high-priced hobby farms for the well-heeled of Victoria. The 5.6 hectares (14 acres) of real estate purchased for the Victoria Estate Winery property consumed a sizeable amount of the money that Smith raised. Von Krosigk is candid about why he and Smith are encouraging other land owners to grow grapes for the winery. "We can't afford to buy the land," he says.

In the winery's 2.4 hectares (six acres) of vineyard, von Krosigk has planted three white varieties, Kerner, Gewürztraminer and Schönburger, and two reds, Pinot Noir and Dunkelfelder. The latter is a German variety producing deeply coloured wine and therefore useful for touching up lighter red wines such as Pinot Noir. The vines had a first modest crop in 2003, all of it protected with netting against the island's voracious birds. Meanwhile, von Krosigk made wine with Okanagan-grown Riesling, Chardonnay, Pinot Blanc, Pinot Gris, Maréchal Foch and Merlot, beginning with the 2000 vintage. The winery relies on the Okanagan for about 85 per cent of its grapes. Given its size and its portfolio, Victoria Estate will always need Okanagan fruit. There will never be enough island-grown grapes, even if the varieties were not limited.

For Victoria Estate, von Krosigk started cautiously, making a modest 1,200 cases in 2000. Before the current building opened, Victoria Estate had only a small tasting room in a mousy little house at the end of the driveway. Anticipating growth with the new tasting room, von Krosigk made 4,400 cases of wine in 2001 and 9,600 cases in 2002. Even so, Moyes was worried about running out of wine when the new facility opened. He was right to worry. Most of that production was sold by the end of the summer in 2003. Looking ahead, von Krosigk, scrambling to get enough grapes, almost doubled the production in the 2003 vintage. "We were going to do 11,000 cases and we ended up doing 16,000 cases," he says. In 2004, when he became Hester Creek's winemaker, von Krosigk turned over Victoria Estate's cellars to Ken Winchester, a California-trained winemaker with his own winery nearby.

Victoria Estate is designed theatrically, with tourists in mind, even including a small theatre. Architecturally, the two-storey building echoes the grand barns common during an earlier era on the Saanich Peninsula. The approach is a stately, vine-bordered driveway. A shaded artesian pond across the driveway from the winery is one of the two picnic areas. The other picnic area, on the hillside above the winery, is open to visitors with pets. It is typical of the detail designed to attract visitors of all interests. The winery delicatessen sells food for the picnics.

The theatricality reflects the background of Edd Moyes. A Victoria native, he was running a golf course at Courtenay when he was recruited to manage the winery. Victoria Estate had advertised internationally for a general manager, attracting candidates from Australia, Argentina and South Africa. But most also wanted to make the wine — and von Krosigk was doing that. Fraser Smith was about to launch a new search when he was introduced to Moyes, a marketer with absolutely no desire to make wine. Moyes had not applied for the job.

"It was perfect," Smith concluded. "Edd knows anybody who is anybody down here. He knows the tourism industry." In his career in the Victoria area, Moyes worked in radio and for two advertising agencies before setting up his own marketing company. He also spent eight years as vice-president of sales and marketing at the Oak Bay Marine Group, one of Victoria's major tourist-oriented firms. He has been president of Tourism Victoria and has run or been on the executive of most high-profile volunteer groups related to tourism.

The success of this winery depends on its becoming another of Victoria's high-powered attractions. The parking lot accommodates tour buses. The winery's public spaces include a wrap-around heated balcony with seats for about 200, effectively doubling the capacity of the tasting room inside. A private tasting room next to the 65-seat theatre is large enough for an entire busload of visitors. The tasting area includes both a delicatessen and long bar.

And impresario Moyes directs matters from a glassed-in office at one side of the tasting room. "I'm a little bit of an outgoing guy, so I want to see what's happening on the floor," Moyes says. "I want to make sure that everybody is upbeat and everybody is selling. Everybody's going to be on stage. We will perform!"

VIGNETI ZANATTA WINERY AND VINEYARDS

OPENED: 1992

5039 Marshall Road, Duncan, BC, V9L 6S3

Telephone: 250-748-2338

Web site: www.zanatta.ca

Wine shop: Call for seasonal hours.

Restaurant: Vinoteca on the Vineyard is open noon – 5 pm Wednesday through Sunday, March through December; open for dinner Thursday through Saturday.

RECOMMENDED

※ **GLENORA FANTASIA BRUT**
FATIMA BRUT
ALLEGRIA BRUT ROSÉ
TAGLIO ROSS
DAMASCO
PINOT NERO
ORTEGA
PINOT GRIGIO

IT IS NOT SURPRISING THAT A THIRD OF THIS WINERY'S PRODUCTION SHOULD be sparkling wine since winemaster Loretta Zanatta's post-graduate work in Italy involved making spumante at a relative's winery. But according to Jim Moody, her husband and the winery's vineyard manager, the sparkling tradition began with his father-in-law's home winemaking.

Dennis Zanatta, who grew up in northern Italy but settled on this Cowichan Valley farm in 1958, had been making wines in a rustic style from vines planted in the early 1970s. "Dennis made the wine according to the phases of the moon," Moody explains. Wines would be racked and later bottled during full moon. "Sometimes the wine hadn't finished fermenting because it was out in the barn during the wintertime. Then it would re-ferment in the bottle. It turned out quite well. So when Loretta went to Italy, she perfected it." She put her stamp on the winery's sparklers, beginning with the 1990 Glenora Fantasia, now the flagship wine among the four sparkling wines (including a red one) made at Vigneti Zanatta.

Dennis Zanatta's contribution to wine growing on Vancouver Island goes well beyond sparkling wines. In 1983 he provided a corner of his property, along with farm labour and equipment, for a grape-growing trial begun that year by the provincial government. This so-called Duncan Project tested at least 50 varieties before government funding ran out in 1990 — the same year that Loretta completed her professional training in Italy. Zanatta had learned enough from the Duncan Project that he planted six hectares (15 acres) of vines in 1989 and later doubled that. In 1992, the Zanatta family opened the first new winery on Vancouver Island in about 70 years.

From the very beginning, Vigneti Zanatta has made wine only from its own grapes, never purchasing Okanagan grapes. Unlike some other island wineries, Zanatta is not militant on this point. However, there is a quiet determination that the wines should express the island terroir, even if the climate on Vancouver Island is so capricious that the winery's production can swing between 1,500 and 2,500 cases a year.

Jim Moody understands why many new wineries with young vineyards have accelerated their entry into the business with Okanagan grapes. "You need to make money," is his practical observation. "The danger is that once they are producing, will they stop bringing in Okanagan grapes? I understand — but at the same time, we are on Vancouver Island and our wines are very different. And it would be a shame to have 60 wineries on Vancouver Island that are buying all their fruit from somewhere else. It kind of defeats the purpose."

Moody argues that the style of Vancouver Island wine "is a little more aromatic and the flavours are a little more subtle." The contrast can be seen by tasting Zanatta's crisply dry Pinot Gris alongside one from the Okanagan. The latter, he says, often has bold peachy flavours and higher alcohol. The Ortega grape, which can yield a dry, fruity white with a hint of spice, is a Vancouver Island specialty. A German-created cross, Ortega matures reliably in cool climates to yield no more than 12 per cent alcohol. But in those seasons that are warmer than average, Ortega ripens exuberantly. "One year, we got 13 per cent," Moody recalls. "It was kind of embarrassing really for a white wine."

In some vintages, Zanatta sells grapes to other wineries on the island, in part because its vines yield more fruit than the winery needs to support its sales. The Zanatta vineyard is one of the largest on Vancouver Island, growing not just the most successful Duncan Project varieties (such as Ortega, Auxerrois and Pinot Gris) but also Cabernet Sauvignon, Merlot and Cabernet Franc, the big reds of the Okanagan. The winemaking at Zanatta needs to be more flexible to deal with the lower ripeness of those varieties on the island. The Cabernet Sauvignon has been turned into Taglio, British Columbia's only red sparkling wine. Some of the reds are blended artfully with, if needed, a touch of the vineyard's blood-red Castel grape, a French hybrid that came through the Duncan Project well.

Loretta Zanatta's answer to what she calls "the incredible variability" of Vancouver Island's season is demonstrated by Damasco, a fruity white wine incorporating at least four grapes, including Auxerrois. The Damasco is not vintage-dated because the winery believes it can make a more consistent wine by blending several vintages. On Vancouver Island, a fully ripe vintage can be followed by a cool, high-acid vintage. Consistent quality has made Damasco the best-selling of Zanatta's wines.

As one of the largest plantings in the Zanatta vineyard, Auxerrois shows up in several wines. It goes into the cuvée with Pinot Noir to make another of the winery's four bubblies, the Allegria Brut Rosé. As production has grown, Zanatta has been able to age all of its sparkling wines for four years on the lees before the final bottling, in a quest for complexity.

The winery's flagship sparkler gets the Glenora half of its name from the local district. Fantasia, the second half, is pronounced *Fant–a-ZEE-ah*. It is British Columbia's only wine made with Cayuga grapes. This is an aromatic grape developed in New York state in 1945 by plant scientists looking for a winter-hardy, productive white. Cayuga was included in the Duncan Project because the government's grape expert saw the reliable variety as "a mortgage maker." Other vineyards have not adopted Cayuga because it is not permitted in VQA wines. Zanatta, which left the VQA program in 1996, maintains enough vines to produce about 300 cases a year of Glenora Fantasia.

The best place to taste the Zanatta wines is the winery's Vinoteca Restaurant, which opened in 1996. The restaurant is in a fully restored farmhouse built in 1903, with views from its veranda over the vineyards. Indeed, some Zanatta wines are made in small volumes, to be served only in the Vinoteca.

WELLBROOK WINERY

OPENED: 2004

4626 88th Street, Delta, BC, V4K 3N3

Telephone: 604-946-1868

Web site: www.wellbrookwinery.com

Wine shop: Open daily 11 am – 6 pm. Call for winter hours.

RECOMMENDED:

BLUEBERRY

CRANBERRY

ICED APPLE

TERRY BREMNER'S DEDICATION TO PRESERVING HERITAGE SHOWS AT this winery, where everything glows with the patina of age except for the wines and the fruit juices. The Old Grainery Store, as the wine shop is called, is one of the original buildings on the 100-year-old Delta farm. Formerly used for grain storage, it has been restored meticulously: there is a new roof on the exterior but the underside of the original roof is visible in the interior, soaring four metres (14 feet) above a tasting bar crafted from century-old barn boards. The two-wheeled wooden cart in the corner, now filled with wines and other products, was salvaged from the nearby barn, another original building so dangerously near to collapse when Bremner acquired it that some tradesmen refused to work inside it. Bremner restored it, with the help of a gutsy carpenter. "I love heritage," he says.

Bremner and his mother, Caroline, bought the farm in 2001, becoming only its third owners. It was developed by Seymour Huff, a pioneering Delta farmer who operated it for 50 years before turning it over to his grandson, Gordon, who ran it for another 50 years. As an adolescent, Bremner, who was born in Delta in

1959, delivered newspapers to the Huff home. Later, Bremner was a member of the volunteer fire department when Gordon Huff was the chief. Seeking a farm on which to develop the winery, Bremner was close to buying elsewhere in Delta, when he discovered that the Huff farm was available. "This just had so much character," he says. "It was a perfect match." In the two years that Bremner spent renovating the buildings, including the house with its wrap-around veranda, Huff has been on hand, providing details of the design and the farm's history. One of those details inspired the winery's name: the property was once called Wellbrook Farms because it had one of the few wells in the area. "I have a picture of the old windmill and the water tower," Bremner says.

Bremner's vision of Wellbrook is that of a working farm enriched not only by the wines in The Grainery but also by a petting zoo, a pumpkin patch, an antique store and a display of farming practices. The 22-hectare (55-acre) property, just west of exit 20 on busy Highway 99, grows cranberries, blueberries and soon will have a small vineyard. Bremner and a brother, Alan, also operate a 33-hectare (80-acre) blueberry farm nearby. It was once among British Columbia's larger blueberry producers but a single-commodity farm has become economically challenging. "To save the farm, you have to diversify," he says, explaining the reason for creating the winery. "There were years that we would lose money."

Bremner seems to have inherited his taste for agriculture from his late father. A long-time assessor of the Corporation of Delta, Stan Bremner changed careers in the 1970s to become a meticulous farmer. He once had a flock of 300 to 400 sheep whose lambs were so prized that the customer list developed entirely by word of mouth. The Bremner family farm switched to blueberries in the early 1980s and again, the Bremner trademark became known for quality fruit.

When he graduated from high school, Terry Bremner managed to see the world by becoming a diamond driller. Warm and gregarious, Bremner prefers hands-on experience with cultures when he travels. He worked in North and South America as well as Asia, coming back with colourful stories about the people of the jungles of Indonesia and about living for a month in a Mongolian *ger* (as the country's traditional round tents are called). Those eclectic tastes inform his effort to turn Wellbrook into a memorable destination.

The idea of a winery evolved from the fresh juice business that Bremner started in 2000 to fill a perceived need for ultra-premium blueberry and cranberry juices. "I had tried another juice," he recalls. "It did not taste like blueberries. I found they make juice from juice-grade fruit, which is the lowest grade fruit there is." He created juices from the top-quality berries usually sold fresh in produce stores. He sorts his berries for the juices so rigorously, he says, that the rejects, which are sold to processors, still rank one step above juice-grade.

The juice business was a sheer gamble. "I did all this with no contracts, nothing," he says. "I put away 30,000 pounds of fruit with no idea where it was going." He had a product by Christmas, entered a trade show in January, and just plugged away. He now distributes throughout the Lower Mainland and into the United States, having built a market even though the juices are almost the same price as fruit wine and — reflecting the raw material cost — often double the cost of competing products.

While building the juice sales, he had begun to think of the winery. Bremner had made fruit wines for many years with a friend. Then The Fort Wine Company, which opened in 2001, began buying Bremner blueberries and Dominic Rivard, the winemaker there, praised the winemaking quality of the flavourful berries. In the fall of 2001, Bremner spent two weeks at a small German winery during the vintage. That experience cinched the winery decision. "It was very enjoyable," he recalls.

In spite of Bremner's home winemaking, he contracted the Fort to make the wine. "You want to make a good end product," Bremner says. "In my mind, the ingredients are the most important item and that's what we do. We grow the best ingredients. Then we found someone who is knowledgeable and good at making the wine." Wellborn also makes use of The Fort's processing facility. As the pragmatic Bremner says, it makes no sense to duplicate expensive equipment that another winery already has.

Wellbrook opened with 10 fruit wines, including cranberry, blueberry, peach-apricot, iced apple and fortified examples of several of these fruit wines. The overall style is comparable to the fruit wines offered by The Fort, as one would expect since both use the same winemaker. Over time, subtle differences might reflect the particular flavours of the berries being grown by Bremner. With nine varieties of blueberries on his farms, Bremner already is wondering whether there might be a place in the future for named varietals from the four now blended in the Wellbrook wines: Bluecrop, Hardyblue, Olympia and Spartan.

It might be an uphill battle. "With wines, you can say specific varieties of grapes because people have been educated for 1,000 years about them," Bremner says. "With blueberries, most people don't even know there is more than one variety."

WESTHAM ISLAND ESTATE WINERY

OPENED: 2003

2170 Westham Island Road, Delta, BC, V4K 3N2

Telephone: 604-940-7555

Web site: www.westham-island-winery.com

Wine shop: Open 10 am – 5:30 pm Monday through Friday and 10 am – 6 pm
  Saturday and Sunday.

RECOMMENDED

❋ STRAWBERRY

❋ RASPBERRY

✸ TAYBERRY

PEACH

BLACK CURRANT

FRAMBOISE

WESTHAM WHITE TABLE WINE

JUST DUCKY

SNOGOOS

SOMETIMES, THE ONLY CONSEQUENCE OF BEING FIRST IS BREAKING TRAIL for everyone else. In the late 1990s, Andy Bissett was the first person to seek a winery license in Delta. By the time Westham Island Estate Winery opened in the summer of 2003, three other fruit wineries in the Fraser Valley had opened and two were under development. Sadly, Bissett died the year before. His feisty widow, Lorraine, took his dream through to successful completion, breaking through a log-jam of zoning approvals with a somewhat frustrated telephone call to the mayor of Delta.

Perhaps Andy Bissett had been a bit of a rough diamond who got under the skin of the bureaucrats at city hall. "If you piss them off, you suffer," suggests

Lorraine, who is pretty good herself at getting right to the point. The oil painting hanging in the winery's antique-rich tasting room shows another side of Andy Bissett: an amiable figure in hunting gear with his bird-hunting friends gathered around him.

Besides being a good hunter, Bissett was a successful farmer. His 16-hectare (40-acre) property at Agassiz is one of the valley's larger black currant and rhubarb farms. The rich, 14-hectare (35-acre) Westham Island farm, owned by the Bissett family for a quarter-century, grows a profusion of berries and even a few rows of Concord, Maréchal Foch and Madeleine Sylvaner grapes. The cultured blackberries are menu items on cruise ships. The farm's jams, syrups and produce, which are sold at its fruit stand during the season, have a strong following.

Andy Bissett began laying winery plans about the same time that a farmer friend, John Stuyt, opened the Fraser Valley's first fruit winery, Columbia Valley Classics, in 1998 near Cultus Lake. "He had this vision," Ron Taylor, Westham Island's winemaker, said in a 2003 interview. "Seven or eight years ago, I was talking to someone about cider, who said, 'You should talk to Andy. He is growing cider apples on Westham Island.' I phoned him and said we should meet some day."

They finally met in the fall of 2001 at the Columbia Valley winery, where Taylor was completing a winemaking project. By that time, Bissett had collected most of his winery equipment, including sheets of glistening stainless steel. A long, narrow section of the farm's big blue barn was being converted for wine processing and the steel sheets went on the walls. "It is the only winery I have ever run into that has stainless steel walls," says Taylor. "Andy believed that a winery had to be as sanitary as a meat-processing place. Having stainless steel walls sure made it easier with the health inspector."

For Taylor, making fruit wines is a second career. "Never made fruit wine in my whole life until the last four or five years," he says. "It's been a journey!" Born in Vancouver in 1942, he went to work in 1970 at the Andrés winery in Port Moody after graduating in microbiology from the University of British Columbia. In his 22 years there, the avuncular Taylor mentored many younger winemakers who progressed through his laboratory. After leaving Andrés to work with a bottled water company, Taylor returned to wine, this time with fruit wines. He consulted to Columbia Valley, then helped launch both Richmond's Blossom Winery and the Samson Estate Winery in Washington. "Then projects started falling from the sky," he laughs. One of them was Westham Island.

After Andy Bissett's untimely death, his widow and her family re-evaluated the winery plan. They concluded it was sound because of its strategic location on Westham Island, home to the Reifel Migratory Bird Sanctuary. "We get an awful lot of traffic," Lorraine Bissett observes. Many of the 80,000 visitors to the sanctuary also stop at the winery or the nearby fruit stand. It is the year-round traffic that wineries covet. Bird watchers come from afar in November, for example, to see the thousands of snow geese that come back to the island annually. Never missing an opportunity, the winery's range includes a gooseberry wine called SnoGoos.

Flat and fertile, Westham Island, 648 hectares (1,600 acres) in size, is in the mouth of the south arm of the Fraser River and has been farmed at least since 1870. In the 1920s, George C. Reifel, a successful distiller, bought land on the island for, according to local legend, shipping spirits to the United States during Prohibition. Later he developed a significant farm that, during World War II, produced sugar beets. Ultimately, his family leased, sold and donated the parcels that comprise the bird sanctuary today. Only about five per cent of the island is cultivated now, growing berries, fruits and vegetables.

At the Westham Island winery, most of this profusion — even including pumpkins — has been made into wine by the indefatigable Taylor. One of the winemakers famously involved in the creation of Andrés' Baby Duck, Taylor revisited the idea at Westham with a summertime rosé from the Concord and Maréchal Foch grapes. "It is called Just Ducky," he chuckles. It was one of the most popular wines at the tasting room, selling out before the first summer was over.

Westham Island's tayberry wine, with an exotic spicy perfume and taste, is unique, since the Bissett farm is one of the few places in North America growing this fruit. Tayberry is a cross of blackberry, raspberry and loganberry, so named because the berry was first grown in a Scottish region called Tayside. Taylor has also made wines from red, black and white currants, blueberries, raspberries, peaches, rhubarb, blackberries and cranberries. His personal favourite is a luscious strawberry dessert wine that he calls a milkshake for adults.

Generally, the wines are off-dry to sweet. "I think it's required," Taylor explains. "My rule of thumb is if the fruit or berry is 10 or 12 Brix sugar, you would want to go about a quarter of that in the table wine — just a hint of the sweetness that you would expect in the fruit. I am sure there are some fruits that make interesting dry wines. But historically, if you look at fruit wines, people made them for social wines. Sweeter wines can go very well with spicy foods." While his dessert wines might have about 16 per cent alcohol, Taylor keeps the table wines at a "gentle" 11 per cent to ensure the fruit flavours come through cleanly.

Lorraine Bissett's decision to complete Andy's dream appears to have been a good one. "The wines have been very well received," Taylor said at the end of the winery's first summer. "People have been coming back."

WILD GOOSE VINEYARDS

RIESLING DRY
2002

STONY SLOPE

13.5% Alc./Vol.   **White Wine Vin Blanc**   750 ml

Produced by A. F. Kruger & Sons, Okanagan Falls, BC
Product of British Columbia, Canada   Produit de la Columbie-Britannique, Canada

WILD GOOSE VINEYARDS AND WINERY

OPENED: 1990

2145 Sun Valley Way, Okanagan Falls, BC, V0H 1R0

Telephone: 250-497-8919

Web site: www.wildgoosewinery.com

Wine shop: Open daily 10 am – 5 pm from April 1 to October 31.

By appointment November through March. Licensed picnic area.

RECOMMENDED

- ❋ STONY SLOPE RIESLING
- ❋ GEWÜRZTRAMINER
- ❋ RIESLING CLASSIC
- ❋ TAWNY PIPE
- ❋ PINOT GRIS
- ❋ PINOT BLANC
- MARÉCHAL FOCH
- AUTUMN GOLD

WHEN HIS SON, NICHOLAS, WAS 17, WILD GOOSE WINEMAKER HAGEN Kruger asked him what he wanted to do on finishing his education. "He said 'I want to make wine,'" Hagen recounts proudly. "I was just floored." If the young man perseveres in that ambition, he will be the third generation at this quintessentially family-run winery. "It would be nice having the kids following in our footsteps, if at all possible," says sales manager Roland Kruger, the winemaker's younger brother. "My daughter wants to be a zoologist but I tell her there is no money in it.

Wild Goose is notable for the warmth of the welcome because the Krugers live their family values. The winery's spacious tasting room is usually personally managed by a Kruger or by someone equally affable who is married to a Kruger.

The winery opened modestly in a back room of the house of Adolf and Susanna Kruger, the parents of Hagen and Roland. The business now operates from a purpose-built winery next door and makes about 5,000 cases of wine a year, the right size for a family enterprise. "Once you go beyond a certain size, it gets tough if you want to keep it within the family," Roland Kruger observes. "It's hard to do this all yourself. We've made some projections and 7,500 cases is where we can comfortably grow to."

Truly fortunate visitors have found themselves enjoying cold cuts, cheese and tea at lunch in the family's dining room, listening to Adolf and his sons trading stories about their history in wine. Born in Germany in 1931, Adolf made a career in engineering after arriving in Canada at the age of 20. "Sometimes I think that our success — that we got where we are — is because I worked at engineering and it was fairly disciplined," Adolf says. When an engineering industry downturn threatened his job, he changed careers. A friend made a comfortable living with an Okanagan vineyard. Kruger, who was making wine as an amateur, purchased a rugged four hectares (10 acres) of raw land southeast of Okanagan Falls in 1983. He negotiated a contract with Mission Hill to grow Riesling and Gewürztraminer.

Adolf initially aspired only to be a good grower. Then, the 1989 free trade agreement threatened an uncertain future for Okanagan vineyards smaller than the minimum 20 acres allowed for estate wineries. Adolf joined with several other owners of tiny vineyards, pressing the provincial government to create the license for what became known as farm-gate wineries. Just in case they lost their winery contracts, the small growers now could protect their livelihoods by making wine themselves. The bureaucrats in Victoria were very sceptical. One asked Adolf how much wine he expected to sell in a year. "I had a vision of a little wine shop and doing the vineyard and selling wine on the side," Adolf remembers. "I said I'm looking at least at selling 2,000 to 3,000 bottles a year. And he looked at me and said, 'I don't think you can sell 2,000 bottles.' The vision just wasn't there." Wild Goose now sells close to 70,000 bottles a year.

The vision had not been there earlier either. When Adolf proposed his vineyard, the industry consultants warned him that his chosen European varieties would not grow in the Okanagan. Relying on German technical literature, he ignored that advice and planted Gewürztraminer and Riesling, with just a few rows of Maréchal Foch. He had his concerns as well. "One major consideration at the time was the frost," Adolf says. Thus, he chose varieties known for their ability to survive moderately cold winters. "If we were to plant now, we would probably plant Pinot Noir or Merlot," Hagen Kruger suggests. That is what several nearby vineyards grow, with good success.

Roland, who sells the wine, differs with his brother. "We've had such tremendous success with the wines that if we were doing it all again, perhaps we *would* put in the same varieties," he says. The two white varieties yield full-flavoured grapes in the hot, rock-strewn Wild Goose vineyard. The property is named for a flock of geese that exploded into flight when Adolf chanced upon them during his first walk there. He had bought the rugged land cheaply, for good reason. "You could plant no other crop here," says Roland. "Nothing else would grow. On the surface, there is nothing but rocks and gravel." Visitors sometimes assume the abundant rocks between the vines were placed there deliberately to catch the day's heat. When they planted, they were unable to dig holes with spades for the new vines. Instead, the Krugers wrestled with a high-pressure water gun to drill holes. "Hagen worked this water gun all weekend," Adolf remembers. "On Monday morning, he was eating a bowl of corn flakes and the spoon fell out of his hand ... he couldn't hold onto it." And Hagen is a sturdy, big-boned man.

Nutritionally, this is extremely lean soil in which the vines struggle. "The roots are finding good nutrients down below," Roland believes. "Sometimes we get grape clusters that are sparse. Yet it's amazing how well that fruit develops. The tonnage is really low. The vine has to work really hard to ripen up what is there." The winery's Riesling and Gewürztraminer grapes produce wines with intense flavours, reflecting the terroir. Usually, the Riesling is made in two styles. Wild Goose's Riesling Classic, finished with residual sugar, is an easy-drinking, popular style. The green-tinged Stony Slope Riesling is boldly dry and so full in flavour that it receives an extra six to eight months bottle age before being released. In the early 1990s, dry Riesling was so hard to sell that Wild Goose dropped it for five vintages after 1995. It returned in the 2001 vintage when the Krugers saw the revival in Riesling's popularity and it now comprises about 40 per cent of the winery's Riesling.

Gewürztraminer has emerged as the flagship wine at Wild Goose, with an annual production now of about 800 cases. In style, the wine is powerful in flavour, with spicy aromas that explode from the glass. Rich and full-bodied, it is finished dry, with an insignificant amount of residual sweetness, just enough for balance. Visitors from Alsace in France have compared the Wild Goose Gewürztraminer to similar wines from Alsace, arguably the world's benchmark for this variety. Adolf did some personal research there in 2001. "We stayed at a little winery that had rooms for rent," he recounts. "They had Gewürztraminer — and it could have been one of ours. Almost identical."

Wild Goose now is in the enviable position of having mature vines, capable of yielding fine-flavoured grapes for years to come. "People ask us, when they are doing the tours, 'How old are the plants?'" Hagen says. "Well, they are getting up to 25 years old. People also ask, 'How long will these plants last? When do you have to replant them?' And I say, well, they'll be ready for replanting when our kids are old enough to do it. Because I sure don't want to replant those myself, that's for sure!" In 1999, the Krugers bought a second vineyard — two hectares (five acres) of sandy loam near Oliver. "One of the appealing aspects of that property was no rocks," Roland says. "It is exciting to stick a shovel in it and it actually goes down in dirt."

Again, that vineyard grows white varieties, including Pinot Blanc and Gewürztraminer. The winery's largest-selling brand is an off-dry white called

Autumn Gold, a blend of Riesling, Gewürztraminer and Pinot Blanc. Today, red wines comprise one-quarter of Wild Goose's production and are getting more of Hagen's attention. "We've been very successful with our whites," he observes. "For me personally, improving the reds is kind of a challenge. I don't feel complete."

All of the reds, except for seven rows of Maréchal Foch grown in the Wild Goose vineyard, are purchased from neighbouring growers. Hagen believes that Foch is the ideal grape for making port-style wines. At Wild Goose, it produces a dark, rich wine with plum and chocolate flavours that is released as Tawny Pipe. The neighbours, who are growing Merlot and Pinot Noir for Wild Goose, usually are named on the wine labels. As added incentive, they receive bonuses if their vineyard-designated wines win awards. "They are almost an extension of our family," Roland says.

2003
PINOT NOIR
SHARP ROCK VINEYARD

WINCHESTER CELLARS

OPENING: PROPOSED FOR 2004

6170 Old West Saanich Road, Victoria, BC, V9E 2G8

IN 1996, WHEN KEN WINCHESTER PLANTED HIS FIRST WINERY IN CALIFORNIA'S Paso Robles region, that appellation was just emerging. Eight years later, there were more than 50 wineries there and he was able to sell Winchester Vineyards in a rising market. Now on Vancouver Island, he is aiding another wave of expansion with Winchester Cellars, his second winery. Winchester's role in shaping the future of Vancouver Island wine goes beyond his own winery. Since settling in Victoria late in 2002, he has become president of the Wine Islands Growers Association, has begun to teach an Okanagan University College extension course in viticulture and has become the winemaker at Victoria Estate Vineyards.

Born in New York in 1952, Winchester is the son of a journalist who, in spite of being a war correspondent and travel writer, was not very interested in wine. "I really grew up in a household that did not own a corkscrew," Winchester laughs. He discovered a lifestyle that included wine and good food in Montreal. He came to Canada for a master's degree in environmental science in 1977 at the University of Toronto, liked the country, and took a job as an editor at *Reader's Digest* in Montreal. He lived in that vibrant city for the next 12 years.

When he discovered he could not afford to buy wine for daily consumption, he began making wine at home in 1980, with a friend "who had the proverbial Italian uncle." They bought enough California grapes to fill four used whiskey barrels with wine. "We did everything wrong but darned if we didn't make a decent Zinfandel," he says. "I was hooked on winemaking."

In 1983, he set up a publishing house, St. Remy Press, moving back to New York in 1989 to look after the firm's growing American sales. There, he began buying his wine grapes from the emerging vineyards on Long Island. When the publishing house was sold in 1993, Winchester moved to California to become editorial director at *Sunset Magazine*. His "not so secret agenda" for moving to California, however, was to start taking winemaking courses at the University of California's Davis campus. "I took every course I could and loved every minute of it," he recalls. "It carried my winemaking to another level." He has never applied all the cookie-cutter techniques he learned at Davis, but he insists it is important to have that knowledge. "To break the rules, you have to know what the rules are," he says, quoting an old aphorism.

Two of his favourite wine grapes are Pinot Noir and Syrah. Thus, when he decided to establish his own winery, he looked at Oregon's Willamette Valley, which has a reputation for Pinot Noir; and he looked at various California regions. "Paso Robles had the edge for the wine I was used to doing," he says, referring to the big, full-bodied reds he had made at home.

In 1996, he and his wife bought a 12-hectare (30-acre) farm, planting half of it to vines, mostly Syrah. While his vines were developing, Winchester worked three vintages at nearby Windward Vineyard, a small producer that only makes about 1,500 cases of Pinot Noir each year. Meanwhile, at Winchester Vineyards, his Paso Robles winery, he began releasing wines in 1999. Altogether, he made three vintages there, never more than 500 cases. The wines received favourable notice in the *Wine Spectator* and made it onto wine lists of expensive restaurants.

A number of events in 2001, including California's skyrocketing energy costs and some shattering personal medical expenses, triggered the Winchesters' decision to return to Canada. (Ken had acquired Canadian citizenship and his wife, Fiona Gilsenan, was born in Toronto.) "I felt there was going to be a correction in the California wine industry," he said, judging correctly. They sold Winchester Vineyards just before the wine market correction began and left California after the 2002 harvest.

A gardening writer, Gilsenan had become enamoured with Victoria while researching a book for *Sunset*. Ken Winchester decided against developing his new winery in the Okanagan, figuring he could have more impact on Vancouver Island. "We wanted to go to a place where we could start new challenges," he says.

He appreciates the quality of Okanagan grapes, however, and purchased both Pinot Noir and Pinot Gris from growers there in 2003. The first 2,700 litres (600 gallons) of Winchester Cellars wine was made at Victoria Estate Winery under an arrangement that saw Winchester also handle much of the cellar work that fall in the large winery. After that vintage, he leased a vineyard not far away on the Saanich Peninsula as a base for a winery that is close to its market and to tourism.

Initially, and perhaps for a long time, Winchester will make only Pinot Noir and Pinot Gris. He intends to convert some of the varieties in the leased vineyard as well as source grapes elsewhere on Vancouver Island. He does not think that a small winery should spread its efforts across a large number of varieties and blended wines. Unfortunately for those boosting Ortega as Vancouver Island's signature grape, this is currently not in Winchester's plans. "I have not tasted an Ortega that blows me over," he says.

JUST HATCHED OR IN THE INCUBATOR

Honeymoon Bay Wild Blackberry Winery
Honeymoon Bay, BC, V0R 1Y0
Telephone: 250-749-4681

Seoul Ricewine
208 20167 96 Avenue, Langley, BC, V1M 3C5
Telephone: 604-513-3605

Sonoran Estate Winery
21606 Highway 97 North, Summerland, BC, V0H 1Z0
Telephone: 250-494-9323

UNDER DEVELOPMENT

Celista Vineyards
2319 Beguelin Road, Celista, BC, V0E 1L0
Telephone: 250-955-8600

Desert Falls Vineyard
2273 Oliver Ranch Road
Okanagan Falls, BC, V0H 1R0
Telephone: 250-497-8197

Joie Gastronomic Guesthouse and Farm Cooking School

2825 Naramata Road, Naramata, BC, V0H 1N0

Telephone: 250-496-0093

Web site: www.joie.ca

Summerland Cellars Estate Winery

11612 Morrow Avenue, Summerland, BC, V0H 1Z0

Telephone: 250-494-5423

Vicori Winery

1890 Haldon Road, Saanichton, BC, V8M 1T6

Telephone: 250-652-4820

THE LAST WORD WILL NEVER BE WRITTEN: there is always another winery just opening or being developed somewhere in British Columbia.

Five years in the planning, the Honeymoon Bay Wild Blackberry Winery opened on Cowichan Lake in the summer of 2004, operated by Ray Mogg. The winery was conceived by Merna and Walter Moffat, who had retired to Honeymoon Bay in the early 1990s from Prince George. They saw the winery as a modest economic development project in a community that formerly thrived on forestry and is still a tourist destination. The project was set back after Merna had a heart attack and required surgery. Now recovered, she consults for Mogg, a local resident who took over the project, including 2,700 kilograms (6,000 pounds) of blackberries that the Moffats had in cold storage. The winery's products on opening included a dry blackberry wine and an icewine-inspired dessert wine. Mogg also plans to add other fruit wines.

In the spring of 2004, Korean immigrant Sup Yoo began selling his traditionally made rice wine which he produced in his Seoul Ricewine establishment in Langley. It is made by fermenting rice (California rice in this case) and is produced in two styles: a fresh, milky product with eight per cent alcohol and a clear, dry wine with 14 per cent alcohol. The wines, which can be compared with Japanese sake, are sold primarily to Korean restaurants and the Korean community in Vancouver. Yoo, who operates this winery with his wife, Mi-Yeon, was born in Seoul in 1950. He became familiar with Canada while working as a building supplies importer in Korea and immigrated in 1996. Like many of his countrymen, he made rice wine for personal consumption until, at the urging of friends, he opened Canada's first rice winery.

The Sonoran Estate Winery, which opened in the summer of 2004, north of Summerland, is difficult to see from Highway 97 but rewards visitors with a fine view over Okanagan Lake and vineyard gazebos in which to relax with wine in hand. Located about two kilometres north of Sumac Ridge, this winery is on a narrow bench below the highway. The 2.2-hectare (5.5-acre) vineyard has an aspect similar to the much larger Greata Ranch vineyards, several kilometres to the north.

The winery is operated by Arjan and Ada Smits and their son, Adrian. Immigrants from Holland in 1981, the Smits family were flower growers both in Ontario and in British Columbia's Fraser Valley until moving to this Okanagan property in 2000. They quickly replaced the apple orchard with vines. While waiting for the vineyard to mature, they opened their Windmill Bed and Breakfast. Unlike the winery, the windmill is clearly visible at the edge of the highway. The varieties in the vineyard include Merlot, Pinot Noir, Chardonnay, Riesling and Gewürztraminer, and the winery opened with 2003 vintage wines from these grapes. The consulting winemaker is Gary Strachan. He is mentoring Adrian Smits, who has completed the assistant winemaker's course at Okanagan University College. Born in 1979, Adrian had previously worked with a company providing computer technical support, an office job that had little appeal after his parents involved him with the winery. "I like to be outside all the time," he says, adding that his eyes had begun to trouble him during long days of work hunched over a computer. "Since I have come out here, my eyes have gotten better. I guess I won't need glasses now because they are fine."

There also is a Dutch connection at Celista Vineyards, a property owned by Margaret and Jake Ootes on the north shore of Shuswap Lake near the community of Celista. Jake Ootes — pronounced Otis "like the elevator" — was born in Holland in 1942 and came to Canada as a child. "I work on an eight-year-cycle," he says, describing his rich career before grape growing. First, he worked for eight years as a reporter and photographer for newspapers in the Ottawa area. Next, he became a federal government information officer; then he switched to a similar role with the government of the Northwest Territories just as it was moving from Ottawa to Yellowknife. He headed the territorial government's communications department as well as being executive assistant to the territorial commissioner. Ootes cycled from that to buy a small weekly newspaper in northern Alberta, building it to a chain of three and then selling them. Moving back to Yellowknife, he created a successful magazine for a territorial airline. Then he was elected to the government and served as minister of education, culture and employment. In 2003, he and his wife retired to Celista where Margaret Ootes, who formerly operated a Yellowknife art gallery, had earlier purchased a 65-hectare (160-acre) property overlooking Shuswap Lake. Here, on a warm slope, they have started cautiously with about a hectare (two acres) of vines, including St. Laurent, Maréchal Foch, Ortega, Madeleine Sylvaner and Gewürztraminer. Having begun a new career cycle, Ootes now is immersing himself in viticulture, with the long-term objective of opening a winery.

At Desert Falls Vineyard, Don Gabel is converting into a winery a massive structure that formerly housed the semi-trailers and tractors he once owned when he was in the trucking business. Born in Winnipeg in 1935, he spent 35 years operating a small trucking fleet that specialized in hauling frozen foods. He bought this rural property near Okanagan Falls in 1986, eventually moving there to retire with his partner, Brenda Bond. "A neighbour talked me into a vineyard," he admits candidly. He threw himself into this with the same energy once reserved for the trucking business, spending two years bulldozing the property to create a perfect domed and terraced 2.4 hectares (six acres) for a vineyard. Planting began in 1998. Gabel now has about 13,000 vines, almost entirely Merlot and Chardonnay. The only exception to the neat vineyard symmetry is a planting of about 100 vines of Okanagan Riesling. The variety, all but vanished, used to be the most widely planted white in the valley. Gabel is resuscitating it because he believes it makes a fine sweet wine. That reflects his taste in wine. When the winery opens in 2005, the wines, made by a consulting winemaker, will be unoaked and dry.

On the Naramata Bench, Michael Dinn and Heidi Noble expect to begin selling wine in 2005 from their cooking school and inn, Joie Gastronomic. To learn the art of winemaking (as well as to husband their resources), the couple will make their first three vintages, beginning with 2004, at the nearby Poplar Grove winery under the tutelage of Poplar Grove winemaker Ian Sutherland. The début wines will be whites made from purchased grapes; Dinn and Noble plan to plant about a hectare (two acres) of vines, likely red varieties, on their property in 2006.

Joie arises from the couple's experience in the restaurant and the wine trades, a surprising career turn considering their university degrees. Dinn, who was born in Victoria in 1967, has a bachelor's degree in history. Noble, born in Windsor, is a gold medal graduate from the University of Western Ontario, with degrees in literature. She then trained at the chef's school in Stratford, a leading Canadian culinary school. By the time the couple met in 1999 while completing a course for sommeliers, they had experience in restaurants — Noble in the kitchens and Dinn in wine service. The desire to make wine began when they struck up a friendship with Sutherland in 2000. Both took jobs with wine sales companies for several years, while they looked for property in the Okanagan. In 2002 they purchased a sprawling farmhouse with a small orchard on Naramata Road, converting it into the first cooking school in this hot wine region. Dinn and Noble take an idealistic approach to food that includes using produce, where possible, that has been purchased directly from farms or farm markets. Their approach to winemaking is likely to be equally uncompromising.

Summerland Cellars Estate Winery expects to open its wine shop in 2005 with 1,200 cases of sparkling wine to sell. This winery, which may still change its name prior to opening, is the creation of Eric von Krosigk, the veteran Okanagan winemaker who has developed sparkling wines at most of the numerous wineries where he has worked. Since Hester Creek and Hillside, the two wineries that occupy most of his time currently, make no sparkling wine, Summerland Cellars is an outlet for von Krosigk's passion for bubble. The winery, based on his own small vineyard, has five different sparkling wines: a classic Champagne cuvée plus bubble with Riesling, Muscat Ottonel, Pinot Noir and Chardonnay.

On the Saanich Peninsula, construction company owner A.J. Vickery, who has had a license application pending for several years for Vicori Winery, has been delayed by the viticultural problems in his vineyard, which is located on the road to Newton Ridge Estate Winery. Vickery's 4,000 vines include Ortega and Pinot Gris.

As this book was going to press, bulldozers had just finished contouring a vineyard site on Lakeside Road, just south of Penticton, for the most exciting winery not yet open. In the spring of 2004, John Skinner, a Vancouver stockbroker, marked his 45th year by purchasing a 25-hectare (62-acre) property previously owned by Hillside Estate Winery but not developed. The winery is projected to open around 2010. "That dovetails very nicely with my retirement from the brokerage industry," Skinner says.

The property is immediately south of the Pentâge winery, on a bench that looks westward over Skaha Lake and is bounded on the east by high rock bluffs. This once was part of Braeside Farms, one of the largest apricot farms in the world, but the property has been idle for more than a decade. About two-thirds of the area is suitable for vines. Skinner leans toward planting primarily Bordeaux red varieties but only after getting the best viticultural advice he can. "I've always deferred to the experts," he says. "I'm going to hire good, smart people."

Skinner, who grew up in Comox, was attracted to winegrowing through the experiences of winemaking friends in the Napa Valley. He is planning to build what he calls a "destination" winery with a restaurant attached to the tasting room. It will be a few years before work begins on the architecturally designed winery. "I am looking at developing this carefully," he says. "Time is on my side."

INDEX

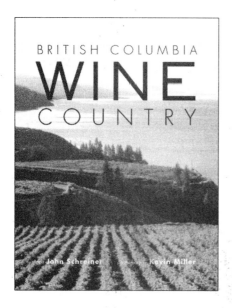